Wild Animals and Wedding Outfits

A voyage of self-discovery around the world

Wild Animals and Wedding Outfits

A voyage of self-discovery around the world

Anna Bromley

authorHOUSE®

AuthorHouse™
1663 Liberty Drive
Bloomington, IN 47403
www.authorhouse.com
Phone: 1-800-839-8640

© 2013 by Anna Bromley. All rights reserved.

Cover design by Anna Bromley
Book design by Anna Bromley
Photos by Bill Jope, Anna Bromley and Markus Fischer

No part of this book may be reproduced, stored in a retrieval system, or transmitted by any means without the written permission of the author.

Published by AuthorHouse   02/05/2013

ISBN: 978-1-4817-8074-2 (sc)
ISBN: 978-1-4817-8075-9 (hc)
ISBN: 978-1-4817-8076-6 (e)

This book is printed on acid-free paper.

Because of the dynamic nature of the Internet, any web addresses or links contained in this book may have changed since publication and may no longer be valid. The views expressed in this work are solely those of the author and do not necessarily reflect the views of the publisher, and the publisher hereby disclaims any responsibility for them.

Contents

Chapter 1:	The Ancestors Are Calling	1
Chapter 2:	Southern India Part I—Lost Temples and Scary Monkeys	5
Chapter 3:	Sri Lanka—Bushman Bandara and the King of the Veddas	42
Chapter 4:	Southern India Part II—Ooty and the Todas	84
Chapter 5:	Northern India—Bear in the Woods	123
Chapter 6:	Sikkim—Yaks, Yetis and Yuksom	158
Chapter 7:	Nepal—Flight to Freedom	186
Chapter 8:	Thailand—Booby, Beaches and Banana Milkshakes	194
Chapter 9:	Vietnam—Sticky Rice Balls	218
Chapter 10:	Laos—Magical Land of the Nagas	264
Chapter 11:	Australia—Hawkeye learns to bodysurf	292
Chapter 12:	Chile—Pisco Sours and Seeing Stars	329
Chapter 13:	Bolivia—No Hay Anaconda	344
Chapter 14:	Peru—Gringos in the Sacred Valley	408
Chapter 15:	And They Lived Happily Ever After	444
Acknowledgements		459

For Bill, my curly headed gardener. Without you, none of this would have been possible.

And in memory of Grandpa, a truly remarkable man, and my inspiration for this journey.

Chapter 1

The Ancestors Are Calling

'Milky, milky!' cried the Milk Seller, arriving at the mission house in Koyyalagudam, North East India. Anna Elisabet Herwig Bromley came to the door. The year was 1907.

'You've been watering the milk,' she said.

'Oh, no, Madame. It is finest quality,' said the Milk Seller, with a bob of his head.

'If you wish to continue selling your milk to me, you will bring your animal here so that I can watch as you milk it. Good day to you, sir,' said my great grandmother, turning on her heel and disappearing back into the house.

'Milky, milky!' cried the Milk Seller the following day. This time he had brought his cow and proceeded to milk it in front of Anna. She tasted the milk. It was full and creamy as it should be.

'That's better. I will buy your milk today,' she said.

For several days, the Milk Seller would come with his cow, milk it in front of Great Granny and then make his sale of fresh milk.

'I don't understand it Eustace,' said Anna a few days later to her husband, as they sat on the verandah taking tea. 'This milk is tasting watery again, even though the Milk Seller has been milking the animal right in front of my eyes.'

'Perhaps he has some trick up his sleeve,' said Great Grandpa. 'Perhaps he is putting water in the bucket before he starts milking?'

The following day, the Milk Seller appeared as usual and commenced milking. Anna watched him carefully.

'Ah ha. I see what you are doing!' she cried. Underneath his shirt, the Milk Seller had a bag of water, connected to a tube that ran down inside his sleeve. Each time he pulled at the udder, he gave the bag a little squeeze with his elbow and squirted an equal amount of water and milk into the pail. Great Granny decided to find a new milk seller—one who would not cheat her. But, being a good Christian, I am sure she prayed for the soul of the dishonest man, and secretly admired his ingenuity.

Bill and I sat on a rug, picnicking by the Thames. It was a glorious June afternoon, and the swaying branches of a grand old willow shaded us from the full strength of the sun. I was telling him the tales of my ancestors.

Bill's head was thrown back. He was laughing that loud, whole body laugh of his, rolling about, clutching his sides. Passers-by were looking over their shoulders to see what all the commotion was about. 'Go on—tell me another,' he said when he had finally recovered, wiping his eyes with the back of his hand.

'Well, I love listening to my father talking about his childhood in Malaya. His other grandfather, Great Grandpa Jumeaux, was the chief civil engineer in Malaya. He built all the main roads and railways there. Dad says that when he and his brother Blake were little, Grandpa Jumeaux would sit them, one on each knee, and enjoy frightening them with stories about fearsome tigers in the jungle. Then, when he had to leave them, he would pop out his glass eye and leave it on a shelf, saying, "Be good boys—I've still got my eye on you!"'

'Blimey—what an exotic family you've got. Have you ever wanted to travel?' asked Bill.

'Oh, yes. All my life I've wanted to go off on a big adventure and see all the places where my family has lived,' I said.

'So what's stopping you?' asked Bill.

'Have you ever felt as if you were waiting for your life to begin? As if you were waiting for something momentous to happen, before all the exciting things you had planned could start?'

'No, can't say I have. If there's something I really want to do, I just do it,' said Bill.

'Well here I am, with all these adventurous relatives and I've never been anywhere more exotic than a two week package holiday to Corfu. I suppose the truth is I've always been too scared to go on my own,' I said.

'Easily solved,' said Bill, 'I'll come with you. When shall we go?'

'Would you? Would you really? I mean I'm thinking about a really big trip. You know, something like a year's round the world trip.'

'A whole year of adventure together—great idea! I'm excited about it already,' said Bill.

'But I'm not as fit or sturdy as you. I'd slow you down,' I said, my head whirling with all the excuses about why this trip could not happen. 'And I'm not very good at roughing it—I like my creature comforts too much. I mean I like a hotel room with an en-suite bathroom and really good shampoo is very important to me.'

'That's OK. We'll go at your pace. And good hotel rooms are dirt cheap in India. You can stay in the height of luxury for a few rupees. The most important thing for me is to have you, the light of my life, by my side to share the experience with.'

So, all my excuses squashed, we spent the next few minutes planning how we could make it happen. Bill, with paper and pen in hand, was sketching it all out in cartoon form. Two little stick Anna and Bill figures got on a plane, trotted round a big globe and then stood by a quaint cottage with flowers in the garden and a big love heart over it. There was also a small object in what looked like a crib.

'What's happening there?' I asked, pointing to the last picture.

'That's when we come home from our trip, get married, have hundreds of babies and live happily ever after,' said Bill.

I looked at Bill. My heart was pounding. 'Bill Jope, are you asking what I think you're asking?'

'Yes,' said Bill, reaching over to take my hand. 'My darling Anna B, will you marry me and have my babies?'

'Oh.' My head was whirling again. Although I had known Bill for nearly two years, I had only realised that I was in love with him three months ago. So, for a serial procrastinator like me, everything seemed to be moving very fast. But when I looked into Bill's dear face, a voice inside me shouted, 'What else are you waiting for? **This** is the moment to SAY YES, SAY YES, SAY YES.'

'YES!! I will!' I finally blurted out.

'Oh, thank God. You had me going there for a while,' said Bill, giving me a rib-crushing hug.

The Song of Solomon

*The voice of my beloved! Behold, he comes,
Leaping upon the mountains, bounding over hills.
My beloved is like a gazelle, or a young stag.
Behold, there he stands, behind the wall,
Gazing in at the windows, looking through the lattice.
My beloved speaks and says to me:
'Arise my love, my fair one, and come away;
For lo, the winter is past, the rain is over and gone.
The flowers appear on the Earth.
The time of singing has come,
And the voice of the turtle dove is heard in our land.
The fig tree puts forth its figs, and the vines are in blossom;
They give forth fragrance.
Arise, my love, my fair one
And come away.'*

Chapter 2 vs 8-13

Great Granny & Great Grandpa (centre) with Anna's Grandpa (top left) and Great Great Granny Katie (bottom left)

Chapter 2

Southern India Part I—Lost Temples and Scary Monkeys

It is 6am and already starting to get hot when we first step out into the reality of India. As we come through customs at Chennai airport, there are crowds of eager faces pressed against the wire barrier, waiting for the return of their loved ones. There is the din of voices, all touting for your business in their rickshaw, or taxi, or trying to take you to a hotel. And the smell—it is a hot smell, a smell of hot dusty earth, mingled with spices and the smell of hot bodies. And there is a background note of the ever-present tang of cow dung and a tinge of rotting rubbish.

As soon as we get into the arrivals hall, there is a clamour of people crowding all around us, wanting to take us somewhere, wanting to sell us something, wanting to part us with some of our cash. I am really excited to be here, but I feel like the new kid at school who does not understand how everything works. I look pleadingly at Bill.

'Diversionary tactics are needed here,' he says. 'We shall do what they least expect us to do.'

'Oh, what's that?' I ask.

'We'll just hang about and wait for them to lose interest,' he says.

'Huh?' I'm confused, but go along with his plan, not having a better one of my own. 'OK, let's get some chai,' I say. A friend told me her favourite thing about India was drinking gallons of the sweet spicy tea out of little terracotta pots. I am eager to try the real thing and, as a person who does not do mornings, I am desperately in need of caffeine to help me cope.

We run the gauntlet of touts and make it to a chai stall outside. To my disappointment, it is served in plastic beakers instead of terracotta pots, but it does the job anyway. The sweet, milky nectar is starting to work its magic. It is breakfast in a cup. I feel like a wilting flower that has been given a deep drink of summer rain. We stand drinking the reviving brew, whilst the most persistent of the touts are eyeing us from a distance, like circling wolves plotting the next phase of the kill.

We finish the chai, then get another. The touts look most perplexed. Some of them start to drift away. We go for a third and they clearly think we are unhinged. This is definitely not normal behaviour. Only the die-hards stay on. After three cups of chai, I feel ready to face whatever comes next.

'Lesson number two in how to keep your sanity when dealing with touts,' says Bill, 'Is to pick out someone with an honest face and go with them. Ignore everyone else.' It seems like a good strategy to me, so we pick out an auto-rickshaw driver and tell him where we want to go.

Our first plan is to get straight out of Chennai and head for Mamallapuram, a small town on the coast about 50km south of here. We chose it because of its ancient history, its reputedly magnificent rock temples and its setting next to the sea. It seemed like a good place to acclimatise ourselves to India.

So we need our chosen driver to get us to the bus stop for Mamallapuram. 'Sir, madam, I can take you direct Mamallapuram. Very cheap—600 rupees. No problem,' he says, bobbing his head from side to side and flashing us an endearing grin.

This does not seem like a good plan. It would take forever in his little underpowered rickshaw and we know the bus will be far cheaper.

'No, just the bus stop is fine, thanks,' says Bill. They haggle over the price of the ride before we squeeze ourselves and our large rucksacks into the rickshaw. This is to be the first of many journeys in strange vehicles around the world.

Known as a tuk-tuk, the auto-rickshaw is a three-wheeled vehicle, more than a motorbike, but not quite a car. Our driver sits on a seat in front, just behind the single front wheel, from where he proceeds to hurl us towards the chosen destination with great gusto and audacity at the greatest speed he can muster, often directly into the path of oncoming trucks and other vehicles, seeming to defy the laws of physics as he squeezes it through impossibly narrow gaps. We sit on a bench seat behind him, over the two back wheels. The roof is enclosed, but the sides are not, allowing for adequate ventilation, but also the unfortunate ingress of dust, mud, water and other unwanted substances onto the persons within.

There is just about enough room for two large people to sit side-by-side on the back seat and a small recess behind the seat for luggage. This however, is not big enough for our rucksacks, stuffed full with all the belongings we have chosen to help us through the next year of travel. This leaves us with the dilemma of whether to:—

a) Sit on them—with heads uncomfortably squashed against the roof,
b) Sit them on us—heavy and cannot see where you are going (often a blessing with the aforementioned driving style common amongst rickshaw drivers, but not so handy when looking out for a landmark), or
c) Balance them in front of us and hang onto them for grim death in case we lurch round a corner too fast—a common occurrence—and they attempt to exit out of the open sides.

On this occasion we plump for the latter option. Oh, and did I mention, there is absolutely no suspension? So every time you drive over a pothole or bump in the road, of which there are an abundance, you are treated to a spine shuddering, bottom crunching, bosom juddering jolt. I would advise any ample-chested woman to wear a high impact sports bra on such journeys. The combination of the speed of the vehicle, the lack of suspension, its open-sided nature, and the need to hang on tightly to one's possessions, tends to lead to passengers arriving at their destination with wide-eyed expressions, dust or mud splattered apparel and hair looking as if it has been carefully backcombed into an ample bouffant.

From the above description it should seem fairly obvious why we decline the driver's kind offer to take us all the way to Mamallapuram. And until he actually drops us off, we are not quite sure whether he will really deliver us to the correct bus stop. But using the honest-faced principle, Bill has chosen well and our driver is as good as his word.

There is some initial confusion about which bus we need, but we eventually climb aboard the right one. It is pretty crowded and we have to sit on our bags up by the driver, but I do not really care—we have successfully negotiated the first part of our journey with no major mishaps and we are on our way. I feel elated at our first small triumph.

As we drive through the suburbs of Chennai, I have time to contemplate my first impressions of India. There are many alien sights, sounds and smells, but I also have an uncanny feeling that it is all strangely familiar. Perhaps hearing Bill talk about his previous experiences here has already conjured up a vivid picture in my mind, or perhaps I am tapping into the ancestral memories of my father, my grandfather and my great grandfather, who have all lived in India for part of their lives.

I look out of the window at the dusty unpaved streets with their shack-like shops and poor houses. There are many people, dogs and cows thronging the sides of the road. Two things strike me most. First, I am surprised by how immaculately clean and neat most of the people look, despite the dusty roads and the heat. The women are so beautiful in their bright saris with neatly combed and braided hair. If I were at street level, I would be a sweaty dishevelled lump covered in dust by now. Come to think of it, I already am.

The other thing that puzzles me is what are all these people actually doing? They just seem to be milling aimlessly about, sitting or standing, sometimes chatting, but rarely performing any task or seeming to go anywhere. This would be a totally alien concept in a large city in England such as London or Bristol, where, at this time in the morning, everyone would be rushing to work or taking the kids to school.

On making this observation to a friend who had visited India, he chastised me, saying, 'Indian people never wander aimlessly about. Only in one thousand years of contemplation, when you have divined their holy purpose, will you know the true meaning of aimlessness.'

Soon the bus is out on the open road. We follow the Coromandel Coast through stands of casuarina trees and coconut and palmyra palms. The landscape is very flat, and inland from the road are paddy fields and sugar cane plantations.

Mamallapuram, nestling on the shores of the Bay of Bengal, was once a port of the Pallava dynasty in the 7th and 8th century, who have left their mark in the many intricately carved monuments and temples around the town. It is known as the land of the Seven Pagodas. But today there is only one of these temples that remains on land, while the myth has persisted that there are six more temples under the sea just off the coast.

The myths of Mamallapuram were first set down in writing by a British traveller, J Goldingham, who visited the South Indian coastal town in 1798. The myth tells of a large city which once stood on this site, which was so beautiful that the gods became jealous and sent a flood that swallowed it up in a single day.

When we first planned our route, we had already decided to come to Mamallapuram, but did not know of this myth. By coincidence, a month before we left home, news hit the headlines that the mythical underwater temples had actually been discovered by a team of divers led by one of my old school friends, Monty Halls.

According to Monty, 'Our divers were presented with a series of structures that clearly showed man-made attributes. I found a carved lion's head and huge blocks of dressed stone that seemed to have been part of a big building, perhaps a temple. The scale of the site is huge. We did 50 dives over a three-day period and still only covered a small area of the overall ruin field. The ruins cover many square kilometres.'

Scientists now want to explore the possibility that the city was submerged following the last Ice Age. If this proves correct, it would date the settlement at more than 5,000 years old. So you can imagine that we were doubly excited about visiting the town when we heard about Monty's discovery.

After one and a half hour's bus ride, we arrive at Mamallapuram, and at Bill's suggestion, go straight to the bus station restaurant. Here I experience my first authentic Indian food. First, I drink more chai—I am getting a real taste for it and my mouth is very dry after a long dusty journey.

I am amazed to see everyone else get off the bus, speedily eat breakfast before getting back on, to go on their way to Pondicherry, or wherever. A scheduled breakfast stop—how civilised—it would never happen on public transport in England.

And my other surprise is that what they are eating looks delicious. Soon we are eating rice with onions, herbs and nuts with tasty dhal, raitha and yummy vadai (spicy lentil doughnuts) all served on banana leaf platters. I really relish this food. I have been told so many horror stories about the food in India that I had worked myself up into a state of nervous tension about eating anything for fear of contracting some horrible life-threatening disease. So I am really relieved to find it is so fresh and tasty.

Bill returns from the bus station toilets to tell me that he has incurred the first of the many mosquito bites of our journey. Whilst otherwise occupied, he was unable to swat it away and it stung him on the hand.

We have finished eating, and it is not long before we are touted by a tuk-tuk driver. He tells us that the best and cheapest place to stay in town is the Lakshmi Lodge. I consult our guidebook and the description sounds OK so we agree to go there. The Lakshmi is fairly mediocre, but I do not have anything to compare it with and we are both very hot and exhausted, so we take a room for the night. I am secretly shocked at how dirty the toilet and bedspread are, but do not say anything, assuming this is the norm. I tell myself it is fine really and that anyhow, the people are very friendly and helpful and it has got everything we need here. So it will do until we are a bit more rested and can go searching for something better. But I substitute one of my sarongs for the dirty bedspread and sprinkle tea tree oil liberally around.

It is stiflingly hot and humid. We both lie about perspiring copiously under the wobbly ceiling fan.

'I think I'm going to die of heat exhaustion,' I tell Bill. 'Every pore in my body is issuing fluid but it still isn't cooling me down.'

'I think we're both a bit jetlagged and it's making everything feel more uncomfortable,' he says. 'I'm sure we'll get used to the heat soon.'

I am sitting at a table outside our room at the Lakshmi now. It is on a long balcony with other guest rooms opening onto it. We have just eaten our evening meal of vegetable thali. It is 7pm and dark has fallen. I am just starting to relax as the evening gets cooler. Other travellers are sitting outside their rooms. Some are chatting, some playing cards, some writing. Everything is very new. I feel green and naïve. The other travellers bandy about the names of places they have visited, boasting about which are the coolest places to go. I still have not got my head round how everything works here. I am very glad I am with Bill.

He tells me, 'Coming back to India after eight years, is like greeting a wild, dysfunctional and rather smelly, but dear old friend.'

Despite feeling naïve and nervous, I am filled with a bubbling excitement. Here we are at the beginning of our big adventure. I have started the trip that I have dreamed about all these years and I am with the man that I love. I have a whole year of visiting exotic and amazing places in front of me. What a very lucky woman I am.

I feel secretly proud of myself to have got here. It seemed that Bill and I had to go through tremendous struggles and upheavals in our preparations to leave England. I sold my flat in London. He sold his share in a house near Bristol. We bought a house together in Bristol. All of this took months to achieve—far longer than anticipated and we had many setbacks. Many times it felt as if we would never get away and we had to keep putting the date of our tickets further and further away. In the end we lived in our new Bristol house for a mere 10 days before having to move all our belongings to my parents' house so that we could rent it out while we are away. And there are the wedding plans. We set the date for 21st June 2003. That is one year and one month away. So if we travel for a year, we will have precisely one whole month to make all the last minute preparations before the Big Day. Some might say we are cutting it a bit fine, particularly my Mum.

The night before my parents came to take us to the airport, we were up till 3am finishing our tax returns. I will never forget the look of shock on Mum's face when she arrived to find the house still in total disarray and we had not even packed our rucksacks.

'Does this look like a house that people are about to move out of?' she asked Dad. He merely shook his head and wandered off to read the paper. Mum, being the stalwart that she is, set to with cloth in hand to scrub the kitchen and bathroom and to repaint the mouldy window frame in the back bedroom ready for the new tenants. God bless my Mum—I do not know what I would do without her.

* * *

We awake on our first morning in a new land. We decide to get up early and explore our surroundings before it gets too hot. We wander along the beach. It is 7.30 am and there are already many people about. Some are fishermen mending their nets and there is a herd of small black and white pigs with their scampering piglets.

'That sea looks inviting, doesn't it?' says Bill.

'Yes it does, but I hear it's pretty much an open sewer and the beach shelves very steeply with a dangerous undertow,' I tell him.

'Perhaps I won't go for a swim then,' says Bill wrinkling his nose.

We walk on into town and go past the entrance to the ancient town temple. A temple attendant greets us. 'You like to come in? There is very beautiful blessing ceremony just starting. You like to take part? Is possible. I show you.'

'I'm game if you are,' says Bill.

'Oh yes, I'd love to,' I reply. So the temple attendant instructs us about buying offerings—a coconut, some bananas, a garland of fragrant white frangipani and some incense.

'Take off shoes,' he says, waving us in. We are ushered into the inner sanctum. It is dimly lit and cave-like. There are carvings of gods and goddesses on the stone walls, stained black by hundreds of years of smoke from incense and candles. The air is heavy with the scent of incense, flowers and exotic fruit. We meet the priest, a young man with shaven head and luminous eyes. He is a devotee of Vishnu, the protector god. We give him our offerings and he performs the blessing ceremony. It is very beautiful and touching. He says prayers and chants for our health and sends blessings to our family. He instructs us how to bless each other and does what he tells us is a purifying fire ceremony to send negative thoughts and bad luck away.

I do not know much about the Hindu religion, but I am really curious to learn more. The ceremony seems like a fitting thing to do, here at the beginning of our journey. There is something about this priest. He seems to glow with an inner radiance like a serene and holy being.

I start to get a shaking feeling, as if energy is moving through my body and it feels as if some healing is happening to me. After the ceremony we sit in the shady courtyard outside the temple. There are people playing drums and pipes. I feel very peaceful.

The priest comes out and sits next to Bill, explaining some of the philosophy behind the ceremony. I am completely entranced by his radiance and just stare at him. Consequently, I do not remember a word he says, which is a great shame as it is a rare opportunity for non-Hindus to attend ceremonies like this one.

It is evening now. Something seems to have changed since the ceremony. The heat does not seem to bother me so much now. My body feels different. The only way I can describe it is that I feel 'comfortable'. I feel happy and full of energy—a complete contrast to the exhaustion of yesterday. Bill says, 'You smell different. There's a sweet fragrance about you—almost as if you have taken in some of the perfume of the frangipani.'

* * *

We have changed hotels and are now in a lovely room at the Luna Magica with a balcony overlooking the ocean, and cooling breezes blowing through. From our window I watch the fishermen on the beach, children making seesaws out of driftwood, the pigs and piglets, dogs and puppies scampering and plenty of people just wandering. On a rocky promontory to the right of the hotel is the ancient temple, the last of the seven temples still standing on land. Its red sandstone glows in the fading light against the backdrop of the beach and the sea.

It is dark now, but the moon is two days off full and casting a silvery light over the waves. The sounds of children's voices and dogs barking waft up to my ears, to the accompaniment of the breaking waves. I look over at Bill. This beautiful setting has put me in a romantic mood and I fall into a reverie about how we first met . . .

British School of Shiatsu-Do, Seven Sisters Road, London

It was a crisp September day and a shaft of sunlight poured in through the long sash window of the North London dojo. I walked across the room and joined the circle of people dressed in white, kneeling on the carpeted floor.

'I'd like you all to welcome our new assistant, Anna,' said Hilary, the tutor, as I sat down. All heads turned my way. Some smiled, some looked at me more critically, judging whether I would be of much help in their studies.

'Congratulations to everyone here for passing your exams. I hope you all feel rested after the break and excited about another year of studying shiatsu. Let's

each start by introducing ourselves for the benefit of the newcomers and saying a little about how things have been going over the summer,' said Hilary.

It was my first chance to get to know this group of people for whom I would be pretending I knew more about shiatsu than they did. I had already completed my three-year practitioner training but had not yet plucked up courage to take my final exams. Hilary had called me to suggest that being an assistant on this second year course would be good revision and build my confidence enough to take my exams. So here I was. I was more than a little nervous. But they seemed like a good-humoured bunch and soon made me feel welcome. There was one person in particular that caught my attention.

'My name's Bill, for those who don't know me, and I'm from Somerset,' he said, looking in my direction. 'Well, it's been a glorious summer. I mean, it's been a joy to be gardening. All this shiatsu must have really helped my liver because the colours of the flowers and the sky and the leaves all have a clarity that I've never seen quite so intensely before,' he said gesticulating wildly to illustrate his point. 'And the smells, oh the achingly beautiful scent of roses, after the sun's been on them all afternoon, it's almost too much sometimes,' he said, placing his large hands on his heart, his copper coloured skin making a sharp contrast with the white of his shiatsu gear. 'And the birds have been in fine voice. There's a blackbird that sits at the top of an oak tree in one of my gardens that's been singing its heart out all summer. It's been wonderful. So I haven't spent much time indoors really.' He smiled a huge, toothy smile that made his brown eyes all but disappear in a wheel of crinkles and fell silent.

I sighed a wistful sigh and thought how much nicer it must be to earn your living that way, than to sit indoors in grey old London writing and editing excruciatingly boring reports about medical equipment, which was how I had been spending my time lately.

Shiatsu is all about creating balance. A shiatsu practitioner is looking to achieve a balance between hot and cold, stillness and movement, light and dark, fullness and emptiness, yin and yang. The universal energy or qi, which flows in our meridians (energy channels) can become blocked or depleted. By gently moving qi, through the use of finger pressure and stretches, a good practitioner is able to help an overactive, stressed person to become calm and move in a smooth and efficient way; or to help a tired, lethargic person to feel energised and active. The same principles can be used to help injuries. A hot, inflamed, acutely painful injury can be helped to feel cooler and more rested, while a joint that feels cold, empty and aching could be helped to feel warmer and replenished. Each meridian is linked with an organ or physical structure and each governs a different emotion, so by balancing the flow of energy in the meridians, shiatsu can help to improve the health of the organs and to resolve emotional imbalances.

I suppose I was looking for some balance in my life too—a balance between a sedentary job using mostly my intellectual faculties; and practising shiatsu which is very physical and helps to develop the intuition.

Among the skills needed by a good shiatsu practitioner are sensitivity of touch, highly developed powers of observation and an empathy with the person they are working on. As I got to know Bill through the shiatsu course, it became clear that he had these qualities in abundance. Observing nature and working closely with the earth and plants in his work as a gardener must have helped, but Bill has two other qualities that make him ideally suited to this work—he has to be the most enthusiastic person I have ever met and he is an inveterate nosey parker.

Part of my role as assistant on the course was to have treatments from the students and to give them feedback on things like their quality of touch, the accuracy of the points they were using and the general effectiveness of the treatment. I was quick to spot what a talented healer Bill is and I was always first to volunteer when he needed someone to work on.

Over the next few months, we became the greatest of friends. Bill was coming up to London from Somerset every month for the course and he needed to find somewhere to stay. I had a spare bedroom in my flat and when he rang to ask if he could stay with me, I was very glad of the company. At the time, I was in love with a man who was extremely bad for my self-esteem and I spent more than one evening crying on Bill's shoulder about my hopeless love life.

A few months later. Plas Taliaris Retreat Centre, Llandeilo, Carmarthenshire

We had spent a week at Plas Taliaris, a lovely Georgian mansion set in acres of beautiful grounds overlooking the Towy Valley in Wales. It was the end-of-year shiatsu residential course. Under the expert tutelage of Ray Ridolfi, principal of the British School of Shiatsu-do and qi-smoothing wizard, we had learnt much and honed our qi-balancing skills to perfection. It had all been very zen.

That night was to be the end-of-term party, which I had a feeling was going to be decidedly un-zen. There is a favourite saying amongst shiatsu people—'Moderation in all things, including moderation.' Having spent a week working and studying hard, there was a determination amongst the group to get rip-roaringly drunk.

The meditation centre was run by a community of people who lived on-site and believed in the practice of mindfulness in daily life. They were very strict about noise and general exuberance levels. They were in for a shock.

The first part of the evening was spent innocently enough with the Five Elements Theatre. Ray had split us into groups and asked each group to put on a performance that illustrated the nature of one of the five elements of Chinese medicine, these being fire, water, earth, metal and wood.

I was in the earth group, our colour was orange, our season late Summer, our theme Mother Earth and the fruits of the orchard. Dressed in robes of orange and garlanded with nasturtiums, we took people on a sensory experience through the grounds of Plas Taliaris, handing out fruit from the baskets we carried and singing a sweet song about Mother Nature's bounty. It seemed to go down well.

Finally, the Wood group put on their performance. We were by now in the drawing room—the oak panelling and oil painting of a pastoral scene above the fireplace providing an appropriate backdrop for their production. They were dressed in green and accompanied by loud pumping music, The Chemical Brothers, over which they had to shout their performance. Bill was the music maestro of their group. It set the tone for the rest of the evening.

The Five Element Theatre now over, Bill took on the role of the bonco-booth man. He had a bottle of tequila, a bottle of champagne, some wedges of lime and a pot of salt. He was inviting anyone to have a tequila slammer in return for giving him an interesting fact. This was causing the inebriation levels and the riotous behaviour levels to rise sharply. Someone started a round of rude jokes, including one about old ladies doing the hokey cokey. This was inevitably followed by an exuberant demonstration of this most beloved of English traditions, for the benefit of the foreign students on the course.

By now I had had a few tequilas, in fact, if I did not think of Bill as such a good friend, I could have sworn that he was following me around with his bonco booth.

'Got any more interesting facts for me, Anna?' he said sidling up with his tequila. I thought for a minute.

'Oh yes, how about this one? I saw a nature programme recently and there was a certain kind of octopus that has a very unusual way of mating.'

'Tell me more . . . it sounds worthy of a tequila slammer so far,' said Bill.

'Well, the male octopus hides behind a rock and waits for a female to come along. When he sees a suitable girlfriend, he takes aim and . . . fires his penis off at her. I mean, the whole thing actually leaves his body.'

'I hope he's a good shot,' said Bill, 'Because he's going to be pretty disappointed if he misses. Anyway, I think that very interesting fact deserves one of my special tequila body slammers.'

'And what might that be?' I asked.

'Well, you bang the champagne and tequila in the glass and down it as usual, and you also get the special privilege of licking the salt off a crevice of my body and taking the wedge of lime from between my teeth.'

'Oh, I see,' I said, blushing and giggling. 'And which crevice are we talking about here?'

'Well some people do belly buttons, but mine's usually full of blue fluff, so you might prefer my clavicle.' By this time a small crowd of eavesdroppers had gathered round.

'Go on, Anna,' was the general murmur as many ribs were nudged. Bill was busy sprinkling himself with salt and putting the lime in place. I had already drunk enough tequila for my inhibitions to be well subdued, so I agreed. Having spent a year practising shiatsu on each other, we were all pretty touchy-feely with each other anyway, so I thought, 'Oh well, why not?'

The heady, bubbly mix of champagne and tequila served to make the slammer a bit of a blur, but I was aware of Bill squirming a lot as I licked the salt and I had to work very hard to get the lime off him.

Bill's friend, Johnny, walked past. He cupped his hand round my ear and said, 'You've just made Bill, very, very happy.' We looked at Bill, who was leaning against the oak panelling with a faraway look in his eye and a huge grin on his face. I scuttled away, not really wanting to contemplate the implications of having just snogged my best friend . . .

Bill

And so it was that we spent the next few months like a couple of crested grebes doing a poetic, circling dance around each other. It was not until the following March that our necks finally entwined and we declared our love for each other. We had a shiatsu class the next day and I was quite astonished at the reaction to our announcement that we were now officially an item. We were greeted with a chorus of, 'Hooray, about time too. We all saw that one coming long ago.'

I come out of my reverie. 'Bill do you remember the day we met?' I ask him.

'Oh yes. I was sitting in the dojo at the Shiatsu School, all excited about starting my second year and in you walked. As you sat down in the circle, a shaft of sunlight fell upon your golden head and I thought an angel had stepped amongst us,' he says looking at me with a little mist in his eyes.

'Ah, you big soppy,' I say giving him a nudge.

* * *

It is even hotter this morning. We wake at 6.30am intending to make an early start to look round the temples of Mamallapuram, but even at this time and even in our breeze-cooled room we are still overheated. We lie about reading guidebooks.

'Bill, we've been here a whole three days and haven't visited any of the sights yet. But I feel so lethargic, I can't muster up the energy to go anywhere today.'

'Look, Anna, it's our holiday. We can do exactly what we want. If you want to lie around drinking cold drinks all day, that's fine.'

'Actually, what I need are some cooler clothes,' I tell him. I am learning that, particularly for a woman, there is a definite art to dressing in this climate and culture. It is not the done thing to wear sleeveless tops or shorts, since displaying your shoulders or legs will have you labelled a harlot and get you lots of unwanted attention. 'I need loose, billowy clothes in a fabric that feels cool to the touch and doesn't cling. Fine cotton or silk is the thing.' But I look in my rucksack and there is nothing that fits that description. I hold up my ever-so practical trekking trousers with the hardwearing, double-thickness backside. 'These are about the last thing I feel like putting on,' I say.

'Well, what a terrible hardship,' says Bill. 'Having to go shopping for beautiful silk clothes at incredibly cheap prices must be every girl's worst nightmare.'

'You're right—even the heat and humidity can't keep me away. Let's go!'

Othavadai Street has several tailors' shops, but my first encounter does not go well. The young man who runs the shop asks what we are looking for. I try to describe the voluminous effect I am after.

'I think Madame will be needing one of these wrap around skirts, since she is so fat,' he says hopefully, holding up one of his ready-made garments. 'Look, the waist is very adjustable.'

I am aghast at his rudeness. Bill looks ready to hit him. 'Come on,' I say, 'I don't think we will be giving him any of our business.' I turn on my heel, gathering the remnants of my tattered self-esteem to me and stalk off.

Bill tries to comfort me saying, 'It's probably because his English isn't very good. He probably meant to say that you are curvaceous, but he didn't know the right word,' then mutters under his breath, 'But I'd still like to punch his smarmy little face.'

After this initial setback, we discover the delights of Suba Silks. We enter the dimly lit shop. Whilst waiting for my eyes to adjust from the bright glare of outside, to the subdued lighting in here, I become aware of that particular smell that emanates from the bales of fabric, a kind of fresh, cool, biscuity smell, intermingled with the usual smells of India, masala spices, incense and a hint of cow dung. As my eyes adjust, the owner of the shop materialises in front of them. He is small and dapper, with an open, friendly face and a lovely smile. He manages to look impossibly cool despite the overwhelming heat. With head tilted slightly to one side, he politely enquires how he can help us. We tell him of our need for billowy clothes to help us deal with the heat.

He points out designs that he thinks might suit us from the array of beautiful garments hanging around the walls. 'I can make these in any colour or fabric for you, and they can be ready tomorrow. Would you like tea while you choose?'

A boy is called to bring us tea while we decide. I choose a couple of tunic tops and loose fitting trousers, and a long skirt in shades of peacock blue and turquoise silk. But my favourite garment is a gauzy dress in magenta floral silk edged in blue and gold. This is the Holy Grail to me—to feel cool <u>and</u> look stylish. Bill chooses a long, loose cotton shirt and matching lightweight trousers.

Whilst having an interesting conversation with the tailor about religious tolerance, he places his tape measure discreetly and expertly against our persons.

'I am Moslem. My neighbour is Hindu, and we all live happily side-by-side. But the troubles in the North, oh, it makes me very sad,' he says.

By the end of the conversation he has both our measurements and designs for our lovely billowy garments that will be ready by tomorrow. It is a pleasure doing business with him. We step out of the tailor's shop into the glare of the mid-morning sun and are beaten into the shade of the nearest café for a cold drink. We are following the advice of our good friend, Pete, in how to deal with this unspeakably hot weather—'Never stand up until you can see where your next cold drink is coming from'.

Wanting to find other local diversions, we hire a moped to go to the Tiger's Cave a couple of kilometres North of town, then retreat to our room to rest and wait until it gets a bit cooler.

The temperature starts to ebb slightly below the brain boiling level by about 4 pm, so we head off for the Tiger's Cave. At first I am nervous about getting on such a vulnerable vehicle because of the state of Indian roads and the madness of its drivers. But Bill is a good driver and has ridden a motorbike all the way from Goa to Ley in the far north, so he has the measure of the hazards that are likely to come our way.

'The law of the road in India,' says Bill, 'Can be summarised as *The biggest vehicle rules the road AND everyone must drive at the maximum speed possible.* For example, pedestrians are the lowliest form of life on the road and must be prepared to jump out of the way of whatever is careering towards them. Often the vehicle's driver will do you the courtesy of sounding the horn loudly to warn you of the impending collision, but usually too late to let you calmly take evasive action, and it will be right in line with your ear, shocking your nervous system and causing you to jump wildly into the gutter (which will be full of rotting food, filthy water and poo). This is probably what the other driver wanted you to do anyway. So, bicycles have the right of way over humans, motorbikes take precedence over bicycles, tuk-tuks are superior to motorbikes and will also cut up other tuk-tuks, especially if they already have paying customers on board, cars have priority over tuk-tuks, and trucks are the Lords of the Road. They can go anywhere and do anything they want. So don't be surprised to round a bend and find a huge truck bearing down on you, on the wrong side of the road. The one exception to this rule is the cow. In India the cow is holy and everything gives way to it. And the cow never hurries anywhere. If you remember all that, you'll be perfectly safe,' he says giving me a wry smile as we climb onto the moped.

In this case, our journey is uneventful and we turn off the main road and head down a sandy track towards the site. In the distance we can see trees and sand dunes and beyond them the ocean. We have a delightful time at the Tiger's Cave, guided by a character calling himself Coconut Raj.

After our tour, we stroll through the trees and down to the beach. We paddle in the shallows, watching the sky darken and storm clouds gather in the North. Will this be the first of the monsoon rains? The storm stalks us as we walk south down the beach. Each time we look up over our shoulders, the ominous clouds seem to have inched a bit closer. It is like playing Grandmother's Footsteps. As heavy rain looks imminent, we decide to head back to town before we get caught in the storm.

The storm is still just about holding off by the time we reach Mamallapuram, so we do a bit more exploring with the bike. We end up at the Old Lighthouse on the southern side of town, another Shiva temple. There are carvings depicting the demons and gods of Hindu mythology, all carved from one giant block of stone.

We climb very steep steps to the top of the lighthouse and negotiate our way along a narrow and precarious ledge, passed by an incongruous young goat. We sit down to admire the panoramic view, when the storm finally breaks — great flashes of lightning striking all around, illuminating the sky and town below us — a fantastic show, until we realise it is probably not the safest place to be so high up with lightning striking so close to us. We go back to our room to watch the light show over the ocean and listen to the beating of the thunder drums.

*   *   *

I never get bored of the view from our balcony in the changing light. This morning the sky is milky pink and orange as dawn breaks. We set off at 6.45 am on the moped, bound for a town nearby, Tiruvukalikundram, where there is an ancient Siva temple. It is a place of pilgrimage for Hindus and the only other temple that we have heard that will let non-Hindus inside. After our beautiful experience in the Mamallapuram town temple, I am hungry to learn more.

It is magical driving through the countryside as it wakes up in the early morning. The locals all smile and wave and shout 'hello' at us as we pass. But Bill's pride is supremely dented as we are overtaken by a whole family on a moped — Dad, Mum, Granny, child and two large bags of shopping. They wave and smile too.

The temple is set picturesquely on a huge rock, which rises 500m above the surrounding plain. It dominates our view as we drive through the countryside towards it. Despite having this gigantic landmark, we somehow manage to get lost. We know that Tiruvukalikundram is only 15 km from Mamallapuram and we have already covered that distance and are still not close.

We see a highway patrol man and stop to ask directions. But try pronouncing 'Tiruvukalikundram' when you are lost and a bit flustered. I am not sure he understands what we are asking. He does that sideways head-bob thing that Indians do which can mean anything from 'yes,' 'no,' 'maybe,' to 'I have no idea what you are talking about, but I am going to humour you anyway' and he sends us down a 20km dirt track.

We bump up and down, in and out of potholes, sending up clouds of dust for a few minutes before deciding there must be another way. We know the bus goes there and it could not possibly get down this lane. At this moment we are met by a carload of smiling Indians going the other way. We tell them of our dilemma. They laugh and tell us how to get there on the main road.

It proves to be the right way and we are soon approaching the outskirts of town. We make our way to the temple entrance. Feeling like old hands at this temple mallarky now, we know that we need to buy some fruit and flowers for the puja and temple offering.

A lady offers to help us, but we end up with a couple of rotten coconuts, some manky bananas and some wilted flowers. She asks Rs 6 for this wretched ensemble and then, seeing that we have no change, ups the price to Rs 40. We are arguing about a few pence here, but it is the principle of the matter. I hate being taken for a ride.

We approach the steps up to the temple. A man attaches himself to us saying he will be our guide.

'Madam, the climb is very steep and difficult. This man can carry you up in a basket,' he says, calling to a tiny little bent man who comes over with his basket. I am mortified by the idea of a man who is half my height and probably about a third of my weight attempting to carry me up the steps in his flimsy looking wicker-work, and decline his offer. Besides which, it is not much of a pilgrimage if someone else has to do all the hard work.

Bill leans towards me and whispers, 'Oh go on, I'd love to see him try!' He gets a swift dig in the ribs from my elbow.

The climb is bearable with a couple of stops to catch our breath and admire the view. We can see all the way across the plain to Mamallapuram along the very direct road we should have taken, but somehow missed.

At the top, we are suddenly set upon by a gang of huge monkeys baring their teeth, growling and trying to grab our bananas. I am terrified by these fierce creatures.

'Bill, help!!' I shriek as the biggest male, the size of a rottweiler, is wrenching my bag off me and trying to bite my hand. Bill grabs a rolled-up newspaper and swats at him a couple of times, but he is not giving up on my bananas that easily. We are saved by the temple attendant, a small skinny man, who seems to shape-shift into the form of an even larger monkey and chases them off. He obviously does that several times a day. He laughs heartily at how scared we had looked.

Inside the temple, it is very dark and the walls are lined with ancient carvings. I would have liked to stay for a while and just absorb the atmosphere, but we overhear our guide being told to rush us through because there are 200 Hindu pilgrims on their way.

The puja is performed (very quickly) by a decrepit old priest with mad starey eyes, hair that stands four inches on end from behind a receding hairline, and one tooth. He does a little chant and blesses our offerings, before looking expectantly at us with his hand out. The guide whispers that we are expected to pay him now and tells us what the usual donation is—around Rs 200 (£3) each—a small fortune in local terms. We pay up and are rushed on. Outside we have another encounter with the vicious monkeys who are beaten off by the temple attendant brandishing the rolled-up newspaper. I feel disappointed that this experience seemed so rushed and commercialised compared to the beautiful ceremony at the temple in Mamallapuram.

By the time we get back to the mundane world at ground level we are starving and find a café where we have breakfast. By now it is 10 am and getting very hot. We head back to Mamallapuram, the right way this time, and are back in no time. The scenery is beautiful, there are lots of smiley, waving people and we feel jolly.

We visit the lovely tailor at Suba Silks. Our new clothes are ready and fit us perfectly.

'I love this shirt. It's fantastic! Can you make me another one exactly the same?' says Bill. These shirts are to become the mainstays of his wardrobe and will endure much pounding on stones by the washerwomen of Asia before our journey is over. We beat a retreat to the haven of our breeze-cooled balcony for the rest of the day and start to form plans for our next move—we have heard it is much cooler in Kanniyakumari, at the very southern tip of India, where the breezes blow in from three directions off the sea.

* * *

My grandfather has always been my inspiration for wanting to travel. Now well into his nineties, he finally put away his passport aged 93 after a bird-watching trip to Chile.

I remember as a child, whenever he was in England, he would come to Sunday lunch and tell us the tales of his latest adventures. Often he would listen to a language programme on the radio with headphones on. I was fascinated by the strange sounds he uttered in Mandarin or Russian, or some other tongue from a faraway land, as he repeated words from the programme. He always liked to be able to speak the language of the countries he visited so that he could converse with the local people on his trip. Bill and I went to visit Grandpa in England before we left, to help us plan our trip . . .

Dulas Court, England

On Grandpa Bromley's lap lay a map of India. Bill and I were sitting in his room in Dulas Court, a residential home in Herefordshire where he had recently moved to be closer to my Dad. It was a month before we were due to leave for the Big Trip. Grandpa was showing us places that had been important to him in his long life.

'There's Ooty,' he said pointing at the map. 'I went to Breek's school in Ooty, and so did your Dad and his brother Blake, many years later. It's a lovely place up in the hills, so it's a bit cooler. It's a good place to escape from the heat when it gets really hot during the summer. And there are lots of places to go walking in the Nilgiri hills. The native tribes people, the Todas, still live there. They are very interesting people and very friendly. They worship the buffalo spirit and have temples dedicated to them, you know. When I was a little boy, I used to go and visit them in their villages. I thought they were very strange—they wore nothing but loincloths and had wild, matted hair. But they were very kind to me and they taught me some of their songs and dances. I can still remember them now. I went to the Breek's school reunion a couple of years ago and I performed a Toda song and dance. People were quite surprised that I could still remember. I think I am probably the oldest pupil from Breeks still alive.' Grandpa's blue eyes were twinkling at the memory of spending time with the Todas.

The sun was shining in through the open window, which looked out over a lovely garden full of spring flowers. The sound of birdsong and the babbling of a little brook at the bottom of the garden created the backing music to our conversation.

'And while you're there, you could visit Bandipur and Mudumalai National Parks—they are very close. They're famous for wild elephants because they're on the migration route through the Western Ghats. And if you're very lucky, you might see a tiger. But I think they're getting very rare and difficult to see now, which is a terrible shame.' His eyes were shining even brighter as the memories came flooding back to him. And we were all getting very excited about the forthcoming trip.

'The mission school built by your Great Grandpa Eustace is over here in Andra Pradesh. They lived in the Godavari Delta area. Now let me see, where is it?' He pours over the map. 'Your nearest train station would be Rajamundry, and there is a hospital named after him there. It's run by a doctor who was orphaned as a boy. Eustace adopted him and his brother and paid for their medical training, so they named the hospital in his honour. Ah, here it is Koyyalagudam. It's a tiny place, quite hard to get to, especially during the monsoon as everything floods for miles around. What time of year are you going?' he asked.

'Well, soon—as soon as the house sale goes through. We wanted to leave a couple of months ago, but there've been loads of delays with selling Anna's flat in London. So we're going at about the worst time to visit India, because it's getting really hot and the monsoon will be coming any day now,' said Bill.

'That's a great shame,' said Grandpa. 'Andra Pradesh is one of the hottest parts of India. I'm sure the heat there was a factor in shortening the lives of both my parents. My mother was German and during the war they wouldn't let her move from the area, even though she was married to an Englishman. So she wasn't allowed to go to the cooler hill stations during the really hot months like most of the other Europeans. And my father wouldn't leave her on her own. I think you may have to leave that visit for another trip. The heat will just be too unbearable now.' He gave a little shudder at the memory of the stifling heat in the Godavari Delta.

My eye was drawn to a huge picture of a bird of prey above Grandpa's bed. 'What kind of bird is that, Grandpa?' I asked.

'It's a Lanner Falcon. Of all the birds in the world, it's my favourite—such a beautiful, graceful little bird, but mustard when it comes to catching its prey.'

The little room was stuffed with mementos of his long life, many of them bird related, for Grandpa's two great loves in life are bird-watching and travelling to far flung places to see birds. A clock above the mantelpiece had a different bird in each place where the numbers would normally have been. As the clock struck 11 am, it made the sound of the bird under the hour hand. Grandpa saw me looking at it and smiled.

'I was given that one when I went to Japan. It shows all the common native birds over there. I've learned to say all their names in Japanese now.' His third great love and talent is learning new languages.

'Grandpa speaks everything from Welsh to Urdu,' I told Bill. 'He always makes a point of learning the language of each country that he visits. He even learnt Pigeon English for his trip to Papua New Guinea.'

'Oh, that puts me to shame,' said Bill. 'I don't even speak English very well!'

Just at that moment, we all looked over to the bureau where there was a picture of my grandmother. She looked so vibrant in the photo, it could have been taken the day before.

'That's a lovely picture of Granny,' I said.

'Yes, it is. She's been gone over twenty years now, but I still really miss her,' and turning to Bill he said, 'Do you know she was the sweetest, kindest person that I have ever met, before or since. She would do anything for anybody. I was very lucky to have her as my wife.'

'She looks lovely,' said Bill, 'She reminds me of my Gran.'

'Grandpa, some of Granny's family were originally from Sri Lanka, weren't they? We are planning to visit Sri Lanka, too,' I said handing him a map of Sri Lanka.

'Oh yes, you must. It's a very beautiful country. We went there as a family many years ago, when I was on furlough from my job as a teacher in Malaya. I'm afraid it's a very long time since Iris' family moved from Sri Lanka and I'm not sure which part they were from, but it's not that big a country and you could probably see most of it in a month. I remember there being very beautiful ancient temples round a place called Polonnaruwa. And the scenery and wildlife are delightful.'

'Mr Bromley,' said Bill, 'You have been to many countries and learnt many languages. But which country would you say is your favourite?'

Grandpa thought for a long time. 'I went to Chile last year and that was very nice. In fact I like the whole of South America. I enjoyed the ancient temples in Peru and I loved the Amazon jungle—so many colourful birds. I had a wonderful holiday there about ten years ago, when I did some canoeing along rivers in the jungle—that was such fun. But I do love India, because it was my home for many years. I didn't like Siberia much, far too cold—spent most of the time thigh-deep in freezing cold water when I was bird-watching there. Japan was nice but it brought back awful memories of working on the Burma Road when I was a prisoner of war . . .' He thought for a little longer and then said, 'Actually, it's hard to beat England. Yes, that's it, I've visited over a hundred countries and England is my favourite. Aren't we lucky to live here?

I must say, you two are very adventurous, doing a trip like this. I wish I could come with you, but I'm afraid my travelling days are over. This arthritic back of mine won't let me go far now. But that's all right, because I'm very lucky living here. This valley is so beautiful, and full of birds. They have a wonderful bird-watching club here, you know. So there are plenty of people with interesting things to talk about. And the staff are so kind to me,' said Grandpa.

I felt a huge pang of sadness as he said this. This man, who had been on the planet for 94 years and travelling to far flung places for 93 of them, who was so full of spirit and still so interested in life, was now confined to Dulas Court in the Golden Valley, beautiful though it is.

'Well, Grandpa, you can travel with us in your mind, because we are going to send lots of letters describing where we are going. And when we get back you can see all the photos too.'

'Yes, I'm looking forward to that,' he said. 'And I'm looking forward to your wedding when you get back too.'

It was time for us to go. I kissed him goodbye and he shook Bill's hand.

'The very best of luck to you both,' he said, as he waved to us at the door.

'What an amazing man,' said Bill. 'I'm very glad to have met him.'

It is full moon tonight and incredibly beautiful. At first the moon rises through the clouds and appears as a huge yellow ball not far above the horizon. We are sitting on our balcony at Luna Magica, watching it getting smaller and brighter as it rises high in the sky. By now it is so bright that I can see the fishermen's boats clearly on the beach and it is casting a huge river of silver across the ocean. 'Finally Grandpa, I'm on an adventure just like you,' I think to myself.

* * *

We get up at 5.30 am to go to the shore temple. This is so unheard of for me. Normally anything before 7am seems like the middle of the night. But we have decided this will be our last day in Mamallapuram and our last chance to see the sight that first attracted us to come here—the Shore Temple—the lone survivor of the seven temples, the rest having fallen to the ravages of the sea. We had hoped to go on a boat trip to see the underwater temples. From September to December, when the sea is calm and clear, it is possible to see the temples from the surface. But we have been told by a local fisherman that at this time of year it is too rough and you cannot see anything as the temples are more than ten metres below the surface. So we will not be able to see Monty's lion's head and underwater temples after all. We will have to be content with this one and the others will have to rest in our imaginations.

We are the first people to arrive and have the place to ourselves for the first half hour. It is wonderfully peaceful. Outside, rows of Nandi bulls, lions and elephants line up to guard the temple. The double-spired temple is unique in that it houses shrines for both the gods Shiva and Vishnu, the destroyer and the protector gods. Five tiers of ornately carved soft red sandstone rise up to the pinnacle of each spire. We pass into the inner sanctum, which has a lovely atmosphere, and contemplate its reclining statue of Vishnu.

Anna at the Shore Temple

When the site starts to fill up with other tourists we decide to head off for some breakfast. Fortified by our meal, we make the mistake of attempting to look round the other sites. It is 9 am and already very hot. We gaze at the impressive sculpture of Arjuna's penance with its carving of a family elephants for a while. It is the world's largest bas-relief sculpture, measuring 30m by 12m. The rock is split by a huge fissure that has been skillfully worked into the sculpture. It represents the story of Arjuna the hero of the epic tale, the Mahabharata. He is a master archer and does penance to get a magic arrow from Lord Shiva that will destroy his enemies. Originally water flowed down the fissure, representing the waters of the Ganges, and among the other carvings on the rock are animals and heavenly beings witnessing the descent of the Ganges from its source in the Himalayas.

After this encouraging start to our sightseeing, we get ambitious and try to do a tour of all the other rock cave temples, including such delights as Krishna's butterball. But the overwhelming heat and the incessant incursions of the postcard touts and guides really gets to me. I am wearing my expensive Oakley sunglasses, purchased especially for the trip, but this does not stop a sunglasses salesman pestering me.

'Madame, you need some sunglasses for this hot weather,' he says, thrusting his cheap products at me.

'No thank you, I already have some,' I reply.

'But these ones are much better,' he says. I look at his sunglasses with their scratched lenses and warped frames.

'I don't think so,' I say, extricating my sleeve from his grasp and moving away. The blazing sun beating on my head is making me feel dizzy. When the next would-be guide tells us about the monkeys who might try to grab our bags—that is really the last straw and I stomp off back to our room. By now I do not give a stuff whether I ever see Krishna's Butterball, which is surely melting in the heat like me.

Later, we visit an Internet café to check our e-mails. There's one from Mum:—

My darling Anna-B,

I hope you and Bill are both enjoying India and not finding the weather too hot. I have checked with the vicar at St Mary's, and yes, the 21st of June next year is free, so I've booked it for your wedding. I've just realised that it's the Summer Solstice. I hope you're not planning to do anything pagan!

We are all well here, and dying to hear your news. So many things to organise for the wedding. Do give us a call when you have a moment. It would be lovely to hear your voice.

Bye for now.

Lots of love to you and Bill
Mum and Dad xx

We originally set the date for our wedding before all the house selling/buying problems delayed our departure. Now, here we are gallivanting round the world, whilst Mum is left to organise everything at home. The excitement of finally going on our travels made me oblivious to how much pressure this would put on Mum. Organising a daughter's wedding must be one of the highlights of a mother's life and I have gone and made it ten times more difficult by putting myself on the other side of the world. Sorry, Mum.

Still, the stresses and strains of travelling together will be a good test of my relationship with Bill, and so far we have not fallen out—a good sign for the future I think.

* * *

We make our way to the bus stand. We are bound for Pondicherry, a French colonial town, three hours further south from here. The bus which pulls into the stand is already crowded and we jostle and vie with the other passengers to get on. There are not enough seats and we have to stand in the aisle for the first part of the journey, clinging tightly to a pole as we lurch along and acutely aware of our huge packs blocking the gangway, which everyone getting on or off the bus has to negotiate past. Eventually, enough people get off the bus for us to have a seat for the rest of the way. It is mid-morning and heating up rapidly. All the bus windows are open, and the breeze is very welcome, but we are covered in a thick layer of dust by the time we arrive at our destination.

I have a romantic notion of what a French colonial town will be like, but by now most of its Frenchness has all but disappeared. The beach-front reminds me of a rather faded version of Brighton. We take a room at the Ajantha guesthouse, one of only two or three facing the shore and the only one in our price range. Our experience from Mamallapuram was that, in this stifling weather, a little breeze from the sea can make so much difference.

Pondicherry is unbearably hot, dirty and smelly, with an open sewer running through its centre. I cannot wait to get out of here. It is really only a stop to make railway connections and buy plane tickets. The normally exuberant Bill is very quiet. We wander the sun-baked streets trying to find an ayurvedic pharmacy to get medicine for Bill's pooey bum.

But amongst this unpleasant environment I have a vision which has haunted me ever since. Walking down the street towards me is an old lady dressed in long white robes. She catches my eye and gives me a radiant smile. She is the image of my grandmother who has been dead for twenty years. I say to Bill, 'Did you see that lady? She looked just like my granny.' Bill says that he had not seen her, so we turn to look behind us, but there is no-one there . . .

When I was a little girl, my mother used to buy our tea from Sainsburys. I remember sitting in the trolley looking at the packet, which had a picture of a lady in a sari picking tea. The packet said it was from Ceylon. I loved that picture and dreamed that one day I would go to Ceylon and see the beautiful ladies who picked the tea. Years later, my Aunty Beryl did some research into the family tree. She discovered that a branch of the family had fled France during the French Revolution and had ended up as tea merchants in Ceylon (now Sri Lanka). One family rumour is that our ancestors were actually responsible for introducing tea into Sri Lanka. Years later, one ancestor married a local girl, a bit of a scandal at the time, but it accounts for the exotic dark looks of my grandmother, and perhaps my own longing to see the country. I took it as an omen that I had just seen a mysterious lady who looked just like Granny on this day, and in this city with its French colonial origins.

So, despite the government warnings about the terrorist activities of the Tamil Tigers in Sri Lanka, I am determined to go there. We have done some research and it seems that we are very fortunate in our timing. In December 2001 the Tamil Tigers declared a temporary ceasefire, which was made permanent in February this year because of the success of peace talks with the Sri Lankan government. So we go to a travel agent and book our flights to Sri Lanka for the 8th June. We also book tickets on the overnight sleeper train to Kanniyakumari, which will be the next leg of our journey.

By the evening I am very hungry and we go to the Ajantha's rooftop restaurant where we are served by the Maître D, who has a most superior air about him. But Bill has soon worked his charms on the man, whose demeanour towards us is now decidedly softer. He is a most extraordinary looking man with luxuriant tufts of hair jutting out horizontally from his ears. I try not to stare.

Poor Billy is still not feeling well. He has a bad dose of exploding bottom. So he does not feel very hungry. The Maître D sympathises and recommends a plate of plain rice and curds as a cure. This simple recipe has a miraculous effect at calming Bill's intestinal grumblings.

By contrast my appetite and toilet habits have been exceptionally good since we got here. In fact I seem to be positively thriving on Indian food. I feel a little guilty tucking into Mutter Paneer—'cheesy peas'—as we have grown to call it, with Bill feeling so queasy, but it is deliciously set off by its masala sauce and swimming in ghee—yum! The reputation of Indian food for causing terrible diseases of the digestion is legendary, and in a masochistic kind of way, I was quite looking forward to this enforced way of losing weight. I do not know whether I have some inherited immunity to the bugs here, but it seems a tragic irony that I may be the only traveller to actually put on weight in India, while Bill cannot afford to lose much more from his slim frame.

* * *

Boy, is it hot here in Pongicherry. We carefully prepare ourselves for the onslaught of the heat of the day by having cold showers and then lying, still wet, under the ceiling fan to let the evaporation cool us down. It is 10am when we venture forth to change travellers cheques and to pay for our Sri Lankan tickets. As we step out, we thud into a solid wall of heat. It is like being slapped in the face with a boiling hot flannel. Within minutes I feel as if I am being roasted alive. It is so vicious that we almost turn on our heels and go back to the hotel, but the Ajantha's restaurant is not open in the morning and we need to find somewhere for breakfast. We decide to go to Le Café Pondicherry on the beach, where we hope there will be a bit of shade. Sounds nice doesn't it? I had romantic illusions of croissant, good coffee and perhaps some chilled orange juice in a shady, breezy, café full of old world charm. I was sadly mistaken. It is the most filthy, fly-blown hovel in town—another duff recommendation from the guidebook.

We beat a hasty retreat to our room at the Ajantha until it is time for our train to leave for Kanniyakumari at 7.30pm. Poor Bill really needs to rest and be close to a toilet at the moment. Later we find out that the temperature in the shade when we made our ill-fated venture to Le Café Pondicherry was an astonishing 49°C.

We are at the station waiting for the overnight sleeper train to Kanniyakumari the southernmost point of mainland India. I am so looking forward to the breezes that blow in from three different directions, and hoping it is as cool and delightful as we have heard.

We are like excited children about to go on a school trip and stay away from our mums overnight. We sit on a bench watching the hustle and bustle of the station. There are young men in claret coloured uniforms getting our train ready and taking on supplies. They come and sit with us, eager to practice their English. The boldest young man introduces them,

'I am Tea. He is Milk.' They are very proud of their work. We tell them we will be glad of their services when we get on the train.

We board the train at 9.40pm and already people are asleep. Our bunks are at the top. We clamber up, like children late for bed. Our friend, Tea, comes to give us some bedtime drinks. The train is blissfully air-conditioned. The respite from the heat and humidity is heaven. The hypnotic motion of the train soon lulls us to sleep. Tomorrow we will wake in another land.

* * *

We are in Kanniyakumari now — the Land's End of India, the southernmost tip of this great nation. The breezes do indeed blow in across three different oceans, the Bay of Bengal, the Indian Ocean and the Arabian Sea. There is nothing but sea between us and the Antarctic. It is a place famous for its sunsets and sunrises over the ocean. The town is named after the Goddess Kumari, the virgin, and is a place of pilgrimage for millions of Hindus.

We are staying at a wonderful hotel — the Sea View Lodge. We have a palatial room with ornately carved wooden bed-head, large bathroom, balcony room and even a very grand sofa. Our balcony has a fantastic view of the harbour and the Vivekananda Memorial temple on a rock 500 metres offshore. But the view from the shore is dominated by a magnificent 130 feet high statue of the sage and revered poet, Thiruvalluvar. The bearded saint stands watching us from a rock just off shore. Two thousand years ago, he wrote his classic work, the Thirukkural, which instructs mankind on matters of Virtue, Wealth and Love. It took 500 sculptors to create the 7,000 tonne statue, which was unveiled at the dawn of the new millennium.

The town is full of plastic tourist tat and a slightly unnerving religious fervour. There is a place at the confluence of the three oceans where there is a strange hollow formed in the water. It is said to be a sacred place and people like to take a dip in this 'dip' in the ocean. They throw themselves in fully clothed with great gusto. I have not been tempted to do the same, despite the temperature, but there is definitely something magical about this place. I have felt blissfully happy since we arrived, and Bill is feeling much better too. As I drift off to sleep for an afternoon nap, I have a vision of an island of light moving in towards me across the ocean.

It is evening now. We take a tuk-tuk to sunset point. Our tuk-tuk lines up with all the other tuk-tuks disgorging tourists who are making their way en masse towards the edge of the headland. It is obviously the thing to do. I had been worried how we might get home afterwards, but the tuk-tuk drivers are in no hurry to get away. They sit around smoking and chatting. 'You don't need to worry about them going anywhere. This is where the business is,' says Bill.

We watch the sun go down over Kovalam, a picturesque village just along the coast from where we stand. The houses, all painted lavender blue, are set around a curving sandy beach with the waves of the Arabian Sea crashing in and a backdrop of the foothills of the Western Ghats. This beautiful scene is bathed in the myriad colours of the sunset. Bill is leaping about and climbing to the top of huge rounded boulders that lie here and there on the beach. He looks out to sea and strikes a manly pose silhouetted against the sunset. As we turn to walk back, there is an eerie light from the luminous velvet blue sky and the bright pink sand glowing beneath our feet.

The place is full of Indian tourists—it is the school holidays at the moment. Everyone wants to take our photo with their family. 'I don't think I've seen another westerner since we arrived,' says Bill. 'The Indians seem as excited to be here as we are. It's very sweet.'

It really is a marvellous hotel here. Whenever you need refreshment, tiny Umpa Lumpas come to the door and cater to your every need. The only problem is that they seem to think we have a penchant for cheese sandwiches.

Umpa Lumpa: 'What is your order, Sir?'

Bill: 'We would like one omelette, one mutter paneer and two chais please.'

Umpa Lumpa: 'Very good, Sir, so that is one omelette, one mutter paneer, three chais and a cheese sandwich.'

Bill: 'No, we don't want a cheese sandwich. The order is one omelette, one mutter paneer and <u>two</u> chais please.'

Umpa Lumpa: 'Yes, Sir, so that is one mutter paneer, three chais and a cheese sandwich.'

Bill: 'No, we want an omelette, not a cheese sandwich and its two chais, not three.'

Umpa Lumpa (with sideways head bob and glazed expression): 'Yes, very good, Sir.'

Order arrives—everything is there, including a cheese sandwich and three chais.

* * *

I am over-excited about watching the sunrise and get up at 4 am, convinced that it is about to happen at any moment. But I have to wait another 2 hours for the great event. Bill is not particularly pleased to be woken so early. 'Go back to sleep Anna. It will be at least another hour yet,' he grumbles, turning over in bed.

Finally, what I have been anticipating so eagerly begins, the colours in the sky changing every second—blues, purples, reds, orange, turquoise, all reflected in the cloud formations and in the ocean—a feast of colour. The Indian dawn chorus starts—a lonely car horn sounds out to mark the beginning of the overture. It is joined by a rising crescendo of other assorted toots and trumpeting. This reaches fever pitch and goes into the second movement—the guttural sound of lungs and throats being cleared all around town, a prelude to dogs barking and much shouting later. Ceiling fans whirl, bottles clunk, more dogs bark—an Indian morning is born.

It is time for our first dip in the Indian Ocean. We thought that Kovalam looked so enchanting in the sunset last night, that we have hired a tuk-tuk to go there. Our driver, Gladius is a very earnest man with 'God Bless You' on the front of his tuk-tuk. He looks after our bags whilst we swim. The bathing bit is fun, but changing into our swimmers is a bit of an ordeal. A large and curious crowd gather round to stare at us. Gladius takes pity on me and asks a local lady if I can change in her hut. Meanwhile, Bill has to battle his way out of his underpants whilst the wind threatens to whip his towel away and more than 20 onlookers crowd round him. I do not think they would be too surprised to find what is in Bill's pants, but they are determined to check anyway.

'God, it feels good to get in the sea at last,' says Bill jumping about in the water and shrieking. He is right—it is a huge relief after ten days of sweltering heat. The waves are foaming and boiling after their long journey across the ocean, but the beach has a nice gentle slope and we have fun jumping about in the shallows.

* * *

I have just phoned home to check in with Mum and Dad. They gave me the sad news that Aunty Beryl died suddenly of a brain aneurysm. It is such a shock, she seemed so healthy and bright last time I saw her. I have been thinking about her a lot lately, with our impending visit to Sri Lanka and what she discovered about the family there. My lasting image of her is the photo she sent with this year's Christmas message. She and Uncle

Blake smiled out of the photo, sitting on a tandem, about to go off on one of their bike trips. They looked the epitome of happiness and fitness.

* * *

I wake up feeling sad about Aunty Beryl. It feels strange hearing this news when we are far away from home. I would have liked to go to the funeral and say goodbye, but I cannot do that. A book that I am reading falls open at a page with this quotation, 'The bond that links your true family is not one of blood, but of respect and joy in each other's life.' It seems pretty apt.

We take the ferry to visit the Vivekananda Memorial Temple. It was built to commemorate Swami Vivekananda, a Bengali religious leader and philosopher. In 1892, he swam out and sat in deep meditation on one of the rocks and was inspired to preach the message, 'The Lord is one, but the sages describe him differently,' at the Parliament of religions in Chicago. He is the founder of the Ramakrishna Mission in Chennai, which now has spread all over the world. People also come to see the Sri Pada Parai, the footprint of the Goddess Kumari, where legend tells that she did her penance on the rock.

We take our shoes off and leave them at the entrance before we are allowed to walk round the temple. The stones are very hot under foot, but there is a lovely peaceful atmosphere. We walk to the southern side of the rock and lean against the railing gazing out at the ocean.

'Just think, there's nothing between us and the Antarctic except sea. And that's a very long way,' says Bill.

'Yes and a very different temperature,' I reply, thinking wistfully of cooler climes.

The temple is made from acres and acres of skilfully worked marble. We wander inside and find a room where people of all faiths can meditate and pray. We sit for a few minutes, enjoying the dark, cool, serene atmosphere.

Back on dry land, we walk through the back streets of Kanniyakumari, trying to find a way to a church we saw from the ferry. After the news about Aunty Beryl, I feel the need to say some prayers. The streets get more and more narrow and teem with life. Everywhere we go, people shout, 'hello!' — we must look so out of place. The children run out to greet us — 'Hello, what's your name? Do you have any school pens?' They want to hold our hands and stare at us with big bright eyes, beaming smiles and giggles.

In one street, we are greeted by a silver-haired man who speaks very good English. He tells us his name is Joaquin. He wants to shake our hands and ask us lots of personal questions:

'Are you married? Why not? Do you have any children? Why not? etc, etc.' His family and neighbours are gathered tightly around us whilst this is going on. They all have broad smiles, with red stained teeth and glazed eyes. They have been chewing betel nuts. Joaquin is a comical little man. There is a very tall giggly lady standing behind him and doing hand gestures making fun of Joaquin's diminutive stature. The whole experience is rather surreal.

* * *

Yesterday evening we made a snap decision to leave the luxury of our palatial room-serviced apartment with the breezes from three different oceans and a view of the sunrise, to start out on new adventures. So, this morning we got up early and went to the train station. We both went to the ticket desk and Bill asked for two tickets to Varkala. The conversation went like this:

Bill: 'Two tickets for Varkala, please.'

Ticket salesman: 'Three?'

Bill: 'No, **two** tickets please.'

Ticket salesman: 'Yes, three sir.'

Bill (speaking very slowly and patiently): 'No-o, <u>TWO</u> tickets. Look — one (points to himself), two (points to me).'

Ticket salesman: 'Yes, OK, sir.' Sideways head bob. Hands us three tickets.

This is a strange phenomenon we have encountered before. The Indians, despite in general having very good English, seem unable to distinguish between the numbers two and three. If in doubt, they always seem to plump for the higher number. It has happened so many times that we are beginning to wonder whether there is some person, invisible to us, but perceived by the locals, following us about. Or perhaps they are just really keen to make that extra sale?

Varkala is on the coast, about four hours direct train ride North West from Kanniyakumari. It is on this journey, that I first become aware of Bill's penchant for all things fried and sold in the aisles of the train. The first vendor approaches along the gangway, with cries of, 'Tea, coffee, iddly. Iddly, iddly, iddly.' Bill eagerly beckons him over and orders five of everything he has on offer.

'Why've you bought so much?' I ask.

'Because they were only five rupees each and I bought enough to share with you,' says Bill.

I look in dismay at the unhygienic array of deep fried indescribables, turn up my nose in disgust and say, 'Uh, I don't think so!'

What Bill has not yet worked out is that there will be another hawker along every five minutes of the journey. Inevitably, the next hawkers' food looks better than the stale offerings from the first guy, so Bill spends the whole journey looking at all the other food passing by and saying peevishly, 'Oh, those look much fresher than mine.'

Apart from Bill's food vendor envy, our trip is fairly uneventful and we arrive at Varkala station with great expectations about how wonderful this place will be.

* * *

In the cool of the evening we stroll on the beach. There are a lot of Indian families doing the same and some people are swimming. The Indian women, wearing what resemble Victorian nightdresses—floor length, long-sleeved and complete with neck ruff made from the thickest of fabric—have gathered in little groups segregated from the men to paddle in the sea.

Yesterday, I was in revolt about being here. It is ten-fold hotter and more humid than breezy Kanniyakumari. All day I felt incredibly tired, lethargic and nauseous and in the frame of mind where I could never imagine feeling better.

We stayed one night at Panchavadi, down in the valley where it is unbearably hot, humid and infested with mosquitoes, before discovering that there are lots of good apartments up on the breezy cliff top overlooking the beach. As I was feeling really dreadful, my hero, Bill, moved all our belongings to the Sea View Lodge, while I had a shower and lounged about on the bed. We have our own private balcony looking out to sea with a view framed by coconut palms. The world looks very different from up here. And Bill is really happy since Stephen, the Manager, told him he has a big TV to watch the World Cup football matches on.

* * *

Bill's favourite Salomon sandals, in fact, his only pair of sandals, have ripped away from the sole. He is very upset, but thinks hopefully that they can be mended.

'Indians can mend anything for a few rupees. That's what I love about this country—everything gets recycled,' he says.

'I'm not sure they can do much with these,' I say doubtfully. But I had not counted on the ingenuity and craftsmanship of Indian cobblers. A kindly rickshaw driver takes us to the cobbler and later picks up the finished article for us. They come back perfectly mended for the princely sum of Rs10 (about 13p)—how marvellous!

Bill and I are sitting in the Internet café. I am checking e-mails and he is reading the paper. There has been a lot of talk of war between Pakistan and India over Kashmir. We have been following the escalation in hostilities in the papers and wondering whether we should be concerned about it. There are lots of e-mails from worried friends and family back home, who seem to think that India is about to be annihilated by a nuclear bomb from Pakistan.

I tell Bill that Dad has e-mailed to say, 'The latest advice to all British nationals from our Government is 'don't travel to India' and British nationals already there are told to consider leaving the country. You are advised to contact the High Commission or your airline. You are also advised not to travel to North or East Sri Lanka due to the terrorist activities of the Tamil Tigers.'

'Great. We picked a really good time to come—not only is the weather the hottest and most humid it could possibly get because of the monsoon, but war is about to break out!' I say to Bill.

'To be honest, down here in the South, I feel a million miles from it all. The locals seem pretty laid back about it, except for the fact that it's spoiling the tourist trade. Apparently we are two of only 1,000 British people in the whole of India,' he says reading from the paper. 'The Indian government can keep close tabs on us because we have to give our passport number and next destination every time we book into a hotel or change money. We've left a trail a mile wide since we got here and it wouldn't take them long to track us down in Varkala. I find that quite reassuring somehow. I think we're pretty safe here for now. Let's face it, if India or Pakistan were to start a nuclear war, we wouldn't be much safer at home in Europe. But I don't think it will come to that anyway.'

'Yes, I think you're probably right. Hey, do you want to hear some other news from home?' I ask him, reading an article in the South India Express. 'Apparently there is a sex-crazed dolphin off the coast of Weymouth, which lures people to go swimming with it and then tries to have its evil way with them. I always wondered why all those people like to go swimming with the dolphins!'

'That's classic, isn't it? War's about to break out and there are articles about sex-crazed dolphins on the other side of the world in Blighty. I s'pose it's a good distraction from imminent war to read about the eccentric English . . . But it's good to hear that World Cup fever is beginning to grip the nation at home and that the Queen's Golden Jubilee celebrations went with a swing, because it's unusually sunny for a British Summer,' Bill tells me after perusing a few of his e-mails.

Back in our room at Sea View Lodge, Bill disappears for a while and then comes back looking decidedly guilty. 'Have you got something you need to tell me?' I ask.

'I'm off to watch football and drink beer,' he says.

'Oh, is that all? Well, have a good time.' He runs off to watch the Germany versus Ireland match. I watch from the balcony as a huge TV is brought outside and placed with great reverence in front of the small crowd of excited men. There is the ceremonial adjustment of the aerial, which takes ages, but never seems to quite get the reception right. The picture is always a bit fuzzy. There is the passing round of Kingfisher beer and the preliminary chat about who supports who. No matter that India is not in the World Cup, men the world over are experts on football and feel qualified to make judgements on who is good and who is not. Finding out that Bill is English, the locals make pronouncements such as, 'Michael Owen is the best player in the world.' 'No, no, David Beckham, <u>he</u> is the best player in the world.' They settle down to watch the match. From time to time, the collective sounds of, 'Hooray,' or 'Ooh,' as goals are scored or missed, filter up to me on the balcony. I look over to see rows of happy male faces engrossed in the match and sipping beer.

In the evening we like to wander along the cliff top, taking in the sea air and the delicious smells issuing from the restaurants, which line the path. We have got to know most of the restaurant owners who are friendly and chatty and vie for our business in a laid-back kind of way. One of our favourites is the little man who wears jam jar thick glasses and owns a wobbly wooden shack on stilts. It sways alarmingly as you climb to the first floor balcony for a table looking out over the sea. Only one person at a time on the ladder, please, or the whole thing is in danger of collapsing. The owner boasts that he can cook anything from scratch in ten minutes flat on his two gas rings. Forty-five minutes later the food arrives, but it is always delicious. His range includes Italian, Mexican and French dishes as well as the usual South Indian fare. He has not disappointed us so far and his chilli is particularly good.

I am growing to like Varkala more and more. The people are very friendly and easy going here. There is none of the hassling by touts that was so wearing in Mamallapuram. My eyes are constantly filled with beauty—the contrast between the red earth and the deep green foliage; iridescent beetles, jewel coloured butterflies and dragonflies constantly fluttering by; soaring fish eagles and hawks plummeting into the sea, or swooping just over our heads on the cliff, the view down to the beach and the changing moods of the sea, the coconut palm fronds waving in the breeze and changing the pattern of sunlight on the balcony of our room. And in the valley below, buffaloes working the fields; the colourful temple and the washing activities at the temple tank—men bobbing up and down in the water at their morning ritual and the slap-slap of washing being beaten on stones; smiley faces, waving hands and shouts of, 'Hello. How are you? What is your name?'

* * *

I am sad to leave Varkala, but we must start the next leg of our journey. We have a short, but crowded train journey to Trivandrum, in which a fat, sweaty Indian lady wedges herself next to me. Her body is like a bag of jelly held together only by her skin, and oozes all over the people sitting next to her.

On arrival in Trivandrum, we install ourselves in a posh hotel, the Regency, costing all of £7 per night. Bill's most important criteria in choosing our room is that it must have a good telly so he can watch the England versus Argentina match tomorrow night. But it is a good move on other fronts, as we have a cool, clean, mosquito-free room in which to relax and gather our wits for the next country on our agenda—Sri Lanka.

After a very sedate visit to the zoo and botanical gardens, we return to our room to find a lovely pile of fresh clean laundry and then settle down with Kingfisher beer to watch the Argentina versus England football match. It is a really important match and will decide whether we get through to the next round. I will have to be Bill's token man for the match, pretending I understand the off-side rule and trying to make comments in the right places and sound as if I know what I am talking about. I am reminded of an episode of Father Ted when Mrs. Doyle buys a book entitled, *How to watch football, for women*. It teaches her when to chant phrases such as, 'You're not singing, anymore!' and 'Go on, my son.' I wish I had a copy of the book.

Even I can see that it is an exciting game. As the match progresses and the number of Kingfisher beers mounts, the frequency with which Bill leaps out of his chair, shouting loudly increases. When Beckham scores his penalty goal, we both leap out of our chairs and embrace. Bill tells me it is sweet revenge for the fiasco of a match between the two teams in the last World Cup. The final score is one nil to England. We are through to the next round.

Chapter 3
Sri Lanka—Bushman Bandara and the King of the Veddas

We get up very early for our flight to Sri Lanka and have a hair-raising ride through the monsoon rains to the airport. Suddenly the roads are running with six inches of water, which laps in at the sides of the rickshaw, soaking us and stalling the engine. Are we going to have to walk or to change rickshaws to get to the airport on time? But after a quick wipe of the plugs our driver manages to get the engine going again and eventually we arrive safely, if a little soggy, at the airport.

We had been told that we absolutely must arrive three hours in advance of our flight or we would not be allowed on, so we are in a mild panic that we are running late after our problems with the rickshaw. We rush in, only to find that nothing is open, not even a chai stall. Having left the hotel with no breakfast, we have to wait around for nearly three hours, hungry and bored until the check-in desk finally opens. Then there is a chaotic scrum to get wodges of forms, fill them in and queue up to get them processed before we can get onto the plane. Needless to say, the plane does not leave on time.

But the flight is very quick and soon we arrive at the scenic Colombo airport. By now it is 1.30 pm and we are feeling pretty jaded, having had nothing to eat since yesterday. So we head for the airport restaurant. They seem to have run out of everything, so we have to share a tiny plate of anaemic looking chips and are still hungry.

Our plan is to catch the train to Kandy in the hills and use it as a base for exploring. So we take a taxi to Colombo railway station, praying that there might be something to eat at the station café. At the station, we go into the Rail Tours office to find out train times to Kandy, not realising that it actually has nothing to do with the railway and is just in the business of selling tours. In our light-headed state, we are persuaded to book ourselves on a relatively expensive five-day tour around the cultural sights of Sri Lanka. I come away with an uneasy feeling that somehow we may have been conned. I do not like to sign up to something without having time to think about it and look into all the alternatives.

'Don't worry. I'm sure it'll be fine. It sounds great!' says Bill in his usual optimistic fashion.

The train for Kandy is just about to leave and we are rushed into the observation car at the front of the train, still having had nothing to eat or drink. The train ride is bumpy but very scenic. It is a relief to leave the suburbs of sprawling Colombo. We travel through paddy fields and banana plantations, gradually turning into lush forests with outcrops of strangely shaped rocks as we rise higher into the hills. Small neat houses are dotted here and there amongst the undergrowth and people step back from the track to let the train pass.

We eventually arrive at the very grand Hotel Thilanka, where we are booked in as part of our tour. We are both exhausted, dirty and shabby after more that 12 hours travelling on snack rations.

'Ah, this is heaven,' I say to Bill as we sit drinking proper Ceylon tea on the hotel balcony. 'It is the best cup of tea I've ever tasted.' The Thilanka is up on a hill overlooking Kandy. We have a view of the town below, with its lake and forest all around. The air is pleasantly cool, here in the hills. The sun is slowly setting behind a huge white statue of the

Buddha, which sits on the horizon. I take a deep sigh. 'So this is the land of my ancestors,' I say to Bill. 'I like it.'

'Yes, it's beautiful. And after the day we've had, I'm really enjoying the luxury of this hotel,' says Bill, grabbing a towel and heading for the bathroom. 'I'm looking forward to my first hot shower since we left England. And a gin and tonic in the restaurant later would make the perfect end to the evening.'

* * *

It would have been nice to just stay a couple of days relaxing at the luxurious Thilanka and slowly exploring our surroundings, but our tour is about to start and we are picked up bright and early by our driver, Rajan. He is very polite and formal, always addressing Bill as 'Mr William.' I am referred to as 'Madame' and he will only speak to Bill, even if I ask him a question. I find this infuriating. It seems to be the etiquette both here and in India to always address the man in a couple, as if the woman's opinion does not count.

'He's a bit stuffy, isn't he?' whispers Bill. 'I'm going to make it my mission over the next couple of days to get him to lighten up and have a bit of a joke with us.'

Our first visit is to the Perideniya Botanical Gardens. It is Sunday morning and traditionally the time when young lovers go to the gardens to wander round arm-in-arm or sit canoodling under a tree. It is lovely to get carried away with the romantic mood in these beautiful gardens.

Bill, being a gardener, is very excited by some of the specimens in the Botanical Gardens. The giant double coconut, which takes six to eight years to mature and weighs up to 25 kg is a particular favourite.

'Wow, that's BIG!' he says. 'Apparently it's the world's largest and heaviest fruit. Can you just stand underneath while I take a photo, to give an idea of the scale.' It is not until afterwards that it occurs to me that it might have been rather foolish to stand there. I can just see the headline in the paper—'British woman killed by massive nuts falling on head.'

We walk down the avenue of palms, where smelly fruit bats, as big as cats, flap about in the treetops. There is an ancient fig tree, *Ficus Benjamini*, the size of a football pitch and propped up in places with sticks.

'Corr, this is huge too—the biggest one I've ever seen,' says Bill who runs about in excited fascination under its giant canopy.

'And we must see the orchid house. There's nothing quite so amazing as a hothouse full of beautiful orchids,' he enthuses. He is right.

It is full of exquisite flowers that smell of chocolate and vanilla or look like little animals, spiders, bees and deer. Two nuns wander amongst the exotic blooms and Bill giggles as he tries to capture them in the background of our photos. I think he is quite taken with the contrast of their austere black and white clothing set amongst the colourful blooms.

Once we have filled our senses with fragrance, colour and beauty, we go back to the car, where Rajan is waiting to take us to the elephant orphanage at Pinnewala. It is feeding time for the orphaned baby elephants when we arrive and Bill is asked to help by giving one of the two-year-olds a bottle of milk.

'Blimey, he likes his milkies. You have to hold on tight to the bottle to stop the whole thing going down his throat,' says Bill. The keeper thrusts another bottle into Bill's hands, saying, 'Quickly, give him another one.'

But one of the saddest sights is a tiny seven-month-old baby elephant. It is not much taller than our knees and covered in coarse hair. It is wandering forlornly around, looking very depressed and rather frightened by all the people crowding round to take its photo. When all the crowds have rushed off somewhere else, we spend some time with it, just giving it some love and reassurance. It seems to have a real affinity with Bill. As he pats its shoulder, two big teardrops run down from each eye.

We are invited to meet some of the mother elephants who have given birth at the orphanage. I make friends with a mother and her baby. She seems happy for me to pat her on the trunk and stroke her baby, but when Bill comes along, her long trunk zooms straight in on his crotch, as if to say, 'You better have good intentions towards my baby, or I could do you some serious damage.'

There is a stir of excitement—it is time for the elephants to go to the river and bathe. They all gather into a crowd at the top of the hill, trumpeting and hooting in anticipation. Then they charge down towards us and we have to run for cover as a thunderous mass of giant grey bodies gallops past us. We follow behind them at a safe distance as they are let out of the orphanage and stampede through the narrow streets of the village, causing chaos on their way to the river. The shopkeepers are quick to bring their goods indoors and all the other villagers know to dash inside.

We watch them as they bathe. There are lots of play fights and general frolicking about. I love the way they seem to look out for each other—the frisky youngsters are shepherded by the older ones to stop them going out of their depth, and all of them care for the really little babies. Some of the older working elephants lie down in the shallows to get scrubbed by their keepers, the mahouts. Occasionally a bold teenager thinks it might be interesting to try to cross the river and escape into the jungle on the opposite bank. This is greeted by lots of shouting and waving of sticks by the mahouts.

'That was brilliant,' I say to Bill. 'I think I'm in love with elephants and I'm dying to see some in the wild.'

'Yes, me too,' says Bill.

Back in Kandy, we visit the Temple of the Tooth, which supposedly has a casket containing the Buddha's tooth. Occasionally the tooth is uncovered and displayed for important people. Apparently it is the size of a buffalo tooth and seems to be a symbol of political power, since it is always kept in the capital city of the kingdom.

It is the first Buddhist temple we have visited and I am surprised at the fervour with which people worship in front of the tooth relic. I suppose I had imagined that Buddhists would be more serene and detached.

In the evening we go to watch some traditional Kandyan dancing, which is highly entertaining. The dancers are a whirl of colour in their sparkly red and white costumes, with elaborate headdresses and jangly leg bells. They dance to a barrage of belly pulsating rhythm provided by five drummers. There are five male dancers—four young and agile, who amaze us with athletic feats, back flips, leaps and high kicks, often whilst balancing spinning discs; and one old fella. He does a little spin and then wobbles a bit and he is always a couple of beats out of step with the others.

'Ah, bless him,' says Bill. 'He looks as if he might need to go and have a lie down afterwards.'

* * *

Back in the car with Rajan bright and early again. Today we are off to Matale, Dambulla and Sigiriya. Our first stop is a herb garden at Matale. We are not particularly interested in going to the herb garden, but Rajan is most insistent.

We are shown around the garden by an ayurvedic doctor who is very knowledgeable about the plants and herbs and gives us both a very good back massage using some of the medicinal oils made from the plants in the garden. Everything is fine up to this point, but then we are herded into the shop run by a very aggressive man, where we are persuaded to buy two bottles of the massage oil for a hugely inflated price and he tries to get us to pay for one bottle to be sent back to England, packed in our clothes to protect it. Hmm, do we think that package will ever arrive?

Our next stop is Dambulla, which is the setting for the most remarkable Buddhist cave temples in a rocky outcrop. There are five magical grottoes. We step into the first cave and come face to face with the most enormous reclining Buddha carved out of the rock. The Buddha almost fills the whole cave. It feels strangely intimate, like walking into someone's bedroom by accident and finding them doing something they would rather you did not see. We go into the next dimly lit cave and as our eyes begin to grow accustomed to the light, painted images of the Buddha start to materialise. There are hundreds upon hundreds of images, covering the cave from floor to ceiling with the most intricate murals in red, gold and white. And there are yet more Buddha statues sitting serenely about the cave. It is quiet and peaceful and we spend ten minutes meditating completely undisturbed, before some other visitors arrive and we leave to give them some peaceful time of their own.

From Dambulla, we drive to Sigiriya, the lion rock. It rises sheer-sided, 600 feet above the surrounding plain, a vast lump of ochre and amber striated rock, glowing in the afternoon sun. In the caves that honeycomb its base are inscriptions written by Buddhist monks on retreat here in the third century BC. Around the base of Sigiriya are pleasure gardens full of fountains and swimming pools, and on its flat summit, a citadel, built by King Kassapa 1500 years ago. He chose this site as being easy to defend because he had murdered his father and lived in fear of being attacked by his brother, the rightful heir to the throne.

We climb a rickety, rusting spiral staircase up the rock, stopping to admire the beautiful murals of busty dancing damsels, where Bill lingers rather longer than I would have liked.

'I'm looking for the nymph with three nipples,' he says when I suggest we move on.

'I bet you are,' I reply.

We pass along a corridor bounded by a mirror wall coated with a mixture of egg white, beeswax and honey. I think of the hands that long ago must have rubbed and polished so hard to build up this shiny patina.

Now we ascend a perilous rusting iron walkway, which is bolted to the rock none too securely, fearing that it might part company with the rock at anytime. I am in awe of the people who had to carry all the materials up to build the palace. We step out onto a spur of rock known as the lion platform.

'Wow, look at those!' says Bill pointing to the huge hornets nests, which dangle from the rocks above. Our guide points out a cage which is apparently designed for people to hide in if the hornets swarm. We step onto a staircase between two enormous lion's paws, for the final ascent to the summit. The guide shows us a vast rectangular tank of water, in which the people of the palace used to swim. It also created the head of water pressure to power the fountains in the pleasure garden below. We teeter on the edge of the citadel, looking at the vertiginous drop to the plain below. Our guide tells us that ironically, King Kassapa was also afraid of heights. But it seems his fear of being attacked by his brother must have been greater—the driving motivation to create this incredible edifice, a monument to a man's fear. Kassapa's life finally ended when his fears came true. His brother mounted an attack, but instead of retreating to his lofty citadel, Kassapa, with foolish bravado, rode out to meet him on an elephant. Getting cut off from the rest of his army when his elephant bolted, he feared he had been abandoned and killed himself.

Dusk is falling as we drive through the jungle towards our hotel. It is very quiet and the roads are deserted. We round a bend to see a herd of wild elephants crossing the road about 50 yards in front of us. The big mother elephant is acting as lollipop lady, waving the others across the road. They scurry across almost on tiptoe. Big She Elephant hurries the last two straggling youngsters into the bushes and checks both ways up and down the road to see that no-one is following before she too disappears into the bushes. Bill and I look at each other, eyes wide with wonder.

'We've just seen our first wild elephants,' we both say in unison.

Tonight we are staying in another splendid hotel, The Giritale, overlooking Lake Giritale and surrounded by jungle. We have spent so much time in cities and in the thick of civilisation, that it is a real pleasure to be staying somewhere a little wild at last.

Whilst drinking tea on the balcony, we are serenaded by a lovely old man, playing a mandolin and singing traditional Sri Lankan songs. They are hauntingly beautiful and add to the romance of our setting.

* * *

This morning, we wake to find a herd of spotted deer right outside our room. They are making little barking noises and seem quite alarmed. The jungle comes to within a few feet of the room.

'I wonder what is scaring them?' I say to Bill.

'There's something out there. I can feel it in my water,' he says, peering into the trees. Maybe it's a leopard and the deer know that it won't come near us humans.'

'Ooh, how exciting. I've always wanted to see a leopard,' I say straining my eyes into the undergrowth. But whatever it is, it proves elusive.

Today, we are on our way to visit the great ruined city of Polonnaruwa, which dates from 1700 years ago. The large site covers four kilometres. We visit the remains of the seven-storey Royal Palace and the Quadrangle, the religious heart of the city, where the famous tooth relic was once housed. The Thuparama is a pleasantly cool and shady house with a wonderful peaceful atmosphere. It houses eight crystalline limestone Buddhas which sparkle in the dim light.

The Vatadage has a beautiful symmetry. Four seated Buddha statues, flanked by nagaraja (snake kings), lotus flowers and jolly pot-bellied dwarves align to the cardinal points. At each entrance is a semi-circular moonstone of polished granite with carvings of symbolic animals and flowers.

But the site I love the most is the Gal Vihara, the 'Cave of the Spirits of Knowledge.' Here there are four vast statues of the Buddha carved out of the rock. The grain of the rock adds to their beauty, as if there are clouds and sky in them. As I gaze at the statue of the standing Buddha, it seems that the whole universe is contained in it. An ocean of serenity emanates from the 14 metre-long reclining Buddha. This carving depicts the moments before the Buddha's death, as he slips peacefully into Nirvana. As I contemplate this image, memories of Aunty Beryl are flooding my mind and I feel sad that I cannot go to her funeral to say goodbye. I tell Bill how I am feeling.

'Maybe you can find your own way to say goodbye to her. This seems like a good place to do it,' he says.

So I sit on a grassy bank and write a letter of farewell, thanking Beryl for discovering our connection with this beautiful land. Then I put the letter in one of the incense bowls and set light to it, hoping that the smoke will carry my words to heaven.

In the afternoon we visit Anuradhapura. By this time we are feeling overheated and tired. For me, the site does not have the magic of Polonnaruwa, even though it is much older (400 BC). It is a vast site with so many dagobas, that we become quite blasé about them.

'Oh, look there is another 2000 year old intricately carved temple.'
'Oh really? Where can I get a cold Pepsi round here?'
But the most off-putting thing is that the minute you set foot in any of them you are assailed by people wanting donations, despite having

already paid $32 to get in. It spoilt all the feeling of being a sacred place of worship. The place was also overrun by mangy starving dogs, many of which looked close to death. I found it really upsetting that these people purporting to be Buddhists were so greedy, materialistic and uncaring, when all around them were creatures in dire need of their help.

It is our last night with Rajan and he has decided to be sociable with us for once. He invites us to sample some arrack with him. It is the local brew made from coconuts. It is powerful stuff and I only manage a little to be polite, before it gives me a headache. But Bill sees it as a challenge to his manhood and tries to keep up with Rajan, who is hoovering it down at a frightening pace. By the end of the second bottle, they are both bleary-eyed and wobbling about. Bill is starting to get a little over familiar for Rajan's liking, asking him lots of questions about his home and family. It seems that all is not harmonious there—perhaps the reason he has a job that takes him away from them for so much time. I can see that Rajan is getting angry and when Bill slurringly mispronounces his name for about the third time, he tries to pick a fight. Bill pours on the charm and manages to diffuse the situation. We bid Rajan goodnight. Unfortunately Bill has already drunk enough arrack to make him sick in the night and give him a cracking hangover the next day.

* * *

The final leg of our journey with Rajan is a long and bumpy ride to Trincomalee. Each time we lurch in and out of a vast pothole, Bill is in danger of losing his breakfast. Rajan is not looking too fresh either.

We are very lucky that the ceasefire and the peace talks between the Sri Lankan government and the Tamil Tigers has given us the freedom to travel to parts of the country, like Trincomalee, that would have been off limits only a few months ago.

We bid goodbye to Rajan and find a room at the French Gardens Guest House, just north of Trincomalee. It is all slightly run-down because it has been starved of tourist money for so long. But it has everything you could want from an idyllic beach resort—fine, white sand, clear blue sea lapping gently onto the beach and the shade of the coconut trees to keep you pleasantly cool—a little corner of paradise. It is run by a lovely family, including grandpa and ten grandchildren.

'The tour was a great overview of Sri Lanka's cultural wonders, but I think I've had my fill of hot, dry, dusty cultural sites and bone-shaking journeys on terrible roads for now,' says Bill. 'This looks like the perfect place to kick back for a couple of days.'

'Yes, I think you're right,' I reply.

We have made friends with two Germans, Juli and Markus. They are a handsome couple. He is tall and courteous with near perfect English. His wide blue eyes are always alight with the kindest smile. She is tiny and fragile-looking with pale silky hair but an underlying toughness that belies her size. There is football to watch and Bill needs a male friend to shout at the telly with. Despite Germany and England being sworn enemies at football, Markus and Bill have called a truce and it is Germany and England against the rest of the world here in Trincomalee. Markus is very gracious about England's mediocre performance against Nigeria which ends in a nil:nil draw.

There is a tiny puppy which the family have rescued from the street. It nearly died today due to dehydration and lack of food. It is really too young to be away from its mum and no-one has taught it about things like drinking water. But it is now being tenderly nursed back to health in shifts between us and Juli and Markus.

'I have made up zis mixture of mulk and egg,' says Juli. She is a doctor and she has made it her mission to save him. She is sitting in the café feeding the puppy with a teaspoon. 'He seems to like it very much and it will rehydrate him.' It certainly seems to be working.

'I think his name should be Rocky, because he is a survivor,' says Markus. We all agree.

* * *

It is blissful here. This is the most relaxed I have felt since we left home. We swim and eat and swim and do laundry and eat some more and play with the puppy or chat with Juli and Markus, the happy Germans. Juli is covered in fleabites from having Rocky in her room at night, but she still loves him. 'He has **so** many fleas, but I don't care. He is **so** cute. I just cuddle him all night long,' she says. Markus raises his eyebrows, giving us a resigned look.

* * *

One day folds into the next with gentle ease . . . Rocky has made a spectacular recovery and last night was attacking the resident adult dog with great gusto. Fortunately the adult dog was very tolerant of having its ears and tail bitten.

We said goodbye to Juli and Markus today, who were on their way to see the sights of Sigiriya and Dambulla.

There was just enough time to watch England and Germany in their latest World Cup football matches before they went. Both teams won their matches, England beating Denmark 3:nil and Germany beating Paraguay one:nil.

In the evening we sit in the café. 'I miss Markus and Juli,' says Bill. 'They are the nicest Germans I have ever met.

'Yes, me too. I really enjoyed their company,' I tell him. Rocky is sitting in my lap, so I give him a little tickle. 'That's from Juli,' I tell him.

* * *

We travel from Trinco to Kandy on an overcrowded bus that stinks of fish and vomit, driven by a madman who hurls the bus along the terrible bumpy road at break-neck speed. Each time we lurch around another corner there is synchronised puking from all the children, who are overpowered by the smell of rotten fish. In the seat in front of us, a tiny frail old lady is squashed by her husband, who sits on her lap. We are most relieved to get off the bus in Kandy.

We cannot afford to stay in the Thilanka at the prices that they charge directly to foreign tourists, and settle for a less luxurious hotel beside the lake. There is a wedding about to take place and the hotel is full of smartly dressed wedding guests. We catch sight of the bride. She is radiantly beautiful and looks very happy. I give a little sigh and think forward to next June, just over a year away, when Bill and I will be doing the same thing, if we are still speaking by then! So far, so good . . .

Our hotel room is right next to a busy main road and we cannot have the window open without the traffic fumes coming in, so we are going to look at a guest house in a quieter part of town, the Freedom Lodge.

As we walk up the drive to Freedom Lodge, a familiar figure is hanging out washing on the balcony. He looks up. 'Hey you guys!' shouts Markus. Juli comes running out onto the balcony.

'Bill and Anna. How vunderful!' she shrieks, slapping her thighs in excitement.

'Markus and Juli!' shouts Bill. 'What a brilliant coincidence to find you here. We're thinking of taking a room.'

'You should. It is very lovely here,' says Markus. 'Let's take some tea together. Vait there. I'll tell the landlady you vont a room.' He runs off and after booking us into a cool spacious room, the charming landlady brings teas for us all on the verandah.

'How is little Rocky?' asks Juli.

'He is very well and full of mischief,' I tell her.

'Oh I am **so** glad. I was so vorried about him,' she says.

'Vot are your plans for the rest of your time in Sri Lanka?' asks Markus.

'We want to see more of the wildlife and countryside. I've read about a Mr Bandara, who is very experienced in leading nature tours and want to book with him,' I tell Markus.

'Oh, this is another coincidence! We have just booked a tour with Mr Bandara. Shall we see if we can all go together?' says Markus.

'Oh yes, zat vould be **so** fun,' says Juli.

'Great idea!' Bill and I chorus together.

So we all go to see Mr Bandara, who very generously halves the cost for both couples since we are all going together. Known locally as Bushman Bandara, because of his great knowledge of the country and its birds and beasts, he is quite a character. He is a stocky man in his sixties, still with plenty of energy and verve. There is something of the Omar Sharif about him — it must be the exotic dark looks and the rakish charm. He has a twinkle in his eye that tells me he is definitely an old rascal.

In the evening we go out for a drink with Juli, Markus and Althea, another lady who is staying at the Freedom Lodge and who has also booked on the tour with us. We drink gin cocktails and talk about our forthcoming trip and how excited we are. Althea looks like a strong robust kind of woman, but there is something nervy and unsure about her. I hope she will be OK on this trip.

* * *

It is 6am. Bushman Bandara arrives in his minibus to pick us up. The adventure is starting. As we drive out of Kandy, we see a serpent eagle sitting on a post next to the road.

'This is a very good omen for us. I think we will see lots of animals on this tour,' says the Bushman. We drive up into the mountains and have fantastic views over the Knuckles Range. We stop for tea at a little shack by the side of the road. The Bushman disappears out the back for a while and reappears with a plate of what looks like a cross between fudge and toffee.

'This is a local delicacy known as *jaggery*. It is made from crystallised palm nectar and is very is delicious,' says the Bushman. He is right. It tastes like treacle toffee.

After another hour of driving, we stop in the mountains and go for a walk. All around us, the slopes are covered in tea bushes and there in the distance are some ladies picking tea. I have got my childhood wish at last. I am here in Ceylon watching the beautiful tea ladies. I take a deep breath of the fresh mountain air and savour the moment. It is a good moment.

Bill is in raptures about the tea plants. 'They must be at least 150 years old, judging by the size of their trunks. Look, some of them are a foot thick. Just think, each of these bushes must have made thousands of cups of tea—the best drink in the world.'

As we drive, the Bushman chatters away. He has been on many adventures and has many tales to tell. He tells us of a group of people who he took hiking in the Knuckles Range.

'There was one lady in the group whose fitness I was concerned about,' he tells us. 'I questioned her very thoroughly and told her exactly what we would be doing. She told me, 'I am very fit and it will be no problem,' but when we got there, she was scared of everything and she was exhausted after an hour. I had to carry her the rest of the way on my back!' says the Bushman.

'I called her Pipilulu because she kept stopping every few minutes to go behind a bush. She was cured of this habit after the time she went behind a bush where there was a nest of fire ants!' he laughed heartily at the memory of her hopping about.

We stop by a lake in the Victoria Randenigala Sanctuary. We all have a swim. The water is like a hot bath. As we picnic by the lake, Bushman Bandara seems to be sussing everyone out. He has a charming way of picking up on what you feel least confident about and saying things to reassure you. Althea has the air of someone who has had her heart badly broken and has shrunk inside herself. The Bushman is working his magic on her. He lies back, languorously eating a piece of juicy pineapple and, fixing her with his twinkling dark eyes. 'You remind me of a film star. You look just like a young Gina Lollobrigida,' he says. She blushes and smiles coyly at him like a young girl.

The Bushman spots eight wild elephants on the opposite shore of the lake. He has very keen eyes and we can only see them properly through binoculars. Markus and Bill have a little male competitive moment, comparing each other's binoculars.

All too soon it becomes apparent why the elephants are there. They have been startled out of the bush by poachers who have lit a fire.

Bushman Bandara is very angry. 'Where are the rangers from the Wildlife Department who are paid to stop people doing this? They are playing cards and drinking in their hut!'

We finish our lunch and get back in the minibus. We are heading for Mahiyangana, to see the Veddas. They are the Wanniyala-aetto, the 'people of the forest' and the original inhabitants of Sri Lanka who came here 18,000 years ago. They still live as hunter-gatherers, in harmony with the land, worshipping the ancestral spirits.

The Bushman is a great friend of the Veddas, and one of the few people who speaks their language. He first met them forty years ago when he was out trekking in the bush. They befriended him and he became fascinated with their culture and lifestyle. Now he takes people to meet them, to learn of their ways and to educate people about their plight.

We are given a little fast-track course in Vedda etiquette. We want to give them a gift for spending time seeing us, but the Bushman tells us that they will be insulted if we just give them handouts of money, so we are to buy them some betel nuts, which is their favourite treat.

'Until twenty years ago, the Veddas roamed free in the forest, living how they have always lived for 18,000 years,' Bushman Bandara tells us how. 'Then the Americans came and gave the Sri Lankan government millions of dollars to make a national park. And what happens to the Veddas? They kick them off their ancestral land and send them to a reserve. It is tiny and it is on the poorest land in the dry zone. They cannot live like this. So the Vedda King and a few families that are close to him refused to leave and he started a campaign to get their land back. In the end they got 1500 acres. This is a pathetic amount. Not enough for them to find enough animals to hunt for food. The poachers burn the forest around them and the police come with big trucks and steal all their firewood. The piece of land they were given does not even have its own water supply, so they have to buy containers of water, forcing them to trade goods and ask for donations. And of course, the animals do not come to this land with no water.'

We turn onto a track in the forest that leads to the Vedda village and there at the side of the road is a truck with a man looking round furtively before putting an armful of wood into the back. 'See, what did I tell you? Here are the police stealing their wood.'

The Bushman's story makes me imagine that we are about to meet a forlorn people with broken spirits, but I am quite wrong. The Bushman takes us to their village for an audience with their king. They are very beautiful people with shining eyes, radiant skin and lithe, strong bodies. All of them look much younger than their years.

'How old do you think that man is?' asks the Bushman.

'Around 35?' we suggest.

'He is 54 years old. I have known him since he was a teenager,' the Bushman tells us as they greet each other and embrace. This is true for all of them. They all look about twenty years younger than someone of their age who has lived in our culture. Their lifestyle must be very healthy.

They greet us, warmly shaking both our hands. They are obviously very pleased to see Bushman Bandara and make us feel very welcome.

'Hondamai, hondamai,' they all say.

'Hondamai,' we reply. The Bushman has told us this is their all-purpose greeting. It means, 'Hello. You are welcome. I am very pleased to meet you.'

Beautiful Vedda Man

The King appears. It is immediately obvious that he is the King. Although he is dressed exactly the same as everyone else, in a simple checked sarong, he has an air of quiet dignity and authority about him that is unmistakable. He stands very tall with a mane of hair and a chiselled jaw, even in his sixties a devastatingly handsome man. He also greets us with the two-handed handshake. I have never shaken hands with a king before.

We sit around him in a circle, whilst he talks and allows us to ask him questions. Bushman Bandara translates.

The King tells us of his trip to a world conference on the plight of indigenous people round the globe. He says he feels a great affinity with the Australian Aborigines and the Sami of Lapland. He feels heartened that some governments are starting to listen to the native peoples and to give them their land back. He hopes that one day the government of Sri Lanka will do the same.

He tells us about the Veddas' herbal medicine, which he says can cure anything except cancer. He is an expert healer and is teaching his son to pass on the knowledge to future generations.

The normally chatty Bill is for once awestruck, to be in the presence of the King.

'I just can't get over the fact that this man is descended from an ancient line of kings, stretching back thousands and thousands of years behind him. I want to ask him lots of questions, but what on earth do you say to a king?' he whispers to me.

After our audience with the King, some of the young men show us the ancestral graveyard, which is held in great reverence. Then they show us their bows and arrows and let us have a go at firing them. We girls have all gone a bit giggly in the presence of these strong, handsome warriors and they are enjoying showing off their skills. We learn another all-purpose Vedda word. 'Podga' means 'thing' and has a multitude of uses. Tiny Juli is a crack shot with the bow and arrow and the Vedda boys look impressed.

But the atmosphere suddenly changes when they show us two of their spirit dances. One is to summon the ancestor spirits and the other is to ask for help before going hunting. This is serious business. There are two men back in the village who are testament to how dangerous it is living like this. The King's own brother lost an eye and has four great claw marks down his cheek from being mauled by a bear and an eighty year old man has a withered shoulder and dented ribs from being crushed by an elephant. They are both lucky to have escaped with their lives and perhaps it is an indication of the effectiveness of the healing powers of the King's folk medicine.

Everyone falls quiet as the Vedda warriors sing a powerful song to accompany their dance. They dance in a circle, one behind the other, rhythmically bending down to the ground and straightening back up again, throwing their long hair back over their shoulders. A rhythmic wave undulates around the circle of dancers. The Veddas have been dancing and singing like this for thousands of years and it seems that the spirits are still listening. It is as if some great power that had been quietly sleeping is suddenly woken by their dance and is now paying attention.

Something is stirred in all of us—we westerners from over-developed lands, far divorced from nature. A chord is struck in each of our hearts. An ancient memory is awoken of a time when we all lived like this, in harmony with the spirit of the earth.

When it is time to go we all shake hands again. 'Hondamai,' we all say—'very good,' 'go well,' etc. Even though we only understand two words of their language, it feels that on some level there has been a meeting of hearts and spirits. One man looks deeply into my eyes as if to say, 'I am very glad to have met you.' His beautiful face and searching eyes are forever etched into my memory.

Back in the Bushman's minibus, we have a long and tortuous drive up to Nuwara Eliya, Sri Lanka's highest town, at an altitude of 1990m. We rise up from the seeringly hot, dusty plains, through lush forests into the mountains and tea plantations. Suddenly, the Bushman stops the minibus and points up into the trees at the side of the road.

'Look! Up there, a giant squirrel. They are so rare these days, you are very fortunate to see this,' he says. Perched on a branch a few feet from the road, the squirrel is staring right at us and barking angrily. It has a grey-flecked back and cream underbelly with a black forehead. Apart from the angry barking, it is quite a cute creature. The name 'giant' squirrel is perhaps a bit of an exaggeration though, as it is no more than 60cm from nose to tale, and not much bigger than the grey squirrels we see at home. I feel honoured that we have seen such a rare creature and am impressed at the Bushman's sharp observation skills. After taking a few photos we resume our journey.

As the road gets steeper and more twisty, the air grows cooler and the Bushman's driving more erratic. It has been a long, tiring day and he looks exhausted. We are very relieved to reach Nuwara Eliya in one piece.

Bushman Bandara has booked us into a wonderful old colonial building with high ceilings and wood panelling. It is now pretty chilly (10°C) and it makes a welcome change to have to wear a jumper and use a blanket on our bed.

We all dine together. The Bushman has dressed for dinner in a smart navy blazer.

'You look very elegant Mr Bandara. I think from now on I vill call you, 'The Captain,' since you are in charge of our little crew,' says Markus.

'Yes, the Captain, I like that,' says Bill.

The Bushman gives us a wry smile. He seems to like his new nickname too. Despite being exhausted and starting a cold, the Captain entertains us with many stories. He tells us how the cobra never forgets and will seek revenge if you harm its mate. He tells us of strange spirits in the jungle and of the ghosts of Dutch sailors in the port of Galle. Just as he is in the middle of a particularly eerie tale about an encounter with a red-eyed demon in the jungle, there is a power cut and all the lights go out. Unperturbed, the Captain carries on with his tale—how his gun suddenly would not fire even though there was nothing wrong with it and the next day a local man is found impaled against a tree at the very spot where he had met the demon. Bill and I hold hands under the table and shiver with fright like little children. We retire to bed with a candle feeling really spooked.

* * *

Today we are alive and well, despite the ghostly goings on last night. But the minibus has broken down, so we spend some time exploring Nuwara Eliya whilst the Captain tries to fix it.

Nuwara Eliya, founded as a hill retreat for the British during the colonial era, is known as 'Little England' because of its climate, the colonial buildings, the golf course and the racecourse. We look round the Grand Hotel, which is set in immaculate gardens. It is like stepping back in time 150 years. There are stags' heads on the walls, a billiard room and a library full of antique English furniture.

In the town itself are quaint old-fashioned shops selling gems like Ideal Milk and Marmite. Billy is delighted and buys a large jar of Marmite to have at breakfast.

The Captain tells us that the bus is going to take a couple of hours to fix, so he has hired a driver to take us to the Horton Plains. We have a scenic drive, climbing up even higher to reach the plains at over 2,000 metres, crossing the railway at Ohiya, Sri Lanka's highest railway station, on the way. We step out onto bleak moorland. If it isn't for the odd tree fern, we could be on Dartmoor. It strikes me that Sri Lanka is full of contrasts. Within the space of 100 miles you can go from humid, tropical climes up into green, forested mountains and tea plantations, where the nights are chilly, higher still to wind-swept plateaus and back down again to the hot dry zone, which looks like the African savannah.

Before we parted company with the Captain, he told us all about the wildlife to look out for. 'There are deer, monkeys, many colourful birds, bright green lizards and even leopards if you are really lucky, but they of course are very illusive,' he told us. He instructed us how to give the call of the rare bear monkey. 'If you get it right, they will answer you and then you will know where to look for them,' he said. The Bushman praised Bill's impression, saying it was very realistic. Bill looked really pleased with himself.

With Markus & Juli at the World's End

We set out on a three hour round trip across the Horton Plains to see the Baker's Falls and the World's End. After about half an hour of walking, Althea says she has low blood sugar levels and is going back to the café.

We have been looking forward to spotting lots of wild animals, but the Horton Plains on this particular occasion are sadly lacking in the wild animal department. Even when we give the Captain's bear monkey call, we get no answer. In fact, Billy is so pleased with having been praised by the Captain, that he practices his bear monkey call *ad nauseum*.

'Billy, I don't think the monkeys are coming out today,' I say.

In the end, the only large mammal we see is a slightly mangy and very tame sambar deer that begs a piece of fruit from Markus on our way to the kiosk. As we walk, there are noisy and annoying groups of people in front and behind us. We keep stopping to let them get ahead of us, but they wait for us and keep asking to have their photos taken with us. I am sure the animals heard them coming from miles off and have slunk away.

The highlight of the walk is climbing up through shrubby bushes to a look out point at World's End, where the mist suddenly parts to reveal the vertiginous drop of 1000 metres to the valley floor below. It really does feel like peering off the end of the world. The other highlight is spending time in the company of Markus and Juli, who have smashed all our preconceived ideas about Germans not having a sense of humour. There is much male bonding going on between Bill and Markus. They find out that they are both from families of three brothers. The only difference is that Bill is the eldest and Markus the youngest, so they are now calling each other Little Brother and Big Brother.

We rejoin Althea, who has had a lovely time topping up her blood sugar levels with cake at the café.

Back in Nuwara Eliya, the bus is fixed and we head off on another long and bumpy drive to the tongue-twisting town of Tissamaharama. It seems that the Captain is the animal charmer and that we only see the animals when we are with him. Having not seen a single mammal, other than the noisy two-legged variety, in three hours walking on the Horton Plains, we have only driven for ten minutes out of Nuwara Eliya before the Captain spots a bear monkey in a tree by the side of the road. He tells us we are very lucky, as they do not usually come so close to civilisation.

Bear monkey

We are off again, but Althea is still worried about her blood sugar levels and asks the Captain to stop so that she can buy some bananas. It is not the first time she has done this. She does not seem to have the forethought to get enough bananas at the first stop to last her the whole day. She is our version of Pipilulu. She seems to be away ages, causing the Captain to exclaim, 'Where is that Banana Lady?!'

En-route to Tissa, we stop at Ella, reputedly the island's most beautiful village, surrounded by green hills, gushing waterfalls and tea plantations. We have tea in the gardens of the Grand Ella Hotel and are treated to perhaps the finest view in the whole of Sri Lanka. From our vantage point, we can see past the towering bulk of Ella Rock and through a cleft in the hills, known as the Ella Gap, to the plains below. When we have refreshed ourselves with tea, we wander round the pleasant gardens and have our photo taken with the Captain in front of the view. We discover the fattest puppy in living history plodding about in the rose beds — his tummy is so big he can hardly hold it off the ground. Juli picks him up for a cuddle and says, 'I vunder how little Rocky is doing?'

Markus seems to share my enthusiasm for tea plantations and every time he sees anyone picking tea, he shouts, 'Captain, please stop! I vont to take a picture of the lovely tea pluckers.'

A little further along we stop to admire the Rawana Ella Falls, where the water tumbles ninety metres over the valley wall. After the verdant greenness of the hills, we wind our way slowly down to the heat and dust of the eastern plains.

To keep our spirits up on the long journey, the Captain suggests that we sing some songs. We all take it in turns to lead. The Captain seems to have taken a shine to Bill's repertoire and keeps exhorting him, 'Mr William, Mr William, give us a song!' The only two that everyone knows are *I'd like to teach the world to sing* and *Bohemian Rhapsody*, which we all sing with gusto and accompany ourselves on air guitar. The Captain teaches us a Sri Lankan song about a little fishy. It is great fun and certainly makes the time go quicker.

We are to stay tonight at the Tissa Inn and as we will be arriving late, the Captain phones ahead to order a special curry to be ready when we arrive. But when we get there, the restaurant knows nothing of the order. The owner, who is a good friend of the Captain's, asks what number he rang and the Captain shows him the paper where he wrote the number. The owner roars with laughter. 'You have ordered six curries to be ready for you at the Police Station!'

'Well the idiot at the police reception took the order without saying anything,' says the Captain. I have a feeling he is not going to live this one down for a long time.

Once the owner has stopped laughing, he tells his chef to make the special meal for us that the Captain had in mind and by the time we have settled into our rooms and had showers, it is ready. There is a veritable feast spread before us. Known simply as 'rice and curry,' there are many and varied dishes which comprise our banquet. There is *mallung* (green vegetables stir fried with spices and coconut), eye-watering *pol sambol* (chilli powder, onions, grated coconut and shrimps), fiery chicken and fish curry, curried banana flowers, curried potatoes, curried aubergines, tasty dhal and mountains of rice. As if we are not already full to bursting after that little lot, it is followed by delicious Kiribath, a dessert made from rice cooked with milk and served with our favourite jaggery.

After supper, the Captain invites us to share some cocktails with him on his balcony. He turns the preparation of the cocktail into a little ritual. It is a mixture of the best black-label arrack, lemonade and orange juice. Each person takes turns in adding to the mixture in the jug, whilst giving blessings and their good wishes for the gathered company.

'And you, Anna, you look so beautiful tonight. You are like a Russian princess. I would be greatly honoured if you would be the one to pour in the arrack,' says the Captain.

'Well, Captain, how could I possibly refuse, when you put it like that?'

He sings us beautiful Sri Lankan love songs. His voice is strong and haunting. And while he sings, he accompanies himself by tapping his fingers against a strange instrument, which looks like a large ceramic pot. A full moon shines upon our backs and we stay up late into the night telling stories. We have become like one family, and the Captain is definitely Dad.

* * *

The Captain takes us on an early morning safari into Ruhuna Yala National Park. We clamber bleary-eyed from the night's revelry into the jeep, as the sun is only just thinking about climbing over the horizon. We leave poor Althea behind, who is suffering more than most from the effects of the cocktail.

Dawn is breaking as we reach the park office to pick up a park ranger, who will travel with us for our safety. The walls of the park office are covered in photos of the magnificent animals that we are about to see. There are nine tuskers, the giant male elephants, who can be very dangerous and are the main reason for the park ranger coming with us. There are pictures of beautiful leopards and I feel a thrill of excitement that we might see one of these elusive creatures.

We travel along dusty tracks into the park. The dry-zone landscape is strikingly beautiful in the early morning light. The Captain and the ranger have incredibly sharp eyes and spot many creatures that I would have missed—a huge antlered spotted deer in the undergrowth, rare birds, wild boar . . .

We stop the jeep at a watering hole, watching as nervous deer approach to drink in fear of lurking crocodiles. Even the more commonplace animals look magical in this setting—long-legged jack-rabbits, colourful jungle cocks and wild buffalo.

At one watering hole, shrunk down in the hot weather, lurk eight crocodiles. Shoals of bright fish leap into the air each time the crocs go under for a mouthful of breakfast. Pelicans, painted storks, egrets and spoonbills are forced to share the shrinking pool with them. They are not going to pass up the chance of so many fish concentrated in one place, even if the crocodiles are constantly trying to sneak up on them.

We drive down many dusty trails in the hope of seeing leopards and elephants. Sadly the leopards remain elusive. We stop at a lake full of water lilies, watching birds for a while and at first we do not notice the mother elephant and baby who have snuck past us down to the water for a drink and a swim. The mother is very careful to keep herself between us and the baby at all times, but other than that gives no sign that she has actually seen us at all. We watch in silent rapture.

The park leads down to the sea and we stop amongst sand dunes for a swim in the ocean.

'Sometimes the elephants will come to the beach for a swim in the sea,' says the Captain. 'But it looks as if we are not lucky today.'

There is a tree with a big bough that swoops near to the ground like a natural hammock. The Captain stretches himself along it and goes to sleep, looking for all the world like a panther after a hearty meal.

Bushman Bandara

After our swim we get back in the jeep and set off back into the park. We pass a huge mound.

'You see this?' says the Captain, indicating the mound. 'Not so many years ago there was a magnificent twelve foot tusker in this park. But the army started camping here. He got very angry and kept attacking them. So they shot him and buried him in this mound.'

'Oh, that is SO sad—he was only defending his territory,' I say.

The morning grows hot and all the animals are retreating into the shade of their daytime hideaways, so it is back to Tissa for breakfast and a nap.

We set off for Unawatuna, the final destination of our tour, driving along the boundary fence of the Uda Walawe National Park. We stop for a while to watch the wild elephants through the fence. Wild? It seems they are absolutely livid. The Captain is reluctant to go in, telling us about the two rangers who have recently been killed trying to protect the tourists who were being attacked in their jeeps. 'The elephants are not happy to be fenced in, because it disrupts their natural migration routes. So they are getting their revenge on humans,' says the Captain. We do not want to put the Captain in danger and are happy to stay on this side of the fence.

It is a very long drive to Unawatuna, and the roads, as is the case in most of Sri Lanka, are atrocious. They are so bumpy and pot-holey, that we are continually being thrown around and have to cling on tightly to avoid falling off the seats. Often the main roads narrow to a single track, and it requires a great deal of concentration and skill to avoid having an accident as the oncoming traffic hurtles towards us. The Captain who has been progressively sickening since he started a cold in Nuwara Eliya, is now really under the weather. Bill offers to drive for a while and the Captain sits beside him, schooling him in the art of driving Sri Lankan-style, which requires copious use of the horn and nerves of steel.

Finally, Bill manages to deliver us safely in Unawatuna. 'Big Brother, may I congratulate you on your excellent driving. I could not have done this,' says Markus.

'Oh, Little Brother, it wasn't so bad,' says Bill rather modestly. And then whispers, 'I found it more difficult to cope with the Captain's constant instructions of, "More horn, more horn!" than the other drivers. And it was a bit unnerving when his hand kept straying down to try and change gear a fraction earlier than I would have chosen to.'

The Captain has brought us to the Sea View Hotel. It is late and already dark. Despite his ill health, he has organised another sumptuous feast for us and appears immaculately dressed in his blazer to regale us with stories and generally entertain us. But as soon as the meal is over, we insist that he goes to bed and promise to visit him in the morning.

* * *

Unawatuna has been voted one of the world's top ten most beautiful beaches. Over breakfast at the restaurant, which overlooks the beach, we can see why. A narrow strip of soft white sand, backed by jungle, lines a pretty, semicircular bay. To our right a picturesque dagoba on a rocky headland finishes the curve of the bay. Even at this time approaching the monsoon, when all the seas on the west coast are rough and dangerous, the bay is sheltered and gentle waves lap onto the sand.

Markus and Juli join us for breakfast. Markus complains that he got badly bitten in the night by a mosquito, which had somehow found its way inside his mosquito net.

'I cannot understand it because I checked so carefully that there were absolutely no mosquitoes in the net before I vent to bed. And yet in the morning there he is, the one which I know has been feeding on my flesh all night. It must be ven I go to pipilulu in the night,' he says. 'I come back from the bathroom and I 'Open Sesame' vith the mosquito curtains and it must be then that he sneaks in.'

Althea comes to say goodbye. She is moving to a cheaper guesthouse, further down the coast. In our little family, she has been the difficult child. At heart she is a nice woman, but she is terribly insecure and lonely after a failed marriage. She has become self-absorbed to the point of being a complete hypochondriac, constantly telling us in gory detail about her bodily functions. So it is actually quite a relief to part company with her—it has been hard work paying her the attention she constantly craves.

After breakfast we visit the Captain. Doctor Juli has already been to see him, diagnosing bronchitis and possibly pneumonia, and prescribing antibiotics for him. He is cheerful as usual, despite looking tired and drawn. He has enough energy to make cheeky comments about my figure. I was going to give him a shiatsu treatment, but after his comments we think it might be better if Bill does the treatment—we do not want him to get over excited.

We spend the morning on the beach sunbathing and swimming with Markus and Juli. It is wonderful just to relax after the tour. We watch the Sri Lankan families on the beach or larking about in the water. A middle-aged aunty insists on taking a photo of her family who are in the water. She stands on the shore and orders them about, trying to get the right pose. She decides she needs to get closer and wades into the water.

'No, no, get back Aunty, the waves are too strong,' they all shout. But there is no dissuading her. The inevitable happens—an extra large wave crashes towards her and she falls over face first, camera and all. We try not to laugh, but it is impossible. Besides which, most of her family are laughing. They look at us and shrug. We get the feeling that sort of thing always happens to Aunty. I look over to see Markus clutching his sides in helpless laughter too.

Today there are two big world cup matches—the quarter-finals between England and Brazil, and Germany versus the USA. So Markus and Bill have done a little research to find the best place to watch the matches. They have decided on the Thilak café, at the other end of the beach, which has a big screen and serves Lion lager and Elephant ginger beer (my favourite).

We walk along the beach on our way to the café. It is a glorious day on one of the world's top 10 beaches, but we turn our back on all this beauty and step into the darkened café. We want to be in good time to get seats with a good view of the screen. The bar is already crowded with

Europeans and Sri Lankans, but we find a table with a view of the screen and order drinks. Markus knocks glasses with Bill and says,' I vish you good luck, Big Brother.'

'Good luck to you too, Little Brother. May both our teams get through to the next round,' says Bill.

There is an air of excited tension. An over-excited Scouser has already had far too much to drink and is shouting, 'Cume on you England.'

The English face a daunting task against the brilliant Brazilians, hampered too by the heat and humidity of Shizouka, which must be fairly standard weather in Brazil. But England seem to be doing surprisingly well and our goalie, Safe Hands Seaman, does a brilliant save, to avert a goal from Ronaldo. Then mid-way through the first half a small miracle happens and Michael Owen scores a goal.

'We could have a chance of winning this you know,' says Bill in a voice hoarse from shouting at the screen.

'Yes, your team is playing very vell. And I think your goalkeeper is very good,' says Markus.

'He is, but I'm a bit worried after that last save. He landed badly and looked as if he really hurt his back and neck. I think he should have gone off for treatment, but he doesn't want to let the side down,' says Bill.

Then, just before half-time Ronaldinho runs through the England defence and passes the ball to Rivaldo, who crashes it into the England net to equalise. All is not yet lost, they have plenty of time to score another goal. But just after half-time, disaster strikes for poor David Seaman, as he lets in a free kick from Ronaldinho, giving Brazil a 2-1 lead. Seven minutes later there is renewed hope for England, when Ronaldinho disgraces himself and is sent off for a dangerous tackle on Danny Mills. But the heat is now taking its toll on the England team. They look tired and sluggish and fail to capitalise on Brazil playing with one less man. When the final whistle blows, the score is still 2:1 to Brazil and we are out of the World Cup.

'I am so sorry, Big Brother,' says Markus, patting a distraught Bill on the back.

We begin the long slow trudge back along the beach to our guesthouse. It seems a lot further on the way back. Bill's head hangs very low. 'I can't believe it. We came **SO** close,' he says.

'Never mind,' I say, patting him. I do not know what else to say. It is as if someone has died.

'I'm glad we're not in England,' says Bill. 'There would be too many things to keep reminding me.

'Yes,' is all I can say. The beauty of our surroundings is for me a welcome distraction from the feeling of anticlimax, but is not enough to console poor Bill.

In the restaurant at our evening meal, we are entertained by the family whose aunty fell in the water. They are having a jolly old knees up, singing and dancing. Aunty is the life and soul of the party, accompanying the singing enthusiastically with her accordion. It is just the tonic that the mourning Bill needs to cheer him up. And Markus, whose team has just beaten USA to go through to the next round is very gracious and sympathetic towards Bill. He is definitely the nicest German we have ever met, apart from Juli, that is.

The Captain has joined us for dinner. He must be feeling a little better as he has regained some of his mischievous twinkle. 'Doctor Juli, tell me, in your medical opinion, do you think it is possible to have proper sexual intercourse under water?' he asks with an earnest look on his face. Despite blushing deep crimson, Juli handles the enquiry extremely professionally and Markus manages to change the subject quickly onto how well Aunty is playing the accordion. Bill has a look of shocked amusement on his face and I have to kick him under the table to stop him from joining in with the Captain's questions.

* * *

This morning the Captain has perked up enough to hire a driver to get him back to Kandy. We bid him a fond farewell and promise to visit him in a few days.

We spend the morning on the beach with Markus and Juli, enjoying the delights of one of the world's most beautiful spots. Bill, whose hair has taken a turn for the decidedly wild and unkempt since we have been away, decides it is time to get a haircut. He announces that he has spotted a hairdresser not far from here and he will not be long. Half an hour later, I barely recognise the person walking towards me along the beach.

'Oh my God, he's given him a mullet,' I whisper to Juli, although I am not sure that the term 'mullet' would mean anything to anyone outside Britain.

Markus and Juli politely chime together, 'Very nice. You look really smart now.' Perhaps mullets are in fashion in Germany.

It is our last day with Markus and Juli before they fly back to Germany early tomorrow. So in the late afternoon we travel into Galle, all four of us crammed into one tuk-tuk, to see the sights and to have dinner together.

We go to the old part of town and have a romantic walk along the ramparts of the fort. We find a café with a roof terrace that looks out to sea and order gin and tonics. It is very civilised. With Markus and Juli's imminent departure, the conversation turns to home.

'Guys, you must come to our wedding,' says Bill.

'We're looking forward to it already,' says Markus.

'Oh, yes, that would be **so** great,' says Juli.

We have a little toast in honour of meeting up again in a year's time. We leave the café and wander about for a while before deciding it is time to search for somewhere to have dinner. There is nowhere that looks particularly promising in this part of town. We stand outside a Chinese restaurant, trying to decide whether to go in.

Markus goes in search of a cash-point and is away for ages. Ten minutes go by and we start to wonder what is taking so long. Twenty minutes go by and we start to worry that something has happened to him. Half an hour goes by and we discuss sending out a search party for him. Forty minutes later, he turns up. He is riding in an overloaded tuk-tuk full of smiling young Sri Lankans, who are all his new best friends.

'Sorry I took so long, guys. The cash-point voz out of order and I started to panic, because I knew it was my last chance to get money for our journey tomorrow. Then these guys come up and ask what is the problem. They tell me that they know of another cash-point on the other side of town, but that it is difficult to find and they can take me there. I did vunder vether they might be going to beat me up and steal my vollet, but I figure that I don't have any money to lose anyway and decide to trust them. They vurr so kind to me and vould not even let me pay for the tuk-tuk ride.' It is so typical of the kind of thing that happens to Markus, and it is why we love him.

We give up on the search for a restaurant in Galle and go back to Unawatuna for a last night of rice and curry at the Sea View Hotel.

* * *

Markus and Juli flew back to Germany in the small hours of the morning. It already feels strange without them.

We call Mum, who has some bad news for us. 'I'm afraid there may be some problems with you getting married in Clifford Church. Paul, the rector, says that you must live in the parish for him to consider marrying you at St Mary's. I told him that all your belongings are stored in our house here and that all your post is coming here, but he said it would still be difficult for you to prove 'domicile' as he calls it. It's a bit of a blow, isn't it? You might have to get married in your local church in Bristol.'

'Oh, no, that is bad news. We don't really have any connections with the local church in Bristol. We only lived there for 10 days before we left and there isn't anywhere decent to have the reception nearby. Is there any way you can persuade him to change his mind?' I ask.

'Well I'll try, but don't pin all your hopes on it,' says Mum.

'Well, good luck and thanks for all this organising you're doing on our behalf. We really appreciate it,' I tell her. I feel very despondent at this news and pray that Mum can get the rector to change his mind.

We travel back to Kandy on the train, via the fetid station at Colombo, a six hour journey all told. We almost do not make it, as we are pushed for time and arrive at the station with minutes to spare before our train departs. We rush to the platform and a train is just pulling in. Thinking it must be ours, we climb aboard and sit down with a sigh of relief.

As the train pulls out of the station, Bill asks a fellow passenger, 'This is the train for Colombo, isn't it?'

The man gives him a puzzled look and says, 'No.'

'I don't think he understood me,' whispers Bill to me. 'I'll ask someone else.'

'Excuse me, where is this train going?' asks Bill of another man in the carriage.

'It is going to Matara,' he says.

We look at each other with horror—Matara is in the opposite direction from where we want to go. 'Oh, no. What on earth are we going to do?' I say in despair. 'It'll add hours to our journey to get off there and wait for another train to Colombo.'

But then the train comes to a juddering halt and to our utter amazement actually starts to go backwards towards Galle. There must be some guardian angel looking after us today. The train arrives back at Galle station and we scramble off with the help of the other passengers. We have to cross the tracks and clamber up several feet to get back on the platform, but we do not care. We have just saved ourselves about five hours unnecessary travelling. We look round sheepishly at the other passengers waiting for the Colombo train who are giving us odd looks. I want to say, 'We meant to do that, actually. It was all part of the plan—just adding a bit of excitement to our journey!' We must be the luckiest people in the whole of Sri Lanka today.

In Kandy, we meet up with the Captain again and are finally introduced to Mrs Captain, the long-suffering woman we have heard so much about. She is very forthright, giving the impression that she does not suffer fools gladly. But she has a rascally sense of humour—you would need to have a good sense of humour to live with the Captain! And Bill's verdict? I think his exact words were, 'She's as mad as a badger.'

The Captain is still a little unwell, looking very tired, but improving all the time and still busy organising everyone's lives for them. We decide to stay at the Captain's guesthouse, the Expeditor Inn, this time. He gives us his best room in the new block just across the way from the main building.

We came to Sri Lanka knowing of its reputation as a place for having beautiful gems and hoping that we might find something special to make into an engagement ring. But owing to the preponderance of touts and conmen, we are both very nervous of getting ripped off. As we trust the Captain, and he seems to know everybody who is anybody in Sri Lanka, we ask for his advice.

'I know just the place. I'll call my friend Mr Gamini for you, if you like. He owns a gem shop and jewellery workshop. All his gems come from his own mine and I know that he is a very trustworthy person,' says the Captain.

Mr Gamini picks us up in his minibus—the preferred form of transport in Sri Lanka—and takes us to his shop. A very small man with a square head and an earnest face, he sits behind his huge desk and proceeds to produce box after box of sparkling gems in every size, colour and variety. He spends a long time showing us the different types of gems and carefully explaining about their different properties. I am dazzled by all the sparkling jewels. This place is like a cave of treasures and Mr Gamini is guardian of the hoard. I did not realise that sapphires came in so many different colours.

'I've fallen in love with the cornflower blue sapphires,' I tell Bill. 'And it seems quite special that they are only found in Sri Lanka.'

'How about this one?' says Bill picking up a beautifully cut oval-shaped stone which sparkles like the sky on a crisp September day. We spend a long time comparing it to many others, but finally we decide that the one Bill first picked up is the most beautiful.

I have an idea of a design, but it is so hard to put the picture in my mind onto paper. With lots of prompting from Mr Gamini and Bill, I finally come up with a drawing which captures what I am looking for. The craftsman is called in. He is a tall, handsome young man, but he has the furriest ears I have ever seen. Silky black hairs grow out from the whole surface of his shell-likes. He redraws the design to show that he understands what I want. His drawing is much more graceful than my cartoon-like effort. Finally satisfied that the ring will be perfect, Bill and I sit in Mr Gamini's garden drinking tea. I am shaking with nerves. I have never had so much money spent on me before. Bill squeezes my hand and reassures me that I deserve it and that it will be a fitting emblem of our love.

As if I have not been spoilt enough today, while we are waiting for work to start on the ring, we visit Mrs Gamini's clothes shop upstairs and I am treated to a batik dress and a top and trouser set with little elephants on it.

After these purchases, we are taken deeper into the cave of treasures where we are shown our very own gem being crafted into its setting by the little elves that work there.

The ring is delivered later that evening to the Bandara's house. It is even more beautiful than I imagined. I try the ring to ensure it fits, before Bill whisks it away, wanting to present it to me at a special place later on. Mrs Bandara coos over the ring, saying what a thoughtful future husband I have, to buy me such a beautiful thing and batting her eyes at the Captain, who seems quite oblivious to her hints.

* * *

From Kandy we set off on a pilgrimage to the magical mountain of Adam's Peak, which is sacred to Christians, Hindus, Muslims and Buddhists—a very holy place indeed. One of the things I have looked forward to most about this trip is to see the sacred places of the world. Here in the land of my ancestors, I want to give thanks for finally meeting Bill and to ask for blessings on our future life together.

In distance, the journey is not that far, but in logistics very complex. Part of the pilgrimage seems to be in managing to negotiate the tortuous journey to get to the base of the mountain. First, we catch the bus from Kandy to Gampola, a half hour ride. It is lunchtime and we have time to kill before we catch the train on the next leg of the journey. We look for somewhere decent to eat. There is nowhere appealing. We choose a café which seems to be the lesser of the evils, but even in this one, there are bowls of cooked food lying around everywhere in the heat and thousands of flies.

The next phase of our journey is a two hour train journey from Gampola to Hatton, the filthiest fly-blown place we have had the misfortune to come across so far. We have more time to kill before the next connection and ask a tuk-tuk driver if there is somewhere that does a good cup of tea in town. He thinks for a moment, then looks at us with pity and says, 'No, none of them are good.' He is right, everywhere is skin-crawlingly awful.

We catch the bus to Maskeliya, a 45 minute journey. Here we find that because it is the off-season, there are no buses running from here to Dalhousie. So we take a half hour rickshaw ride to the bottom end of Dalhousie. Our spirits rise on this last part of the journey. The scenery is stunning. We skirt a lake, with Adam's Peak rearing its pyramidal head through the clouds in front of us. The air is cool and dry and all around us the slopes are covered with tea plantations. The road finally runs out and we have to shoulder our packs and walk the rest of the way to our chosen guesthouse.

The Greenhouse is set in a beautiful garden full of flowers such as impatiens and hydrangeas. Our hosts are very welcoming. It feels good to finally arrive after the messy journey and at last we get our good cup of tea sitting under a quaint wooden pagoda in the garden.

Peter, the guesthouse owner, describes the climb to us and tells us the legends of the mountain. 'This is a place of magic, where miracles can happen,' he says. 'Many crippled and sick people have been cured when they come to the mountain.'

There's something mysterious about Peter, as if he is the guardian of the path that leads to the Holy Mountain.

'Peter, I've heard that the weather's pretty unpredictable at this time of year and it's dangerous to climb if there is heavy rain or strong winds,' says Bill.

Peter says, 'It is best to get up in the night, and if the weather is clear, start walking at 3am. If the weather is bad, go back to bed and try again the next day. It should take you about 3 hours to climb at a steady pace, so if you start at 3am, you should be able to see the dawn break from the top. Sometimes it is possible to see a very special pyramid-shaped shadow of the mountain cast into the sky. But you will be very lucky to see it at this time of year.'

Peter has laid everything on to make our climb easier, including leaving a flask of tea, a midnight snack and leech repellent for us on the table in the night. So we go to bed at 8.30pm, not knowing what the night will bring and sleep intermittently in our excited state.

We get up at 2.30 am to find clouds racing across the sky and a stiff breeze. 'I don't think it's going to rain,' says Bill looking out at patches of starry sky and bright moonlight. 'This might be our best chance, shall we go?' he asks. His many years of gardening have given him a sixth sense about predicting the weather, so I trust his judgement. After our flask of tea and jam sandwiches, we set off into the moonlight, liberally smeared with leech repellent.

The path to the Holy Mountain is very clear and well lit for the first portion. All is quiet and calm, except for the Mexican wave of barking dogs that we set off as we pass through the outskirts of the village. The air is surprisingly warm as we spring eagerly along the gentle slope of the path.

After a few hundred yards, we pass through a huge ancient archway and come face to face with a reclining Buddha flanked on either side by a shrine to Ganesha and to Shiva. As we stop to light incense, we are passed by another lone pilgrim who shouts, 'Good morning!' on his way passed. He is wearing only a T-shirt, shorts and flip-flops, whereas we are in full mountaineering gear with thermals, walking boots, waterproofs and a backpack full of rations, just in case we get caught out on the mountain. Just behind this man trots a three-legged dog who comes to greet us. He knows we have biscuits. He hypnotises me into giving him one and then accompanies us for the rest of the journey. We name him Tuk-tuk. Flip-flop Man obviously does not carry snacks.

The path gets increasingly steep until it becomes continuous stairs. I am finding it surprisingly difficult. I had not considered how much thinner the air is up here—the peak is at 7,000 feet. Tuk-tuk is doing rather better on his three legs than I am doing on two. Bill on the other hand is springing up like a gazelle.

I am wearing thermal leggings under my zip-off trekking trousers, a vest, a long-sleeved T-shirt and a fleece jacket. I am far too hot and my trousers seem to drag at my sweaty knees each time I try to raise a leg onto the next enormous step. After about an hour of struggling along like this, I have the bright idea to zip off the legs of my trousers, to reveal my baggy long johns underneath. I look ridiculous, but hey, it is dark and there is no-one else around.

The going is easier for a while in my new outfit, but the steps are getting steeper and steeper and the air thinner. I feel dizzy, nauseous and as feeble as a kitten. The weight of my holy intention seems like a heavy burden. Sometimes I can only manage about five steps before I have to stop and rest. And there are two more hours of climbing to reach the top. What on earth am I doing? It is the middle of the night. I should be snuggled up in bed.

Bill gives me the option of sitting in a shelter and waiting whilst he goes to the top on his own. For a brief moment it seems very tempting. I ponder on all the goodies in the backpack and how nice it would be to sit scoffing biscuits and sweets. But then my fighting spirit comes back and I have a stern word with myself. I tell myself that there is no way that I have come half way round the world to just sit stuffing myself and miss out on getting to the top.

Soon there are railings on either side of the stairs and even though the steps are steeper than before, it feels easier to haul myself up using my arms to help my feeble legs.

The wind is getting stronger. It is still dark, but our climb is accompanied by the strange noises of frogs that sound like wooden glockenspiels, and the splash and gurgle of unseen streams and waterfalls. Leaves flap and flutter in the wind and my laboured breath joins all the sounds of the mountain.

We are in the clouds by now. It is misty and damp. It is also much colder and windier and now I am glad of my extra layers. Just at this moment, we meet the flip-flop chap coming back down from the top. He tells us cheerily that it is not much further to the top. He is from Hawaii. They must make them from stern stuff over there.

Finally we arrive at the gates of the temple in thick, wet cloud and biting wind. I am surprised to find that it has only taken us three hours to climb. The place is eerily deserted. Dawn is creeping through the gloom—no spectacular sunrise for us.

We find the 'Sri Pada,' the holy footprint. We say prayers and make offerings. As the wind buffets and bites us and the cold gnaws at our tired bones, Bill gets down on one knee. He takes the beautiful sapphire ring out of his pocket and holding it out to me says, 'Anna, the first time I saw you in the shiatsu classroom, a beam of sunlight came in through the window and fell upon your golden head. It lit up your beautiful face so that I thought an angel had been sent to walk among us. I have loved you from that moment on. We have travelled through many strange lands to get here and we will travel through many more before we reach home. It is my dearest wish that you will become my wife and share the rest of life's wonderful adventures with me. In the presence of the Holy One I offer you this ring as my sign that I will love you forever.'

'Billy, from the first time I met you I have been impressed over and over by your generosity of spirit and your innate and unquenchable cheerfulness. You have treated me with the utmost care and respect. I have never before felt so honoured and cherished. There is no other crazy pilgrim that I would rather spend my life with than you, and I know that with you I will always be loved, always cared for and that laughter will never be far from my lips.'

'I take it that's a 'yes' then?' says Bill and we both laugh heartily. He places the ring on my finger. We embrace in the driving wind and rain. It is a special moment, but not a physically comfortable one. Perhaps it is symbolic of all the obstacles we have had to overcome in order to come together in our lives.

Billy runs off to ring the temple bell vigorously, which clangs strangely in the fog. He does this partly to send our prayers up to heaven and partly to rouse the old man who we have heard will make a cup of tea for pilgrims.

We leave the temple thinking that we will be disappointed on the tea front, but then we hear a tentative, 'hello' and a wrinkled old face appears in a doorway.

'Tea possible?' says Bill hopefully.

'Yes, yes,' is the reply and he beckons us into his warm but sparsely furnished room. The old man has a wonky leg, a wonky eye and not many teeth. I feel ashamed that a young healthy person like me found it such a struggle to get up here, when this old man obviously does it regularly. He tells us that Tuk-tuk belongs to him. It fits—they seem to go together perfectly.

The sweet black tea that he makes us tastes like nectar after our climb. It is wonderful to sit in his room out of the wind and the rain, despite the accompaniment of the squeaky radio, which he has turned up to full blast for our benefit. We share some biscuits and donate the rest of our snacks to him in return for the tea. He seems very pleased with the loaf of bread, tomatoes and onions that we have brought. Did we really think that we would bother to make a sandwich at the top?

After this pit-stop, I feel completely refreshed and practically race down the mountain. Well, actually, I kind of wobble down on jelly legs, but at least my spirits are much revived.

Soon we are rewarded by the sun coming out to reveal the most spectacular views of the valley and the lake below. Markus would have been delighted by the sight of plenty of tea pluckers at close quarters.

Almost at the bottom, we come across a river, the start of the Mahaweli Ganga, Sri Lanka's greatest river. It looks so inviting. I cannot resist the urge to get my hot tired legs in it. We strip off boots socks and trousers and sit on a rock with the delicious cool water flowing over our aching limbs.

A little further on, we are shouted at by a Buddhist monk, who is beckoning us to go into his house, probably wanting money. He does not sound very friendly.

'I think that tops it all—being touted by a monk!' says Bill. We pretend we do not understand, because breakfast is calling to us and we are eager to get back.

Back at the Greenhouse, Peter has made a feast for our breakfast and then prepares us a hot bath, which he fills with special herbs from his garden. It seems to magically take the aches out of my legs. Billy decides to do his laundry in the herbal bathtub.

'Oh Bill—that's such a travelling thing to do,' I say.

'Waste not, want not,' he replies, scrubbing his smelly socks. I crawl into bed and fall asleep, leaving Bill at his washing.

After we have rested, Peter shows us a video of what we should have seen if the peak had not been shrouded in cloud. There is the strange phenomenon of the rising sun casting a perfect triangular shadow of the mountain into the sky behind it. But it seems that this is a pretty rare occurrence and usually only happens at the height of the pilgrim season, when you have to struggle up the steps hemmed in by thousands of other people and jostle for a good place to view the sunrise at the top. I was glad to see the video, but I much preferred the experience of our quiet journey to the top, accompanied only by Tuk-tuk and the wooden glockenspiel frogs.

Once more we travel back to Kandy, with mixed feelings. Somehow it always seems to be the central hub of things for us and it will be wonderful to see the Captain again, but there is a certain atmosphere to the place that I find really unpleasant. It is the place where we have fallen foul of the touts and conmen most often.

And the more time we spend in Sri Lanka, the more badly behaved Buddhist monks we come across. Several times we have seen young healthy monks get onto a crowded bus or train (for which they do not pay) and people give up their seats for them, whilst old ladies have to stand in the aisles, being thrown from side to side as the buses lurch along the pot-holey roads. I even saw one Buddhist monk wearing Ray Ban sunglasses, carrying an expensive looking briefcase and talking on a mobile phone. Of course, I am sure he was not at all attached to these possessions! As Mrs Bandara said to us, 'There are very few true Buddhists left in Sri Lanka—most of it is about politics, money and power.'

Today we have decided to go for a walk in the Udawattakelle Sanctuary, a densely forested hill to the north of Kandy's lake. We walk along Lovers' Lane amongst the trees to the accompaniment of the strangest sounding creatures. There is something really spooky about their rising and falling wail, especially as we cannot see the creature that is making this sound. It seems to be coming from the trees and we guess that it may be some kind of bat or frog. But perhaps its one of those red-eyed demons of the jungle that Mr Bandara told us about?

A little further on, we come across a large brown snake. We decide it is not dangerous, more to comfort ourselves than from any great knowledge of the creature, but we give it a wide berth anyway, just in case.

We stop for a while to sit on a bench and admire the view. It is here that Bill has his first encounter with a leech, which had crawled up his shoe and attached itself to his ankle. He emits a loud shriek when he realises what it is. Now he is running round in panicked circles with his arms flapping. It is a good few minutes before I can stop him long enough to squirt it with insect repellent and remove it. For the rest of the walk, he adopts a strange kind of gait, which consists of hopping, skipping and tip-toeing, in a vain attempt to keep the amount of time that his feet are in contact with the ground (and available to leeches) to a minimum.

* * *

We liked Unawatuna so much when the Captain brought us here, that we are back, but a lot has happened since then. England is out of the World Cup, beaten 2-1 by Brazil. The final, Brazil versus Germany is tomorrow. Bill is missing Markus and would have loved to watch the match with him. In the cricket, England has beaten Sri Lanka several times, which is a great talking point with tuk-tuk drivers.

The situation between India and Pakistan over Kashmir seems to be settling down. We are very relieved to hear this, as we are about to return to India in six days and hope to make our way slowly north, closer to where the worst of the troubles have been happening.

It feels so good just to stay in one place for a few days after all the rushing about and bumpy journeys. The tuk-tuk driver found us a really wonderful room at the Rock House and the family that run it are very nice. My favourite thing about the room is that the bed has a mosquito net arranged like the curtains on a four-poster. Once I am inside I feel safe from the onslaught of the horrid little marauders and it is much less claustrophobic than the usual nets that drape right over you. The other thing I love here is that the bathroom is massive. In India and Sri Lanka, no-one uses shower curtains, so for once I can have a shower without soaking the toilet roll and my towel. And unlike most of the rooms we have stayed in, there is somewhere to hang your clothes and store your belongings. There is a big balcony with tables and chairs. There is even a fridge. These things may seem trivial, but when you have been away so long, it makes all the difference to have a few home comforts.

We sit on the balcony to eat our favourite breakfast of Sri Lankan hoppers. They are delicious bowl shaped pancakes made from rice flour and coconut milk. You can have them with an egg cracked in the middle or plain and fill them with butter and marmalade, or Marmite in Bill's case. From here, we can watch a troop of bear monkeys that live in the forest behind our room. It feels wonderful to be so close to nature and I love the sound of their calls echoing through the mist in the early morning.

Billy has just gone to watch the World Cup final. I can hear the commentary in English on the telly downstairs. I have lost interest in the competition since England went out. The final result—Brazil beats Germany 2-0. I can almost see Markus' disappointed face in my head and I mourn the break up of our little family.

I received an e-mail from Mum today, which gave me a bit of a shock. We have been having our post re-directed to her while we are away. She is a devout Christian and she and Dad are very active in the local church. It seems that one or two things that arrived in the post have worried her. She has asked me to explain my connection with shamanism and to say why I want a Christian wedding in her church.

Whilst Billy is downstairs watching the World Cup, I take the opportunity to write a letter in reply to Mum's e-mail. But I am finding it very painful. I pace the floor in our room, my heart thumping loudly in my chest and my face flushed with anxiety. A torrent of words whirls round my head as I try to compose a letter that will explain my innermost feelings and heartfelt beliefs. Why does this bring up so much fear for me? I suppose I fear being rejected by Mum and the rest of my family. But there is also a deeper unconscious primal fear instilled by all the Christian teachings that I have heard over the years. Perhaps my eclectic beliefs and relationship to God and the realm of the spirit are 'wrong' and 'evil' and perhaps I will go to hell.

I suppose I must tell Mum that I am a very spiritual person and the idea of declaring my love and lifelong commitment to Bill in the eyes of God and in front of our gathered friends and family is very important to me. And finding a suitable venue for this sacred ceremony is equally important. The little ancient church set on the hill in Clifford, which has been a place of worship for hundreds of years seems like an ideal place.

Finally I manage to assemble my jumbled thoughts into some semblance of a message that I hope will not send Mum off into paroxysms of fear in the way the word 'shamanism' seems to.

* * *

Unawatuna is beautiful and our room is perfect. Life here would be completely idyllic except for the BLOODY MOSQUITOES. I have been so careful, wearing long sleeved shirts and trousers and putting insect repellent on all exposed areas, but I am still being bitten. These Unawatuna mozzies really are the sneakiest of creatures. I cannot work it out—they must be biting me **through** my clothes. Today my mosquito bites have reached critical mass. It feels like my whole skin surface is alive and prickling. It is driving me nuts.

Billy imprisons one of the evil creatures under a piece of sellotape in his journal and writes a poem about it. It is his way of getting revenge. It reminds me of the Vogon's in the *Hitchhiker's Guide to the Galaxy*. They write the worst poetry in the universe then torture unwitting victims such as Ford Prefect and Arthur Dent by making them listen to their awful verses. Sorry Bill, your poetry is not bad enough to be a fitting punishment for the mozzies.

Had a restless night, full of nightmares. I think it is because of all the mozzie bites. Woke at 8 am still feeling exhausted, with my eyes all swollen and gummed up. Had a long shower and hair wash and then Billy gave me a shiatsu. I feel loads better now, thanks Billy.

Time seems to be doing a strange thing here. At other places, we have stayed two or three days and it has seemed like a very long time. But we have been here four days already and it seems like no time at all.

We awoke to the calls of the bear monkeys again. There is one big male declaring his territory, but if I had not seen him with my own eyes, I would have thought it was a gorilla by the sheer volume he was creating. The jungle is teeming with life. There are parakeets, owls and pariah kites. And last night I saw the most enormous bat. I had to do a double take, because at first I thought it was a flying ferret.

* * *

It is our last full day here and I am sad. Tomorrow we go to Negombo and the following day we fly early in the morning back to India. Unawatuna has been a wonderful haven and I have not had my fill of it yet. I will miss the Thilak café, where they serve delicious Sri Lankan curries and we have made friends with the staff and the other travellers that are regulars there. I will miss the long stretch of silver sand and swimming in the tranquil bay. I will miss the relaxed dress code—being able to wear a bikini on the beach or shorts and sleeveless tops around town without being branded a hussy. I will miss the family that run the Rock House and our lovely room here. I will miss eating eggy hoppers on the balcony. I will miss the exotic greenness of the jungle and all the wild animals that live there. But I will not miss the evil mosquitoes.

* * *

Today we are to catch the train from Galle to Colombo, ready for our flight back to India early tomorrow morning. I have a bad feeling about this trip. In general, we have found travelling around Sri Lanka very stressful. There seems to be no easy way to do it. The roads are terrible—pot-holey, narrow, bumpy, twisty and full of mad drivers hurtling towards you. To venture out on the roads in Sri Lanka is to take your life in your hands. The buses are always overcrowded and full of vomiting children. The trains are worse. It appears that no maintenance has been done on any of the tracks or rolling stock since the British left in 1948. Stopping at junctions to change tracks, I watch in horror as a man in the signal box hauls on a big lever, which is connected to the track by a series of rods and bolts which are distorted by rust almost beyond recognition. The area that the connecting rods cross is thoroughly overgrown with weeds and grass and the signalman has to heave with all his might to get them to move through these impediments. The trains are shabby, rickety, slow, almost never on time and desperately overcrowded and hot. When the train pulls into the station there is always an unseemly scramble and much elbowing to get on the train first and get a seat.

    We arrive early at the platform, tickets in hand, in an attempt to get a good seat. The train rolls up to the platform. It is quite full, but we are lucky and find a seat. It is hot, very hot. We wait a long sweaty hour and a half before the great metal beast finally stirs into action. The carriage has been getting more and more crowded in this time as latecomers and people waiting for the next train get on this one. The carriage clears momentarily as the guards move through checking tickets and the fare dodgers creep back to third class.

    At each station, more people squash into the enclosed space. The atmosphere is stifling and tense. A woman starts screaming because she is being crushed. The only people able to move are the food vendors, who, with calls of, 'Waddy, waddy, waddy. Tea, coffee, iddly,' somehow defy the laws of nature and manage to squeeze through. But no-one is hungry. Not even Billy, who is a renowned train-food junky. An old lady sitting opposite us gives us a resigned smile and shrug of the shoulders. She has done this many times before.

At last we reach Colombo station and I look in dismay at the sea of bodies between us and the exit door. I can hardly squeeze myself through, let alone manoeuvre my rucksack through the crowd. There is a real danger that if we do not get off quickly, we will be stranded on the train as it leaves the station for its next destination. More people are forcing their way onto the train without letting anyone off. We fight against a tide of human ignorance.

A child in front of me is panicking and spread-eagling herself across three or four people and blocking the whole aisle. In the nick of time, a kind gentleman helps Bill pass the bags out through the carriage window. But now there is the danger that someone may steal our bags before we are reunited with them, or that the train will pull off and separate us from them. I start to panic and shout, 'Let me out!' first bodily lifting the poor child to one side and then forcing my way through the crowd. There are screams as I trample on feet and ankles, but there is no other way. I nearly lose my shoe in the melee and am knocked sideways by a woman trying to force her way onto the train as I climb down the precarious steps onto the platform. Eventually we are reunited with our bags on the platform, trembling and sweating, but in one piece except for Bill's last packet of rolling tobacco, which has been pilfered out of his back pocket.

I have been claustrophic since I was a child, trapped in a tunnel in the hay bales at my grandfather's farm, and what we have just experienced is my worst nightmare. I am so glad to be with Bill, who is always good in a crisis. He finds me a seat and runs off to get me a cup of tea. It takes me a long time to calm down enough to continue our journey. We are touted by a taxi driver and Bill shovels me, still trembling, and our bags into the back. I am really happy to shell out Rs1000 (about £7) to be driven all the way to Negombo, rather than face the ordeal of getting on another train.

We are much relieved to arrive at the Silver Sands Hotel in Negombo, run by one of the Captain's many friends, Mr Francis, who makes us very welcome.

Chapter 4
Southern India Part II—Ooty and the Todas

We are in India again now and the weird thing was that flying back was like coming home. It is strange to look back and realise we were only in India for a mere two and a half weeks before our month in Sri Lanka, and yet how familiar it feels. As we drove through the streets of Trivandrum, my heart rose to see the familiar sights of the chai stalls and whole families on motorbikes.

As cities go, Trivandrum is one of the more pleasant I have encountered. It is full of beautiful old buildings, with lots of greenery and is relatively clean.

An inexpensive luxury that I wasted no time in making use of here at the Regency Hotel is the laundry service. You can hand over your filthy garments to a lovely smiley woman in the morning and it is back by the evening, spotless, neatly pressed and folded with leaves of tissue paper, for a mere handful of rupees—bliss!

Our one and only laundry experience in Sri Lanka was taking a rickshaw ride to the grandly named Queen's Laundry. At the front desk, an irksome man held up and examined my dirty smalls in front of a shop full of people, whilst deliberating how to describe them on his form, with a look of utter disdain on his face. He then totalled up the bill, which came to a small fortune. It would have been cheaper to throw the clothes away and buy new ones. When we went back to collect them later, I stupidly did not check my clothes as we were being hurried out of the shop which was about to close. But when we got back to the guesthouse, I found that they were all badly pressed and what was even worse—they had written in indelible black pen on the front of each of my white blouses. They could not have chosen a more noticeable place to write if they had tried. I was livid, but we were leaving town early the next morning. So I was even cheated of the satisfaction of storming in there and giving them a piece of my mind.

Billy lies on the bed wearing the batik sarong we bought in Sri Lanka. He looks very peaceful. I am full of love for him. Even in the scariest moments, I feel safe with him by my side. I cannot imagine anyone else I would rather share all these experiences with.

We spend the day doing chores, catching up on the news and e-mails and planning the next leg of our journey. E-mail was a lot less common in Sri Lanka and we have not written to anyone for a whole month, except for the letter I sent in reply to Mum's questions about my spirituality and our choice of venue for the wedding. But it seems that she cannot have received that yet and has gone into a complete panic. We have several very worried e-mails from her. She had convinced herself that we have been blown up or kidnapped by the Tamil Tigers, and was about to send a search party over. But finally she writes:—

Dear AnnaBill,

Hope you are both OK and still enjoying your trip. I do so miss being able to pick up the phone and talk to you. I spoke to Marian (Revd M. Morgan) and she was very helpful—she said the good thing was that you wanted to be married in church and that she would be happy to marry you, and she thought that proving domicile was a lot of hooha. She said that all you need is a suitcase of your clothes in our house. I said we've got rather more than that! She also said that she'd recently married a couple at Hardwicke whose only connection was a grandmother in the churchyard, and that Rector Paul was leaving in March anyway. So there you are—fixed.

Lots and lots of love

M&D

Well thank goodness for the Reverend Marian Morgan, who seems much more open-minded than stuffy old Rector Paul. I wonder if he was the real reason behind Mum's e-mail, asking us to justify our beliefs in order to grant that he would deign to marry us at Clifford?
    My best friend Karn is to be my 'Maid of Dishonour' at the wedding. There's an e-mail from her with some bad news, 'I came back

from Ecuador with Dengue Fever, a mosquito-transmitted disease that makes your joints ache and leaves you half crippled (temporarily, thank God).'

I write to let her know how things are going at this end. It is really good to have a girlfriend to get excited about these things with. I love Bill dearly and we are very close, but he just does not get as excited as I would like about things like the design of the bridesmaids' dresses. But poor Karn, the dengue fever sounds pretty dire.

The advent of the internet is a mixed blessing. It is wonderful to be able to keep in touch with people, especially because of the plans we need to make for the wedding. But once you open the lines of communication, people expect you to keep in touch no matter where you are or what you are doing. You can never quite leave the rest of the world behind anymore.

The other drawback is the absolute tediousness of sitting in Internet cafes, when there are far more exciting and interesting things beckoning. It always seems to take at least an hour, even to send a short message, having lost what you have written a couple of times due to the frequent power cuts here. Poor Billy, who types with only one finger at a time, finds this particularly infuriating.

'I haven't heard much about the Pakistan/India situation since we got back,' I say to Bill.

'No. It's fine here in the South, but it looks like a trip to Manali and Leh are off the cards—they're too close to the border,' says Bill. 'I'm really disappointed. Leh was my favourite place last time I came to India. I was absolutely astonished when I first saw Leh. It's this city right in the middle of nowhere, in seemingly inhospitable landscape. It's totally inaccessible by road for most of the year, because you have to go over the highest navigable pass in the world to get there and it is closed by ice and snow for months of the year. Everything in that city has either been grown or made there or has had to be dragged up a mountain or flown there. The people are very versatile and ingenious. They manage to grow a huge range of crops in the short summer. They even grow apricots. And they are really warm, welcoming, lovely people. There's a Tibetan feel to the place. The people look Tibetan. I remember having a fantasy about getting snowed in there and having to snuggle up with a local family for the whole winter. It's such a shame we can't go there.'

'It sounds amazing. I hope we can still travel to Darjeeling and Sikkim. Grandpa says they're really lovely. They're at the other end of the Himalayas and we might get a bit of that mountain flavour there instead,' I say.

'Yes, I hope you're right,' says Bill.

We arrive in Cochin after a five hour train journey on the Trivandrum-Ernakulam Express. And then we have a long tuk-tuk ride from the station in Ernakulum, Fort Cochin's noisy modern twin town, to our final destination. We cross the Vendruthy Bridge onto Willingdon Island and then across the Palluruth Bridge onto the spit of land between the Arabian sea and the Kerala backwaters, that houses Fort Cochin. The hotel we have chosen from the guide-book is closed for refurbishment—we are not having much luck with this guidebook. So we end up at the Hotel Delight, a 400 year old Portuguese house, full of ghosts of the past. The owner, David, must be Freddie Mercury's long-lost twin brother. He is an ex-stockbroker who wanted a quieter life and decided to let out some of the rooms in his house. His English is immaculate. We sit in his neat clean office and he says, 'I am sure you do not want to do much more than explore your immediate surroundings today, as you must be tired after your long journey. But when you are rested I can arrange everything for you to go on a backwater trip, or to the theatre, or to get a lovely massage from an ayurvedic doctor. He is very good and has even been asked to go and lecture in Germany . . .'

In the evening we wander the streets, exploring. Fort Cochin is a beautiful old town on the edge of the Kerala backwaters, its complex history is reflected in the assortment of mouldering buildings and quaint little streets. There's a feeling of ancient decrepitude, the moss and damp left over from Vasco De Gama's time in the 1500s.

Since 1341 it has been the chief port on the Malabar coast, an important link in the spice trade. European involvement in Cochin began in 1497, when the Portugese navigator, Vasco de Gama, pioneered a sea route to India around the tip of Africa. The Dutch and then the British followed the Portugese, all wanting to get their hands on the lucrative spice trade.

The architecture in Fort Cochin is European, full of houses built by wealthy British traders and Dutch cottages with wooden doors, whose top and bottoms open independently.

We walk to the harbour mouth to see the Chinese fishing nets, believed to be brought here by Chinese traders in the 14th century. There are many men working the huge cantilevered nets.

'They seem to be catching more tourists than fish,' says Bill. Most of them want you to give them money to have a go at hauling the nets up or to have your photo taken with them. 'But of course I want to have a go,' he adds.

We wander on along River Road and find a restaurant where you can sit on the terrace and look out over the harbour where narrow spits of land and coconut covered islands jut out into the bay. We are served a meal of fresh fish steamed in a banana leaf with coconut and spices by a very enthusiastic waiter. It is sublimely delicious.

* * *

Today we are taking a boat trip into the heart of the Kerala backwaters. A short minibus ride and a slippery walk through mosquito-infested woods, delivers us to where our dugout canoe is waiting. We climb aboard and sit incongruously on plastic chairs that ride precariously high above the dugout. Our guide, Badikh, knows everything about everything. An elegant little man in a linen suit and flip flops with smiley eyes and little round glasses, he carries a large umbrella against the monsoon rain. He is quite young, no more than twenty five, but dresses and has the mannerisms and knowledge of someone much older.

Everything is peaceful and serene, just watching life on the river slide by. People are fishing or washing in the river, there are ladies making coir, and people doing many other things with coconuts. Coconuts are the lifeblood of this area. In fact, the name Kerala means, 'Land of Coconuts.' You can use every part of them and the people here do. You can get a sweet syrupy drink from the young tender coconuts, you can press the mature ones for oil and use the flesh in cooking. The shell is used to make cups and spoons and the fibrous outer husk is used to make coir.

Coconut anyone?

We stop at a village and watch as the women spin the coir. It is like magic. I cannot understand how it happens. Two women each have a bundle of fibres wrapped in a cloth, which is tied at their waists. They pull out a few fibres and attach them to a hook. The hooks are attached to a bicycle wheel, which is being rotated by a third lady. The two ladies walk backwards and the fibre magically twists itself into a thin rope, which emerges from the bundle at their waists. The spinning thread seems to automatically pick up more fibres onto itself as they walk. When they each have a length of about 30 metres, they run an ingenious wooden triangular device along the two lengths, which twists them together.

We are back in the dugout now, heading off down narrow tributaries, accompanied by every colour of iridescent butterfly, tiny green and black frogs hopping over the water lilies and bright red dragonflies skittering by. The banks of the river are lined with wild pineapple, coconut palms, cocoa, coffee beans, creepers and many other plants used as ayurvedic herbal medicine. The land is very fertile and productive.

* * *

The monsoon rain is coming down as if forced under high pressure from a fireman's hose. It is the first really heavy, sustained rain we have seen so far. I feel cosy in our room with the rain beating down outside.

We go to a favourite café, Sabala at the Elite Hotel, where the décor is very basic but scrubbed within an inch of its life, and the food is cheap and tasty. Bill has a whole fruitcake for his breakfast. I am always amazed at how much he can stuff into his slim frame. Eating fruitcake for breakfast seems rather decadent somehow, but Bill has never been one for following rules. He tries very hard to persuade me that it is perfectly possible to live a healthy life on fruitcake alone.

'It has all the nutrients needed to sustain life,' he says, 'Carbohydrates for energy, fruit for vitamins and minerals, protein from the eggs and nuts and essential fatty acids from the butter.'

'Sorry Bill, I'm still not convinced.'

We have just changed rooms to one with a balcony in the modern annexe of the house. It is lighter and airier than the room we had for two days in the old part of the building. The old room was damp and dim and neither of us slept well there. There was a feeling of unquiet spirits, echoes of things that have happened over the last 400 years. I kept feeling as if I was just catching a glimpse of something out of the corner of my eye and then I would turn my head and there would be nothing there. I had a feeling of a young woman, perhaps a servant, being really sick with a fever there. This morning Bill told me the main reason he wanted to move was because it reminded him too much of another damp dark room where he lay very sick with amoebic dysentery last time he was in India.

The rain eases off enough for us to go to another favourite, the Kashi Art Café, where we drink a cafetière of really good fresh ground coffee, a rare find in India where everything is made by Nestlé.

David has booked tickets for us at the Kathakali Centre. Kathakali is a dance form which originated in Kerala. It is one of the oldest forms of theatre in the world. The themes of this dance-drama are based on Hindu Mythology, particularly on the epics, the Ramayana and the Mahabharata. The performance we are going to see is an extract from the Mahabarata.

We arrive early to watch the actors applying their elaborate make-up. They grind natural stones with coconut oil to produce vivid, intense colours. They pile on thick layers of the bright colours. Each colour is symbolic—representing good, evil, spirituality, male, female, god, goddess, etc. They change into huge, heavy costumes and headdresses which make them sweat profusely—a great challenge to keeping their make-up intact.

The narrator describes the meanings of the special hand positions, known as mudras, and the myriad of facial expressions. It takes years of meticulous practice to develop the muscular control needed to perfect these intricate movements, which convey so much meaning. The actors do not speak, but each expression and mudra signifies a specific phrase or emotion. The meaning of the mudra showing a bee sucking honey from a lotus flower, can be taken in a number of ways! Billy is very taken with the expressions and practices the eye-rolling and facial ticks with comic effect, while we are waiting for the performance to begin.

The play begins. The action is accompanied by two types of drums, cymbals, song and a squeeze box. All the elements combine to make an entrancing performance. The evil Kichaka tries to force himself on the beautiful Draupadi, wife of Bhima. We are both totally emotionally involved in the story. The climax, when Bhima disguises himself as Draupudi and kills Kichaka, has us on the edge of our seats.

Kathakali

Billy has been practising the facial expressions and body postures ever since. His rendition of Kichaka getting excited about meeting Draupadi is now quite convincing.

David of Delight has booked us an ayurvedic treatment with his friend Dr Subhash. So we take the ferry to Vypeen island where he lives. Dr Subhash, a quiet shy man, meets us at the bus stand and takes us to his house overlooking the backwaters. It is a tranquil oasis. We sit on his terrace drinking lemon and ginger tea whilst he explains the choice of treatments. I choose a full body massage followed by a herbal steam bath. Bill plumps for the body massage followed by half an hour of having warm oil poured in a continuous stream onto his forehead.

    Dr Subhash's wife, Jancee comes to do my massage. She is very good, but for the first few minutes I find it hard to relax, remembering a terrible massage I had from an aggressive woman in Varkala. My muscles are tensed ready to leap off the table if I do not like her style. Eventually I relax enough to enjoy the treatment and feel quite soporific by the end of it. I lie dozing on the table, while Jancee prepares the steam bath. When it is time to get in, I slither off the table like a slippery fish and then sit in a strange box with just my head peeping out. As the herbal steam wafts up, I feel as if I am being lightly poached in basil, which Dr Subhash has suggested will help my mosquito bites.

After the treatment, we shower and have a Kerala-style lunch, prepared by Jancee on the terrace. 'How was your treatment? I ask Bill.

'It was wonderful! The warm oil pouring onto my forehead was like having liquid light poured into my head. It feels like all the corners of my mind have been washed clean,' he tells me.

'That sounds great. I'm having that one next time,' I say.

The monsoon is really set in now. It has been raining heavily on and off all day. The rain does not make me feel closed-in like it does sometimes in England. In fact, it is quite exciting when you get a really heavy downpour, and of course it is much cooler. There is a power, an energy, to this monsoon rain unlike the dreariness of a rainy day in England. The only snag is that it seems to drive the mosquitoes into a biting frenzy and nothing seems to keep them away—they bite through clothes and insect repellent alike. I asked the lady at the Kashi Art Café if she could suggest anything and she said, 'Yes, it is a real problem at this time of year. There is not much you can do except endure it, and you will get a bit used to it in the end.' To my great relief, since the ayurvedic treatment, I find that the intensity of itching has eased.

We bought a local SIM card for our mobile phone and Bill has been playing with it ever since. He texted some friends in England, but no reply yet. About an hour ago, the phone started to ring. We got very excited about receiving our first phone call, until a voice said, 'Hello, is Mr Chandraba there, please?' It was a wrong number.

It is evening now. Opposite our dwelling place is the Parade Ground, where all the local boys gather to play football. Billy has been watching them with interest from our balcony and says they are really rather good. I think he has been half tempted to go and join in. But today the rain has turned the Parade Ground into a swamp and we are being serenaded by a chorus of frogs. They get excited when it is about to rain and their song suddenly gets louder, then you know you need to have your umbrella handy. They remind me of a TV programme I watched as a child—they sound just like the Clangers, and I keep expecting to see the Soup Dragon coming in to land at any moment.

* * *

More rain today. It was stormy during the night and I actually woke up feeling cold. After weeks of sweltering heat, it felt SO good to be cold. I never thought I would see the day when I take pleasure in such a thing!

We finally brave the rain to dash out for breakfast at the Elite. The sun breaks through as we eat and it is starting to heat up now. Today I feel rather sleepy and thirsty. I think I am detoxing after yesterday's treatment.

We have been in Fort Cochin for five days and I feel as if we have thoroughly sampled its delights. It is time to move on.

* * *

We set off today for the hill station of Ootacamund, better known as Ooty, at 2200m in the Nilgiri hills. This is the place where my father, uncle and my grandfather went to school and so it is a must-see for me. But it is a formidable journey and will take us the best part of two days to get there, because there is no direct route and there will be much chopping and changing of transport.

The first stage is a five hour train ride from Ernakulum Junction, where a huge cow lies nonchalantly on the platform—a strange sight to our eyes, but commonplace here, where the cow is a holy being. The train guard comes and asks us if we would like to order lunch. It seems like a good idea and very convenient, so we agree. At the appointed hour, a piping hot and fresh vegetable thali arrives. We arrive in Coimbatore and have an hour to kill before we catch the next train to Mettapulayam. Another hour's train ride brings us to the one horse town where we will catch the narrow gauge steam train to Ooty in the morning. We enquire about booking tickets for tomorrow and are told that we cannot pre-book. We are advised to get to the station an hour before the train departs at 7.10 am to make sure of a place.

We look despondently around. It is late and the sun is beginning to set. The dusty streets are strewn with rubbish. All the buildings are poor looking and run-down. Mangy dogs wander about. I do not hold out much hope of finding somewhere decent to stay. We follow the crowds down onto the high street. But further up the road is a large modern hotel, looking incongruous amidst the shacks and squalor. It looks very luxurious and we are not sure whether we can afford it, but it is worth a try and it is only for one night. Bill goes to the reception of Ems Hotel and enquires about a room. To our great relief, they have a double en-suite available at a reasonable price. It has been a very long day and we sink gratefully onto the bed in our room.

* * *

We rise at the unearthly hour of 5 am and make our way to the station. We queue for a ticket to Ooty, until a man behind me says that ladies can go straight to the front of the queue. It seems rather unfair, but there are others doing it, so I take advantage of being a member of the fair sex and quickly get our tickets.

We breakfast on *vadai* and *dosas* at the station café, a quaint, checkered tablecloth kind of place. There is a buzz of excitement in the air. Lots of other people are waiting for the same train.

The toy train pulls into the station, but we unhurriedly finish our breakfast, thinking there will be plenty of space in the first class carriage, as is usually the case on most of the trains we have taken in India so far. Wrong—we squeeze ourselves into the carriage, which is much more crowded than the 2nd class carriages behind. There is much snobbery attached to a trip to Ooty and there are many rich families from Chennai and other big cities on their summer vacation. They can afford to pay top whack. Ah well, at least we have padded seats and a better view. Wrong again—people open the windows and sit with their bums hanging out of them, almost entirely blocking the view for the majority of the journey.

I feel tired and sleepy after the previous day's travelling and the early start. I know that the train will take five hours to complete the 46km journey into the mountains. We chose to do it this way because of the novelty of catching a steam train and because the scenery is said to be very beautiful. In my tired state, with the view blocked, I envy the people on the bus who wave and smile at us as they pass on the road which runs parallel to the train tracks. They will be in Ooty in less than 2 hours.

Bill is like an excited little boy on his first train ride, so I try not to moan too much and spoil it for him. The train crawls along at a snail's pace. We are overtaken by a lame cow and an old man on a bicycle. The train stops frequently to take on more water, at which point half the passengers jump off to admire their surroundings or have a cigarette. Then the whistle blows and there is a mad scramble as everyone tries to board the train. The train sits there for another five minutes, so the people in the know just amble back to their places.

At the second station, we stop for half an hour. Again, those in the know have a leisurely breakfast, whilst the rest of us grab a quick chai and stand nervously next to the train door, ready to jump back on. Next stop Runnymede—same thing. Next stop Coonoor—same thing, next stop Lovedale, etc, etc . . . plus more stops for water.

Eventually people get tired of hanging out of the windows and sit in their seats allowing me a better view. The scenery is indeed spectacular. A myriad of colourful wildflowers grow by the track—trailing daisies, morning glory heaped up over the trees, red salvias, huge agaves and orange and pink lantana.

Sometimes the train crosses impossibly spindly bridges spanning vast ravines. When I look down out of the window, all I can see is a dizzying drop hundreds of feet to the valley floor below. We pass through many tunnels hewn into the rock. Each time, people whoop and cheer to hear their voices echoing off the tunnel walls.

The air grows cooler and thinner as we climb and I begin to wish I had put some warmer clothes on. Finally, we arrive in misty Ooty. I think of all the people on the bus, who have probably been drinking chai and strolling about already for three hours.

As we pull into the station, the narrow gauge steam train track is joined by many other big grown up tracks. Making his way confidently across the tracks towards our train is an Indian man. He is dressed in sharply pressed trousers, pulled up slightly too high over his small-checked shirt and beige acrylic tank top, and fastened with a narrow belt. His shoes are highly polished and his dark hair is oiled and carefully combed. In contrast with his neat appearance he holds in front of him two huge bunches of fluorescent pink candyfloss on long sticks that seem to float above his head like helium-filled balloons. I fear that any minute now a gust of wind might come along and carry him off by his candyfloss balloons. But he makes it safely to our train where many takers for his wares hold money out of the windows to purchase some of the sugary fluff.

I have been looking forward to visiting Ooty ever since we first began to plan our trip. My father, uncle and Grandpa all speak fondly of it — a hill station in the Nilgiri Hills, with tribal people called the Todas living close by. My father used to reminisce about wandering through the forest with his brother to visit the Toda village and Grandpa, in his nineties can still give a good rendition of the Toda tribal dances and songs, as he told us when we visited him at Dulas. Ooty was one of the first hill stations of the British in India. There is a myth that it is the place where snooker was invented. With all this in mind, I had built up an image of a quiet town full of old colonial houses and surrounded by tea plantations and forests. I imagined it to be India's version of Nuwara Eliya. But I am sadly disappointed.

The town has been growing at a colossal rate. It is noisy, dirty and full of traffic pollution. The once beautiful lake has receded to a tiny puddle. The few remaining colonial buildings that have been converted to hotels are dilapidated and full of damp.

We drive about in a tuk-tuk, despondently trying to find somewhere decent to stay, that does not cost a fortune. We are taken to one place that from the outside has all the old colonial charm that I had imagined and the tuk-tuk driver assures us that it is good value. Bill goes in to investigate, but comes back out with his nose wrinkling.

'How is it? I ask.

'Smells like a wet sock,' says Bill.

Eventually we settle on a modern building at the top of Charing Cross, the commercial area of Ooty even in my father's time. It is relatively pricey at Rs600 (£7.85) per night, but at least it is clean, dry and warm with hot water in the bathroom. We are feeling decidedly chilly by now.

We wander about, exploring our surroundings and slowly, Ooty begins to grow on me. The views to the surrounding hills are beautiful, the people are friendly, but not as pushy as in other places we have been. We find Breeks School, set up a grassy hill overlooking Charing Cross. The red-brick, St Pancras-Gothic building with its turrets and spires, is exactly as I had pictured it, and seems to be the only thing that is the same as in my father's day. We walk up through the school grounds. I have the strangest feeling. I am excited and a little fearful, but feel more than anything that I am intruding—intruding on my father's past.

'Hello. Is anyone about?' shouts Bill. I want to shush him, not to draw attention to myself, but the school is deserted anyway. It must be the summer holidays. I picture my father, coming here as a five year old boy, with Blake, who was only a year older—two little boys, dwarfed by the pith helmets they wore to keep off the sun.

The story of how they came to be here is a traumatic one. The family had been living in Malaya, where my grandfather was a teacher working for the Colonial Civil Service. When the Japanese invaded Malaya during the Second World War, my grandfather joined the Johore Volunteers. He was taken prisoner and sent to work on the Burma railway, the infamous 'Road of Death'. Miraculously, he survived, but it was to be three and a half years before he saw his family again. Meanwhile, my grandmother, Dad and Blake managed to get on the last ship to leave Singapore as the Japanese bombed the city in February 1942. It was a long and arduous journey to India, with cramped conditions and food in short supply, the boat being frequently shelled by Japanese aircraft. But several weeks later, they arrived in India in one piece. Great Grandpa Eustace used his influence to arrange a place for Dad and Blake at Breeks School, where he had sent his own sons a generation before.

We walk across the playground and look in at one of the windows. The desks and chairs in the classroom seem so small. Idyllic as it is here, I think about how much of an ordeal Dad's first day at Breeks must have been. After parting from his father, the terrible boat journey and a three-day train journey from the north of India, now some strange teacher was trying to part him from his mother. And my father's reaction? Uncle Blake tells me that Dad swung back his little five year old leg and kicked the teacher as hard as he could in the shins, before they both burst into tears and wailed for their mother, who was leaving to stay at the mission station in the Godavari District with Great Granny and Grandpa. Perhaps the teacher, Mr Fisher, was a little sympathetic towards the boys, since he remembered teaching their father twenty one years earlier.

We are about to leave the school grounds when we spot a plaque on the wall. It reads, 'In memory of late Mr Willy, Principal (1945 to 1960).

'He must have been made Principal in the last year that Dad and Blake attended the school,' I say to Bill.

'Take a picture of the plaque,' says Bill. 'I wonder if your dad will remember him?'

After this poignant dip into my father's past, I feel in need of refreshment. Bill tells me that one of the delights of Ooty is that hand-made chocolate is a speciality. It is one of the few places in India where chocolate does not melt into a gooey mess. So we waste no time in finding a suitable eatery to sample the local delicacy. Accompanied by a glass of chai, it is heavenly—so creamy and melt in the mouth delicious.

So from the poignant to the shallow—for a woman who likes to shop, Ooty is divine. There are lots of Kashmiri shops selling bargain pashminas and embroidered wool jackets and shirts. There are general stores which sell ready made clothes that are actually big enough to fit me. Since Indian women are very petite, I have found it a problem finding anything big enough on the shoulders and chest. So I buy two shalwar kameez sets. These are long cotton tunics with matching baggy trousers—very comfortable and practical for travelling and have the added advantage of being acceptably modest in this culture.

* * *

Bill has finally remembered the name of the guesthouse where he stayed last time he came to Ooty eight years ago, so we are moving there as it is much cheaper than where we are currently staying. It is a little way out of town on the road that runs next to the lake, or should I say former lake. It is in a quiet location away from the noise and pollution of the town and it is run by a lovely old lady, who seems strangely familiar to me.

The rooms are basic but very clean and functional. Our room reminds me of a school dormitory, with its slightly wobbly steel-framed beds and checked woollen blankets. We are in a little annexe at the top of the garden. Meals are served in the main family house, where a log fire warms the dining room. All the guests sit down to eat at a set time and there is a friendly atmosphere amongst the collection of different nationalities—French, Dutch, Danish and English.

The owner has arranged for us to go trekking for the day with a Toda guide and we have been provided with a generous packed lunch for our trip, by the tiny little ladies who do all the housework here. We finish our breakfast and, bulging packed lunches in hand, we go out to the roadside to wait for our guide. I am so excited about meeting the Todas that I have heard so much about from my father and grandfather. A tall man strides towards us, a trail of smoke billowing behind him as he puffs on a beedi. He greets us with a radiant smile full of pearly white teeth. He is film-star handsome with a perfect jaw and large clear eyes.

'Hello, my name is Rajiv. I am very pleased to meet you. I am your guide for the day,' says Rajiv holding out his hand to shake ours. 'We need to catch the bus for the first part of the journey, so please follow me,' and he leads the way to the hustle and bustle of the Ooty bus stop.

While we wait for the bus, Bill asks him about his background. 'My family are Toda, but my grandfather became a Christian and had to leave the village. I went to university and got a degree in Marketing. For some years I worked for a big company in the city. But even though I was very successful, I always felt restless and wanted to come back to the Nilgiris. So eventually I left my job and became a guide. I love more than anything just walking in nature, so now I am very lucky and have the perfect career.'

'I can understand that,' says Bill who gets cabin fever if he stays indoors too long.

The bus arrives and we have a twenty minute journey out into the hills. We need to change buses to get right out into the wilds, so there is time for a quick chai at a roadside hut before the next bus comes. I am enjoying this haphazard adventure already. The next bus drops us in the middle of nowhere and we walk from here. Our path climbs steadily through shola forests into a pristine wilderness set aside many years ago by the British as a Nature Reserve. It seems that the Todas have been treated much better than the poor Veddas in Sri Lanka.

'It is the law that the Todas are the only people allowed to live on this land and they are only allowed to sell their land to other Todas,' Rajiv tells us.

'For once, the British have left something good behind,' says Bill.

'Yes I think it is a very good thing. It has saved this land from being ruined like so much of India,' says Rajiv.

The trees give way to a view of rolling hills and low shrubby woodland. There is a special micro-climate that exists here in the Nilgiris, Rajiv tells us. He points to a patch of small shrubs and ancient rhododendrons. 'See here, the vegetation will colonise whole areas and then for no reason it stops and there will be gaps where only grass will grow. Then over there the shrubs will grow again.' As a gardener, Bill is fascinated by this concept.

The Todas are the perfect guardians of the land. They live in harmony with their surroundings and you would not know that they had been there except for their occasional neat houses in isolated hamlets.

We arrive at a Toda village where they have had a celebration the night before. When I say village, it is only a collection of two or three dwellings, one of which is a new bricks and mortar house and the others are the traditional domed wooden long houses, coated with a mixture of mud and buffalo dung. Many people are visiting from surrounding villages. The headman greets us warmly and invites us in for tea and sweets made from cassia. Everyone is very friendly. The children are still excited, running about in their party frocks and coming to gaze and smile at us. It seems like a thriving community. I think of my father as a small boy, visiting villages such as these and it strikes me what he must have liked about them—in his fractured young world, the sense of community and happy families must have been very attractive.

'They are vegetarians and grow most of their own food,' says Rajiv, indicating the fields. The headman shows us around his land. He has a couple of small fields of neatly growing vegetables. I can see carrots, potatoes and salad crops. He takes us into one of the traditional long houses. I feel shy to enter a stranger's home—there is a cosy intimate atmosphere and the smell of wood smoke from the log fire. But the family are very friendly and make us welcome, showing us how they sleep on wide benches that run the length of the house, and where they keep all their possessions and cook their food.

'The Todas have a very close relationship with the buffalo,' says Rajiv. 'They worship the buffalo spirit. Here is one of their temples' he says, showing us a long low domed timber building, carved with images of buffaloes. On the door is a carving of the Buffalo god.

Toda Buffalo Temple

'The buffalo are wild animals. They wander in the hills all day, but they choose to come twice a day to be milked. The Todas do not give them food or anything to encourage this. But they help the buffaloes when they are having their calves. And in return, the buffalo give their milk to the Todas.'

'That's amazing. No wonder the Todas worship the buffalo spirit,' says Bill.

We leave the village, thanking the headman for his hospitality and walk on through the hills — the Nilgiris, the Blue Mountains, named because of the misty haze that surrounds them, looking blue from a distance. Over the crest of a hill, we enter a beautiful valley. A river runs through its bottom and a herd of buffalo graze the river meadow. 'We shall stop here to have our lunch,' says Rajiv. The weather is perfect. The sun is out but the air of the hills is a pleasant temperature. Everything is quiet and peaceful as we munch contentedly on our sandwiches and the buffalo munch contentedly on their grass below us. From time to time, Rajiv mimics the greeting sound made by the buffaloes and they greet him back.

'My heart is in the hills,' says Rajiv, 'And I am much happier now that I walk amongst them every day. I love the Todas and I envy their quiet, simple life. But once you have tasted another lifestyle, it is impossible to quiet your mind enough to be satisfied with this basic life again,' says Rajiv wistfully.

'Rajiv, my father and my grandfather went to school at Breeks in Ooty. They have both told me how they used to go walking in the hills and visit the Todas, who were very kind to them,' I tell him.

'Really? How wonderful. I would love to meet your father if he ever comes to India. Tell him he must come trekking with me and I will take him back to meet the Todas again,' says Rajiv.

'I will. I know he would love it.'

After lunch we begin a slow steady climb. Our goal is the summit of a mountain we can see in the distance. We meet a couple of young Toda men on the way. They greet Rajiv with beaming smiles and share a smoke together. They do not speak English and seem a bit shy, but Rajiv explains who we are and with their customary hospitality, they offer us some buffalo curd. It tastes like slightly rancid yoghurt, but seems to have a strangely fortifying effect. I had been experiencing that after-lunch drowsiness, but suddenly my limbs feel full of energy as if I could run up and down ten mountains.

We set off again, climbing through woodland, where ferns and orchids drip from the ancient trees. We reach the top of the mountain in what seems like no time at all. The wind is blowing mist over the ridge. We are all very exhilarated and run about whooping. I feel that I am on top of the world and close to God. Then we all flop down for a rest, panting and laughing.

I feel a huge sense of achievement getting up here. We gaze out at the incredible view and chat with Rajiv some more. He is a deep thinker and a sensitive man. It feels like one of those rare meetings with a kindred spirit. We put the world to rights for a while, enjoying his company enormously. But sadly, our day with Rajiv is coming to an end and we must now set a quick pace to march down the mountain and through the lanes to take us to the bus stop. There is time for one last sweet chai in a smoke-filled hut as we wait for our bus back to civilisation. It has been a magical day and we both thank Rajiv warmly for giving us this experience. We have only been with him for one day, but he already seems like an old friend.

* * *

We wave goodbye to Ooty, the place of noise and smells and handmade chocolate and spices, where we trekked in the hills to visit the home of the Todas. We board the bus for a one and a half hour journey to Masinagudi. The bus winds its way slowly through 36 hairpin bends down the Nilgiri Mountains onto the plains below. The Mudumalai National Park is laid out before us. My excitement mounts at the prospect of a few days in the wild, in search of elusive creatures and getting back to nature for a bit. Our days' trekking with Rajiv has whetted my appetite for getting out in the countryside.

We stop at a chai stall in Masinagudi for the regulation cuppa on arrival at our destination, a habit we have got into since our very first experience at Chennai airport. It is good to just pause for a moment, to gather your wits after the journey and take in the atmosphere, before making the final push to your accommodation for the night.

As we stand at the chai stall, a calf approaches us and enjoys being scratched under the chin. Next there is a fluffy dog that does the same.

'The animals are very friendly round here,' I say to Bill. 'Let's hope it's a good omen for our wildlife spotting.'

'Yes. I can't wait to meet this Kumar fella that Rajiv has recommended,' says Bill. 'It sounds as if he really knows the animals round here. Maybe we'll get to see elephants in the wild again.'

'Or even a tiger. Now, that would be exciting!' I say. There are lots of young jeep drivers, touting to give us a ride and all of them tell us that they are wildlife guides and try to get us to book them for a tour. But we are holding out to meet Kumar.

Tonight we are staying at the Log House, a government run guesthouse in Masinagudi, on the outskirts of the Mudumalai Wildlife Park. It is a timber building with a large wooden verandah on the upper deck. We are greeted and shown to our room by our host-come-forest ranger, a tall, strong man with a gruff demeanour, but a sparkle of humour just glinting under the surface.

From the verandah outside our room, we gaze out on the savannah spreading out before us to the Nilgiris in the distance. There is a watering hole not far away, but so far no animal sightings other than the odd fish jumping. I think it is too noisy and too close to civilisation.

We are called to dinner by our host who has cooked us mountains of delicious curry.

'Eat, eat!' he exhorts Bill, 'You need strength for trekking tomorrow.' He is proud of his cooking and is delighted to have met someone like Bill who is up to the challenge of eating it all.

We retire to bed with full bellies and climb into the safety of our mosquito net. We drift into peaceful sleep until I am rudely awoken by a loud buzzing, whirring sound. Something heavy, with scratchy feet lands on my eyelid . . .

'Oh my God, I've got a cockroach on my eyelid!' I scream out, waking the whole Log House. The cockroach is soon despatched by Bill's sandal and I feel a bit of a girlie for making such a fuss, but it is not the most pleasant way I have ever been woken.

* * *

It is not permitted to go on foot inside the park, so we set off trekking through the forest and the savannah just outside the park. We are guided by Sanjay, who brought us to the Log House in his jeep. It is wonderful to be walking in the wilderness amongst forests of teak and rosewood with a backdrop of the Nilgiri Mountains.

We sit for a long time on a rock overlooking the savannah and watching a herd of spotted deer, the chital, who pass quite close to us in the undergrowth. We also see the larger sambar deer, some beautiful blue and green parrots, a woodpecker, squirrels and rabbits. As we walk, there is plenty of evidence of wild elephants — large piles of dung and tree rubs — but no sightings. We come across a termite mound, which has been dug out by a sloth bear, but again no sighting of the animal itself.

Bill asks Sanjay, 'How did you get all your knowledge about the animals?'

'From my father. He was guide for many, many years. He know everything about the animals,' says Sanjay.

'So your father doesn't guide any more?' asks Bill.

'No, he was killed by elephant last year. Now I best guide in the family.'

'Oh, I am sorry to hear that. You're very brave to do the same job after such a tragedy,' says Bill.

'I love the animals and there is no other work here for me.'

It is pretty clear that we are not going to be going anywhere near elephants today, if Sanjay can help it. So we get in the jeep and go to Moyar Falls, a local beauty spot. We come to the top of a ridge called Suicide Point and there in front of us is a dramatic drop hundreds of feet to the valley floor and a waterfall cascading down the mountain on the opposite side. From our high vantage point we look down upon bright blue rain birds, flying to beehives hanging from the rocks to drink honey. It seems ironic that such a piece of paradise has a macabre name like Suicide Point. Perhaps people are so enchanted by this vision that they are seduced into stepping through the veil into the other realms.

We climb down to a small waterfall and pools halfway down. It is too steep and dangerous to get right to the bottom. Besides which, our guide tells us that there are crocodiles in the river below. We strip off for a swim. Bill plunges under the waterfall only to emerge covered in what looks like hundreds of leeches. I shriek in fright, which sends Bill into a panic, frantically trying to swipe them off. Sanjay laughs and assures us they will not bite, but it puts a bit of a dampener on the fun of our swim.

On the way back, we come across a chameleon—a very strange little creature which sways back and forth three or four times before carefully opening a two-toed foot and placing it on the ground. It is not going anywhere in a hurry. Perhaps it is trying to fool predators into thinking it is just a leaf swaying in the breeze.

So far, we have had a pretty exciting day, but the best is yet to come—an elephant ride through the park. We go to meet the beast who will carry us on his back. His name is Ganesh, the Lord of all elephants. We climb up a platform and get onto a seat strapped to his back, known as a howdah. His mahout sits on his neck and guides him by pushing a bare foot behind either his left or right ear depending which direction he wants to go. We are off, swaying regally through the forest. We are surrounded by colour—the pink and orange lantana filling the forest floor. It is quiet and peaceful except for a huge bull bison which looks like something you might see in the ancient cave paintings in France. We see plenty of langur monkeys, but none of those elusive stripy felines that I am so longing to see. Ganesh's rhythmic movements send me into a magical dream-like state. Finally our ride is over and it is time to return to earth. We rub Ganesh's bristly domed head and say thank you.

Langur monkeys

Tonight we are staying at the Sylvan Lodge in Mudumalai Wildlife Park. The lodge is in a pretty setting overlooking the River Moyar. Outside our room, grey-faced langurs play in the trees. As I look out of the window, to my right I can see a huge male elephant chained to a very substantial tree. He looks agitated and is doing his level best to break free from the giant chain around his leg. The ranger at the lodge tells us that he has to be chained up for now because he is in 'musth' and is a very naughty elephant. In the elephant world it is the males who come into season and become very rampant. They will do anything to find a female who is ovulating. The story goes that before the keepers realised that he was in musth, the naughty elephant was still working at the park, giving rides to tourists. One day he was giving a ride to a 10 year old boy and his mother. Suddenly, Naughty caught a sniff of an available lady elephant and he was off. The mahout and the mother managed to get off, but the boy was too frightened and ended up going on more of an adventure than he had bargained for when his mother booked the elephant ride. It was eight hours before they could catch up with the elephant and get the boy off. This was finally achieved by a ranger climbing a tree and grabbing the boy from above as the elephant went past. The poor boy was very distraught and probably rather hungry and thirsty. It took them another day to catch the elephant and so they are taking no risks in letting him get away again.

It is dark now and I have just been outside for a breath of air. I wandered down to the river and saw strange moving lights, like little fairies flitting about. Thinking they were animal eyes glinting in the dark, I ran back to the room to tell Bill and get the torch. On the way I was aware of dark shapes moving about just in front of our room. When we shone the torch we discovered a family of wild boar, which can be quite dangerous, especially when they are protecting their young. So we did not linger and were careful not to get between the mother and her babies. The lights I had seen turned out to be fireflies.

* * *

We enjoyed our elephant ride so much yesterday that we booked another one for this morning, hoping that perhaps we might see more wildlife earlier in the day. That was before we had heard the story about the naughty elephant. Our elephant this time is Naseem, even bigger and stronger than Ganesh. He has a will of his own and his mahout is helpless to stop him from going exactly where he pleases, which is usually in pursuit of the choicest and most tender shoots. We have an exciting and sometimes hair-raising mystery tour going up and down some very steep banks and almost out of the park at one stage.

Back at the Sylvan Lodge, we are about to try and track down the guide recommended to us by Rajiv, when we meet a dapper gentleman in a cream linen suit with little gold-rimmed spectacles

'Pleased to meet you, my name is Subbu,' he says, proffering one hand and pushing his glasses back up his nose with the other. 'How are you enjoying Mudumalai?' he asks.

'It's very beautiful, but we haven't seen as much wildlife as we would like to,' I tell him. 'Oh, would you be interested in doing some trekking with a guide?' asks Subbu.

'Yes, but we already have the name of someone who has been recommended to us,' I say cagily.

'Perhaps I can help you find him. What is his name?' asks Subbu.

'His name is Kumar and we have been told that he is based at the Green Park Hotel.'

'Oh, you are in luck. He is my colleague and I am going to Green Park very soon. I can take you to meet him if you like? You have been given a good recommendation. He is the best guide around here—he knows everything about the animals,' says Subbu. At first I feel a little sceptical—you always have to be on alert for a con, but Subbu has such an innocent, smiley face.

'What do you reckon?' I whisper to Bill.

'I think he looks pretty honest. Lets go along with him.'

So we get into Subbu's jeep and he takes us to the Green Park Hotel, the place we had planned to stay next anyway.

Kumar is sitting in the Green Park restaurant talking to a German lady, Sabbine.

'Hello, Kumar, this is Anna and Bill, they are interested in doing some trekking with us. Can you tell them a little more about it?' says Subbu.

Kumar holds out his hand and motions for us to join him. Subbu goes to get us some tea. A short stocky man dressed in a green polo shirt and khaki shorts with a thatch of dark hair and luxuriant moustache, Kumar has a very serious air about him. Over tea he explains what he has on offer. He is a man with a commanding presence and gives us the utmost faith that he is an expert on the animals and their habitats. We have found our Indian version of Bushman Bandara. With a trek booked for early the next morning, we take a room at the hotel and relax for the rest of the day. It really is the most perfect spot here. The daytime temperature is a pleasant 20°C and cooler at night, and we are surrounded by teak and rosewood forests with the Nilgiri mountains rising in the background.

We take a night safari in Kumar's jeep, hoping to get our first glimpse of wild elephants. We are not disappointed—there are lots in the area. Having heard so much about how dangerous they can be, I am personally shocked at how close they come into the village.

Kumar says, 'There are panthers also in this area. They are nocturnal so you may be lucky to see one tonight.'

We see no panthers, but there are several people walking along the road back into Masinagudi. One man is cycling along in the dark with no lights and another is asleep at the side of the road.

'What's going on here, Kumar?' asks Bill.

'Oh, this is very bad,' says Kumar sucking his teeth and shaking his head. 'The people in Masinagudi have rounded up the village idiots and taken them to the next village. Now they are trying to find their way home. It's very dangerous. The elephants hate bicycles and will attack. And this poor fool asleep in the road. He is in great danger. The elephants will attack if they are surprised to come across someone like this. Many people are killed each year around here when they are out gathering wood or fruit.'

'Can't we help them?' asks Bill.

'It is too dangerous for us to get out of the jeep in the dark,' says Kumar. 'We will just have to trust that fate is kind to them.'

After our glimpse into Indian-style care in the community, it is time to go home and turn in for the night. We have an early start tomorrow and our appetites have now been whetted for our on-foot trek tomorrow, although I must admit to being a little nervous after all the talk about how dangerous the elephants are.

* * *

We rise at 5 am. It is still dark. 'Wooh, hooh, I'm really excited,' says Bill. 'I've always wanted to go trekking like this.'

We are picked up in the jeep by Kumar. We have a quick stop in Masinagudi for a cup of chai and a banana to get the blood sugar levels up. It is so early that the chai stall has only just opened, I am sure just to catch our business. The owner looks sleepy and ruffle-haired. Unusually for India, no-one else is about and all the dogs lie sleeping in the road or in doorways. It is not even properly light yet and there is a delightful chill in the air.

Kumar is impatient to get away, 'Let's go. It is the best time to see the animals,' he says as he bundles us back into the jeep. Subbu and Sabbine are also with us. She has obviously been before, as she talks with familiarity to Kumar and Subbu. We have a five minute drive to the area where Kumar wants to start the trek. From here, we set off on a four hour trek through the bush led by the intrepid Kumar.

Dawn is just breaking as we pull up in a clearing amongst thorn trees and teak. Our arrival in the bush is greeted by the whoops of the langurs, as they dash between trees to get away from us. Soon we see a herd of spotted deer—such beautiful elegant creatures.

'The spotted deer and langurs are usually found together', says Kumar. 'The monkeys are an alarm system for the deer. The deer can relax while they are eating because they know the monkeys will shriek if anything dangerous comes along.'

We are moving out of the forest now and into more open grassland with the occasional acacia tree and scrubby bushes. As we walk, we see many birds, including a vivid red hawk-owl, but the prize we are really after, wild elephants, remain elusive. We walk in silence, trying to make each foot fall as quiet as possible, so as not to disturb the animals. The excitement and tension builds till it is almost unbearable.

After two hours of walking, we sit down on a rock to rest and have a snack. It is getting very hot by now. The smell of the hot baked earth is in my nostrils and the back of my throat. I am beginning to think we will not see many animals today, when we hear a snort from behind a group of trees. It turns out to be a buffalo rather than an elephant, but the reason it is snorting is because a family of foxes have been bothering it.

'Oh, you are very lucky to see this,' says Kumar. 'These foxes are very rare in this area.'

The Indian foxes look more like jackals than the British fox—fluffier, with a speckled grey coat that graduates to a gingery belly. Our animal spotting luck has changed for the better. A little further on, we walk into a clearing and come face to face with a pair of hyenas with their young cub. My preconception of hyenas, based on the mean-looking African spotted hyena, are shattered. They have full, soft-looking creamy coloured coats, and lovely faces. They are shy of us and run as soon as they see us. We follow them, hoping for another glimpse, but they have vanished into the bush.

Luckily for us, they have taken us right into the path of the elephant trail. Kumar leads us along this trail until we come across a watering hole with lots of fresh dung. He tests it with his hand but says that it is cold.

'They probably spent the night here and moved on early this morning,' he tells us.

We follow the trail of broken twigs and footprints, barely perceptible to us, but obvious to Kumar's expert eye. He sticks his finger into another pile of dung and immediately motions for us to stay still and silent.

'It's warm. They are very close,' he whispers. He listens very carefully until he hears the tiniest sound of a snapping twig. 'Over there!' he says in a hoarse whisper, pointing to a shrub-filled dip about 50 metres away. 'Wait here,' he says, moving silently away to investigate.

Kumar comes back and beckons us to follow. We creep on tiptoe, hardly daring to breath, lest we give our presence away. And there he is—a magnificent tusker in a small hollow, quietly eating his breakfast. We watch for about ten minutes from a safe distance, until he moves off deeper into the undergrowth. I cannot believe that such a huge animal can move so quietly through the forest.

'The dung by the watering hole did not belong to this male,' says Kumar. 'It must have been a large group of females with babies. I want to try and find them.'

On the way, Kumar stops and points up at a tree. 'Look up there. Giant squirrels,' he says. They have thick red fur and fluffy tails, around the size of a large cat—a lot bigger than the 'giant' squirrels in Sri Lanka, but still not the four feet tall rodents I have created in my imagination.

Suddenly Kumar points out another tusker. This time we are upwind of him and pretty close. We are in real danger if he becomes aware of us. We watch for a while and then he moves, catches a sniff of us and looks directly at us. His ears come forward as if he is about to charge. In an instant of panic, I realise that Kumar has not told us what to do in this situation. But as quickly as I think this, I get my answer. Kumar disappears into the distance, his heels a blur in a cloud of dust. We all run for our lives in hot pursuit of Kumar. Finally at a safe distance we look back to see that, content with giving us a scare, the elephant has not bothered to give chase.

After this exciting episode, we all return to Green Park for a hearty breakfast. 'How did you enjoy your first trek?' asks Subbu.

'Well, it's been quite a morning—fresh air, beautiful scenery, good exercise and rare beautiful creatures all around us.' I tell him. 'In fact, we liked it so much, that we would like to book another trek for this evening.'

Breakfast is a chance to get to know our fellow trekkers a little better. Kumar is a man of few words and puts most of his attention into tucking giant platefuls of food away. Sabine tells us she has a son at the Kodai International school in Kodaikanal and she is over here visiting him. She has been on several treks with Kumar.

'Kumar really is the only guide to go trekking with round here. He is so knowledgeable and you will see far more animals with him because he knows what to look for,' says Sabine. Kumar smiles and looks slightly embarrassed by the compliment.

As the afternoon begins to cool in preparation for the coming of evening, Kumar comes to pick us up for our second trek. We go to a different area this time. It is more heavily wooded and there are clumps of bamboo and thick undergrowth everywhere.

Some Indian bison stare at us for a while from the bush before leaping off into the undergrowth. They are fine looking creatures, big and powerful, with their glossy red coats.

We come across a shaded riverbank, where there are fresh tiger prints in the mud. Just up river from us a herd of spotted deer leap from one bank to the other, sometimes pausing to stare at us, and then hurrying on. As we walk on, I have a strong feeling that the creature that made the prints in the mud is watching us. As I look down a side-track, I am sure I catch a glimpse of something orange and stripy slinking into the bushes. A thrill of excitement runs up my spine.

Kumar suddenly realises that we are very close to a group of elephants and they are coming our way. We have to run through the tight undergrowth, as quietly as we can, getting scratched and bitten by fire ants on the way. Kumar tries to find a place for us to view the elephants, but it is too dangerous. We have to walk a long way out of our way to keep down wind of them and night is starting to fall. The forest becomes a scary place in the increasing darkness, especially with the thought of large stripy felines on the loose.

At last we hear Subbu call to us from the opposite bank of the river, where he is waiting with the jeep. There is a bridge up ahead and soon we are safe again after our adventure.

'Phew, it's a bit of a relief to know that we will get home safe after all,' I say to Bill.

'Yes, but I wouldn't have missed a minute of it,' he says.

'No, neither would I.'

* * *

We set off on another early morning trek with Kumar. As well as Subbu and Sabine, we are joined by a Dutch couple, Anna and Rudolf. Rudolf, a tall gangly chap, chats incessantly in the jeep. His babble is punctuated every minute or so by, 'Oh, there's a spotted deer! How beautiful!' or 'Oh, there's a monkey! How beautiful!' with a look of rapture on his boyish face.

Anna, by contrast, is very quiet and all her movements careful and considered.

Bill leans towards me and says, 'He's definitely a badger, but I like him.'

We start walking into the bush and soon we come upon an ancient ruined temple. We climb it to get a better view of our surroundings. The temple is on a high outcrop of rock, overlooking a wide expanse of flat land below, which stretches away to the blue hazy Nilgiri Mountains in the distance. The land below us has a dense covering of low trees. The Flame of the Forest, the Indian silk cotton tree and the Indian coral tree add a dash of orange, yellow and red to the green tones of the forest.

Just below us, a large group of elephants are moving through the bush. It is so exciting to see these wild elephants at close range and we feel safe up here in the temple. Once again, I am struck by how quietly these giant beasts can move through the forest. All you hear is the occasional tiny snap of a twig and a faint rustling of leaves.

Kumar checks the wind direction and says, 'If we walk round behind them with the wind blowing our scent in the other direction, we will be able to get a better look at them in the open.'

We creep along, one behind the other, with Kumar in front and Subbu bringing up the rear, carefully keeping an eye on the herd to our left. The smell of the elephant herd is coming to me on the breeze. It is a strong heady smell a bit like sweating horses, but muskier. I suddenly spot another elephant going in the opposite direction to our right. She is the big matriarchal vanguard leading another large herd. At first I think we can get by without her spotting us, because elephants have notoriously bad eyesight. Kumar has not seen her and if I shout to him I will definitely give us away. But suddenly, she catches our scent. I see her big head swivel towards us. Ears out and trumpeting, she starts to charge at us. A general cry of, 'Run for your lives!' goes up. We all scatter in different directions. Not knowing which way will take me to safety and which way will take me into the path of the other herd, I blindly follow on the heels of Bill, who is weaving in and out of the bushes at top speed, his body leaning this way and that as he swerves around obstacles. As I run, I dare not look back, not wanting to know whether the elephant is on my shoulder and death is imminent. The primal fear of being chased by wild beasts fills my whole body.

After a few minutes of running at top speed, it seems that we are out of danger and I slow down. My heart is pounding out of my chest and my lungs feel as if they are about to burst, not only from the exertion, but also from sheer fright. We all regroup. It is interesting (with hindsight) to think about people's reactions in that situation. Everyone bar Subbu ran for their lives, without a second thought for anyone else. But Subbu hung back to make sure that I was all right and to check which way the elephant was going. He is a very gentle, sensitive man, but in that moment he showed incredible bravery and caring for others.

Bill puts his arm round my shoulder and says, 'Anna, I'm <u>SO</u> sorry that I didn't stop to check that you were OK.'

'Thanks for the sentiment, but hey, don't worry about it—what could you have done to protect me against a huge elephant?' I reply.

'Oh my God! We all nearly died!! That was **too** exciting!' says Rudolf.

'I saw the elephant coming and I didn't know what to do, because Kumar hadn't seen it and he was too far ahead. I was so scared,' says Anna.

'Yes, I saw it too and I thought we might get past without it seeing us. I didn't want to shout to Kumar, because then it would definitely hear us. But it smelt us anyway. I think that was the most frightening thing that I have ever experienced in my life,' I tell them.

After our brush with death, Kumar comes back from checking where the elephants have gone. 'I'm sorry about that. I didn't see her coming the other way. I think we will get out onto more open ground, where we can see what is going on.'

Just as we are about to step out into the open, Kumar motions for us to hang back and be quiet. We hide behind some bushes with a good view of the clearing. To our left the original group of elephants that we were following is about to step out into the clearing. The Big She Elephant, who has been leading the herd, steps out from the cover of the bushes. She is being very cautious, looking this way and that, sniffing the air and listening. She is not aware of us and decides it is safe. She motions for the others to follow and they come out, lined up in formation with five big females in the front row. In between theses big elephants are the smallest of the babies, four in total, flanked on each side by a big adult. Behind this line come the rest of the youngsters and teenagers, surrounded by adult females chivvying them along and keeping them all together. And then, forming the rear guard comes the Big She Elephant's second in command, making sure there is nothing dangerous creeping up behind them. We watch as they cross the open ground safely and then disappear silently into the bushes again. It is a wonderful display of their intelligent and caring behaviour. I feel very moved.

'That, was SO beautiful!' says Rudolf, a look of wonder in his eyes. I have to agree with him.

We let the herd carry on and then follow at a safe distance. On the way, we see much evidence of tigers—footprints and a kill so fresh it still has a look of surprise on its face. All that is left of this young sambar is its head and hooves. Its head is resting on the ground and still so life-like that it appears the creature is emerging from the earth. We make our way up into the hills and find a high rock to act as a vantage point. As we climb, Kumar's foot slips and he gashes his knee badly on the rock. He tries to make light of it, but it is clearly very painful and bleeding profusely.

'Oh, Kumar, let me put a dressing on that. It is bleeding everywhere,' says Sabine, getting out the first aid kit.

'Ai, ai,' whispers Bill, winking at me.

'Oh, it's only a scratch,' says Kumar, but he lets Sabine tenderly clean and dress the wound. His knee is swelling up badly and it's going to be difficult for him to walk on it.

'Kumar, I'm a shiatsu practitioner. I have a few tricks up my sleeve to help with injuries like this. I could do something to help the swelling go down if you like. It's a long way to walk back from here with an injury like that,' says Bill.

Kumar looks embarrassed by all this attention, but sees the sense in helping the injury heal quicker and lets Bill give him some treatment. Bill uses a technique called v-spreading which helps to take the trauma back out of the injury. He points one finger at the centre of the injury and uses the thumb and forefinger of his other hand to form a triangle behind Kumar's knee. A look of concentration comes onto Bill's face. We all watch as the swelling on Kumar's knee goes down before our eyes.

'Wow, that's amazing!' says Rudolf. 'How do you do that?'

'Oh, it's just a little trick I learned on a cranio-sacral course. I'm always bashing myself when I do tree surgery, so it's very useful to help with that,' says Bill. 'How does it feel now, Kumar?'

'The pain has almost gone. Thank you, Bill,' says Kumar, with a look of astonishment on his face.

We are all up on the rock now. Below us is a beautiful valley filled with splashes of orange, yellow and red from the silk cotton trees and the coral trees. In the distance a huge tusker is happily grazing on the undergrowth. Kumar estimates that he is around 12 feet tall. I prefer this kind of distance between myself and wild elephants!

In the evening, we join Sabine for dinner at Green Park. Bill, being the nosey parker that he is, pumps her for information about her relationship with Kumar. After a beer or two she starts to open up.

'I met Kumar last time I came to visit my son, Pieter. He loves animals and we were recommended to go with Kumar by one of the other parents from the school. Pieter loved it so much that we came several times. He became very fond of Kumar. I think he looks up to him. He misses having a man's influence since I split up with my husband several years ago. Subbu and Kumar have been very kind to Pieter. They have been to visit him at the school when I am back in Germany. I'm very glad for this. It reassures me that Pieter is OK and not too lonely,' says Sabine.

'And what about you and Kumar? Do I detect a little romance blossoming there?' asks Bill cheekily.

'Kumar is a wonderful man and yes, I can't deny that I find him attractive. But I see no future in that kind of a relationship between us. You know what the culture is here. He would be expected to marry an Indian girl. I am too old for him and I already have a child. I would not be the best match for him,' says Sabine.

'Yes, but you can't help the way you feel, can you?' says Bill. Sabine sighs and looks into the distance.

'I feel really sad for them,' says Bill when we are back in our hotel room. 'She's in love with him and I reckon he feels the same, but the odds are stacked against them being able to make a go of it.'

'I know, the cultural differences would soon split them apart, poor things. His family would probably disown him and families are so important over here.'

'Subbu's a nice man, isn't he?' says Bill.

'Yes, he is. He was very brave today. He's always looking out for other people.'

'He reminds me of a cartoon character. Do you remember Dangermouse had an understudy called Penfold? Well Subbu is Penfold. He's very intelligent, but he'll always be the side-kick to the Great Man, Kumar.'

* * *

Sabine and Kumar invite us on a trip to Bandipur, a neighbouring National Park to Mudumalai. It is officially Kumar's day off, so this is a freebie and I feel very honoured. Kumar knows that I would dearly love to see a tiger.

'Bandipur is much drier. The land is more open—less vegetation. You will have a better chance of seeing those tigers,' he says.

We set out early and have breakfast en-route at a roadside café that serves particularly good puris. It is great to have local knowledge.

'Did you know the elephants were right outside Green Park last night?' asks Sabine. 'Kumar says it is a good job there are high walls and a good gate around the hotel grounds, or they could have done a lot of damage.'

'Oh, I thought I heard some strange noises in the night,' says Bill. 'That's what it must have been.'

After our breakfast stop, it starts to rain and we do not have much luck with animal spotting, other than a couple of bison in the distance. Everything else is sheltering from the rain. As Kumar is off duty today, he allows himself to let down his guard and we see the softer side of his nature. When we stop for a break, he and Sabine huddle under an umbrella, looking very cosy. Bill says, 'Oh, what a lovely picture that will make,' and gets out his camera. They both giggle shyly.

* * *

Our next destination is Mysore. Kumar and Sabine are driving there today and have offered us a lift. Sabine is going back to Germany tomorrow and Kumar is taking her to the train station. The air of sadness between the two of them on the journey is poignantly tangible.

So from the serene setting of Mudumalai National Park, we arrive in the bustling city of Mysore, home to the Maharaja's palace, and to silk and sandalwood oil production. We decide to 'do' Mysore in style and hire a driver with an old ambassador car to take us round the main sites. Our driver, Vishnu, gives us a whistle-stop tour of a sandalwood oil factory, where sadly there is a shortage of local sandalwood and they are importing inferior sandalwood from Australia and putting a limit on how much oil each person is allowed to buy. Next stop is a silk fabric manufacturer, where people work amongst the cacophony of the looms clackety clacking away. Their shuttles of iridescent thread fly back and forth to create the most amazing vibrant fabrics with intricate designs. Then he takes us to visit the temple on Chamundi Hill, dedicated to the goddess Chamundi who slew the buffalo-headed demon, Mahishasura. As usual, doing pooja seems to be big business and we are besieged by people trying to sell us things to leave as offerings. We join the queue to enter the temple and see the solid gold figure of Chamundi. The woman in the queue behind me is so desperate to earn her merit by doing her pooja, that she pushes and jostles me, continually ramming me with her bag. After a few minutes of this, I turn around and tell her that I would be more than happy for her to go in front of me. 'I don't think she is going to earn much spiritual merit behaving like that,' I say to Bill. When we arrive at the altar housing the goddess, there is a bank of priests parting people from their cash before performing the most cursory of prayers and waving the next person along.

Then it is back to town to look around the Maharaja's Palace. I have a very romantic notion of how I will find the Maharaja's Palace. I imagine I will wander serenely around a building which is the epitome of beauty and good taste, breathing in the scent of jasmine and sandalwood, wafted in my direction by the punka wallahs. But this 'fairytale spectacle topped with a shining brass-plated dome' has nothing to do with good taste and everything to do with making a flashy show of the Maharaja's great wealth. This seems quite sickening by comparison to the millions of people in India who live in poverty. The Kalyana Mandapa, the royal wedding hall, seems the embodiment of this ostentatiousness, with its Bohemian chandeliers, the Belgian stained glass peacocks and the cast-iron pillars, especially commissioned and made in Glasgow, which must have cost a fortune. But more is to come, as we pass the life-like figure of one of the Maharajas, Krishnaraja Wadiyar IV, reclining with his bejewelled feet on a stool, to enter the Public Durbar Hall. Here the maharaja used to give audience, seated on his throne made from 280kg of Karnatakan gold and surrounded by more stained glass and everything else dripping with gold leaf. Finally, we leave this room through huge doors made of solid silver.

The city with its noise and smells, seems a real shock to the system after Mudumalai. Despite the beauty of the city, and the many and varied shopping opportunities, I am pining to be out in nature again. Our hotel is made entirely of marble. It is beautifully clean and cool, but the downside is that even the tiniest sound is amplified and seems to reverberate around our room—the noise from the street below, religious processions at 5am, the noisy TV in the room next door and the man hawking in the bathroom early in the morning. There is also the constant blare of the tinny radios playing squeaky Hindi music at you from all directions. The frenetic activity of this city is really wearing my nerves.

But there are some saving graces to Mysore. Rudolf and Anna have joined us from Mudumalai. We have spent hours wandering around the wonderful bazaar, breathing in the heady scent of stalls heaped with garlands of white, orange and red flowers, past stalls heaped with every kind of fruit and vegetable, through lanes where stalls sell strange coloured powders in vivid pinks, oranges and reds all heaped into piles and daring you to sneeze on the way past, and stalls selling perfumed oil extracted from many exotic plants and flowers. It has been fun just to sit with Rudolph and Anna at one of the many chai stalls in the market, to chat and watch this strange and wonderful world go by. Spending time with these two has been the best bit of Mysore for me. Anna is quiet, thoughtful and sweet, whilst Rudolf is hysterically funny, matching Bill in his enthusiasm for anything and everything.

Today I went shopping for saris with Anna. Since Mysore is such a mecca for silk production I thought it would be a good place to start looking for one for my wedding outfit and one for Karn's bridesmaid outfit. But I needed Anna's moral support because with all this choice, I was feeling the pressure to get the very best ones and I was worried about getting ripped off.

We go into shop after shop and nothing seems right. They are either horrible colours or the fabric is too coarse or the embroidery too gaudy. Anna gets a couple of simple ones in muted colours which suit her pale complexion very well, but I give up on getting **THE** wedding ones.

We go to meet Bill and Rudolf for lunch and I tell Bill of my confusion about the saris. 'We need to hone down the search a bit,' he says. 'We need to get a recommendation for a really good shop. Local knowledge is always the best thing in these situations.' So we ask around and the same name comes up a couple of times. So we follow the directions given to us and end up in a very posh looking sari shop with suitably snooty shop assistants. We ask to be shown a selection of their saris. The shop assistant brings one out of the shop window, telling me this is a very special one made for a festival.

'It was specially made for the customer. They ordered two, but only take one, so I can give you this for very special price,' he says, holding out a beautiful sari in rich indigo blue and cerise. 'It is very highest quality. Here let me help you try it on.'

We go into the fitting room and fortunately Bill comes with me. The assistant wraps the skirt section around me, but then spends rather too much time arranging the section that goes over my chest and whilst tucking it in, his hand lingers rather too long on my breast. I cannot quite believe the cheek of the man doing this right in front of Bill.

'Hey, watch what you are doing there,' says Bill pulling his hand away and giving him a pointed look.

'I am merely showing you the correct way to wear the sari,' says the assistant.

'Well, I think we've got the gist of it,' says Bill. 'Anna, are you interested in this one?'

'Yes, it's a beautiful colour,' I tell him, taking off the sari. It is by far the best sari I have seen today, but I am not going to say that out loud in front of the assistant, because it will be ammunition for him to hike up the price.

'Well, let's get it and get out of here,' says Bill to me out of earshot of the assistant.

Back in the hotel room, I get the sari out to admire it. 'Oh, my God. It's got a huge fade mark right across it. That must have been from when it was in the window. He was really careful to hide that when he tried it on me,' I say to Bill.

'The cheating git. First he tries to touch up your boob, then he sells us a faulty sari for a hugely inflated price. Right, we're going straight back to get our money back.'

'Too right,' I reply.

In the sari shop we show the assistant the fade mark and ask for our money back.

'Oh, no. This is just starch. It will come out when the sari is cleaned,' says the assistant.

'Rubbish, it's faded because it's been in the window,' says Bill.

'I assure you sir that it is starch and will come out as soon as you clean it. There is nothing wrong with this sari,' says the assistant.

'It's a fade mark which won't come out when it is washed. We want our money back,' says Bill.

'Not possible,' says the assistant.

'If you don't give us our money back, I'm going to stand outside your shop and tell everyone who tries to come in here how you have cheated us. And I'm prepared to stand there for a very long time,' says Bill.

Eventually the assistant grabs the sari off Bill, takes some money out of the drawer and throws it at us.

'Better count it to make sure he has given us the right amount,' I say to Bill. 'I'm beginning to despair of finding anything for the wedding,' I wail.

'Don't worry, there are plenty more sari shops between here and leaving India,' says Bill.

Thought for the day:—

> 'Anger is no way to be happy. If you are angry you cannot sleep in a comfortable bed and food is tasteless. But anger is our best friend. You should rejoice when someone makes you angry. How else can you practice tolerance and compassion?'
>
> Geshe-la, Tibetan Lama.

We are staying in a cottage at the Mayura River View Hotel just outside Srirangapatnam. We have both been feeling tired and out of sorts for the last couple of days so we thought we would get out of Mysore and stay somewhere quiet.

Our cottage overlooks the river Kaveri—a very beautiful spot, but unfortunately not as peaceful as we had hoped. It is the weekend and lots of people have come for functions and parties. Last night Bill was kept awake by loud music, shouting and singing. I must have been very tired, because I slept right through it.

* * *

So from Srirangapatnam we travel to Bangalore. The city is modern and cosmopolitan and serves the best coffee we have come across so far in India. I feel dowdy wearing a salwar kameez, compared to most of the young Bangalore women all dressed in the latest fashions.

Our hotel is just off the MG Road, which is the main shopping street with designer clothes stores and cafés serving real cappuccinos everywhere. It is such a contrast to everywhere else we have been in India.

In the window of one of the men's shops, we see an outfit in cream silk that would be perfect for Bill to wear at our wedding. The outfit consists of a long tunic-style shirt and waistcoat, matching trousers and scarf, with subtle embroidery on the front of the shirt and waistcoat. We go in to get a closer look and the sales assistant urges Bill to try it on. He emerges from the changing rooms, transformed from the well-worn traveller to a picture of fresh elegance.

'Oh, you look wonderful,' I tell him. Then the sales assistant brings out the matching turban and pointy shoes. They are very shiny and decorated with lots of gold.

'I've just got to try these on,' says Bill. 'What do you think?' he says parading up and down. In an instant he has turned from elegant to comical. I think it is the turned-up ends of the shoes that does it. We are both trying very hard not to laugh. We do not want to offend the shop assistant.

'Very fetching, but I'm not sure my mother would approve,' I say.

'No, I think you're right. We'll just take the suit,' he says, turning to the shop assistant, who takes it away and wraps it beautifully.

'So we've really set the intention for our wedding day now, Anna. But I feel guilty that I've bought my outfit before yours,' Bill says.

'Don't worry. I am really happy that you have found something so elegant at a reasonable price,' I tell him.

'Come on let's have a look for something for you. I'll feel a lot better when we find yours,' says Bill.

Deepam's sari shop is recommended in the guidebook. So far we have not thought much of their recommendations, but as we are bewildered by the amount of choice in Bangalore and it has some beautiful saris in the window, we decide to go in. On the way in, I whisper to Bill, 'Whatever you do, don't tell them it is for our wedding. It will just be a licence for them to charge more and then try to make us feel guilty if we quibble about it.'

'OK, good idea,' says Bill.

We are ushered to a counter, and three sales assistants simultaneously ask what we are looking for. 'We're looking for something for Anna to wear at our wedding,' blurts out Bill.

'Oh, well done,' I snarl under my breath at Bill, as £ signs light up in the sales assistants eyes and they start fawning even more. Out come the most sumptuous fabrics I have ever seen. They are all exquisitely beautiful, but nothing seems quite right so far. Then the more senior sales assistant says, 'We have just had a delivery of a very special sari Madame. It has been hand-woven by hundreds of tiny little elves. The crystals alone took three years to apply. Would Madame like to see it?'

'Well of course I would!' He disappears for a moment before returning with the most incredible fairytale sari that sparkles and glows with dazzling crystals and gold embroidery. But dare I ask the price?

'Never mind the cost Madame, it's for your wedding and you deserve the best,' says the sales assistant. Well, when you put it like that how can I possibly quibble about paying a few thousand rupees?

'Go on, try it on,' urges Bill. 'It's fantastic.'

I go to the other side of the store so that Bill will not see me and two of the assistants help drape the exquisite fabric about me. It is alive with magic and has put a spell on me. I have to have it. I meet the eye of the female sales assistant and if I had not already been in love with it, the look on her face would have persuaded me. She is looking at me as if I am the most beautiful creature she has ever seen. Either she is a very good actress, or the fabric is very flattering.

So out come the credit cards and the deal is done. I am starting to feel sick about how much it has cost and to worry whether it will reach England safely but the shop people assure me that their courier service is very safe and they have sent many items to England with no problems.

Outside the shop, Bill says, 'I am really impressed at your ability to always choose the best.' I misinterpret this as meaning that he thinks I have been too extravagant. I burst into tears. Bill puts a reassuring arm round my shoulders. 'Oh Anna, I'm not angry. I really meant that you deserve the best and I'm glad you've found something so beautiful. We're only going to get married once and the cost doesn't matter. Come on, let's go for a drink to celebrate.'

After my second whiskey at a posh rooftop restaurant, I start to feel better and to get excited about the sari. I cannot wait to hear Mum's reaction when she opens the parcel.

* * *

We check our e-mails to find there is one from Mum writing about our wedding plans. I rush off to phone her with the news about our wedding outfits. She seems as excited as we are.

For the rest of the day, we potter about, getting chores done, like posting Bill's wedding outfit, getting shoes mended, shopping and drinking cappuccinos.

In the evening we go to Bangalore station and board the Rajdhani express train. We are heading for 'hot and smelly Delhi,' as Bill calls it from bitter experience last time. Our journey will take 38 hours—it seems pretty daunting. We are now heading north. Our final destination is the foothills of the Himalayas, but there is no way to avoid a short sojourn in Delhi. Bill waxes lyrical about his time in the Himalayas on his trip eight years ago. He and a friend rode an old Enfield motorbike all the way from Goa to Leh. The highlight of the journey for Bill was crossing the high passes into the Himalayas.

'When I stood and looked out over that vast bleak landscape, it made me feel small and made we want to cry. It was so devastatingly beautiful. We must go their again,' he told me.

Looking out of the train window, I am amazed at how green the landscape is. I had imagined that the middle of India would be dry and brown. In fact the fields are full of crops and deciduous trees. The only way to tell that it is seeringly hot, is to leave the cool of the air-conditioned compartment and stand by the open doors of the train. It is like standing in front of a fan heater turned up to maximum. It is hard to comprehend how the locals can tend the fields without keeling over.

I have been dreading this train journey for days. Thirty-eight hours seems an interminably long time to be cooped up in a small space. But actually, it has been rather fun. The Rajdhani Express has come up trumps. The air-conditioned sleeper is a very pleasant temperature, with comfy bunk beds and spotlessly clean sheets and pillows. We are fed copious amounts of delicious food at regular intervals, in fact more than one person can physically put away. Bill has given it a damn good try, but even he has had to admit defeat on occasions and just could not fit in that final piece of cake. Our fellow passengers are good company. There is Deejay, a biologist, Sanjeev, a computer whizz who writes programmes to model molecular processes (at least I think that is what he said) and Sheela a trainee journalist. We have introduced them to the great game of Scrabble to try and while-away a few hours. They are embarrassingly good, despite having never played before. Bill won both games, but mostly through his sneaky strategy of closing up the board with tiny words squeezed in everywhere and the fact that he managed to hog all the triple word scores.

Chapter 5

Northern India—Bear in the Woods

It is 7 am and we are due to arrive in Delhi in a couple of hours. The long, long train ride will soon be clickety-clacking to an end. We have just finished breakfast and the train staff are eager to get the bedding cleared away. The pillows are counted back in.

There is a queue for the washing facilities, but our friend Deejay who has done this journey many times has beaten the queue. He has spent most of the journey casually dressed in jeans, a T-shirt and a baseball cap. Now he reappears, immaculately dressed in a shirt, tie and smartly pressed trousers and with a turban wound neatly into place on his head.

'Deejay, I am most impressed with how you've managed to look so fresh and dapper after this long journey,' says Bill.

'I am going to see my parents and have some difficult news to break to them. I had an arranged marriage which didn't work and we are going to get a divorce. I wanted to look my best to give me some confidence,' he tells us.

Our arrival in the steaming metropolis of Delhi is smoothed considerably by Deejay, who negotiates a tuk-tuk ride for us. The negotiation seems to involve much dispute and heated words. Deejay tells us that the rickshaw driver does not want to take us to the place we are asking for and keeps saying that he knows of a much better hotel, no doubt that is paying him to take people there. So Deejay kindly comes with us to make sure the driver takes us to the right place. I am so grateful for his help. I have heard of so many people being taken to the middle of nowhere and dumped without a clue where they are and the only option is to stay in the hugely overpriced hotel that has paid the rickshaw driver. In fact Bill tells me that was exactly his experience the first time he arrived in Delhi.

We get out of the tuk-tuk at the Main Bazaar, thanking Deejay and wishing him luck for the meeting with his parents. Tall buildings crowd in on the narrow streets of the bazaar, which are thronged with people, rickshaws, bicycles and the usual assortment of dogs and cows. The streets are lined with shops and stalls selling goods of every description in any colour or size you could possibly want. The air is thick and acrid from the fumes of diesel generators pouring out into the street. Along with the noise they are making, there is a general hub-bub of voices, traffic, blaring horns and loud Hindi music issuing from cheap radios. It is now around 9.30 am and unbelievably hot.

We make our way to the Anoop Hotel. For once, the guidebook has brought us to somewhere half-way decent and we take an air-conditioned room for Rs350. The hotel is a quiet haven from the chaos of the bazaar outside, with its breezy rooftop restaurant, where we retire for a cool drink after showering and unpacking.

I am surprised to find myself mildly excited about being in smelly Delhi and suggest a little expedition into the bazaar. It is a retail dream of brightly coloured, sparkly things—clothes, shoes, bags, etc, etc—and all unbelievably cheap. But I am sent into a frenzy of too much choice and cannot make a decision on anything. All I manage to buy is about five years' supply of bindis, because they are so pretty and glittery and only Rs15 a packet.

Delhi is inescapably hot and humid. We have chosen the worst possible time to come here—just before the monsoon breaks. I feel imprisoned by the heat. I cannot even lift my little finger without breaking into a sweat. In fact, rivulets are pouring down me just in the effort of writing this journal. Even the local people seem to be wilting in the heat.

I got bitten all over by nasty midgy things yesterday evening and the heat is making me insanely itchy. I feel really irritable and cannot even face the idea of braving the heat of the bazaar to get my hands on all those lovely goodies.

'You must be feeling really unwell if it's bad enough to put you off shopping,' says Bill.

Our air-conditioning is not working, because there is a power cut. This happens on a regular basis. Bill spent an hour writing an e-mail and lost it all when the power cut out. He was not pleased. So now we are sitting at the rooftop restaurant, where there are life-saving air coolers powered by a generator. The waiters all look fit to melt and they spend as much time as possible positioning themselves in front of the air coolers.

The only person that looks as if she is coping with the heat is one of the other travellers staying at the hotel. She wafts about in a long white gypsy skirt and camisole top, with a beautiful silk scarf draped casually round her tiny hips and trendy ethnic jewellery gracing her slender neck. I do not think I have seen one drop of perspiration marring her pretty brow. I am insanely jealous. I feel like a big sweaty dumpling by comparison. She cannot possibly be English.

I am now desperate to get away from Delhi with its heat and choking pollution. Since Mudumalai, we have been continually moving every day or two. I feel unsettled and homesick. The constant noise, pollution, grime and intrusions into one's personal space are really getting to me. I am longing to find a quiet, peaceful, clean place to settle and just do nothing for a few days. I am reminded of a verse from the poem *I Am* by John Clare, which sums up exactly how I feel.

> *I long for scenes where man has never trod;*
> *A place where woman never smil'd or wept;*
> *There to abide with my creator, God,*
> *And sleep as I in childhood sweetly slept:*
> *Untroubling and untroubled where I lie;*
> *The grass below—above the vaulted sky.*

Before going to the Himalayas, we want to experience one of the holy towns on the Ganges. At Rishikesh, the Ganges leaves the mountains and flows out onto the plains. It is also the place where my father, my grandmother and my uncle were first sent when they arrived in India after fleeing from Singapore. So it will be interesting for me to see where they gained their first impressions of India. We hope to travel on from there to the Himalayas. But the train to Rishikesh is fully booked for several days and we cannot face the thought of staying in Delhi for that long, so the helpful man at reception has booked us on the night-bus tonight. Hopefully it will be considerably cooler and quieter there.

It is time to leave for our overnight bus to Rishikesh. We are met in the foyer of the Anoop Hotel by a man from the bus company. He says he will guide us to where we need to get on the bus, as this street is too narrow for it to get down. So we shoulder our rucksacks and follow him through the crowded streets. Unencumbered as he is, he is setting a cracking pace down the street, weaving in and out of the crush of people. We almost have to run to keep up—not easy with a 20kg pack, which keeps catching on people as we fight our way through. It is dark and we are in danger of losing sight of him if we do not keep up—this would be a disaster, as we have no idea where we are headed. By now we are panting and sweating profusely. It seems particularly unpleasant to have to breath in increased quantities of the fetid air.

He stops several times at other hotels en-route to pick up other customers for the bus. We are gathering quite a throng, all trotting after our guide. Twenty minutes later we arrive to meet the bus and have to hang around for half an hour before we are allowed to board the bus. Everyone is muttering about having been made to hurry in this heat only to have to wait for ages at our destination.

The bus is a desperately dilapidated old jalopy and Bill questions its roadworthiness to carry us through the night and up into the hills. But it is too late to turn back now, so we climb aboard. The only seats available for two people together are towards the back, a most undesirable place to sit, as we are soon to find out.

The bus sets off and we feel a sense of relief that we are on our way out of this place. But when the bus passes the same restaurant for the third time, we begin to realise that we have just spent two and a half hours circuiting the suburbs of Delhi in order to pick up more passengers. It is not until the bus is absolutely jammed to the roof that we will finally get out onto the open road.

It is stiflingly hot. All the windows are open, but the only thing they are venting onto us is hot, dust and pollution-laden air. The dust coming in from the windows has soon adhered to the film of sweat we are covered in, giving us a lovely prickly coating. The seats are really hard and do not recline. The driver has the radio on at full volume, playing squeally music, which is not quite tuned in properly to the radio station. We are in for an uncomfortable night.

Each time we stop, there is the usual selection of food and drinks vendors who jump onto the bus and vie for our business. At one stop, a man selling ice creams has boarded the bus carrying a handful of cones. The cool creamy substance seems particularly appealing to my parched, dust-filled throat. I am about to put my hand up to beckon him over, when Bill catches hold of my arm and says, 'Not a good idea. Just watch what he does when he gets off the bus.'

As the bus revs up, ready to set off, the ice cream man realises he is out of time to make any more sales and gets off the bus with his remaining cones. The bus pulls away, showering the man and his ice creams with a good layer of dust. But even worse than this, I watch with horror as he tidies up the drips on his surplus cones with his tongue, before popping them back in his chiller bin to await the unsuspecting passengers of the next bus. Bill has saved me from almost certain dysentery.

The bus driver sets off at a bone juddering pace along the bumpy road and we are soon to discover why it is such a mistake to be sitting at the back of the bus. There is a long overhang behind the back wheels and this acts like a cantilever, launching us eight inches off our seats every time we hit a pothole—roughly about every 20 seconds. Having fought me to sit in the window seat for a better view, Billy is bitterly regretting his decision, because a strategically placed electric fan clonks him on the head every time he is thrown into the air. The irony is that the offending fan does not even work.

There is an Indian lady who has got so fed up with being launched off her seat that she has decided to lie down in the aisle of the bus and get some kip there. But she has only really succeeded in getting stepped on and kicked by everyone going up and down the aisle, which people do at regular intervals. There is no real answer other than to accept the discomfort and the fact that getting any sleep is most unlikely.

A few hours later, and it is Bill's turn to make a food-related mistake. By now we are around four hours into our journey and the driver stops for a comfort break. As I am returning from the toilets, the horror and stench of which I try to blot from my memory, I see that Bill has been up to his usual tricks of purchasing deep fried things from unhygienic looking road-side stalls. But he has excelled himself this time. Clasped in his hot little hands are two of the most disgusting looking items masquerading as food I think I have ever seen. The closest way of describing them would be to say that they vaguely resembled battered and deep fried sandwiches with unidentifiable fillings. It could have been some kind of luncheon meat, but I do not care to speculate, really.

'Blimey, your capacity for deep fried junk food never ceases to amaze me,' I say to Bill indicating the sandwiches.

'Oh, they're not both for me,' he says looking hurt. 'I bought one for you.'

'You have to be kidding. I would no more let that pass my lips than dog poo,' I say, feeling decidedly queasy as I watch Bill biting into the first of his purchases. His expression turns to a grimace and I am sure I can see his stomach heaving a little.

'God, you're right. It's vile. I don't know what came over me.'

'Let's just stick to chai,' I say and we wander off, trying to find the least unhygienic looking of the stalls from which to purchase our beverage.

After our chai, we reboard the bus and resign ourselves to several more hours of torture before we arrive at our destination.

It is 7 am when we finally arrive in Rishikesh, with aching backs and foul tempers. By now, we are covered in such a thick layer of dust that we look as if we are about to audition for the black and white minstrel show. When the driver tries to charge us Rs5 for having stored our luggage in the boot of his death-trap of a vehicle, it is the last straw and we stomp off without paying him.

The area around the bus station is noisy and filthy. We look around in dismay, beginning to think we may have made a terrible mistake by coming here. Fortunately, some of the other Westerners who came on the bus, tell us that the area around Lakshman Jhula is much prettier and more peaceful. So we share a taxi with them, and to our great relief they are right.

The road is too narrow for the taxi to take us all the way, so once again we have to shoulder our packs and walk the last way into town. Our first priority is to find a hotel and clean off the disgusting layer of filth and grime that has accumulated over the journey, but we are both exhausted and it seems like there may be a fair bit of trudging around involved. So we plump for plan B—find a café and fortify ourselves with breakfast before attempting to make a decision about a hotel.

This turns out to be a good plan, as we quickly find a sweet little café with a wooden balcony that looks over the river. This part of Rishikesh is beautifully set along the banks of the Ganges and surrounded by forested hills. As we breakfast, we watch the morning mist slowly rise from the river and drift away.

Breakfast over, Bill announces, 'Man go hunt place for woman to rest weary head.' He leaves me to guard the bags and goes scouting for a good hotel. It is one of the things that I love about Bill. Whenever we have had some sort of physical ordeal and I am feeling exhausted and out of sorts, he seems to be able to dig into hidden resources and look after me.

He comes back ten minutes later, having found us a room at the Hotel Ishan. We cross a narrow footbridge that spans the Ganges and take up residence in our room. Bill has come up trumps. It is spacious and spotlessly clean, with a huge marble bathroom and a balcony that looks back across the river to the main town. I waste no time in diving into the shower to scrub off the layer of filth from the journey and get my clothes to the laundry.

So we have finally found somewhere to rest our weary heads for a few days. The Hotel Ishan is a joy. The staff are all smiley and helpful and the food is great, with a lot of variety. I am so sick of curry and I have been longing to eat something bland. Already it feels as if the horrendous journey was worth it. It is a pleasant temperature here—cool at night and in the early morning, but warming up in the middle of the day—a bit like a good day in an English summer. By comparison to Delhi, the air is clean, flowing down the river valley from the mountains. Ah, I can breathe again.

Rishikesh is a holy town. Our balcony looks over the Ganges to the many colourful Ashrams on the opposite bank. There is an atmosphere of religious fervour—many crazy things going on here, mostly centred around the river and the ashrams. There is a constant ringing of bells and circambulation of the devotees around the tiers of the orange and white striped Trayambakeshwar Temple opposite us. There are ghats down to the river where people throw huge elaborate and brightly coloured offerings into the water or bob up and down doing pooja to wash their sins away. All very interesting to watch from a distance, where the sounds are muffled and the frenetic activity does not impinge on us.

The rain fell heavily here until about 3 pm, but it was the perfect thing for freshening the air and forcing us to chill out at the hotel. We have been doing some stretching and shiatsu exercises, followed by meditation. The spiritual atmosphere here must be rubbing off. I felt an enormous sense of well-being afterwards and Bill's eyes were shining and clear.

The rain has stopped so we go wandering round the town in search of Kashmiri shawls to keep us warm on the next stage of our journey. It can get a bit chilly in the evenings—ah bliss!

A man from a jewellery shop comes over to chat to us. At first I think he is trying to sell me something, but it seems that he just wants to tell us about his recent trip to Kashmir and show us his photos.

'How beautiful it is!' he says. 'And it is perfectly safe to go there now.'

'You're not the first person to say this,' says Bill. 'It is very tempting to make it the next stage of our journey. From your photos, it does look incredibly beautiful. So you didn't see any fighting?'

'No, nothing at all. It was very peaceful.'

'It would be wonderful to go. We'll just have to keep an eye on the news,' I say.

Our balcony looks down on a small temple on the opposite side of the street. We watch with amusement as a cow saunters down the street and sticks its head in at the door and eats all the offerings of fruit that have been left by the worshippers. The cow is a welcome guest, as a holy being and this must be a daily event, because we saw the same thing happening yesterday. Meanwhile, the monkeys on the roof are not such welcome visitors. There is a priest who seems to do constant battle with them. They sit on neighbouring roofs or telegraph poles, eyeballing him and daring him to turn away for a second. As soon as they think his guard is down, they all rush onto the roof and pull at his washing or throw things about, looking for food. He chases after them shouting and throwing stones. It seems to be a great game for the monkeys. One of them even picked up a stone and threw it back, driving the old man into a frenzy of temper. What is that saying? 'Monkey see, monkey do'!

Checked our e-mails today and there was one from Mum about wedding plans. She wrote:—

Dear AnnaBill

I've been waiting to write to you until Bill's outfit came, but it hasn't and we are off on a canal holiday tomorrow, so I must let you know Anna that your fabulous sari arrived last Wednesday, another hand stitched parcel. It is so beautiful with all those Swarovski crystals and gold, I do hope that you can remember how to put it on when the time comes. It is now hanging in a wardrobe suspended from 2 skirt hangers, wrapped in white cotton, parcelled up with pearl pins. It was so tightly packed that when it was opened the crystals from one layer had been pressed into the next, looking like rows of chads on an American voting card. I'm sure they will hang out. They have plenty of time.

I've been speaking to Rev Marian again—all she asks, she says, is that the promises at your wedding are made in good faith. They are the usual ones—Love, comfort, honour etc., but she will need you to be home 7-8 weeks before the wedding to allow for talking to Bill and yourself and then for the banns to be called which can take 4 weeks. You will have to decide whether to stick with June 21 and come home a little earlier or have a later date for the wedding.

We are looking forward to our 3 days away—I'm Quarter Master in charge of food. Dad will probably be working the lock gates and we hope we don't have to spend too much time fishing Humph out of the canal. He's had a tea tree shampoo today and all his bedding washed and cleaned. Goodness knows what he'll be like by tomorrow evening. We come back

Wednesday evening. Hopefully Bill's outfit will be here by then. It was good to hear you on the phone a week ago.

Lots of love to both,

H & H

To Mum and Dad re wedding and sari arrival

Dear Mum and Dad

Thanks for the e-mail. We're very relieved to hear that the sari arrived safely and glad that you like it. There are many ways to wear a sari, but I think I've got the general gist of it. Bill's outfit will take a little longer. We sent it registered airmail on 29th July and it will probably take about 2 weeks (should be there around 12th August).

So the outfits are sorted and it's just the reception, venue, date and the vows that we need to decide on! The vows to love, comfort and honour each other sound fine. I'm sure we can say those to each other in good faith.

We have also been thinking about the time-scale and agree that we need a little more time between arriving home and walking up the aisle. Financially, it would also benefit us to come back a bit sooner and not be completely stony-broke in the lead up to our big day. So we thought if we come back mid-April, that will give us just over two months till 21st June, and will only be a month earlier than planned. How does that suit you?

Lots of love
Anna and Bill

Also wrote to Karn updating her on wedding plans and asking her what sort of bridesmaid outfit she would like . . . 'Maybe you'd like a sari in another colour, or maybe an empire line dress like the one you wore as Lady Gluteus Maximus at the Summer Ball last year? And what about colours? . . .'

* * *

Oh the irony of how I waxed lyrical about Rishikesh when last I wrote! It has been such a strange experience for me here. Initially it was a wonderful contrast to the horrors of the heat and smog in Delhi. And it is true that the beautiful setting and this hotel with its wonderful staff have been a haven. But unbeknown to us, we arrived a day or two before the start of a major religious festival and the fervour seemed to mount in pitch as the days went by. The worst thing has been the motorbikes, roaring along the narrow streets, their engine sounds amplified and reverberating off the tall buildings. They drive by in their hundreds, continually blasting their horns and then driving across the narrow footbridge to the ashrams. The majority of the pilgrims seem to be young men going around in gangs and behaving more like football hooligans than spiritual adepts. They all wear orange shorts and t-shirts, chanting, 'Siva, Siva!' and punching the air with their fists. They may as well be chanting, 'Arsenal, Arsenal.' It is the same kind of energy.

So our longing to stay in a peaceful place was not met. The continual frenetic activity has been driving me slowly spare. It strikes me that the reason meditation is so popular in India is because the place is so crowded, noisy and generally intrusive on your personal space, that the only place to get some peace and quiet is by going within.

I also got bitten very badly by mosquitoes, which reactivated the nasty midge bites from Delhi and spent two days in bed feeling very sorry for myself. I feel so disempowered by the mosquitoes. No matter how hard I try to avoid getting bitten by them, wearing long sleeves and long trousers, and smothering myself in insect repellent, they always find the chink in my armour. They are my persecutors and I hate being their victim. I want to shout at them, 'How dare you drink my blood. How dare you make me feel so ill, you evil, alien creatures!' But it would be pointless. They are just insects. They just do what they do—and therein lies the most frustrating part about it.

So it is time to leave and we have decided that our next move will be to Dharamsala, the home of the Dalai Lama and of the Tibetan people in exile from their homeland. Since toying with the idea of going to Kashmir, we have been following the news carefully and there have been several articles about the continuing violence. Only a couple of days ago, several people were killed near Srinagar. So it seems wise not to risk it at the moment and Dharamsala is probably the furthest north that it is safe to go.

We catch a taxi to Haridwar, the nearest railway junction, to embark on our journey to Dharmsala. We made the mistake of ordering the taxi far too early and after a white-knuckle ride with the craziest Indian driver we have had the misfortune to come across so far, we arrive two and a half hours before our train is due to leave.

Haridwar is another holy town on the banks of the Ganges, but what a horrendous place. It will forever be etched in my memory as Horridwar. Take all the worst things about Rishikesh—the noise, the crowds, the religious fervour and the heat, and quadruple them. Then take away the beautiful setting amongst forested hills and add a large dose of filth and grime. Add to that unfriendly shop and café owners that try to charge you double what you should normally pay, lots of aggressive beggars and throngs of people that crowd around and stare at you—that is Horridwar. We wait at the station for our train. The time crawls by in this hideous place. The only distraction is a Western girl with a bag of apples. She offers one to a monkey that has been hanging around—mistake. Five more monkeys descend on her. One grabs the bag and runs off with it. The others pull her hair and pinch her, frustrated that they did not get the apples. She screams and tries to pull them off. Finding there is no more food they give up on her and run away.

A beggar demands money from Bill. 'I don't have much spare change,' he says to me, giving the beggar what small coins he has left. The beggar looks with disdain at the coins Bill has placed in his hand and then spits at him before walking away.

'Bloody charming,' says Bill, wiping the spit from his shirt. 'God, I want to get out of this place.'

Eventually it is time to board the train for our overnight ride to Pathankot on the way to Dharamsala. We go to find our platform and we are surrounded by filthy people that press against us and stare into our faces from inches away. There are no air-conditioned sleeping berths available on this service, so we find our cabin and sit dripping with sweat and already covered in a thick layer of dirt. This is no Rajdhani Express.

To try to take our minds off things, we decide to play Scrabble—very bad move—it only draws more attention to us. People crowd round us, leaning over the board and making unhelpful suggestions as to the words we should make. It is hot enough already, without having to share extra body heat with these people that are intruding on our game.

We give up on the Scrabble and I attempt to read a book. Another bad move. The man sitting next to me leans over me, reading my book. His face is so close to the page that I cannot see round his head to read it myself. He is practically lying on top of me. I have an extreme urge to shout, 'Just fuck off, will you!' But I am too polite and English, so I make do with snapping the book shut in a pointed fashion, hoping that I will catch his nose in it.

* * *

We spent an uncomfortable and fetid night getting very little sleep and I am SO glad to get off the train at Pathankot. We make our way through ankle-deep mud to the bus station to await our bus for Dharamsala. Fortunately we do not have to wait long. 'Ah, it is only three more hours to Dharamsala. I think you're going to like it there,' says Bill.

'Let's hope so. Then it might make this journey worthwhile,' I say.

As we travel along, the scenery gradually changes from grotty, grimy places to sweet little villages with vegetable stalls lining the sides of the road. The road starts to climb slowly into the hills, crossing many rivers with lush vegetation and we pass scenes of people tending the fields or leading mules laden with produce.

There is a distinct change in the looks and demeanour of the people getting on the bus. People here seem much more relaxed and cheerful. The women are very beautiful, all looking fresh, clean and well groomed, in bright salwar kameez outfits. A happy middle-aged couple get on in front of us and sit arm-in-arm talking lovingly to each other. Bill and I are starting to relax too. Bill takes my hand and gives it a little squeeze. As all these things change subtly, I feel my spirits rising. The horrors of last night are soon forgotten. By the time we get to Dharamsala I am glad that we made this journey.

We have been given a recommendation for a place to stay by our friends at the Hotel Ishan. So we jump in a taxi and head for Bhagsu, a few kilometres further into the Himalayan foothills. Finally, our journey ends at the Oak View Guest House. There is only one room free, which has just been vacated. It has a huge balcony with a view into the valley and is only Rs200 (£2.70) a night, so we take it.

Showered and changed after our journey, I sit contemplating the scene from the balcony. I can hear fast running water going over a waterfall just hidden from view. The river emerges to my left and flows off down the valley to my right. Steep slopes covered in deodar forest rise up on three sides. The buildings have an alpine feel to them, built on many different levels, with red roofs. Flocks of doves rise into the air, or potter about on the rooftops, cooing contentedly. The air is pleasantly cool and my thoughts turn to the possible purchase of a lovely pashmina to snuggle into on chilly nights.

* * *

The village has several cafés and German bakeries serving a wide range of food and there are a handful of shops selling local art and handicrafts, all colourfully displayed. The local people are a mixture of Tibetan, Nepalese and Indian hill people—so quiet and laid back compared to what we have encountered of late. There are lots of Westerners here, all dressed in the hippy mixture of traveller-type clothing and jewellery, with the addition of striped blankets swathed around their shoulders for added warmth.

Not many Brits, but lots of young Israeli's here, all letting their hair down after their stint of National Service.

There is a lot of pot smoking and smiley, slightly glazed-eyed faces around—people saying, 'Man' a lot. Whether they mean woman, man, girl, boy, dog—everyone gets called 'Man' round here. 'Hey Man. I love you, Man, but you are getting on my nerves, Man.' Lots of people having profound conversations about nothing in particular.

We have found a favourite restaurant in Bhagsu. It is a little further up the hill and not frequented by the glazed-eyed people who say 'man' all the time. It does a wonderful lasagne and Mexican enchiladas, but there is one thing on the menu that we do not fancy trying—'mixed fruit craps with chocolate sauce.' I think Bill had some of those back in Pondicherry.

We walk to McCleoudganj. It feels good to use my legs again after all the sitting about on long journeys. It feels good to breath in the fresh air of the deodar forest and to look out over the view down the valley.

McCleoudganj is a kind of satellite town to Dharamsala. It is home to the Dalai Lama and many other Tibetans that have fled over the mountains, to escape the Chinese oppression in their home country. In fact, in McCleoudganj, Indian residents are outnumbered by Tibetans. The town has a distinctly Tibetan feel, with its prayer flag bedecked buildings and the distinct style of the Buddhist temples. Bill tells me it is barely recognisable as the place he came to eight years ago. It has grown so much. It is also has some wonderful shopping opportunities. My head is on a swivel, my eyes dazzled by the choice of clothes, blankets, jewellery, books, music, Tibetan artefacts, etc.

In contrast with the delightful shops, the town is full of beggars, many of them in a pitifully deformed state. Leprosy is rife in this area. It is so hard to resolve how to handle this situation. You cannot possibly help everyone—it would be a lifetime's work and I know I would be an emotional wreck.

'My way of dealing with it is to set myself a budget of how much I can afford to give away each day. I keep it in loose change in an easily accessible pocket. I choose to give the money to someone who touches my heart and when the daily budget has run out, I stop worrying about it,' Bill tells me. 'I still have nightmares about being chased down the street by a leper, last time I came to McCleoudganj. I decided on this plan, to help me deal with that experience,' he adds.

Having decided to adopt Bill's plan, my guilt dies down enough to resume shopping activities. We go into the Tibetan Green Shop, the proceeds of which go to the Tibetan cause. We buy beautiful notebooks made of handmade recycled paper. They have flower petals and herbs sandwiched in their layers, and are fastened with golden cords and cowrie shell toggles. Ever since I was a child, I have always been inexplicably excited by shops full of beautiful paper. I would much rather have spent my pocket money in a stationery shop than a sweet shop or a toy shop. It seems that Bill shares my excitement about paper too.

Next we go in search of pashmina shawls. We have looked at many shops, searching for the perfect shawl, but so far, we have not found the right combination of colour, quality and price. Perhaps we will be lucky this time. It would be lovely to buy something so special from the home of the Dalai Lama. I notice a shop with very colourful jackets and shawls of the softest quality hanging outside.

'Look Billy, these ones are nice. Oh, they are SO soft,' I say, as I touch the downy fabric to my face. 'What a shame, it looks as if the shop is closed.'

Just at this moment, the shopkeeper appears at the door and invites us in. 'I am sorry, I was praying when you came. But please come in,' he says.

We explain what we are looking for and out come bundles and bundles of the beautiful shawls in a rainbow of colours and in the softest, purest quality of pashmina we have seen so far. The shopkeeper unwraps a huge emerald green shawl, as soft as clouds. Bill's eyes light up. He wraps himself in it. We both know at once that this is the one for him. He sits snuggling in it while I look through different colour combinations. They are all so lovely. It is hard to choose. I put on a deep red shawl covered in tiny flowers, hand embroidered in fine ochre coloured thread. I look in the mirror. This is definitely the one for me.

So we have chosen, but what about the price? The initial figure, although reasonable for the quality and the amount of work, seems way out of our budget. After some hard bargaining, we get £20 knocked off and everyone is happy. The shopkeeper tells us that he had been praying for more customers when he heard us outside his shop — so we have answered his prayers, and he has answered mine. We chat with him for a while after the deal is done, and learn that the Dalai Lama is out of town for two weeks. So our hopes of seeing the great man are dashed. I would so love to meet him. He looks so lovely in the pictures I have seen of him. I just want to give him a big squeeze. Even though he is not here, his presence is felt all around the town, in the initiatives he has started towards the environment, towards peace and towards looking after the Tibetan people in exile. Just to be in his presence would have been wonderful. But it is not to be this time.

Back in our room in Bhagsu, Bill spreads his pashmina out on the bed and lies face down on it, nuzzling it and squirming about. Then he wraps it round himself and swans about the room. It is wonderful to see how much pleasure it gives him. It was worth every rupee. I love mine too. It makes me feel very regal.

'Billy, are we so very shallow to get so much pleasure from material things?' I ask.

'I don't know, but it feels good,' he says, nuzzling away.

I know what he means. It makes me feel good to surround myself in something so beautiful. And I know that this extra layer of warmth, that weighs no more than a feather and rolls up into a tiny ball, is going to be indispensable whenever we are in the mountains.

Billy enjoys his new pashmina

Today we had intended to go for a walk, but the valley is full of rain and mist. Everything seems quiet, subdued, muffled. We find quiet things to do in keeping with our surroundings.

But the peace does not last for long. There seem to be a lot more tourists arriving today. And the noise levels start to mount. Bill has taken a particular dislike to a group of Indian lads who have moved into the hotel on the opposite side of the street. Their balcony is directly level with ours.

'Every time I go out onto the balcony, they're there, just staring at me. They just seem to sit around drinking beer all day and staring at me,' says Bill.

'Just ignore them,' I say.

'I don't like them and I don't like the way they stare at you, either,' says Bill, who will not be dissuaded from eyeballing them back.

Karn and I exchange e-mails about wedding outfits:—

From Karn:—

... 'As for my dress, I would love to wear a sari! Solves a lot of problems too—bridesmaids dresses are so predictable and uninspired usually. Think it's probably best if you choose it, as you'll know what will compliment your dress best, but for some reason I had in mind a very pale, pastel lilac or lavender or pinky/blue.?????? Does that sound weird? But hey, you know what colours suit me, and I'm sure you'll know when you see it, and I love your taste ... Anyway, let me know if you want me to do anything about my dress or if I can help in any way with the wedding plans ...'

I reply:—

'Thank you for your lovely e-mail. You're right, it's hard that we're separated at a time that so much is going on for both of us ...

Anyway, on to the exciting subject of bridesmaid outfits. I'm so pleased you want to wear a sari. I know how fantastic you look in them. I think lavender or lilac would be perfect. In fact I was already thinking along those lines myself. Don't worry about trying to find something in England. I will enjoy hunting out something wonderful for you. I had wanted to buy you one as a present anyway, but was a bit dazzled by the choice of colours and styles. So now I know what to look for ...'

* * *

As beautiful as Bhagsu is, it seems to be getting noisier and noisier. It is Indian holiday time and hordes of Punjabi tourists are heading up from the sweltering plains to escape the heat. There are lots of people driving about in huge four-wheel drive vehicles or on motorbikes, revving their engines and blasting their horns at every possible moment.

Our guide book tells us that Bhagsu 'has a temple to Bhagsunath (Siva). Outside the rainy season lovely walks are possible. The mountain stream here, feeds a small pool for pilgrims, while there is an attractive waterfall 1km beyond. It is a relaxing place with great views . . .' As the weather is good today we decide to have a walk to escape the crowds and explore these pleasant sounding surroundings.

To get to the start of the walk to the waterfall, you have to walk through the grounds of the temple. People are queuing to get through the gate and inside it is crowded with pilgrims, so we do not linger. On the other side of the temple, the path follows the side of a steep hill, with the stream chasing over rocks in the valley fifty feet below us. After a few minutes we round a bend and come across a young Buddist monk washing his robes in the stream. He looks so peaceful at his work as the sunlight sparkles on the water jumping over the rocks and the vivid orange and maroon of his robes contrasts with the white of the rocks and the greenery on the banks of the stream. We smile at him and pass quietly by.

A little further on the peace is shattered by men shouting. The path turns another corner and there are around twenty young men coming down the valley towards us. When they spot us, they start shouting at us. I cannot make out what they are saying, but it does not seem very complimentary, judging by the way they are all whistling and sniggering.

We try to pass them. They stop and make it very difficult to get by, blocking the path, staring and sniggering. We manage to get by, but now they have decided it will be much more fun to follow us than go to their original destination.

We are nearly at the waterfall and next to it there is a café.

'We might lose them if we go into the café,' says Bill.

'Good idea. I could do with a drink anyway,' I reply.

Behind the counter in the café is a smiley Tibetan man. We pass the time of day with him and order a coke and a lemonade. By the time he has given us our drinks and we have found a seat, the youths have followed us in. They crowd around us, staring and asking to take our photos. They have no sense of personal space. A couple of them are standing over me with their faces inches from mine.

'Not so close, please,' says Bill putting his arm between me and the space invaders. They either do not understand or choose to ignore what he has said and carry on staring.

Bill decides to roll a cigarette—very bad move. They all crowd closer and peer at what he is doing. I am sure they think it is drugs. He lights it and immediately they all want to try some. He hands the cigarette over to the most persistent starer.

'Ooh, another bad move,' I say. 'They're all going to want one now.' And they do.

The café owner has been watching what is happening and comes over to intervene at this point. I am not sure what he says to them, but I think it is along the lines of, 'Leave these poor people in peace to enjoy their drinks.' They back off but carry on staring at us from a few feet away.

'I am very sorry for this. It's such a problem. These people have no manners,' he says to us.

'Well, thanks for helping,' says Bill.

'Come on, let's get out of here,' he says when the owner has gone back to the counter. We swig back our drinks and leave the café, but it is not long before they follow us again.

'Let's climb the mountain,' says Bill, 'They won't follow us up there.' But they do. We walk uphill for half an hour and they follow us all the way, shouting, sniggering, whistling and throwing coke cans and other litter around. We finally give up on our 'lovely walk' and go back to our guesthouse. We leave them behind at the crowded temple, where their mummies are waiting for them.

* * *

We have moved to Dharamkot which is further away from the four-wheel drives, the revving and tooting and the youths who stare at us from the opposite balcony. We have a big spacious room with a balcony and a wonderful view down the valley. It is a good job the room is big. It looks like we will be spending a lot of time in it. The rain is really set in today.

Bill has started reading Lord of the Rings. I am jealous because I am bored and do not have a good book on the go. I offer to read the book out to him. It turns out to be a lovely cosy way to spend the day as the rain beats down outside.

Dharamkot has not turned out to be the peaceful haven we had hoped for. How many times have I said that lately? The café opposite our room is always busy and playing loud music till late at night. Dharmakot is full of partying Israelis who smoke cannabis continually and play techno music till 2 or 3 in the morning.

But the sun is finally out and we can explore our surroundings today. We set off into the woods, not really knowing where we are going. We follow a well-paved walking track into the deodar. All is peaceful and quiet—not another soul around. The solitude is glorious.

After 20 minutes or so of walking, we start seeing signs painted on rocks pointing to a café and waterfall. We both laugh.

'Wherever you go in India, you are never far from a cup of chai,' I say to Bill.

'I can't quite work it out,' he says. 'It's pointing in totally the wrong direction for the Bhagsu café and waterfall.

Twenty minutes later, we round a corner to find a tiny Shiva shrine, a café and three guesthouses on a ridge, looking out over a wonderful view. The café is closed, but we spot someone sitting in front of one of the guesthouses and make our way over to him. He offers to make us chai and tells us that he has rooms available if we are interested. We sit chatting to him for a while and both warm to this quiet-natured man. After our chai, he shows us around. The facilities are very basic, but spotlessly clean and freshly painted.

'I do not allow Punjabi youths or Israelis to stay here. They are too noisy. I like peace and quiet and I like to have guests that enjoy peace and quiet,' says Azie. We get the feeling he is checking us out, to see whether we would be troublesome guests. As Bill has a reputation for being somewhat on the noisy and excitable side, I dig him in the ribs and whisper, 'Better be on your best behaviour.'

'I made the mistake once, but never again,' Azie tells us. 'I let three young Punjabi men stay here for a week. They were all from good families, but as soon as they are away from their mothers, they think it is OK to behave like hooligans. They drink beer all day and throw garbage around. They play loud music all the time and drive my other guests away. They have no respect for people or their surroundings.'

After his little rant, he talks of the wildlife in this area. When he tells us about the bears and leopards that roam in the woods nearby, we make our decision to move here.

'Just two days ago I saw a leopard in the night. I was crossing the lawn to go to the toilet and there she was. She was as surprised as I was. We looked at each other for a minute before she slipped away. She was so beautiful. I know she lives up on that hill there, to our left. One of my guests saw her there with three cubs last year. And the male leopard lives up there on the hill to the right.' I am entranced by Azie's story. How exciting to live so close to these beautiful wild creatures.

When we have finished our chai, Azie points the way to the waterfall. We follow a narrow, winding path, quite precarious in places. It snakes around the spurs of the hills through rhododendrons, moss, ferns, masses of wild flowers, and shady nooks under tall chestnut trees. From time to time, small streams cross our path and make their way down the valley to our left. There is no one else about. Everything is misty and magical.

The sound of the waterfall is gradually getting louder and louder, but we cannot see it, as it is hidden from view by a spur of the mountain. Finally we round a corner to find crystal mountain water gushing over rocks into pools of emerald green.

'I just have to get into those pools,' I tell Bill.

'Yeah, they look so inviting,' he says. 'It's going to be tricky to get in though. Do you think you can do it?'

'I'm determined to,' I tell him.

'Good, let's do it then,' he says. We have to climb up slippery rocks and traverse a narrow ledge with few hand and footholds. There is a nasty looking drop onto rocks below if our grips fail. But with some good teamwork and mutual encouragement, we make it onto a huge smooth boulder with a gentle slope into the pool. We tear off our clothes and slither in. It is icy cold but sublimely refreshing. We splash around laughing and shrieking. We are two water sprites at one with nature.

When finally the cold gets too much for us, we climb out, dress and sit on the rock. The sun shines brightly to warm and dry us. We both sit in an awed silence. I have a sense of supreme well-being and of oneness with everything around me. It is one of those peak moments which happen but a few times in life. It makes all the struggle of travel seem worthwhile. Finally it is time to tear ourselves away. Bill voices just what I have been thinking, 'Wow, we're about to come and live on the doorstep of such beauty!'

'Yes, I could not be more delighted,' I reply.

So we are on the move again. Somehow Bill managed to fool Azie into thinking he is very quiet and we are heading for his isolated guesthouse, the Horizon. Here, we hope that we will find peace at last, for a little mountain contemplation. It is only accessible by jeep track, and sometimes not even the jeeps can get through in the rainy season, as it is now. At least we will be spared the noise of tooting horns and revving engines. We go into McCleodganj to see the man who hires out the jeeps. But he tells us the roads are too slippery to get through today. There is nothing for it, but to walk.

The jeep man offers to hire a porter for us. Bill says he can manage his pack, but I am grateful for some help with mine. Our porter arrives. He is a fresh-faced boy of around sixteen. His name is Hassan. He is very short but with a muscular, stocky build.

'He is very strong,' says the jeep man, squeezing the boy's shoulders. 'He can run up a mountain with 60kg, no problem.' I am impressed. I stagger under 20kg going up even the smallest incline. We take a tuk-tuk back to Dharamkot where we have left our luggage. From here we have a steep, slippery 45 minute climb to the Horizon. I am so grateful to Hassan, who is skipping lightly up the path in front of us like a mountain goat, carrying my pack. The day-pack full of books is quite enough of a burden for me. Bill is doing well. The weight of his pack is no problem, but he is not as sure footed as Hassan and keeps twisting his ankles on the wet rocks, in an attempt to keep up with him. It is a matter of manly pride not to be outdone.

When we arrive, Azie makes us feel very welcome and makes us one of his special chais—the best I have tasted in India.

* * *

The conditions here are extremely basic. There is no ensuite bathroom. There is no running hot water and no heating or electricity. The toilet is a hole in the ground in a little wooden cubicle. To get to it, you have to cross the lawn, go down some steps and around the corner. The bathroom is another little cubicle next to the toilet, where you take a bucket of hot water to sluice yourself down. Azie has to heat the water in a strange metal contraption, like a portable wood-burning emersion heater. He lights a fire in it, which heats the water in the outer jacket. So wash time has to be planned well in advance. It is pretty cold here, so you have to brace yourself to strip off in the cubicle, and washing my long hair in these conditions is nearly impossible. Our room is pretty damp and it takes us a while to get warm in bed at night. The pashminas have come in very handy.

I never thought I would be happy living in conditions like this, but I am. The peacefulness and beauty of our surroundings more than make up for any physical hardship. The guesthouse sits on a little saddle between two peaks—the peak on the left where the female leopard lives with her cubs, and the peak on the right where the male leopard lives. There are woods that stretch off in all directions, giving cover for the bears, leopards and other wild creatures that live here. And from the edge of this saddle, the world just seems to tip down a vertiginous drop, before the angle of the slope grows a little more gentle, allowing people to build houses and plant crops. The scene before my eyes is laid out like a green silken cloth of many shades, pinned between the two peaks and draped in many folds down the side of the mountain.

Moon bears roam the woods surrounding us

Azie is a charming and attentive host. His cooking is excellent and the meals he prepares seem healthy and nutritious. His trademark is a breakfast of very unusual porridge with nuts, fruit and spices drizzled with local honey. He is a very inventive man and is trying his best to minimise his impact on the local environment—hence no flushing toilet or shower. He has created a precisely measured lifestyle for himself. All his routines run to clockwork, allowing him time to just sit and stare out at the fantastic view in front of his house. But the sadness of his situation, to my mind is that he lives here alone, while his wife and child live in McCleoudganj. They come to visit him once a week and he visits them in town occasionally. He does not make it clear why they have this arrangement. Perhaps his wife is not prepared to live in such basic conditions, or perhaps he just likes it this way.

We walk into McCleoudganj to reserve our train tickets to Darjeeling. In a café, we meet a Tibetan monk. His name is Venerable Bagdro. He was a political prisoner of the Chinese in Tibet, but managed to escape to India. He has written a book about his story to raise awareness about the continuing atrocities. He tells us that the problem is still going on and that he was very lucky to get away. There is a warmth and a radiance about this man that is so endearing. I buy his book, *A Hell on Earth*, and wish him *tashi delek* (Tibetan for hello and good luck).

Later I read of the terrible things that were done to him by the Chinese. I can hardly finish reading it, for the tears that course down my face. It is hard to equate the warm, smiling man we met in the café, without a trace of bitterness about him, with the pain and suffering that he must have endured. The Tibetan people we have met here in McCleoudganj are gentle, kind, honest and incredibly stoic given the difficulties they have had to live through.

Finally we have found that peace and tranquillity that we have been searching for. The noisy Bhagsu of a week ago seems a million miles from here. We go for a lovely walk along a mule track that leads to the other side of the valley. We see bear and leopard footprints on the path, and last night Bill heard the leopard roaring. At one point on the path, where an animal track goes up into the dense undergrowth on the upper slope of the path, we both have a chilling sense of being watched by something that is trying to decide whether we will be good to eat or not.

At a place where we do not have the sense of being watched by a large predator, we sit down to meditate. I think of Bagdro and the people of Tibet. I remember a Buddhist meditation which is about sending out loving kindness to the world and I make it my focus to ask for healing for the Tibetan situation. I have that same feeling of blissful oneness that I had experienced at the waterfall. It is hard to come back, but when I eventually open my eyes, they are filled with the beauty of my surroundings, which seems all the more sharply focused for my heightened state. I am glad to be alive and I am glad to be here in this moment.

Bill and I walk back in dreamy silence and finish our trip with a chai at the café, which has now opened. Our timing is immaculate. Just as we finish the last sip of chai, fat drops of rain start to fall. So we make a dash back to our homestead.

We sit on the verandah to take off our walking boots.

'Bill, there's something warm and sticky in my socks,' I tell him.

'Oh, my God, your foot's bleeding,' he says. I look down to find that the warm, sticky substance that has filled my sock is my own blood. I discover that I have three fat, fully fed leeches attached to my foot, and a couple more on the other foot.

'Quick, get the insect repellent, Bill.' As Bill runs to get the insect repellent, Azie comes out to see what all the fuss is about and quickly goes off to get a jar of salt. We discover that Bill has several clingons too. The insect repellent makes them let go, but does not dispatch them, so Azie finishes the job with the salt.

'I'm sorry, I forgot to warn you about the leeches. They are a real problem at this time of year. I keep them off my lawn here by sprinkling salt, but there are plenty in the woods. It is when you stop walking that they get you.'

'It must have been when we sat down to meditate that they crawled on,' I say. A look of horror comes over Bill and he disappears into the bedroom to check his more delicate parts for clingons. Fortunately, he does not find any and looks very relieved when he comes back out.

After a delicious lunch cooked for us by Azie, we have a blissful nap and wake to see bright sunshine and rain at the same time, accompanied by rumbles of thunder. We sit on the verandah, sheltered from the rain with a wide view of the mountains in front of us. Towering dark clouds rise over the rim of the valley and the thunder rolls continuously from peak to peak, booming and roaring like the war drums of the gods. We are entertained to the most fantastic show. A huge thundercloud has gathered over the peak to our left. The sun is slowly setting and as the great dark cloud rolls over us, lightning flashes and flickers, neon pink, lit by the sinking sun behind it. And now a great yellow moon has risen into the last patch of azure sky, still accompanied by the pink flickering lightning over the peak. I can feel the electricity in the air. It makes my skin tingle and the hairs on the back of my neck stand up. The finishing touch is the sight of a huge eagle which flies above us and then soars straight into the eye of the storm.

Later that evening, Bill goes to the other guesthouse, which has a phone. He calls the travel agent to ask about our train tickets. The travel agent says that the train is fully booked till the 27th August, 10 days from now. Bill comes back and relays the news.

'Oh, so we don't have much choice other than to stay here longer than we planned. That's disappointing. I'm quite eager to get going because we won't have much time to see Sikkim, or Nepal, if we stay here much longer. Our flight to Thailand leaves Kathmandu on 20th September, so we will have a lot to cram into three weeks,' I say.

'Yep, fate has decreed that we have to stay put for some reason. I'm keen to get to Sikkim and Nepal too, but I can think of worse places to spend a few days,' Bill replies.

'You're right. This place is definitely full of magic,' I say.

* * *

We set off for a walk again, just following our noses without any real plan. We follow a steep rocky path to the North and eventually realise we are on the path up to Triund, the highest peak in the area at around 4,000 metres. The scenery is much more rugged than our previous walks, but beautiful in its own way.

It is a cloudy, misty day and we do not get much of a view into the valley below. Now and then the mist parts long enough for us to look down into deep ravines and get the feeling that we are almost toppling off the end of the world.

After an hour and a half of walking, we come to yet another mountain café, where we stop for chai. For a remote café, with no vehicular access, it is remarkably well stocked and even sells umbrellas. Someone has had to bring all these goods up here on their back. We decide to buy one of the umbrellas, having left our last one on a bus. They are very handy for this steamy monsoon weather.

We foolishly think we are nearly at the top, only to be told by the boy serving in the café that we have another 4 km to the top. We set off again, just intending to go as far as we can before we get tired. Our fitness levels (or certainly mine—Bill is pretty fit anyway) must be increasing because despite the climb being enough to make me sweat profusely, and the increasing altitude making the air much thinner, I feel surprisingly full of energy. We climb for another two and a half hours, talking all the way about life, death and the universe. Bill is reading a book about Dr Usui, the founder of Reiki and I am reading 'Freedom in Exile' by the Dalai Lama. Both books are thought provoking and inspiring.

It is interesting that as we have moved further away from the general hubbub and frenetic energy of the towns and villages, both of us have felt more peaceful, more connected spiritually and more inclined to spend time meditating. It is no wonder that the Himalayas are considered sacred mountains—after all they do bring you closer to God.

We have been climbing steadily for four hours now and feel that we have left civilisation far behind in the valleys. I am convinced that we must be near the top. The mist is swirling about us as we step out onto a ridge, or is it the peak? But, as the mist lifts, I cannot believe my eyes. Lo and behold we are confronted with not one, but two chai shops and another guesthouse. Outside the first chai shop sit two bored-looking young men playing cards. They are playing the usual terrible tinny music at full volume. Outside the second chai shop sits an old man and a one-eyed dog, which glares at us from its one remaining orb and growls territorially. The old man says he can do us an omelette or toast if we are peckish. It is quite unbelievable to think that to stock his shop with goods, it is a five hour uphill slog from anywhere resembling civilisation, because you cannot get a vehicle any closer than that. How on earth does he make a living? He has even got competition.

We decline the food, but take another chai. We decide that we have had enough exercise for one day and are satisfied not to push on to the top. Our descent takes around two hours and once again, our timing is perfect. We are just within sight of the guesthouse when the first fat drops of rain begin to fall. It is not that I particularly mind getting a bit wet, it is just that in this damp weather and with no form of heating at Azie's, it is impossible to get anything dry. It will just end up going mouldy. Our room is very damp and I have watched with mild disgust as the outside surface of my rucksack, sitting on the floor next to my bed, is slowly gathering a furry layer of light blue mould.

We tell Azie about our journey and ask him how much further it would have been to the top. He tells us that we had only just made it to the base camp of the Triund peak, just before the snowline. I was comforted to hear that unless you are extremely fit and start very early in the morning, it is not possible to reach the top and back in one day. Most people stay at the base camp for the night and climb the peak the next day. So I am not a total weakling after all — I did manage to climb to 3,300 metres.

Often at night-time we can hear lots of banging and shouting in the fields below us. Tonight there is a frenzied kafuffle going on.

'It is the villagers trying to frighten the bears away from their crops. They are very fond of ripe yellow corn,' Azie tells us.

* * *

We have various business that we need to do today, so we trek into McCleoudganj and spend a pleasant couple of hours at the Tsug Lakhang Temple and the Namgyal Monastery. The temple is full of minutely detailed and brightly coloured murals of Tibetan religious art and mandalas. There are shrines to Sakyamuni, the historical Buddha, Padmasambhava, who introduced Buddhism to Tibet and Avalokitesvara, the bodhisattva of compassion, where devotees can leave their offerings. The atmosphere is wonderfully quiet and peaceful, in contrast to many other temples that we have visited so far in India and Sri Lanka.

We circumambulate the temple in a clockwise direction, as we have observed others doing, and we spin the huge red and gold drums covered in prayers, sending them spinning out into the world.

We are about to leave the monastery, when the heavens really open. We are forced to stay a bit longer and shelter until the storm is over. This coincides with the young monks gathering to practice their debating skills. We cannot understand what they are saying, but it is fascinating to watch their animated discussion. One young man sits on the ground whilst the one who is proposing the idea stands up opposite him. He holds one arm outstretched and makes his point most vigorously by circling the other arm, as if bowling overarm, and bringing his second hand down with a slap against his upturned palm. The seated monk practices calm and restraint in the face of this onslaught of forceful argument. There is much humour in this process and laughter bubbles under the surface.

When the young monks have finished their heated discussions, Bill says, 'I really enjoyed that. It's a great way of channelling the energy of boisterous young chaps. I can think of some other young men who would benefit from that kind of training.'

The rain is still falling, so we make a dash for the Namgyal café, attached to the monastery. It is here that I first discover tsampa, the Tibetan dough made from roasted barley flour. For someone with a wheat intolerance, it makes a tasty and welcome change from always eating rice.

Finally, the sun comes out and we are able to make our way on to Dharamsala. We are going in search of a lavender coloured sari for Karn to wear at the wedding. Earlier, I had met two very helpful Indian ladies in the Western Union Money Transfer office in McCleodganj. They told me there is only one sari shop in Dharamsala and gave me the address. We thought it might be our last chance to get a sari before leaving India, so we make our way to this shop.

The shopkeeper gets out all the saris in this colour range and we find one which is the perfect colour. It has a pretty, but simple gold border, and the pallu, the section that drapes over the shoulder, has a gold floral design. Unfortunately, the dye is rather uneven for the first one and a half metres. The shopkeeper assures me that this section will be hidden inside, but then he would say that anyway, wouldn't he? Without Karn here to try it on, I have no way of telling. So I am thrown into a quandary—'Bill, d'you think this is the right sari, or am I just buying it out of desperation because there might not be another chance? D'you think Karn will be upset if I buy her a faulty sari?' I ask.

'I think you should just get it. It's a lovely colour and it's not that much money. I'm sure Karn will be fine about it. There's so much fabric I'm sure you can do something with it,' says Bill, eager to be off. His patience for shopping is shorter than mine and his gardener's instincts are telling him that we need to get going too. In the end I buy it, but I've been agonising over it ever since and kicking myself, when I think of the hundreds of sari shops in Mysore and Bangalore.

Whilst I was pondering the decision, the skies were darkening and now the heaviest rains we have seen so far descend on Dharamsala. Within minutes, water is pouring off the hills, turning the roads into muddy rivers. We had ordered a taxi to get us back to McCleoudganj, because it is a long steep walk and we still have to get from there to our guesthouse via Dharamkot before dusk. The taxi ride is a perilous journey through the driving rain and steep, hairpinned, narrow, slippery roads. But our driver handles the appalling conditions with great skill and we are relieved to arrive safely, if a little soggy, in McCleodganj.

We pick up our train tickets and then head for Dharamkot to pick up laundry and get something to eat. Supper in Dharamkot is a rushed affair, as dusk is fast approaching. We still have a forty five minute walk up a steep rocky path through the bear infested woods. Even so, Bill says, 'I'm so glad we're living away from the loud music and the rowdy atmosphere.' I have to agree.

We set off up the trail in the gathering gloom. About halfway up the hill, we meet another man with a porter walking our way. We fall into conversation and he turns out to be Azie's cousin, who runs the guesthouse just above ours. It is comforting having some company. I figure there is safety in numbers when it comes to scaring off marauding moon bears, which have been known to cause human fatalities. Besides, he is a local and is more likely to know what to do if we come face to face with a large furry creature. I have heard conflicting advice.

'Bill, if we see a bear, am I supposed to bark like a dog, or shine my torch in its face? I know that one scares them away and the other makes them aggressive and more likely to attack. But I can't remember which way round it is,' I say.

'I don't know. Let's try both—that'll confuse it,' he says.

Just as the last of the light is fading, we step out of the forest onto the track that crosses open ground for the last part of the journey. Here we meet a man who is clearly very frightened. He is jabbering away and gesturing with his arms to our right and up the hill to our left—exactly the direction we are heading. It seems he has just had a close encounter with a bear, which is still close by in the woods and wants to walk with us for safety. We might soon find the answer to my question, torch or bark? Fortunately, the bear must have decided we are too big a gang to confront and slunk away further into the woods, leaving us to reach the guesthouse in safety.

'I wish we had seen the bear,' says Bill. 'I love bears and it's very exciting to know that they're about.'

'Hmm, I'd love to have seen him from a distance,' I say, 'But that was a bit too close and very scary in the dark.'

* * *

Bill has been very inspired by his new book, *The Tao of Reiki*, by Lawrence Ellyard, and decided to put some of it into practice. He gave me a wonderful treatment, which really helped my back and hip. I have dysplasic hip joints and they have been giving me a lot of pain lately because of all the walking we have been doing. Towards the end of the treatment I gave a big cough, as if I was coughing something out of myself. Bill told me that just at that moment, he had visualised a horrible many-legged insect (a mosquito, perhaps?) that he was trying to pull out of my lower back. The cough was the last impetus needed to shake it free.

The weather is overcast and there have been intermittent showers all morning. We are reluctant to go walking because of the difficulty in drying things out. So we are staying quietly round the guesthouse.

A couple of days ago, we read in the paper that there has been a terrorist massacre of some politicians in Jalpaiguri, near Darjeeling. Now there is a big search going on for the terrorists and the borders with Nepal and Bhutan have been closed. This is very disturbing news, as we are due to arrive in Jalpaiguri in five days time on our way to Sikkim.

We have both been wondering whether it is still safe to go and I suppose that is why I had what felt like a prophetic dream last night. In my dream a Tibetan monk stepped forward. He pointed to the east and was looking intently in that direction. The message seemed to be, 'Keep your eyes and ears open.' He made it clear that we should still go there. As I looked in the direction that he was pointing, I saw beautiful images of snow-capped mountains.

He took me to the top of a spiral staircase, and as we wound our way down, I felt myself to be a novice Tibetan monk. I was getting younger and younger, until I was a little child of around two years old. The older monk picked me up and carried me in his arms. We stepped down onto a high ledge in the mountains and below me I could see a beautiful valley with a stream running through it.

The monk told me not to fear and to just leap off into the mountains. I leapt, and as I glided down, I looked back at the monk, who was smiling at me and saying, 'Don't worry, we will always protect you. Just go and walk in the mountains.'

I landed gently in the valley and walked beside the stream. It was very beautiful and I felt Bill walking by my side. The words, 'Just walk in the mountains,' kept echoing in my head, as I woke up in our room in the Horizon Guesthouse.

I tell Bill about my dream. 'Well we should definitely go then. If I've learned one thing on our journey, it's that your intuition is always right,' he says.

It is the afternoon now, and the weather has cleared up, so we have decided to go for a walk. Our destination is Naddi village and beside it, Dal Lake. The walk through the forest on a gently sloping ridge is very beautiful. The green of the forest and the mountain plants is intense and the sides of the path are crowded with wild flowers. We come to a tiny pool, fed by water dripping from a mossy alcove in the bank. Bill floats some flowers on its surface and it looks like an enchanted fairy pool.

The village and the lake by contrast are rather disappointing. The village is full of cow shit and groups of sullen men. The lake is not much more than a muddy puddle. It is the site of an animal fair and Shaivite festival in September, but it has nothing to recommend it at this time of year. The women of the village, on the other hand, are lovely. We walk along a twisting path that winds past people's vegetable patches on the outskirts of the village. The women working in the gardens meet my gaze, smile kindly and say 'Namaste,' with their hands steepled in front of them.

On the way back, we have an intense feeling to stay quiet, as if the forest is watching. We come across bear tracks and feel the presence of the leopard above us in the woods.

* * *

For two days now it has rained incessantly. Yesterday, Azie told us it was officially the last day of the monsoon, but as it was late this year, it feels like there is still some way to go before the rains are over. I am beginning to feel frustrated and imprisoned by the rain. It is our last full day at the Horizon guesthouse and we both had hoped to go to the waterfall again before leaving. In some ways I think that it was one of those outstanding experiences that can never be repeated. Perhaps by trying to go there again we would spoil the memory of it.

So we have been forced to find other ways of occupying ourselves. It is as if we have been given the opportunity to do a retreat. I had been thinking that during our travels we could spend some time with a spiritual centre of some sort. Rishikesh turned out not to be the right place for us and I was wondering if McCleoudganj would prove to be the right opportunity. What I have come to realise is that we actually have all the tools at our fingertips to do our own retreat. And instead of feeling frustrated, I should be using this time to meditate and pray. So this is what we have been doing. But it is amazing how much my ego is rebelling against doing these things and I am finding it easy to create distractions, despite having so much time on my hands.

I decided to try one of the meditations from the *Tao of Reiki* book. The purpose of the meditation is to feel empowered and protected. With our imminent journey to Sikkim, it seemed an appropriate thing to do. The instructions are to imagine yourself surrounded by a circle of duplicates of yourself. These duplicates are full of vitality, spiritual empowerment and healing energy. The idea is to imagine them merging into you and filling you with these qualities. But I was quite surprised at what happened.

The duplicated selves which I saw in front of me were beautiful golden beings, but I had a sense that I had not achieved imagining these selves behind me. So I imagined turning to face what was behind me and there I encountered a number of shadow selves. But they were not scary and bad, as I might have imagined my shadow side to be. Instead, they were mysterious, slightly secretive selves, but full of feminine power and wisdom.

The shadow selves merged into one and the golden beings merged into one. Then the shadow self met the golden self. They embraced and merged into each other to form a powerful whole being. This being then embraced and merged into me. Words are totally inadequate to describe how I felt afterwards. The only two that spring to mind are 'whole' and 'empowered' but they simply do not do justice to the immensity of the experience.

'To climb high into the mountains is to rise above the mundane into the magical, to leave behind the smog of disillusion and to breath the clean air of the gods.'

- Bill's feelings about the experience we are having here in the mountains.

Five things that I am grateful for today:—

1. A good night's sleep in a warm comfortable bed
2. To wake up beside, and spend the day with my beloved Billy
3. The view of the mountains from the verandah
4. To feel healthy and strong
5. To drink delicious masala chai

* * *

And so begins four days of travelling that will take us from the foothills of the Himalayas in the North West of India, right across the breadth of the country to Sikkim in the North East. We bid farewell to Azie and his quiet mountain hideaway.

'Come again to visit, anytime,' he urges, 'But maybe not at monsoon next time. April is beautiful here.' It seems really tempting. But would everything be the same? Something tells me not. There are plans to build a hotel on the peak where the female leopard lives. Where will she go then? And as soon as the hotel is built, they are bound to improve the road up here and then Azie will be powerless to stop the weekend hooligans driving about and tooting their horns. I hope my pessimism never comes true.

So we move out of Azie's, carry our luggage down the slippery path through the forest—this time I manage to carry my own rucksack—and spend the night in Dharamkot in preparation for the next leg of the journey.

We will be out of contact for a few days on our long journey to Sikkim and I am worried that we have not heard from Mum whether Bill's wedding outfit has arrived. There is a place to make cheap international phone calls from our guesthouse in Dharamkot, so I take the chance to call her.

'Hi Mum, how are you? I'm a bit worried—has Bill's wedding outfit arrived yet?'

'Oh, hello dear. Lovely to hear you. It's a bit early in the morning here, but apart from that I'm very well. Yes, Bill's outfit has arrived,' says Mum.

'And . . . What do you think of it?' I ask

'Well, erm . . . It's not exactly what I expected,' says Mum.'

Bill is looking at me expectantly to hear Mum's reaction. I put my hand over the receiver and whisper, 'She hates it.' His face crumples.

'How do you mean—not what you expected, Mum?' I ask.

'Well, it's not exactly the right colour, is it?' says Mum. 'It clashes a bit with your beautiful sari.'

'Oh, I thought it was quite neutral.'

'Well, yes exactly. You need something a bit darker to contrast with the pale sari' . . . and so the conversation goes on.

When the phone call is over, I turn to Bill. 'I had hoped she would love it as much as the sari,' I say to him.

'Well, I suppose we should have guessed—it's not exactly your classic morning suit and waistcoat. I think we were pushing it to get away with you wearing a sari. But I'm gutted all the same,' says Bill.

'Well, maybe she'll come round to the idea when she sees how gorgeous you look in it,' I say hopefully.

We catch the overnight bus from McCleoudganj to Delhi. The journey is not as horrendous as the Rishikesh experience, because we have a good driver and comfy seats, but even so it is impossible to get any sleep cramped up like this. We have to stop twice in the night because of punctures and get off the bus for an hour while they are repaired. I turn to Bill in my sleepy state and say, 'Billy, why is that man banging that big wheel with a hammer? It's a funny time of night to be doing motor mechanics.'

'Yes, dear, that's the wheel of our bus. He's repairing it. Did you not notice the bus being jacked up?'

'Oh, is that why we all had to get off?'

Well you can tell how dozy I am feeling and it is little wonder that we lose our beloved Travel Scrabble, as we hastily change buses on the outskirts of Delhi.

We arrive in Delhi at 7.30 am and lug our bags through the main bazaar, to spend a few hours at the Anoop Hotel, where we can shower, change, have breakfast and snooze for a while. Then it is a mad dash across town to the Sikkim Tourism Office to get our 15 day visitor permits. Although Sikkim has been a protectorate of India since 1950, and is now a fully-fledged Indian state, it is still treated like another country and there are special rules which apply. Like all Indian bureaucracy, the procedure for obtaining these permits seems interminably long. We wait, nervously looking at our watches and hoping that we will not miss our train. We conclude our business just in time to rush headlong back across town to catch the 2pm sleeper train to New Jalpaiguri (NJP).

Chapter 6

Sikkim—Yaks, Yetis and Yuksom

(In which we lose Lars)

Sikkim is a tiny jewel of a country, lying sandwiched between Tibet to the North, Nepal to the West and Bhutan to the East. Nestling between the peaks of the eastern Himalaya, it measures just 64 km from east to west and 112km from north to south. Flat land is virtually non-existent in this mountainous region and getting from one part of the country to another is torturously slow as the spindly roads wind in and out of the mountain valleys.

We both managed to sleep relatively well, since we were already exhausted after the nightbus and the dashing about. It is just as well, since the time would have dragged interminably without the aid of the Scrabble board. And once again, good old Rajdhani has come up trumps with the quality of food and standard of cleanliness.

We arrive at NJP at 10.30am, after a 20 hour journey. Having become used to the cooler climes in the mountains, we are assaulted by a wall of heat and humidity as we leave the air-conditioned train and step out into the plains of West Bengal. We are surrounded by a barrage of tuk-tuk and taxi drivers, all screaming at us to get our business. I feel quite freaked out by this after our long journey. I should be used to it by now, but fatigue has lowered my tolerance levels. Bill decides to take the situation in hand and have a bit of fun with it.

'OK, we want to go to the bus station in Siliguri and we will give our business to the lowest bidder.'

'100 rupees,' shouts the first man.

'No, that sounds like too much,' says Bill. 'Who can do better?'

'I take you for 100 rupees,' shouts someone else.

'No, you see, you have to offer less to get the business,' says Bill.

'90 rupees,' says a third bidder.

'That's better. Now you're getting the idea. But still too high. It's only a few minutes drive.'

'Me, me, I take you for 90 rupees,' shouts a chorus of new bidders.

'They're not getting the hang of this are they?' Bill says to me.

Try as he might, he cannot get anyone to offer less than 90 rupees. At this point, people are trying to drag our bags from us to make us go with them. Others are trying to grab the bags off them. It is turning into an all-out scrap, so we have to make a decision.

'OK, you were the first one to offer 90 rupees. You can take us,' says Bill. 'Now let's get out of here before the others tear us to shreds.' Our chosen driver bundles us into his tuk-tuk and we set off.

The bus station turns out to be a 'share jeep' stop next to the tourist office, where we show our passports and Sikkim permits before booking our place on the jeep bound for Gangtok. There is no set departure time, so we have to wait until the jeep has its full quota of passengers before we can set off. This seems to take forever whilst we sit melting in the heat amongst the filth and the beggars. There is a threat of violence in the air. Tempers are flaring and fights break out on more than one occasion. Eventually the jeep is full and we are extremely glad to be leaving Siliguri.

We are told that the jeep ride to Gangtok will take around four hours. On the way we are entertained to ever changing scenery of incredible beauty. The monsoon rains have all but washed the road away in many places and brought down mud and rock slides in others. The road clings precariously to the teak forested hills, winding along the edge of a river-filled ravine.

We pass lots of road gangs repairing the monsoon-damaged sections of the road. There is a high percentage of women among these gangs, doing just as heavy work as the men. We round a corner to see three beautiful young women in brightly coloured salwar kameezs. They are chatting and laughing with each other as they heave great stones on to their heads and lug them about. They are all wearing make-up, including immaculate bright red lipstick. They look too delicate, too clean, to be doing such heavy work, but they seem to be happy.

The roads are repaired by the Border Roads Organisation, the BRO. They are proud of their work. The roads are a lifeline to link all the isolated communities of Sikkim. There are signs all along the highway urging people to drive carefully with witty phrases like, 'It's not a rally, enjoy the valley,' or 'Driving is risky if you have been drinking whiskey,' and 'Better to be Mr Late than "the late Mr."' We find out later that the job of repairing the roads is a risky business and many people are killed each year while they work.

Despite the beauty, I feel exhausted, overheated, dehydrated, nauseous and have a splitting headache. I am so glad to finally reach the Hotel Tibet in Gangtok, where the staff are friendly and welcoming, and everything is clean and cheerfully decorated. Once again, our guidebook has let us down — the hotel we had chosen from it is closed for refurbishment. We spot the Tibet from its doorway and although it is way over our usual budget at Rs 1100 (£14.70) per night, I cannot bear to move another inch.

The sheer bliss of stripping off my filthy travel worn clothes and having a hot shower cannot be described. We have a quick supper and an early night, hoping to feel refreshed in the morning.

The day dawns bright and clear, but I do not. I have a throbbing head, pains behind my eyes, nausea and dizziness. We have a fantastic view of the snow-capped Himalayas. Bill stares in awe out of the window at Mount Kanchendzonga, the world's third highest mountain, at 8,586m. But this spectacle is sadly wasted on me.

'Can't even manage a morning cuppa? Blimey, you must be feeling bad,' says Bill as I push away the cup he proffers me. I go back to bed.

Later I rally enough to check our e-mails. There is one from Mum elaborating on her comments about Bill's wedding outfit.

Hi, A'n'B

Hope all still going well with your trip. Thanks for phonecall re wedding outfits. You said you would be out of contact for a while. Talking about Bill's outfit, at 8am I wasn't ready for the direct question—I thought it might be a dark colour as a foil to the Magnificent Sari. Karn phoned the other day, wanting to come up to see the wedding outfits. I said she and Abava were welcome to stay if they wanted . . .

Much love, H & H, M & D.

Bless her, she still hates it but is trying to be polite.

Lovely as this hotel is, we cannot afford to stay here, so we are having to move across town to the slightly less plush, but considerably cheaper Sonam Delek. In its favour, the Sonam Delek is in a quiet part of town and still has views of the mountains from our balcony.

I woke this morning thinking, 'I just want to go home.' Part of the reason for this crisis of homesickness is, I am sure, due to the horrendous four-day journey from Azie's idyllic pad to get here. It left me feeling unwell, unsettled and fed up. When I am ill, I just want to be in my own bed at home, not halfway around the world. I know that Bill has been quite distraught by me feeling like this. Even though he has not said so, I can tell. He has been so quiet and just does not know what to say to me. I know that he would be utterly disappointed if we had to abandon the trip and go home now.

Another part of my homesickness is my anxiety about the wedding plans. Not that I am really worried about something going terribly wrong. It is just that every time I call home, Mum seems completely despondent about the latest crisis.

It is the afternoon, now. Earlier, Bill gave me a wonderful shiatsu treatment and I am just starting to feel OK again. The other thing that really helped was a bit of shopping therapy. A pair of gold earrings and a new top cheered me up a surprising amount—how pathetically shallow I am!

Our plan had originally been to head up to Yumthang, which is a beautiful secluded valley in the north of Sikkim. It is about as far as you can go into the hills before you get to Bhutan. Unfortunately, the monsoon rains have washed the road away just beyond Singhik, so that is as far as we can go. We have been told that Singhik has the best view of the Kanchendzonga and that it is a nice quiet place to spend a couple of days. So on impulse we decide to hire a jeep to take us there.

The only way to get around in Sikkim is by jeep. The driver waits till his jeep fills up with passengers who all want to go in the same direction and then they share the cost, which seems like a good system to me. We make our way to the jeep stop and ask if anyone is going to Singhik. There is only one driver going that way. He is a strange little pixie of a man with pointy ears and a big strawberry nose.

'I reckon he likes a drink or two,' whispers Bill. This seems pretty common in Sikkim. There are many breweries and distilleries. Alcohol is very cheap here. Bill is greatly amused by the fact that a bottle of beer costs less than a bottle of water.

'Should we trust him?' I ask.

'Well, he seems sober enough at the moment,' whispers Bill. 'He says there won't be anyone else going that way and that we have to pay to hire the whole jeep. I'm keen to get on with our adventure. If we're going to go, he's our only choice.'

'Yes, so am I. Let's do it,' I say. So we strike a deal with the funny little pixie man and climb aboard his jeep. As we drive along, the scenery is beautiful. Everything is green and luscious, refreshed by the rains. We wind along the sides of steep valleys, with dramatic hills rising on all sides. We pass many idyllic villages and farms. The houses are made of wood, raised up on stilts and propped precariously against the hillsides. Around the houses there are terraced fields of crops, but above them, the slopes are too steep to cultivate and the verdant forest takes over in abundance. Along the way, the driver stops to pick up many people and charges them for the journey. Now he has stopped at a café and we all get out for a drink.

'This wasn't part of the deal. The jeep was hired just for us,' says Bill.

'I know, but it doesn't bother me too much. It's good to have some local company,' I say.

'Yes, but the thing that does bother me is that whenever anyone asks where we're going, he says 'Singhik' and then laughs like a maniac,' says Bill in a hushed voice. 'Is there something he isn't telling us about the place?'

'Or is he planning to drop us in the middle of nowhere and then rob us and drive off with all our belongings?' I say. I size him up against Bill and say, 'If it comes to a scrap, I reckon you could overpower him.'

'I'm not a violent man,' says Bill. 'But if it came to it, yes, I think I could 'ave him. And what's worrying me more is that every time we stop at a café, he gets back into the jeep smelling like he's had a couple of snifters. His driving's getting more and more erratic. To put it mildly, these aren't the safest roads we've ever travelled.'

'I know. I hope we get there in one piece,' I say.

The Alcoholic Pixie takes us as far as the road holds out. A couple of kilometres beyond Singhik, the road simply disappears into the ravine. There is a gaping chasm about 20 yards across. There is a queue of traffic on either side of this gap, waiting to get through. Most of the traffic on this side comprises of supply trucks trying to get food through to the towns of Chungthang and Lachen further up the valley. A bulldozer and dozens of people are working really hard to mend the road, but it is going to be days before it is passable. We stop for a while and Bill gets out of the jeep to get a closer look at the proceedings. A dusty young lad of about 13, who has been helping out with the manual labour comes over and climbs into the jeep beside me.

'Hello, where you from?' he says, all smiles and enquiring eyes.

'England,' I reply.

'Where you going?' he asks, studying me closely. I am obviously a great curiosity to him.

'We want to go to Yumthang,' I say, 'But we can't because of the road.'

'No, not possible one week,' he says. 'You stay one week Mangan, then possible Yumthang.'

'We're going to stay at the Tourist Lodge in Singhik,' I tell him.

'I think not possible. I think is closed for monsoon. You stay Mangan,' he says.

I look up at the driver. 'Is that true?' I ask. He just gives his malevolent laugh.

'Must go work now,' says the boy. 'My English good? I learn in school,' he asks.

'Yes, very good. You understand a lot. Thank you for your help.'

'Good luck, nice lady,' he says getting out of the jeep and sauntering back to work. Bill gets back in the jeep and I tell him of my conversation with the boy.

'Well we might as well try the tourist lodge anyway. It's on our way back to Mangan. The boy might have made a mistake,' says Bill. He asks the driver to call in there on the way to Mangan. But just as the boy has told me, the Tourist Lodge is closed and Mangan is our only hope of getting a bed for the night.

The Inebriated Goblin drops us off, snatches our money and drives away cackling. We look around in dismay. Mangan is a filthy, awful dive of a place. People are coming out to stare at us. They are sniggering and muttering, 'Strangers,' under their breath. The one decent looking building which we had seen on our way through and hoped to be a hotel, turns out to be a school. We sit down to have a late lunch at the one café in town, wondering what to do. By the end of the meal, we have decided to get a jeep straight back to Gangtok and Bill goes off in search. He comes back with head down and a frown wrinkling his forehead.

'Well, there are plenty of jeeps and drivers around,' says Bill, 'But none of them are going back to Gangtok today. They say we'll have to wait till 6 am tomorrow morning,'. No-one even took up my offer of an extortionately inflated amount of money for the ride. I reckon they've all been at the pop and don't want to drive because they're three sheets to the wind, unlike the bloody Goblin man.'

So we are faced with the prospect of spending the night in the decidedly insalubrious town of Mangan. A reconnoitre of the three 'hotels' in town, shows the Lachen Valley to be slightly the lesser of the three evils, in that it has an adjoining Indian style toilet and cleanish looking sheets.

I announce to Bill that the room is not too bad after all, as much to try and convince myself as to pass comment to him. Actually, it makes my flesh crawl and I can hardly bear to touch anything. I keep trying to tell myself that I am being irrational, that I won't catch any nasty diseases from the room and that I can bear anything for one night. But I am not very successful at fooling myself.

The lady that runs the ~~hovel~~ hotel seems pleasant enough and we have a reasonable supper of vegetable curry, then sit watching an American film with her, her friend and her daughter in the front room that doubles as a bar and dining room. All is going relatively well, till I see a family of cockroaches marching about on the food serving counter.

Bill and I retire to our room, where we play endless games of cards to try and take our minds off the horrible surroundings. We discover that the previous occupant has just chucked all his fag butts on the floor and no-one has bothered to sweep the room before letting it to us.

It has been pretty hot all day and I am very sweaty and covered in a fine layer of dust from the road. I feel sticky and uncomfortable. I go into the bathroom, which looks as if it has never been cleaned. I somehow manage to wash my face and hands without gagging and I lie down to sleep in the fetid little room. I am still fully clothed, feeling that the less of my bare skin that touches anything, the better. I know I am being irrational, but this place has given me such a fit of the horrors that I just cannot relax and go to sleep. And to add to the discomfort, all night long I am convinced that I am being eaten alive by mosquitoes.

We get up at 5am to make sure we do not miss the first jeep out of town. It is no hardship to rise at this time, since I have not slept anyway.

Just as we have been told, there is a fantastic view of the Himalayas, rose tinted by the first strike of the morning sun. We gaze in awe and take a few photos, before the beautiful sight is once again shrouded in cloud. It seems all too brief a reward for our long journey and fetid night.

As we are so early, we have our pick of the jeeps. 'I like the look of that plush new comfy one,' says Bill. 'And the driver is a smart young fella, who obviously takes great care of his vehicle.' Thankfully, Bill has chosen well and he turns out to be a very good and safe driver. It is an altogether different journey from yesterday and he delivers us swiftly and safely back to Gangtok.

We check back in at the Sonam Delek and we are delighted to find that the room we had before is empty. It feels as if the room has been waiting to welcome us back. It feels like home. I waste no time in having a long hot shower and changing into fresh clothes.

As the day wears on, I begin a streaming cold, sore throat and fever. Perhaps I did catch something from that nasty room after all.

Gangtok is the capital of Sikkim, set on a ridge at 1870m, on the old trade route to Tibet. I really like the place, despite feeling out of sorts. For a capital city, it has a relaxed, quiet feel. Sikkim feels very different from the rest of India. It is like entering another country. There is such a mixture of different racial types—Lepchas, Nepalis, Bhutias, Tibetans, Indians and Westerners, that everyone is used to seeing people that look different or dress differently. It makes a refreshing change not to be stared at or continually asked to pose for photos.

The architecture, like the people, shows a mixture of influences. There are traces of the Tibetan influence in the brightly painted arches over some of the roads and in the pagoda style red roofs of some buildings, but there are an increasing number of concrete nasties springing up among the more traditional buildings as the town expands.

So we have had a peaceful couple of days relaxing, visiting the market, walking in the deer park, shopping, e-mailing and eating delicious food at the Hotel Tibet, including our first try of Tibetan momos, which are tasty little dumplings made from barley flour and filled with vegetables or chicken and eaten with soup and chilli sauce.

My fever and cold are feeling a little better today. We have decided to leave Gangtok to try and see a bit more of Sikkim before our permits run out. But I have a great deal of trepidation about launching myself once more into the unknown and undertaking a four hour jeep ride to the other side of the country. What if it turns out to be just as awful as Mangan and we wish we had never left Gangtok?

In the meantime, I have bought myself a more detailed guidebook to Sikkim. The author is local and everything he has said about the places we have visited so far has proved to be reliable. So I am putting my trust in him that our next destination, Pelling, has at least two hotels with 'well-appointed' rooms. After all, no-one could have described the Lachen Valley as being well-appointed, unless you are a cockroach of course, in which case you would probably think it the height of luxury.

So we catch our share jeep and the journey to Pelling is about as uneventful as can be expected during four hours on single track, monsoon damaged, landslip-prone roads. We are very relieved to discover that Pelling does indeed have two well-appointed hotels. We plump for the Norbu Gang, because it looks cosier and the room we are shown has a balcony facing a view of the mountains.

But Pelling is a strange place. Like Mangan it has the most amazing setting with views of the Kanchendzongas. But it has no heart—it seems to have just mushroomed up around a crossroads. Virtually every building is a hotel and there are many more under construction or being extended. The quality of workmanship is appalling and looks as if everything might come tumbling down in the first winter storm. I am told that Pelling has become popular with honeymooning couples from Calcutta. Even so I cannot imagine how all these hotels can sustain enough business to keep going even at the height of the season.

We have a wander around town and bump into a man that we have seen in Gangtok. We strike up a conversation with him and find that he is a well-seasoned Aussie traveller named Warren. As we walk passed the Alpine café, Warren shouts, 'Have you chucked your husband out yet?' to the lady who runs it. She comes out and flips him with her tea-towel.

'You men. All same. All talk, no work,' she says with a smile. 'But we ladies decide not to beat or kill husbands yet. They still good for some things,' she adds with a twinkle.

We go in for a cup of tea and Warren tells us how he had gate-crashed a ladies meeting in the café earlier.

'Apparently all the blokes are in the next valley at a funeral getting totally lashed. She says the lazy bludgers won't do any work for days now.'

It seems that the women of Sikkim are much more emancipated than in the rest of India. But the men are happy to take advantage of this and let the women run the businesses, giving them more time to drink and play cards. We girls, we just cannot have our cake and eat it!

'Hey, what's the food like in your hotel?' asks Warren. 'It's pretty shit in mine. No fresh veg and no meat. They don't even know how to cook an omelette properly. I had to go in the kitchen and show 'em how it's done. I'm a chef back at home and I can't stand bad cooking. I've told the woman who runs the hotel she needs to get down the market and get some fresh veg and maybe a nice chook. I don't mind paying for it, just so long as it's fresh.'

'Sounds like a good plan,' says Bill. 'In our hotel, the restaurant has this big long menu with all these tasty sounding meals on it, but when you order, they haven't got half of it. You ask for the chicken lasagne but it's, "Sorry, no chicken, Sir." Or you ask for the veg fried rice and it's, "Sorry, no veg, Sir." After this has gone on for about five minutes, you ask, "What do you have?" "We have dhal or bean curry, Sir." I'm sick of dhal and bean curry.'

We spend the afternoon playing cards and chatting with Warren, the latter of which is his favourite occupation. As Bill puts it, 'Donkeys have to take good care of their back legs when Warren's around.'

We have decided to hire a jeep to visit the Kechopalri Lake with Warren and a Slovenian man named Peter, who Warren has befriended. Sikkim is a land full of waterfalls, bursting into the valleys from the Himalayan Mountains above. On the way to the lake, we stop off at the Kanchendzonga falls, which are a particularly impressive example of Sikkim's many waterfalls. The falls split into three different torrents and we climb up to a viewing point where I feel totally surrounded by the power and noise of the water pounding down all around me. Warren has a professional looking camera and an array of other photographic equipment. He is in raptures over the waterfall and spends ages trying to get the perfect shot to capture its atmosphere. Eventually we have to drag him away, as we are all keen to get to the lake.

Known as the 'Wishing Lake', Kechopalri Lake is sacred to the local people. It is beautifully set in a bowl in the mountains, amongst dense forest, temples and multitudes of prayer flags. Because of its shape, it is said to be the footprint of the Buddha. It is easy to see why it is thought to be a special place. A legend says that you will not see a single leaf floating on the lake's surface, despite it being surrounded by trees, because birds fly down to remove them and keep the water pure. It did look amazingly clear, but call me picky if you like, I did spot one or two round the edges that the little birdies had missed.

Buddhist Temple at Kechopalri Lake

We attempt to walk round the lake, but we are beaten back by thick mud and legions of leeches that come lurching towards us at every step. Bill and I learnt our lesson at Azie's and still have itchy scars from our first leech encounter, so we persuade the others to turn back.

We have lunch at the café near the jeep stop. Provisions are low at this rainy season of the year and the only thing on the menu is the Sikkimese equivalent to Pot Knoodles. We buy lunch for our driver and tell him of our disappointment about not being able to walk round the lake. The café owner overhears and tells us that there is a nice walk up the hill to Kechopalri village and the monastery on top of the hill. The driver says he is happy to wait for us if we want to walk. By now a group of villagers have gathered after a hard morning's toil in the fields. Even the little children have been helping out. There is one little girl — she cannot be more than six years old — carrying a heavy iron mattock. So we all agree to walk up the hill to the monastery and village. Many of the local people who have gathered at the café are walking up that way and we chat to them as we go. They are friendly, cheerful people with a relaxed air about them.

The tiny village is the most idyllic place, sitting on its ridge above the lake, with magnificent views all around. The dear little houses are made of wood with wattle and daub walls and thatched roofs. There are crops of maize, runner beans and potatoes around the houses and everything is abundantly green. Happy children play Oranges and Lemons on an open grassy area, and tumble about together in little heaps. At the end of the village is a monastery which has a feeling of ancient sacredness about it.

There is a little teashop in the village. Dressed in striking vermilion, the proprietor, Mr Palas prepares us a cup of smoky flavoured tea over an open fire.

'You know Dalai Lama like visit this monastery when he come to Sikkim,' says Mr Palas. 'Is very special because is centre of big circle of monasteries—Pemayangste, Tashiding, Rumtek and Dubdi. These children you see playing here—many are monks at the monastery.'

'What, even the little tiny ones?' asks Warren.

'Yes. They are orphans. The monastery look after them.'

I watch the tiny snotty-nosed ones tumbling about laughing on the grass. It is hard to imagine them being monks at such a young age, but they seem very happy.

Children from Kechopalri village

Mr Palas says he has rooms to rent and shows us two sweet little rooms in his house. Peter is so taken with the place that he decides to stay the night.

'But how will you get back to Pelling?' I ask him.

'I will walk. It is not so far as by road. I can walk down into the valley and back up to Pelling. They say it takes about four or five hours.'

We say goodbye to Peter and make our way back down to where our jeep driver has been waiting patiently. He seems happy enough, having spent his afternoon playing cards and drinking tea with the café owners.

Back in Pelling, we are settling down for the night. Despite the setting, Pelling is not a restful place. As well as the usual revving of cars and tooting of horns, there is the construction work going on night and day, and the dogs that bark through the night. Bill is looking out of the window.

'There's **always** someone banging something,' he says with a sigh. I think of Peter spending the evening with Mr Palas' family and I envy him staying in that little corner of paradise.

* * *

Today we are going to Teacher's Day at the local school. It is a National day when all the children do something to say thank you to their teachers. And the children at Pelling School have gone to so much effort, decorating the hall and making coloured rosettes for all the guests. They have prepared a big curry, which they will serve to the teachers later on. All this has been financed out of their own pockets. Warren arrived before us and I reckon he has been in the kitchen supervising the curry.

The school captain comes over to greet us and to show us to our seats. Then we are served tea and biscuits that the children have prepared. We watch songs, dances and sketches that they have created. There are folk dances performed by pretty young girls in traditional costumes, there are young dudes breakdancing to the latest Sikkimese pop songs, and there are budding comedians telling jokes. But my favourite performance is the potato dance. This involves a group of little boys who have pulled their shirts up over their heads and painted faces on their bellies, which they wiggle about in time to the plinky, plonky, crackly music. All the children are so well behaved. Even the tiniest little beans sit so quietly during the performances. It is a really heart-warming event.

Later we walk up the hill to Pemayangtse Monastery, which perches on a ridge above Pelling. Culturally and spiritually, Sikkim's strongest links are with Tibet and for centuries, it was an independent Buddhist kingdom. Although Hindu Nepalis, who have migrated into Sikkim, now form the majority of the population, the geographic isolation of the country has contributed to preserving its Tibetan Buddhist culture. The 17th century Pemayangtse, the Perfect Sublime Lotus, is a good example of this. It is painted inside and out with bright glossy colours, depicting scenes of the Buddhist deities and scriptures. Pre-Buddhist shamanistic imagery is also incorporated in the artwork.

A young monk shows us around the monastery and we watch for a while as some of the other monks quietly shape lumps of dough to be used as offerings in a ceremony the following day. These monks have all been recruited from the leading families in Sikkim, as Pemayangtse is the headquarters of the Nyingmapa sect.

On the third floor of the monastery there is an incredibly elaborate wooden sculpture, which practically fills the whole room. It must be 12ft high. It is known as 'Heaven' and was shown to Dungzin Rinpoche, a former abbot, in a vision. It has layer upon layer of the most intricate carving, all painted in bright glossy colours. Its pyramidal shape seems to show a progression from the humans, demons and other creatures having a hard time on the lower tiers, to blissful celestial winged beings at the top. I wonder at how much detail the lama managed to remember. Apparently it took him only five years to sculpt and paint his masterpiece of demons, animals, birds, bodhisattvas and flying dragons, a remarkable achievement.

As we wander back down the lane from the monastery, we meet a very large blond man and a petite dark haired woman. They introduce themselves as Lars from Denmark and Itzell from Mexico, who met in Darjeeling and have been travelling together ever since. Itzell wastes no time in making it clear that Lars is not her boyfriend.

Later, we meet up with Lars, Itzell, Warren and Peter for a drink and game of cards in the Alpine café. I ask Peter about his night at Kechopalri.

'It was beautiful and the family are so nice,' says Peter. 'But the bed bugs were not so nice and there was not much privacy. There was no door on the toilet and the family just coming and going as you do your business. It was a good experience, but one night was enough.'

This is about the last thing that Peter manages to say. Lars is equally as garrulous as Warren and there is some real competition going on here. The poor donkeys of Sikkim!

'Listen, listen, hey English (Lars' nickname for Bill), listen to this,' exhorts Lars as the attention wavers from him. Itzell rolls her eyes in mock exasperation.

'See what I put up with,' she whispers to me. 'Now you know why he is not my boyfriend.'

'What's that Mexico? Come on, it's rude to whisper,' says Lars.

'Just girl's talk. Nothing for your ears,' says Itzell.

We turn in for an early night. Bill is feeling particularly rotten with cold. But the sounds of Pelling are not conducive to a good night's sleep. I am vaguely aware of Bill tossing and turning and hurrumphing, as each new sound disturbs his slumber. Now there is some inconsiderate person in a jeep in the street below our window. He is revving and tooting with particular vigour, and now he is shouting to someone inside the hotel.

'Right, that's it, I've had enough,' says Bill, storming across the room to the window. He throws open the window and bellows, 'Will you SHUT THE F**K UP!!!' There is no response from below. Eventually we hear the jeep pull away and drive into the distance. I am totally shocked. I have never heard Bill speak to another human being like that before. I have never seen him so angry.

'If it is getting to you that much, Billy, I think it's time to leave,' I say.

'Hmm, maybe you're right,' he mutters despondently.

* * *

The conversation with Warren about the lack of fresh food has inspired him to organise a special meal for our last night together in Pelling. He has asked his hotel owner to do roast chicken and steamed vegetables. It is a real treat after spending so long eating nothing but dried food. The party starts out as just Warren, Peter, Bill and me. But soon Lars and Itzell catch wind of it and join us. The word gets round and eventually there are 12 westerners at the table comparing travel stories, or travel lies, as Bill calls them. I really enjoy the chance to talk to other women for a change and realise how much I have been starved of female company lately. Come to think of it, I have not had a good girlie chat since spending time with Anna and Rudolf in Mysore, and that was six weeks ago.

Over the five days we have spent in Pelling, I have grown really fond of Warren. He is one of those people, who, within a few hours of being somewhere, knows all the right people to know, is completely in on all the village gossip and knows exactly when and where the buses run. He is off on new adventures and setting out for Bhutan today. We are on the move today, too. We are catching a share jeep to Yuksom, 40km north of here. We bid Warren farewell at the bus stop and set off.

Arriving in the sleepy village of Yuksom, our local guidebook informs us that the Tashi Gang Hotel is the best place to stay. Set a little apart from the village, it certainly looks plush from the outside and we wonder whether we can afford it.

'Right, time to lay on the charm and do some negotiating,' says Bill. 'I reckon we could get a good discount as it's the low season.'

We wander into the echoing corridors and shout, 'Hello.' There doesn't seem to be anyone about. 'Excellent, there aren't any other guests and they're going to really need our business,' says Bill, warming to his task. Eventually, the assistant manager greets us. Bill's charm and persistence leads to us getting the best room in the hotel for half-price. We go to our room and settle in. It is probably my favourite hotel room so far—very spacious, with lots of polished wood and decorated with Tibetan thangkas. The bed is very comfortable, with no need for mosquito nets at this altitude. And, oh joy, it is cool enough at night to need blankets. We have a posh marble bathroom with a wonderful hot shower. There is a little wooden balcony with wicker chairs, from which we can look out over the hotel garden and have a view towards Mt Kanchendzonga—perfect!

Yuksom is everything that Pelling is not. It is a traditional village with a community that is not wholly dependent on the tourist trade. It is the ancient capital, where the first king of Sikkim was crowned in 1641. The site where the king was crowned by three lamas is still preserved. They came from three different directions to enthrone Chogyal Phuntsog Namgyal, the Great Religious King. He was the founder of Tibetan Buddhism in Sikkim. We visit the site at twilight and it is very atmospheric. The thrones for the king and the three lamas are still there, next to the peaceful monastery. A pine tree was planted behind the thrones at the time of the coronation and now it has grown into a huge tree, which is 360 years old.

We buy take-out momos from Mrs Norling, a big jolly Tibetan lady, and set off for Dubdi monastery. We walk past the leprosy hospital and out of the village past a small river and water wheels. Then the path winds up through the forest to the monastery perched on the hill overlooking Yuksom. Set in a pretty garden amongst roses and other flowers, the brightly painted monastery looks very welcoming, with its red pagoda roof and porch painted with flowers and geometric patterns in blues, greens, oranges and reds. The monastery is locked, so we sit on the porch to eat our momos, before continuing on our walk through forests, hills, farms and villages back to Yuksom. We have to cross a ravine on a rickety wooden suspension bridge. It gives us a wonderful view down the valley, but is in a bad state of repair, so we do not linger. We pass another beautiful waterfall on the way and Bill fills our water bottles with delicious water flowing down from the Himalayas. It is a really hot day and it is tempting to strip off and swim in the waterfall, but we do not have our swimmers and we do not want to offend the people who live at the farm nearby. The possibility of leeches is an added deterrent.

Anna on the rickety bridge

We are getting to know a few of the locals. There is Mrs Norling, who does the best momos in town. I love her shop with its weird and wonderful mixture of food provisions, handicrafts and Tibetan curios—lightning dorjes, offering bowls and a magnificent yak harness covered in bells which make a delightful chiming sound. Bill has taken a real fancy to the yak harness, but it is incredibly heavy and not very practical in the absence of the accompanying yak. There is Mr Gupta, who runs an Indian restaurant. He is very helpful and the best person to go to for information about the comings and goings of the jeeps and local transport. In between Guptas and Norlings, there is another Tibetan style restaurant run by a lovely young couple.

James and Thomas, two Scottish students who we met at Warren's party in Pelling have arrived in town. They suggest meeting up for dinner later. Lars and Itzell come on a later jeep, so we have a bit of a reunion. It is nice to see them again, but with their arrival, the peaceful village atmosphere has gone.

After our lovely walk to Dubdi Monastery, we fancy trying something a little more adventurous today. There is a yearning in me, to get further up into the mountains. It seems that there is a wild land just beyond my reach where the yaks and the yak herders roam, where the red pandas and the snow leopards hide out and where the stories of yetis may come true. The mountains hold secrets that tantalise me to find out more. But we do not have the time or the right equipment to go on a major trek. We know that there is a trail heading towards the Dzongri trek, which leads into the Kanchendzonga National Park and up into the Himalayas. We do not have the special permits that are needed to go trekking, but we are hoping that we will be allowed to just dip our toes in the water of the wild lands. Luckily, there is no guard at the checkpoint, so we saunter by.

There is a small village at the start of the trek, where we stop for a cup of smoky chai. The shop cum café is my favourite of our whole trip so far. You can buy everything you could possibly imagine there—bags of rice flakes and beans, candles and other everyday provisions. You can even purchase a tweed jacket and a quilt, should you feel inclined to step out on an impromptu trek and find that the weather is more inclement than you expected—marvellous!

But somehow we manage to miss the path that leads to the start of the trek, so after about an hour of stumbling our way through maize fields and leech-infested bushes, we decide to sit on a rock and eat our take-out momos. Just as we are finishing our lunch, the heavens open. It seems that the wild lands are not opening to us today and we give up on the trek and go home to the cosy luxury of our room at the Tashi Gang Hotel.

Today it is Thomas' birthday. The little pup has just turned 22 years old. 'Wouldn't it be fun to organise a surprise party for him?' says Bill. 'We'll secretly get James in on the idea, and we'll invite Lars and Itzell too.'

'That sounds like a great idea,' I say. 'We could order a cake from Mr Gupta and buy surprise presents and cards for him. We could ask the young couple with the restaurant between Norlings and Guptas if we can have a meal with a few drinks and some music there.' They are both delighted with the idea.

The evening starts really well. Thomas is very pleased with his presents and cards and the restaurant owners present him with a white silk kata, a ceremonial scarf, in honour of his birthday. Unfortunately, too much alcohol is consumed and the party gets louder and louder. I can see that as the hour gets later, the owners are starting to get nervous about disturbing their neighbours. Bill suggests that we go up to the Tashi Gang, as it is further away from the village and we will not be disturbing so many people up there.

At first the manager of the Tashi Gang is friendly and co-operative, but as more and more alcohol is consumed and the atmosphere is getting more rowdy, I can see that he too is getting anxious. The problem centres around Lars' unrequited passion for Itzell. It turns out that Thomas' mother is Spanish and he speaks the language fluently. Itzell, delighted to find someone to talk to in her native tongue, spends most of the evening chatting away with Thomas. Lars, insanely jealous and put out that he is not the centre of attention, starts hurling abuse at Thomas.

'Scotland, you're an asshole, do you know that?' slurs Lars.

'F**k off, Lars, you big Danish twat,' retorts Thomas.

'Guys, guys, come on. This is supposed to be a celebration. Don't spoil it,' says Bill. Things calm down for a while and then for some reason, unbeknown to woman, all the boys decide to have a male bonding session rolling about together on the lawn. It reminds me of summer days at school, when the playing field would be littered with piles of little boys all wrestling each other. Itzell and I look at each other in bemusement. The Tashi Gang waiters look on with an equal look of bewilderment.

Anyhow, the wrestling does seem to dissipate the tense atmosphere for a while and everyone settles back into a general rhythm of chitchat. But Itzell is chatting to Thomas again. He is a handsome lad and there is a lot of eye fluttering going on. Suddenly Lars snaps. He grabs Thomas and throws him to the ground. He jumps on top and starts pummelling him. Lars is a huge man and it takes all the rest of us to drag him off. James, who is very slightly built, gallantly jumps in front of Thomas to protect him. Eventually, Bill and I manage to calm Lars down enough to persuade him to go back to his hotel and sleep it off. Itzell escorts him home. James is crying because he thought Lars was going to kill his friend. Thomas looks stunned and shaken. We stay with them long enough to calm them down a bit before apologising profusely to the Tashi Gang staff and retiring to bed.

'Bill, I feel so ashamed that we've caused so much trouble after everyone has been so kind to us here,' I say.

'I know, I feel really bad too. We're going to be the talking point of the village for all the wrong reasons,' says Bill.

I wake feeling guilty and ashamed for being part of the debacle last night. It feels so disrespectful of the hospitality we have been shown and of the community that we had the pleasure to be part of for a short time. The worst thing is that it was Bill and I who organised the party. We apologise again to the manager, who is very gracious and says that he knows we were not the ringleaders of the trouble.

We check out and go down to the village to arrange our jeep ride to Tashiding. Mr Gupta gives us a knowing look, but is otherwise pleasant towards us. I am acutely embarrassed and feel as if everyone is watching us from doorways and whispering about what happened last night.

There is no sign of Lars. Itzell says she woke to find that he had gone. We figure that he must have stomped back to Pelling where he had left most of his stuff. Thomas and James share the jeep with us to Tashiding, whilst Itzell has to go back to Pelling to pick up her stuff. I give her a hug and wish her luck, telling her to e-mail to let us know she is all right.

In the jeep on the way to Tashiding, there is a general post-mortem of last night's goings on.

'I don't think Lars was such a bad guy underneath it all,' says Bill. 'He just couldn't hold his drink.'

'No. The problem was that he just couldn't hold his Itzell,' I reply.

In Tashiding, we find a little family run guesthouse, where Bill befriends the owners' young son. He has the sweetest, most innocent little face and serves us tea with a beaming smile. But Bill seems determined to corrupt the boy by showing him naughty tricks. Bill shows him the one where you press your nose with one finger and let out a fart at the same time. The little boy seems absolutely delighted with this trick. But unfortunately, his mother is just coming up the stairs behind Bill at the time. The boy animatedly describes to his mum what Bill has just done, which is rather unnecessary as she has already seen the whole thing, and was regrettably close to Bill's bottom at the time. At first the mother cannot quiet cover-up a smirk, but then manages to put on a stern look of disapproval, telling the boy off for getting too familiar with the customers, while Bill shuffles from one foot to the other, going red with embarrassment. I think that is what you call instant karma, for trying to corrupt a young innocent.

In the afternoon, we walk in the rain to Tashiding Monastery up a steep and slippery path. Again, we run the gauntlet of the leeches. I have made the mistake of wearing sandals instead of boots and they manage to get me, despite checking every few steps.

'Tashiding is reputed to be the most sacred monastery in the whole of Sikkim. It is known as the Devoted Central Glory and was built in 1717, after a rainbow was seen to connect this site to Mount Kanchendzonga. It is the site of the Bumchu festival in the Tibetan New Year, when devotees come to be blessed with water from an ancient bowl, which is said never to dry up. Just the sight of this monastery is supposed to wash your sins away,' I tell Bill, reading from the new guidebook.

'Well, I think we both better stare at it for a very long time after the events of the last couple of days,' says Bill.

'Yes, and we better imagine some blessings going to Lars too,' I reply.

As we arrive at the monastery, we are greeted by a little dog, who seems to want to show us around. At first it looks as if everything is locked up, but the dog leads us to an old man with one eye and a wonky leg, who sits spinning a prayer wheel. He speaks no English, but indicates that he has a key and can show us around. The old man takes us into the entrance porch of the main temple and shows us some paintings depicting the Wheel of Life. With animated sign language, he explains to us the meaning of the painting. He seems to like the fire-breathing demons, who torture the poor human beings the best.

He unlocks the door and motions for us to go inside the temple. There is definitely something special about this place. There is a feeling of immense power emanating from the seated figure of the Buddha at the centre of the altar. The old man leaves us alone and we say some quiet prayers in this lovely, holy place. So we hope that we have now been absolved of our part in the disturbance at Yuksom and that Bill has been forgiven for trying to corrupt a little boy with his farting jokes.

We leave Tashiding with clear consciences and head out of Sikkim and across the border to Darjeeling. I am sad to be leaving Sikkim, despite some of the difficult experiences we had there. It feels as if we have spent a few days in a magical hidden kingdom cut off from the rest of the world by the mountains, rising on all sides. My lasting memory will be of a land of steeply terraced paddy fields, spectacular waterfalls, giant bamboos, colourful monasteries, sacred lakes and prayer flags, yaks and red pandas, and always towering in the background, the mighty, inaccessible, snow-clad peaks of the Himalayas. It is a land where people still live in a simple way, with a thriving spirituality, still honouring the spirit of the land and the turning of the seasons. Long may Sikkim stay that way.

And so to Darjeeling . . . set on a ridge at 2,200 metres, it was once part of Sikkim. Its name, *Dorje Ling*, meaning 'the place of the thunderbolt,' is taken from the monastery that sits on top of Observatory Hill. The town was conceded to the British in 1817, when it became a hill station and major tea growing area. It reverted to India at Independence and so it is a strange mixture of Sikkimese, British and Indian influences. Like Sikkim, its setting is stunning with views of the Kanchendzongas on clear days. The upper part of town is like walking back 200 years in time to some forgotten corner of England. It is dusk as we wander around looking for a hotel and it gives me a strange, eerie feeling, as if ghostly spirits are on the prowl.

The bottom end of town is filthy and noisy, with heaps of rotting rubbish in the streets and open sewers running by. Somewhere in between the two, there is a transition—round about where our hotel is. It is a nice clean hotel, but the road below is extremely noisy, whilst the one above is cleaner and quieter.

Today we pay a visit to Darjeeling zoo. It is a chance to see some of the animals that lived tantalisingly just beyond our reach in Sikkim. Despite the animals being in captivity, it seems a happy place. They have big enclosures, which mimic their natural habitat and they seem quite content.

The tree-climbing red pandas, the symbol of Sikkim, are extremely fluffy and cute. The magnificent Siberian tigers, the biggest of the world's cats, are an imposing sight as they run across their enclosures. There are Tibetan wolves, who prowl their enclosure, licking their lips in anticipation as they stalk two boy monks walking past.

The black moon bear is Bill's favourite. 'That's the kind of bear we nearly met on our walk home to Azie's. Blimey, I'm shocked at how big it is—it must be nearly 2 metres tall by the looks of things,' says Bill.

At the top of a hill in his enclosure, there is a big rock shaped like an armchair. The bear sits in his armchair, feet sticking straight out in front of him, one hand on his knee, contentedly sunning himself. Occasionally he sniffs the air and looks down with disdain on us mere mortals below.

'There's something almost human about him. If I didn't know better, I'd think he was a man in a bear costume,' I say to Bill.

But my favourite animals are the snow leopards . . .

> *'In the high mountains of Central Asia, a snow leopard awakens.*
> *Residing in one of the harshest environments on our planet . . .*
> *It walks among the jagged rocks with a soft step and a regal grace.*
> *So elusive . . . we almost never see them.*
> *And just knowing this . . . we realise such a creature deserves*
> *A place on our earth.'*

The International Snow Leopard Trust

These elusive creatures, prefer to live above 5,000 metres. Their thick soft fur, scattered with silver rosettes, helps to keep them warm at this altitude. Their huge furry paws and long fluffy tails allow them to balance on the snow and make spectacular leaps when catching their prey. Known as the 'Ghost of the Himalayas', there are many myths from Tibet, Nepal, Pakistan and Ladakh about them. They are seen as messengers from the spirit world. But now they have become an endangered species, because of the loss of their habitat and through being poached for their luxurious fur.

> *'For epochs to come, the peaks will still pierce the lonely vistas,*
> *But when the last snow leopard has stalked among the crags . . .*
> *A spark of life will be gone,*
> *Turning the mountains into stones of silence.*

> George Schaller, 1977

Snow leopards are notoriously difficult to breed in captivity, but here in Darjeeling, the breeding programme has been a major success and so we are very privileged to be able to see these beautiful animals at close quarters. We watch in awe as a mother and her three cubs play together and chase each other round the enclosure. In another enclosure, there is a mother with two very young cubs. They look like over-sized tabby kittens with huge fluffy paws. One of them lies close enough to the bars to touch.

When its mother is not looking, I cannot resist putting my fingers through the bars and touching its soft fur — a foolish thing to do, I know. The little kitten reminds me that it is a wild creature with a fierce hiss and snarl. I withdraw my fingers rapidly.

After the delights of watching the snow leopards play, we visit the Himalayan Mountaineering Institute, one of India's most important training centres for mountaineers. The museum there tells the history of the conquest of Everest, with photos and displays of some of the equipment used in the early expeditions. It is amazing what they achieved wearing only tweed jackets and woolly hats. Tenzing Norgay, the chief sherpa of the first successful Everest conquest led by Sir Edmund Hillary in 1953, was the first director of the institute. He lived and died in Darjeeling and is buried nearby.

There is much conjecture about who actually reached the summit first, and Hillary and Tenzing themselves have always kept quiet about it. No matter who it was, it was a fantastic achievement.

The display describing Mallory and Irvine's ill-fated expedition in 1924 is particularly poignant, since Mallory's body was recently found where he lay with a badly smashed leg after a fall. It was perfectly preserved by the frost and dry wind. He was wearing four thin layers — a woolly vest, a viyella shirt, a hand knitted pullover and a tweed jacket. Things have come a long way since then and in 1998, a Nepali, Kaji Sherpa, climbed Everest in a record 20 hours and 24 minutes.

If the weather is clear in Darjeeling, which is rare at this time of year, you can see the western Himalayas dominating the horizon. Bill is captivated by the mountains and has been longing to see Everest. We are very lucky today, and the noble mountain is just visible as a tiny peak among the closer mountains. He stares for ages, imagining what it might be like to climb that immense mountain. At last he tears himself away quietly saying, 'Amazing . . . amazing . . . that's the highest mountain in the world . . .'

Among the other enjoyable things to do in Darjeeling, is to have a spot of tea and tiffin. The tea in Darjeeling, not surprisingly, is excellent and makes a refreshing change from sweet spicy chai. Tiffin seems to mean a mound of cakes, and Bill, having a penchant for such things, is in heaven. Glenary's with its smart waiters, impeccable service, and high-ceilinged dining room, is a reminder of bygone days and the perfect place to enjoy one's tea and tiffin.

'Bill, it's not long till we leave India and I'm worried about the sari I've got for Karn's bridesmaid outfit. I think I'm going to have a last look for another one. I want to have a back-up, just in case the first one's not right,' I say as we sit in the tearoom.

'Good idea. 'I've seen quite a few sari shops in town,' says Bill, tucking into his little cake mountain. 'Mind if I don't come?'

'No, that's OK. I've got my eye in now,' I say and set off for a shop that I saw on the way to Glenary's. The shop has one reasonable sari in lilac. Although it is not as pretty a colour as the lavender sari from Dharamsala, at least it has not got any faulty dyeing. So I buy it and feel a huge sense of relief that I have found something suitable.

Darjeeling is also full of shops selling Tibetan and Himalayan artefacts. We have both been really tempted to buy something as a memento of our travels, but feel vary wary about the provenance of the goods. Some of these things are very special items, used for spiritual purposes, or the family heirlooms of some poor family that has been ousted from their homelands. We want to know where they came from and if the person selling them was given a good price. We have been into several shops and walked out again, because we did not like the feeling there or the attitude of the shopkeeper. But today we found a shop that we were happy to buy from. The owner of the shop is a lovely Tibetan man who knows the provenance of every item in his shop. He can tell you exactly where it came from, what it was used for and how to look after it. Bill has been wanting to buy a conch for ages and asked the shopkeeper to tell him about the conches in the shop. This is what he told us:—

'Hundreds of thousands of years ago, before the Himalayas began to rise, Tibet was once under the sea and these conches lived in that sea. As Tibet began to rise and become dry land, the conches were left on the land. So they are very old—at least 150 thousand years old. They are rare and precious things. When they run out, there will be no more. Some are decorated with coral. This also is found in Tibet, left over from the sea. The conch is a living creature and each has a special voice when it is blown. The conch is a sea creature and it will lose its voice and die if it is not fed with water. Some conches that have become dry will never produce a note, no matter how well they are blown. The conch will sometimes choose its owner and only produce a note for that person.'

He shows us three beautifully decorated conches and instructs Bill on how to blow a note on them.

'You must put your lips in the right shape and you must blow from here,' he says putting his hand over his heart. 'The conch will like someone who blows from the heart,' he tells Bill. Bill takes each conch in turn and blows a note. Two of the conches sound flat and unresponsive. Bill looks disheartened. But when he puts the third to his lips, he sounds a note so pure and clear that it resonates throughout the shop and everyone turns around to look. It seems that this conch has chosen its new owner.

'Oh, I am surprised,' says the shopkeeper, 'I have never heard anyone get a good note from this one before. I always thought it must be very hard to play. It is a special one. It comes from the North West of Tibet and has been blessed by a high lama. It has been used in many ceremonies.'

'It's beautiful,' says Bill, turning it over in his hands. 'I liked it best, even before I played it.' The conch is decorated with a thick layer of finely worked silver which spirals from its thin end to around the 'ear' of the conch and forms a mouth piece at the other end. The silver work depicts many animals—rabbits, monkeys, deer, horses, birds and leopards amongst a scrolling background of leaves and flowers. The silver is also studded with Tibetan turquoise and the precious Tibetan coral that the shopkeeper has told us about. He quotes us a price, which is very reasonable, considering the amount of silver in its decoration. It is around half the price quoted to us in other shops for less decorated conches. So Bill shakes hands on the deal.

'I am very pleased it has chosen you, Sir,' says the shopkeeper. 'I know you will look after it and use it well.'

Outside the shop, Bill says, 'I want to make a special bag to protect the conch on our travels.' So we find a shop that sells fabric and buy some red velvet and a golden cord to make a drawstring. It will make a fine bag to house our new treasure.

We go to our favourite restaurant, Dekevas, to celebrate finding the conch. It is run by a friendly Tibetan family. Here the lady of the family makes momos and thukpa to rival even Mrs Norling.

It is our last night in India. Tomorrow we head for the Nepalese border and catch an overnight bus to Kathmandu. Bill and I are sitting in our hotel room talking about our imminent departure.

'I can't say that I'm that unhappy to be leaving,' I tell Bill. 'I think I've had my fill of India by now. We've had some wonderful times here, but my nerves are frayed to pieces by the constant assault of noise and intrusions into my personal space.'

'Yeah, I'm pretty fed up with the awful ear piercing music they play on radios that are never quite tuned into the station properly, the car horns tooting constantly, people banging things all day and all night long and the way everyone has to shout above the din,' says Bill.

'I'm sick of the smell of piles of rotting rubbish in the streets, the stink of open sewers and of cowshit. I'm fed up with the stress of trying to find somewhere reasonably clean to sleep and eat,' I tell him.

'Indian people are very tolerant of other peoples' noise and activity. They seem to be able to sleep through anything. I can't and I'm fed up with having my sleep disturbed,' says Bill. 'And I hope I never have to eat another veggie curry and rice in my life.'

'I'm fed up with the inefficient, chaotic bureaucracy. I'm fed up with having to traipse round town every time I want to send a parcel to England, looking for someone who will charge me a small fortune for sewing a piece of cloth round it and blobbing some sealing wax on. I'm fed up with having to queue up to get lots of forms to fill in at the post office. Then having to queue again, and wait around for ages while five different people pour over ancient, tattered lists trying to decide how much to charge me.'

'Yeah, we've seen some amazing things here, but it's definitely time to move on,' says Bill.

After Bill's angry outburst in Pelling, my own was precipitated by such a parcel packing fiasco. I went out this morning to post Karn's saris to her, and having been charged a small fortune to have a parcel sewn into cloth last time, I decided I would buy some cloth and pack them myself this time. But this resulted in a fruitless search round town for white cloth. Eventually I found the only place in town that had the right kind of cloth, so I went in to make my purchase. But the shopkeeper refused to sell me just the cloth, insisting that I pay him to do the packaging.

After about 10 minutes of wrangling with him, during which he was looking over smugly at his partner, who was also enjoying joining in, I was getting really fed up. So I said, 'How much would it cost to have it packed by you?'

'Ninety rupees,' he replied. That's about £1.30, and a small fortune in India.

'Alright, just give me the cloth and I'll pay you ninety rupees anyway,' I said, just wanting to get out of the shop and get back to our hotel.

'OK,' he said with a smirk, thinking he had made a very good deal. Then suddenly his face changed and he snatched the cloth back from me.

'No, I won't sell it to you,' he said petulantly. It was if he knew the game was up and it was no fun for him anymore.

'Well thanks very much for wasting my time,' I shouted and stomped off. What made me so angry was that he was treating me as a stupid, rich western woman, who was ripe for the conning. It's not even the money that bothers me, it is the fact that he thought he had got one over on me. I stormed home and ranted to Bill about it. Bill was equally affronted on my behalf and went off to see if he could get the cloth. But he came back empty handed too, saying that the shopkeeper must have sussed that we knew each other and wouldn't back down.

Things are not that much better this evening. We want to get a good night's sleep, in preparation for our journey tomorrow, but no such luck. The priest at the local mosque is shouting through a loudspeaker and making sure his voice is being heard all over town. He sounds so angry, it is impossible to tune the noise out of my head. It goes on for hours and hours and hours. At about 2.30 am I think I finally passed into unconsciousness for a while.

Chapter 7
Nepal—Flight to Freedom

From Darjeeling, we have booked a jeep ride that will drop us at Raniganj, from where we can cross the border into Nepal. This involves filling in the usual hundreds of forms at the Indian customs office. Then we have a hot, sweaty walk, packs on our backs and the sun beating down on our heads, as we cross a long bridge which spans a river in no-man's land. On the other side, we visit the Nepalese customs office, where there are many more forms to fill in and we have to pay $30 for our visas. Now we are allowed to walk into Kakarbhitta, the first town in Nepal. And if it was not for the process of going through customs, we would hardly know that we had changed countries, since Kakarbhitta and its people look much the same as in India.

In Kakarbhitta, we ask around for jeeps or buses that can take us on into Nepal. Our ultimate goal is Kathmandu, where we have a flight to Thailand in 5 days time, but first we fancy a spot of wildlife watching in the Royal Chitwan National Park. We find out to our alarm that there is a strike across the whole of Nepal for 2 days and absolutely no transport is running anywhere. It is too dangerous to even bribe anyone to take us to Kathmandu, since Maoist rebels are threatening reprisals against anyone who breaks the strike. So we are stranded and look about in dismay at this rundown town.

After a little shopping around, we manage to find a reasonably clean guesthouse, where the owner, Mr Rajat is very helpful and speaks good English. All is well, except the bedroom furniture, which has seen better days. Bill's bed collapses as he gets onto it in an overenthusiastic manner (well jumps on actually).

The next day, we are still under siege in Kakarbhitta. It is hot and humid, and we are glad to make use of Mr Rajat's shady garden. We are back in the realm of our old friends the mosquitoes, which comes as a rude shock after so much time at altitude. There is not much to do here except play cards and rest. Oh, how we mourn for our lost Travel Scrabble.

It seems that the country's instability was precipitated by a tragic event a year ago, in June 2001. Nepal was thrown into constitutional crisis when the royal family was all but wiped out by Crown Prince Dipendra with a machine gun. The rumour is that he flew into an alcohol and drug-fuelled rage when his father, King Birendra and mother, Queen Aiswary, refused to let him marry the girl that he loved.

According to some, the reason for the King's refusal of this marriage was that astrologers had advised that the Crown Prince should not be allowed to marry or have children until he reached the age of 35. They had warned that the king would die if this advice was ignored.

So Dipendra mowed down nine of his family at a banquet. The dead included King Birendra, Queen Aiswary and the king and queen's other two children—Prince Nirajan and Princess Shruti. Dipendra then turned the gun on himself and died a couple of days later. The late King Birendra's brother, Gyanendra, who was away from Kathmandu at the time of the shooting, was then crowned King.

Monarchy has long been considered the symbol of unity in this multi-ethnic and multi-cultural country. The Nepalese kings have been credited with success in maintaining the independence of Nepal, sandwiched between its two powerful rivals, India and China. But it seems that these events have created the climate for such factions as the Maoist rebels to prosper.

Another day passes and at last the buses are running again and we get on the first one to leave town. It is 4 am as we walk to the bus stop, but many shops are already open for business and we manage to get a takeaway chai to kick start us in the early morning. A little man checks our tickets and shows us to our bus amongst the maze of other buses. We find our seats and sip sweet chai before the bus speeds away into the dawn.

The road is a good one as we cross the hot subtropical plains, known as the Terai. We stop at a roadside café for a mid-morning break and both rush to the loo for different reasons. The café is skilled at serving vast quantities of food at high speed to large numbers of travellers. Bill's bad tummy does not prevent him tucking into puri and curds.

Back on the bus now, the journey continues and we begin to wind up from the Terai, into the mountains. At the lunchtime stop, we try to make a phone call to check that our flight will still be leaving on time. But we are told that there are no phones working in this region, as the Maoists have blown up the telecom centre.

Altogether it is a tense 13½ hour bus journey, during which we are stopped at frequent intervals to be checked for bombs and terrorists by police carrying machine guns. Finally we reach the outskirts of Kathmandu and take a taxi into the centre of the city as dusk is falling. We are both exhausted.

'What a horrendous journey that was,' I say to Bill.

'Yes, I'm very relieved to get here in one piece. I think our guardian angels must have been working overtime today,' says Bill. We check in at the Hotel Prince in Thamel, shower and change, get some supper in a nearby restaurant and then fall gratefully into bed.

Our flight to Thailand is now confirmed for two days time, but in the bustling centre of the city, life seems to go on as normal. There are many restaurants and shops still full with tourists and trekkers who have just returned or who are about to go.

'I really wish we were going on a trek,' says Bill. 'And it's such a shame that we missed the Royal Chitwan Park.'

'I know, but we don't have enough time now and it's too dangerous.

'Ah well, there's nothing for it then, but to indulge in the thing that Kathmandu does best—a spot of shopping,' says Bill. 'You're going to love it, Anna.'

In the 60s, travellers first flocked to Kathmandu to visit its ancient shrines, temples, and palaces set against the backdrop of the beautiful Himalaya. The next wave of visitors came to enjoy adventure tourism—trekking, rafting and mountaineering. But now shopping is the new tourism product in Nepal. Avid shopaholics can find their Nirvana amidst the bustling and colourful markets of Kathmandu. And I am going to join them.

This, of course, is nothing new. A 6,000 year old Sanskrit tome, describes Nepal as a good place to buy such luxuries as pashmina shawls and a variety of leather goods. Kathmandu has always been on the trade route between India and Tibet, and the craftsmen of Nepal were well respected at the royal courts of ancient China and in India thousands of years ago. But now the range of choice is staggering—from international brand-names to original Nepalese products. Among the Nepalese crafts, shops selling hand-made garments in cotton, silk, wool and leather are everywhere. Kathmandu has one of the widest selections of loose gems in South Asia and Tibetan jewellery abounds here. Other shops sell decorative metalware and statues; products made from traditional Nepalese kagaj paper; thangka paintings, depicting Buddhist deities; woollen carpets, hand-knotted using the traditional techniques and the best Himalayan sheep wool; oh yes, and the Newars are experts at wood carving. My, my, where to start?

'Of course, when I really thought about it, the only real problem I had with my rampant desire to buy stuff was how the hell would I fit it all in my suitcase?'

From **'Drive Thru America'** *by Sean Condon.*

And who says men are no good at shopping? Bill gets stuck right in and buys himself a lovely yak hair jacket, two Tibetan style shirts and lots of books. I find a good tailor and get measured for a cholu, a traditional Nepalese jacket.

I wake early, excited about two things—

1. Tomorrow we start the next leg of our journey. We are leaving West Asia and flying to South East Asia, starting with Thailand. This will be new territory for both of us. I am looking forward to roasting my bones on a beach for a few days and then going off to explore places I know very little about.
2. Nepalese shopping opportunities.

We breakfast at a nearby café, before going to the tailor's to pick up my cholu—an excellent start to the day. Then we set off through the morning traffic for Durbar Square to do the cultural thing round the temples. We make our way through a frenetic scrum of cars, rickshaws, bikes, people, schoolchildren, noise, smells. We pass a butcher's shop with a fat dog looking on in hopeful expectation. A man leans out and scrapes something from a goat's head, brains open to the world, before tossing the scrapings to the dog.

We walk into a throng of people in Durbar Square—commuters on their way to work, sales touts, men carrying impossibly heavy burdens on their backs, tourists and white bearded Saddhus dressed up especially for the occasion in orange robes, faces painted with daubs of white and red, smiling serenely . . . 'You want picture? Only one dollar.'

Saddhu in Durbar Square

The UNESCO world heritage site of Durbar Square is filled with a complex of palaces, courtyards, and temples. They were built between the 12th and 18th century and used to be the seat of the ancient Malla kings of Kathmandu. Altogether, there are around 43 rose-brick temples and palaces that have sprung up on either side of the old trade route to Tibet. With their stacked pagoda style roofs and intricately carved windows and doorways, they create a magical sight.

One of the most important buildings in Durbar Square is the rambling Old Royal Palace, which is known as Hanuman Dhoka. Its oldest, eastern wings date from the mid-sixteenth century, but it is likely there was a palace on this spot before then. It is the historic seat of royalty where the kings of Nepal are crowned. Nepal's royal family last lived here in 1886, before moving to the northern end of town, retaining the complex for ceremonial and administrative purposes.

Another interesting building is the Temple of the Living Goddess, Kumari, known as the Kumari Ghar. We are lucky enough to catch a glimpse of a tiny young girl, the physical embodiment of the Goddess, when she comes to the window to bestow blessings on those gathered below. She wears an enormous red headdress that matches her red painted lips and sets off her heavily kohled eyes. Her forehead is also painted in red and in the centre she wears a large white and black tika to symbolise her third eye. She is five years old.

According to tradition, she must have the body of the Banyan tree, legs like a deer, a neck like a conch and eyebrows like a cow. She must never have lost a drop of blood. She should have no physical blemishes or deformities and be from a pure Shakya family. She should also show no fear when spooked with scary objects in a darkened room as a part of the selection process.

Kumari lives an isolated life in luxury. Her feet must not touch the ground, and the 4 or 5 times she appears outside the palace she will be carried in a covered palanquin. The day when she has her first period, she must leave the palace and go back to her poor family, which must be difficult after having lived in luxury. It will not be easy to find a husband for her either. Men are usually afraid of her. After all, how can a man live up to a woman who has been a goddess? Even worse, rumour says that a man who marries a Kumari will die young.

The little girl that we see is Preeti Shakya, who was only four years old when she was selected to be the new goddess, just over a year ago. This is considered young by the standard of living goddesses who are usually five or above. But the priests encountered a few problems during their search for a new Kumari. Many families were not willing to give their daughter away to become the living goddess, hoping instead that their daughter would have a good career in a profession such as medicine. But the parents of the new Kumari, Surendra Man Shakya and his wife Reena, were said to be overwhelmed with joy. The tiny goddess withdraws from the window, and we move on.

Interestingly, the greatest site of active worship seems to be at the tiny, insignificant looking Ashok Binayak shrine. It is one of the most important Ganesh shrines in the Kathmandu valley and is worshipped by both Hindus and Buddhists.

A tree grows out of this tiny shrine

My favourite building in the square is the temple of Banasgopal, which means 'Krishna in the act of playing the flute'. Like many of the other buildings in the square, it is built from weathered rose-coloured bricks. It is an interesting octagonal shape with steep steps up to a brick pillared verandah, supporting its three pagoda style roofs stacked one on top of the other. This monument to love was built in 1649 by Pratap Malla in memory of his two dead queens.

Visiting Durbar Square is rather an ordeal and we are almost driven back by the onslaught of the exceedingly persistent touts. But next to the Banasgopal, is an ancient building with the most delightful array of colourful and sparkly dresses, draped from the windows. So we take refuge from the onslaught in the square by going into the sparkly dress shop. A tiny Gujarati woman, very pretty and vivacious, comes to greet us. I gaze in wonder at the amazing array of twinkly, dazzling clothes, trying to make some kind of decision about which garments to try. The Sparkly Dress Shop Lady knows her stock well, and helps my decision, by showing me the garments in my size and colours that will suit me. Whilst I am having so much fun with all these wonderful garments, Bill is having a lovely time keeping the lady's two tiny daughters amused. We leave the shop with my purse considerably lighter, but my wardrobe definitely enhanced by the beautiful garments that I have purchased.

We are at the airport now with three hours to kill and no rupees left, having blown the last few hundred on some Tibetan turquoise jewellery to give as gifts. We have just read in the paper that the Maoists are busy blowing up helicopters, kidnapping people and killing soldiers. So we are very glad to be leaving.

Everything seems pretty calm here at the airport and the security seems surprisingly relaxed. As we arrived, a soldier asked to look at our tickets. But the young pup did not seem to know what he was looking for.

'That's the flight number. That's the date. Those are our names,' said Bill, trying to make things easier for him. He seemed very grateful for the help and gave us a beaming smile.

We finally board the plane and make it safely out of Nepal without being blown up by Maoist bombers. We are blessed with a clear day and have a fantastic view of the Himalayas as we leave the country. There is Everest, standing proudly above the other mountains, our first really good view of the world's highest mountain.

Goodbye Nepal, Goodbye India. South East Asia here we come.

Chapter 8
Thailand—Booby, Beaches and Banana Milkshakes

We are in Bangkok now, where everything is clean and efficient. There are no car horns tooting. The people are relaxed, polite and friendly. There is such variety in the food and it is all delicious.

At the airport we formed an orderly queue to catch a metered taxi for a prearranged amount to Banglamphu, the budget guesthouse district. How different from our experiences in India of arriving somewhere to be surrounded by screaming rickshaw and taxi drivers, all trying to bundle you into their vehicle. The taxi was clean, modern, quiet. The suspension worked, the steering and the brakes all worked as they should. There were no potholes in the road. The driver was quiet, but friendly and drove safely. There were no clapped out buses or trucks hurtling towards us on the wrong side of the road. The journey took about 45 minutes right through the heart of Bangkok and in all that time I did not hear a single person sound their horn. It was bliss.

The Lonely Planet Guide is quite scathing about Bangkok, saying that most people hate it because it is so busy, noisy and polluted. It seems like a tranquil oasis to me after the dirt and noise of India.

The pooey bum has struck poor Billy down once again, so he stayed in the hotel today while I went out exploring. I never thought I would take such delight in finding a shop that sold decent bras and to be able to chat on equal terms to a **female** sales assistant about the size of bosoms and which particular style of bra suits the more amply proportioned torso. This would not have been possible in India because a) they do not have any decent bras, b) the shop assistant would have been male and probably would have had a superior attitude, telling me that he knew what suited my bosoms better than I did and c) they most certainly would not have had any in my size, the average Indian lady being considerably smaller in the bosom department, but the sales assistant would undoubtedly have tried to persuade me to buy something that was too small anyway.

There is one thing for which we have to be very grateful to Lars (whatever did happen to Lars?). Most budget travellers head straight for Khao San Road, where there are lots of cheap guesthouses, travel agents, restaurants and shops. But Khao San Road is a frenetic hub of activity, night and day—a sort of Asian flavoured cross between Soho and Glastonbury festival. It is a good place to arrange the next leg of your travels, but not a restful place to stay. Lars' tip was to go a little further, between the Wat Chai temple at the end of Khao San Road and the river, where there are quiet lanes with equally good guesthouses and much less noise. We are staying at the Siam Guesthouse, which is very new and very clean and the staff are lovely.

This afternoon Bill is feeling miraculously better after taking some ayurvedic herbs, so we go for a stroll and have lunch at a little café down our road. Ah the food, ah the choice, ah the fresh vegetables, ah the light fragrant sauces without a trace of greasy ghee, ah the fresh fruit juices that we can drink without getting tummy upsets (it was a watered down mango juice that did for Bill in Mamallapuram). We sit and watch the world go by. There are many travellers, in all shapes, sizes and nationalities. It seems strange after being the only westerners in so many places we have visited.

After lunch we stroll by the river, the Mae Nam Chao Phraya, the celebrated River of Kings, which separates Old Bangkok from Thonburi. It is now the river of commerce, where the River Boat Express, river taxis, industrial-looking tugs and private boats crowd the waterway. Given all the traffic, the lack of collisions seems quite miraculous.

There is a waterside park where lots of local people are strolling, taking the evening air, socialising and taking photos of the sunset over the river. We stroll too, enjoying the atmosphere. A little further on, a huge crowd of people are gathered for an open-air aerobic session. The exercises are led by a very fit, energetic young woman dressed in bright coloured lycra. She is on a podium with a head set and microphone. Everyone from young trendies to middle-aged businessmen and even old ladies are joining in.

'That looks like fun. I want to join in,' says Bill, mimicking some of the arm movements. But the sequences are quite complicated and he finds it hard to keep up. 'They're all so good,' says Bill. 'I feel a bit of twit not being able to keep up.'

'I expect they've all been doing it for ages,' I say, patting him on the arm. 'Let's go and find somewhere to eat.'

Supper is a wonderful meal of grilled snapper and vegetables in delicious sauce at a waterfront restaurant, watching all the comings and goings on the river. Then we wander back to our immaculately clean and quiet hotel room. 'What a wonderful evening. I've decided I like Bangkok,' says Bill.

'Me too,' I reply.

* * *

Today it is my turn to feel under the weather. It seems to be a pattern that happens whenever we arrive anywhere new after a long journey—the first day Bill feels tired and/or poorly and I feel lively; the second day Bill perks up and I feel lethargic and need to sleep.

Anyhow, we managed to make some decisions about our next travel plans and booked an overnight train to the island of Ko Pha-Ngan. We weighed up whether it was better to spend a couple of weeks seeing all the cultural sights of Thailand or to spend a couple of weeks lounging on a tropical beach. The beach won. Two weeks on a beach sunning ourselves, swimming and resting—bliss!

The travel agent where we bought the tickets was a ladyboy called Tom, complete with full make-up and gold nail polish. He was like a wind-up toy. When he first started talking he was very animated and spoke very quickly, and then he seemed to run out of steam, his speech slowing and his head drooping towards his chest as if he were about to nod off to sleep. Then he would jerk upright again and carry on exactly where he left off. Anyhow, he managed to issue our train tickets OK, so that's the main thing. We have heard so many horror stories about travel agents running off with your money and passports, never to be seen again. So we were very relieved to have an uneventful transaction.

There was a beauty salon next door to the travel agent, so on the spur of the moment, I decided to go in and get my legs waxed. I had never had them done in a salon before, so it was a novel experience for me. Fortunately the girl in the salon was very swift, efficient and thorough, even waxing my toes. So as leg waxings go, it was quite a pleasant experience. It cost 150 Baht (about £2), the same price as a tube of hair removing cream in the supermarket and frankly, I would much rather lie down and have someone else do it for me.

Whilst I was being waxed, Bill popped next door for a Thai massage. His masseuse was reassuringly large and middle-aged, so I was not jealous—not that I have any reason to distrust him. He came out saying, 'My God, she was strong! I've been thoroughly clicked and pummelled. It was good though. My back feels the loosest it's been for years.'

I was so impressed with the comfort and style of my new bras, that I went back and bought two more. At £5 they are a real bargain, but actually I would pay anything for comfortable bosoms.

We spend the rest of the day wandering from establishment to establishment, eating delicious food. We are both in danger of growing large and lardy if we do not leave this city soon. At one of the cafés, they are showing the film, 'Sixth Sense,' starring Bruce Willis. It is the first film we have seen since leaving England and I must say, I am thoroughly enjoying this whole hedonistic experience.

* * *

We are on the overnight train to Ko Pha-Ngan. I love sleeper trains. I have got that over-excited child feeling again. All but two of the other passengers are western tourists like ourselves and there is an atmosphere like being on a school outing. Everyone else is excited about going to the beach too.

There is a bunch of Aussies just down the carriage, necking back the beers and singing. The train staff are all joining in too. It is quite funny at the moment, but it could get annoying if they carry on till late at night.

The two locals are sitting opposite us—a sweet smiley old lady and a young woman. Bill has been doing this weird thing. Every time we arrive in a new country, his appearance changes and he morphs into looking like one of the locals. In fact, the little old lady sitting opposite could be Bill's granny, so striking is the facial resemblance. It is hard to believe that she has got even bigger ears than Bill.

One slightly scary thing—I have just seen a cockroach uncomfortably close to where I was planning to put my head when I go to sleep. Let us hope the other passengers are not woken in the middle of the night by me screaming, 'Oh my God, there's a cockroach on my eyelid!'

From the train, we board a bus to the ferry terminal, where we wait in excited anticipation of reaching the island. We get chatting to some of our fellow passengers. There is Paul, a very excitable chap and his girlfriend Kirsten, who is the quiet sensible one. They have both been to Ko Pha-Ngan before and Paul tells us with great authority that the best resort on the island is the Seaflower resort on the west coast in the delightfully named bay of Ao Chao Phao (pronounced Ow Chow Pow). He warns us of the barrage of taxi drivers that will greet us on arrival at the port of Thong Sala.

'It's a nightmare,' he says, 'They all run at you screaming—a huge crowd of them, trying to get you to go to their resort. It's really frightening. But don't worry, stick with us and we'll show you where to go.'

'Yeah, we're pretty used to that sort of thing after India. But thanks, it's good to get a tip for a good place to stay,' says Bill.

After what seems like ages, the boat arrives and we all climb aboard. There are plenty of other western tourists of all nationalities and the boat is pretty crowded. People immediately start stripping off and sunbathing. I find myself, to my surprise, feeling mildly shocked by the state of undress, after so many months in prudish India. I also find myself thinking that these people are all going to be burnt to a crisp by the time we reach Ko Pha-Ngan in a couple of hours. How middle-aged does that sound?!

With due warning from Paul, we get ready to leap off the boat and beat the crowds as we arrive at Thong Sala. We walk along the jetty to the shore, and he is right, we are greeted by a crowd of taxi drivers. But they are all sensibly holding up placards with their destination written on them and politely calling out to tell us where they are going. They seem mild-mannered and friendly.

Bill laughs and says aside to me, 'If Paul finds this frightening, he wouldn't survive very long in India.' All the same, we are grateful for his help in locating the driver for Seaflower and for sharing the cost of the taxi with us. I just hope his recommendation is a good one.

We load our packs into the *songtao,* a kind of pick-up truck fitted with benches in the back to ferry tourists around, and climb aboard. We are soon leaving the hustle and bustle of Thong Sala along a newly paved road going north through forests dotted here and there with the odd house at the side of the road. But soon we turn west off the paved road along a rutted dirt trail which heads bumpily for our resort. We are now heading for the bay of Ow Chow Pow, on the West coast.

Finally, we arrive at Seaflower and Paul shows us around. The central feature of the resort is an open-sided octagonal restaurant and bar area, complete with chill out areas, where you can lounge on bean bags or swing in hammocks. It looks very relaxed. The accommodation at the resort consists of little wooden bungalows set amongst the gardens and palm trees that lead down to a beautiful sandy beach lapped by turquoise water. Yes, we like Paul's choice.

We wander about trying to choose a bungalow, for our stay in paradise, but I am feeling really fussy and none of them feel quite right.

Frankly, they are a little rustic for my liking and none of them has a sea view. We find ourselves wandering along the beach and into Seetanu, the next door resort. There is a palatial bungalow with windows which look right out onto the beach. That is more like it. Bill goes to find the owner and ask about the price. It is a bit on the high side for our budget, but with a little negotiation—it is the low season after all—we get our palace at the price we want and move in.

A new day—greeted by glassy water, opalescent sky, shades of pale blue, pink, grey, milk. Islands on the horizon look like icebergs in this milky pearly whiteness. Silver—the water is silver. The sky and clouds are all silvery. All is calm, quiet. No wind. No people. No cars. Just tranquil sea, imperceptibly lapping at the beach. Not even enough breeze to stir the coconut palms.

Bill is sleeping in our high platform of a bed, in the beachside bungalow with the big windows that look out on the sea. Deep mattress surrounded by square mosquito net—so comfortable. I slept a dreamless undisturbed sleep. How hard it is to describe this island paradise without resorting to terrible clichés, and the relief of finally being somewhere peaceful after all the frenetic activity of India.

Dogs barking, mosquito biting. Always these two things on our travels—how pesky they are. I have to wear cover up clothes in the evening because of the mosquitoes, because I do not want to cover myself completely in toxic repellent. Last night we ate next door at the Seaflower restaurant and I looked enviously about at other women casually lolling about with bare arms or bare mid-riffs or bare legs. Do they not get bitten?

The dogs have started a plaintiff howling and there is a cacophony of barking all round the bay. They have shattered this peaceful morning.

All quiet again now. Dogs gone. Glassy sea turning a deepening blue as the sky colours and the iceberg islands appear from the mist, taking on more solid form.

Called Mum and Dad today. I had had a swim, then roasted on the beach for a bit, then swung in the hammock on the verandah for a while, drinking a pineapple and coconut milkshake, amidst the rustling palm trees, gazing out over the ocean. When I had had my fill of all that, I put on my flip flops and flip flapped my way to the little shop down the road where the pretty ladyboy hires out internet access or connects up a phone for you to make budget long distance calls, under the hum of the ceiling fan. He got me a phone connection and Mum answered straight away.

After the initial pleasantries she said, 'Ooh, I'm glad you rang. Now, have you thought who you would like to play the organ at your wedding?'

I shook my head slightly, trying to focus on what she had just asked. Yes, I had just heard her correctly. 'Well no Mum, I can't say that question has been uppermost in my mind. In fact I didn't even know I had a choice,' I said, trying to stifle a giggle.

'Well, yes. There's Jean, the lady who usually plays the organ at St Mary's on a Sunday. Or there's Dr Wilson who is very experienced and he plays beautifully. He can handle pretty much anything you might throw at him. He sort of roves around the parish, filling in when people are away.'

'Well it sounds like Dr Wilson is our man then,' I reply.

'Yes, I thought you might say that. Oh it is going to be embarrassing telling Jean though. I hope it doesn't hurt her feelings too much,' says Mum.

'Well good luck with that one, Mum,' I say, getting the message that the village politics can be quite tricky.

* * *

I wonder what Bill writes in his diary? He is annoyed with me because he is feeling amorous and I am not. I think he feels rejected and thinks I do not love him anymore, but I do. I just need a little space and some rest. I feel worn out, fed up, unable to get excited about anything and unable to see the beauty that surrounds me. I think my nervous system is blown out. Received an e-mail from Karn today. I am glad, because I badly need cheering up.

```
Hello darlings!

How are you both? Resting your jangled nerves by the sound of
your last e-mail. God, it took me back to my first visit to
India—and the beginning of my love/loathe relationship with
the place. Yes, the noise—the noisy bastards!!! I remember
very clearly, and it still brings a tear to the eye, our
great escape to the tranquillity of the lakes and mountains
in Kashmir, where we thought we could leave behind all the
fumes, bustle, hassle and noise of the low country, and catch
up on sleep and oxygen. But all night long confused cockerels
were crowing, and at 2am, then 4, then 6 incessant wailing
through loudspeakers started, as the Muslims were called to
```

their Mosques for prayers. My nerves ended up in such an exhausted, fragile state that one afternoon I sobbed my guts out for an hour, for no particular reason. The moral of this story?—Don't go to India without earplugs. But it sounds as though you had some amazing times there—and you certainly crammed a lot in.

And did some good shopping too, Anna!!! It was so exciting to be woken by the postman banging on the door with a parcel from India in his hand. I love the saris—both of them. I really can't decide between the two—would like to take them both up to Clifford and view them next to yours. I can't wait to wear them—so much nicer than the traditional bride/bridesmaid gear!

OK my dears, I'd better go. Hope you're getting lots of lovely rest and peace and quiet.

Loads of love

Karn xxxxxxxx

Well she is so right about the need for earplugs in India. Sadly they do not seem to sell them there. Believe me, we tried really hard to find some on many occasions.

* * *

It is October now and we have been here at Seetanu for two weeks on and off. It really is about as close as you can get to a tropical island paradise—the powder white sand, the coconut fringed beach, the turquoise water, the coral reef full of colourful fish and sea anemones, where you can go snorkelling 200m offshore, our little bungalow with the hammock on the verandah, the cheerful staff, Booby the bitch and her nine pups, who all need hugging at regular intervals, Ginger Bollocks the naughty cat who jumps in through the window and pats me through the mosquito net, Ben and his restaurant that serves delicious food, coconut and pineapple milkshakes, friendly people—Robert and Catherine, Paul and Kirsten, the Swiss family Robinson, Dyk the steely-eyed diving instructor. It sounds like I love it, doesn't it?

Well I almost do, I am getting there. Today I probably love it more than I have loved it till now. Yesterday I was talking about going home.

I got as far as wondering how much a ticket from Bangkok to England would be. Then I realised that if I cannot be happy here, then I would probably be just as miserable back in England, especially since winter is on its way there.

The unhappiness and dissatisfaction I feel has nothing to do with my environment. It is inside me. So the sobering thought is that no matter how perfect the place, no matter how luxurious a hotel I stay in, there is no escaping this feeling. I have to resolve it for myself.

Why do I feel like this? Well I am putting it down to exhaustion and frazzled nerves after the India experience. My friend Pete pretty much summed it up — 'People who spend too much time in India,' he says, 'Often find they suffer from a residual build up of noise and frenetic activity in their heads, which cannot be excreted at a fast enough rate by ordinary means, owing to the extreme nature of the sensory bombardment they have suffered. This often leads to sudden uncharacteristic bouts of temper or shouting and general feelings of disorientation and dissatisfaction. The only solution is to sing loudly and out of tune, in order to purge oneself of the extraneous noise and energetic intrusions.'

How right he is. I now realise that because I did not perform the necessary purge of the extraneous noise and energetic intrusions, they are largely still trapped in my system, slowly leaking out and souring what should be a beautiful experience here in Thailand.

I think I underestimated how long it would take to start feeling normal again. Anyhow, now that I have identified the cause, I am sure a cure is possible. Dear, sweet Billy has given me a couple of shiatsu treatments and they have really helped. So today for the first time, I find myself looking around and thinking, 'I really like it here and I will be sad to leave.'

Just to give a measure of how disorientated I felt — on the first morning here, I went for a Thai massage to help me relax. After the massage, I went to get my purse to pay the lady. I searched the whole bungalow, but could not find my bag containing my purse and my passport. Bill had just enough money to pay for the massage and to make phone calls cancelling the credit cards. We spent a wretched day asking after the bag, thinking I might have left it in a nearby café, but to no avail. We came to the conclusion that it must have been stolen, so we had to go to the police station to report the theft and make phone calls to ask about how to get a replacement passport and alternative means of withdrawing money. The bank refuses to send us replacement cards as they say the risk of them going missing en-route is too great.

I felt absolutely wretched. How could I have been so stupid as to lose all our money, credit cards and my passport in one fell swoop? I knew that Bill was really angry with me, but he would not say so, which made me feel worse than if he could just get it out of his system. We both felt so terrible that we even resorted to buying a packet of cigarettes and attempting to get drunk, but it just ended up giving me a headache.

Later that day, Bill opened the drawer of the bedside cabinet and—lo and behold—there was the bag, complete with money, passport and credit cards, exactly where I had put it for safe-keeping. I was mightily relieved to get my passport back, but cursed the fact that I had cancelled the cards and made the whole community feel that there was a thief in their midst. We were both so shamefaced about what had happened that we did not own up to the fact that the bag had turned up and we felt terrible every time someone asked us about it. It still makes me cringe when I think about it.

In my state of wretchedness, I made us move from our lovely spacious bungalow into a much shabbier, more cramped, but cheaper one. We stuck it out for three days before the poohy smell that emanated from the bad drains there drove us to leave the resort altogether and head off for Thong Nai Pan on the other side of the island, which promised wonderful cliff viewpoints, a double crescent bay and a coral reef.

Considering the actual distance, the journey to Thong Nai Pan took ages. We had a seemingly never ending, bumpy and hot *songtao* ride during which Bill was in danger of losing his breakfast. Then we had a long hot walk, carrying our rucksacks up and down the first bay looking for somewhere nice to stay before we finally decided that we needed to catch a boat to the other bay, where the accommodation looked better. After walking the length of the bay, we finally settled on the Dolphin bungalows and gratefully moved in.

We were about to dive into the ocean to relieve our hot, sweaty and dust covered bodies, when we noticed to our horror, that the water was infested with jellyfish of the reddy-brown deadly variety with extremely long tentacles. We had already heard rumours of two deaths caused by these jellyfish, but to our surprise there was a girl swimming happily about.

'How are you managing to avoid the jellyfish?' asked Bill.

'Hey, it's all right if you keep an eye out for them,' she said with a strong Australian accent. 'And it's great if you swim with a friend so that one person can look one way and the other looks the opposite way!'

We both decided she was being overly optimistic about the danger—after all, Aussies are used to risking death every time they go into the ocean. So we decided against going into the water.

It was like torture to gaze upon the beautiful ocean, feeling hot and sticky and not to be able to go in the water. So the next day we headed back to Ow Chow Pow. I felt a bit embarrassed when we arrived back, but we had a lovely reception from Ghoum, one of the staff, who gave Bill a big hug and told us that he had cried when we left. All the beach-front bungalows were full, but he found us one a couple of rows back, which was spacious, new and clean, with a nice bathroom and a comfy bed. It is my favourite room so far and we have stayed in it ever since, to Bill's great relief.

* * *

Checked e-mails. There is one from Mum saying:—

Hallo Anna and Bill,

Hope you are having or have had a great beach holiday. It was great to have your news. Grandpa B looks forward to his copy and frequently asks for the next episode. We are off to Cullompton for the w/end of 19th for Great Aunty Millie's 90th, taking Grandpa and Blake with us. No advancements on the wedding front but it is definitely booked in for June 21st at the church so the Churchwarden says. We seem to be very busy all the time but it is all boring stuff compared to your great adventure.

Much love, M & D, H & H

I love to hear that Grandpa is enjoying our e-mails and it is such a relief to have the wedding confirmed at St Mary's. Also received another cheering e-mail from Karn. She wrote:—

```
Dear Anna

So good to get your e-mail. How are you now? I hope this
finds you more rested and happier. I really, really, really
understand and sympathise with your travel weariness and
fed-upness. Apart from my year in Australia, I don't think
I've ever gone through the 3 or 4 month travel 'barrier'—it
seems to be my personal limit, when I've been saturated with
```

all the foreign sights, sounds and ways, soaked up as much as I could handle, and have to come home to process it all. There comes a point when you just want, more than anything in the whole world, to sit in your own kitchen and drink a cup of normal tea, chat with friends and family, sleep in your own bed, just immerse yourself in familiar, wholesome, healing normality. Oh, the simple joys of home. Think that's why I love travelling so much, because it really makes you appreciate coming home—even the rain, the dark evenings, the traffic jams start looking appealing! Travelling is exhausting!

But perhaps you just need to rest up for a bit longer. India is one of the most invasive countries on your nerves. If your enthusiasm hasn't rallied in the next couple of weeks, perhaps you should consider going straight to the States, or New Zealand, or some other culturally familiar country, but still incredibly beautiful, where you can get a decent cup of coffee and egg and chips, and an English paper and all the other little home from home things that you start to miss so much. Or come home! My God, I for one would be extremely happy to have you back! I know you've got Bill to consider too, and he sounds right into it at the moment, but you must follow your heart. So, my dear, let me know how you're feeling now. Really wish you lots of joy again.

Lots of love to both of you, and write soon and let me know how you are.

Karn XXXXXXXX

You see the reason Bill is coping better than me is that he knows how to make himself at home wherever he is. He has certainly made himself right at home here. He is always the first one up in the morning and just wanders into the kitchen at the Seetanu restaurant to make himself a cup of tea. The staff do not seem to mind, as long as he leaves the money for it on the counter and I love being brought a cup of tea first thing in the morning. As Karn says, it is part of my healing.

Bill on the beach at Seetanu

Now that I am feeling better, I find I am able to appreciate certain people and happenings that have made our stay here far more tolerable. One of these is our friendship with Robert and Catherine, an American couple staying in one of the bungalows just down the beach from us. Now, Catherine is quiet, mild-mannered, kind and very sweet. Robert however, while still being extremely likeable is the exact opposite. The first thing that strikes you about Robert is his size. To put it mildly, he is a big fella. And he has a great mane of dark hair flowing down his broad back. There's an awful lot of him to see, and with the heat and the beach and the general state of undress which is *de rigueur* here, believe me we have seen an awful lot of him. Robert and Catherine's bungalow is the oldest one at the Seetanu resort and it has been weathered by many seasons' storms and monsoons. Watching Robert haul his great frame up the steps of his small wooden bungalow one day, Bill remarked, 'Boy is that testing the tenacity of Thai carpentry! Bless him, I've never seen him try to get in a hammock and that's probably a good thing.'

In keeping with his size, Robert never does anything by halves. Bill, on many occasions, returning to our bungalow after a visit with Robert can be heard exclaiming, 'Man, can that fella talk!' or 'Man, can that fella eat!' or 'Man, can that fella drink!'

In fact his ability to drink and his generosity in ensuring that all around him are also amply supplied with alcohol is fast turning him into something of a local legend. He is like the pied piper of drunken people. He can be seen, of an evening, standing in some bar, bottle in hand, swaying slightly and holding forth on whatever topic he feels passionate about at the time. And Robert feels passionate about many things. He is probably talking to the barman, because everyone else is too drunk to stand up. There he is, this giant man, with a trail of broken, drunken people lying in heaps along the route that he has forged from bar to bar—local Thai people and westerners alike, face down on the bar room floor or by the side of the road, all levelled by alcohol. And the fact that Robert is still standing is a very good thing, because if he were to fall over, there would probably be three tourists, a couple of waitresses and a ladyboy flattened on the way down.

As you can see from his following, Robert likes people, and the stranger and more interesting the better. He is a picker-up of waifs and strays. One such character is a man named Zog. He is a local Thai and I have no idea whether Zog is his real name or just a nickname that Robert has given him, but anyway he is very fond of Robert and will do anything for him, following him around like a puppy. Zog must have expressed a desire to Robert to learn some more English phrases because Robert has obliged by teaching him many colourful and fruity sayings, none of which mean quite what Zog thinks they mean. For example, on one night that we were in the Robert entourage—that was just before our livers packed in—Robert was encouraging Zog to repeat his new phrase. 'Come on Zog, what do we say when we're real happy?' asked Robert.

'I've done big jobs in my pants!' replied Zog looking really pleased with himself.

* * *

A tropical paradise it may be, but life on the island is not without its hazards. As well as the jellyfish, there are the highly dangerous coconuts. Everyone has a favourite statistic about the coconuts—apparently more tourists are killed by getting hit on the head by a falling coconut, than any other cause. Another favourite statistic is that more people are killed each year by coconuts than by lightning! In fact we see coconuts falling at regular intervals. Picture the scene—you are relaxing on the beach after a swim, the sun gently warming your body; there is music from the restaurant tinkling in the background and you are sipping on a pineapple milkshake that your generous loved one has just fetched you from the aforementioned establishment; the waves suss, suss up and down the shore and a light breeze delicately ruffles the palm leaves. Then all of a sudden—'Phaddunkk!!' as a coconut hits the ground with a great crash not 10ft away from your ear. It lands with such force that it bounces back up 5ft in the air and the whole beach shudders. Your heart misses a beat and you look nervously above you, trying to work out which one will be next and hoping that it is not the one directly in line with your head.

Being relatively new to Thailand, one thing which we have found a little confusing is that lots of the boys look like girls and the girls look like boys. Thai people have remedied this confusion by having a different way of saying hello or thank you depending whether you are male or female (whether by design or preference!). There is a brother and sister who work at the Seaflower resort next door and, well you would think they should be the other way round. Now the sister has a pair of strong looking shoulders and tiny hips with chunky legs. She has a very square jaw and stomps around in leggings and a baggy T-shirt scowling at everyone. Her brother, by contrast, is very pretty and artistic of temperament. He cooks delicately flavoured food and paints intricate designs of butterflies, flowers and dragons on t-shirts, which he sells for a fraction of what such masterpieces should be worth. Last night there was a celebration night at Seaflower. The owner and some of the staff had been out on a fishing trip and had brought home a good catch, so the brother had cooked a range of special fish dishes and we were entertained to the delightful sight of the sister dancing and swinging her poi around.

'I'm not gay or owt,' said Bill, 'But I'd rather snog the brother than the sister.' Bill is fascinated by the ladyboy concept. The man at the bike hire shop is a ladyboy too. Bill came back from hiring a moped saying, 'Now don't get me wrong, he's a nice enough chap, very helpful and all that, but he's more of a ladybloke than a ladyboy. He's got great big jowls and a bit of a gut, but he's done his nails and a bit of make-up. I mean, jowls and make-up just don't really go, do they? It's quite refreshing to see that no-one here bats an eyelid, but I don't think he's going to get a shag looking like that, is he?'

'You never know, Bill,' I tell him, 'They say there is someone for everyone. After all, we found each other, and we're a couple of oddballs.'

We had about a week in the new bungalow and I gradually began to feel normal again. Billy went off to Ow My Head, just up the coast, where there are lovely quiet beaches and more coral reefs. There he met Dyk, the steely-eyed diving instructor, who would have looked at home wearing a poncho and smoking a cheroot on the set of a western movie. Dyk introduced Bill to diving and he liked it so much that he signed up to do a five-day course and take his PADI certificate. Bill loved the whole underwater experience—the excitement, the adventure, the manliness of it. He and Dyk became bosom buddies. He would go off on his moped early in the morning and come back late in the afternoon all bright sparkly eyed and giggly.

'How was your day?' I would ask him.

'Amazing! The highlight was diving to 60ft in crystal clear water. There were masses of colourful fish, all nibbling and swimming in and out of the coral, giant jellyfish, moray eels and trigger fish (which can be dangerous, you know) . . .' he would tell me.

Later, we would meet up with Dyk in Ben's restaurant for supper and the two of them would reminisce about the day's adventures.

For the first day I agonised about whether I had done the right thing deciding not to take the course with Bill. The two factors that swayed my choice were that firstly, having dived in Australia, I decided that I preferred snorkelling and did not think I would ever use the PADI certificate again. Secondly, at 8600 Baht (£120), it was too much money to do just to keep Bill company.

The first day that Bill went off, I was quite happy to be on my own, getting all my chores done—washing clothes, sewing, etc. It seemed quite fun to kiss Bill goodbye in the morning as if he was going off to work. I was genuinely happy that he was having a great time.

But the second day I got really bored—it rained and was cold, so I could not swim and sunbathe and I had already done my chores. All the people we had made friends with had already left, so I was a bit lonely too. Bill was very late back—long after dark—and I was starting to get worried about him, thinking he might have fallen off the moped in the wet conditions.

That night I asked Dyk if I could come along on the boat and go snorkelling while they dived the following day, but he pooh-poohed the idea, saying the snorkelling was no good where they were going and I would be wasting my money. So I stayed at home feeling a bit miffed and jealous.

The next day, Bill had a day off from his PADI course, so we hired a moped and set off for Chaloklum—a fishing village in the north of the island. Halfway there it started to pour with rain so we turned back, intending to set out again after lunch. But later on Bill said he was just popping out to speak to Dyk about something. He came back hours later, having been for a beach dive and telling me that he had booked us on a trip to the National Marine Park the following day with Dyk's company. It sounded great till he told me how much it was—3,000 Baht (about £50). We had our first proper row of the trip.

'Bill, I'm really annoyed that you've gone and spent so much of our money without asking me. You've already spent loads on the dive course and extra on the beach dive you've just done. The other dive school does the same trip for about half that and Seaflower does a whole 3 day trip for less than 3,000 Baht. I don't want to sound like a miser, but we don't have a bottomless purse and if we spend so much money on a day trip we'll have to economise on something else. The thing that upsets me most is that you didn't even consult me about it and you seem to prefer spending time with your new friend Dyk to being with me.'

'Well, I'm really sorry for trying to organise something nice for you,' said Bill in a sarcastic tone. Before I could stop him, he raced off on the moped to try and find Dyk, to cancel the trip. I sat worrying that something terrible would happen to him on the wet, rutted roads, in his upset state. As I waited in a state of tension, it made me realise how much I love him and how it really was not worth souring our relationship over £50. So you can imagine how relieved I was when he came back in one piece.

As it turned out, the weather was too bad to go to the Marine Park and the water visibility was too poor to see much, so Dyk gave us our money back anyway.

* * *

Room 905—we have moved again. This time it was more Bill's idea than mine. Although the last bungalow was really nice, it was quite close to the restaurant and a new set of people who liked to stay up late and party had moved into the resort. We had got used to going to bed by 10 or 10.30 pm, so when they started playing loud music in the evenings, we felt like real old fuddy duddies asking them to turn it down because it was our bedtime.

So now we are back in the palatial, expensive beach-front apartment for our last few days and actually it is really nice. We can wake up and gaze out at the ocean. We can sit on our verandah and watch the beautiful sunsets. We have a proper wardrobe to put our clothes in and we have a really spacious comfy bed and mozzie net.

So I am finally feeling happy and normal again. It is time to go now. Our visas run out soon so we have to go back to Bangkok to renew them and sort out the next stage of our travels. Tomorrow we leave, but that feels OK. I feel rested enough to want to embark on the next phase of our journey and I am actually quite excited about seeing Laos and Vietnam.

I am swinging in the hammock on the verandah of our little palace. Bill is sitting on the beach in the shade of a coconut tree. Five puppies come to join him and he spends half an hour contentedly grooming and cuddling them in the lazy heat of the afternoon. It strikes me how very lucky we are to have this quiet peaceful time.

At last I have realised I am in Paradise

Another beautiful day dawns on Ko Pha Ngan. The air is fresh and cool. A light breeze comes in off the ocean. Everything is pale and clean in the dawn. The dogs—Scab, No Tail and Gimp (named by Robert) patrol the beach, checking the smells.

It is the last time we will see this scene in the morning. Last night we went to Ben's restaurant for our final meal. He was very sweet to us and seemed genuinely sad that we are going. He gave us both a big hug and offered to store things for us until we come back.

Bill is keen to come back here on our way to Singapore after Laos and Vietnam. Part of it, I think is that he wants to go diving again with Dyk, and part of it is because we both want to feel there is somewhere familiar and safe to come back to after our whistle-stop tour of the rest of South East Asia. I think in my heart I know that we will not come back here. It would be nice, but I do not think we will have time. I do not want to cling on to it. When we go, we go—on to the next phase of our journey.

Puppy on the beach—it is the skinny little black girl with lopsided ears. She is always very bold and adventurous—so cute with her wide-staring blue eyes. I do love those pups, with their rubbery tails and wobbly gaits, all rolling over each other scrapping or scampering about. Most of all I love the way that when you pick them up and cuddle them, stroking them behind their ears, they go all floppy and sleepy in your arms, like it is the best place in the world to be.

I found out that the staff at Seetanu are feeding the pups. It is a huge relief since Booby, their mum will not feed them anymore. She looks so swollen and sore—their sharp little teeth must be agony.

From Mum and Dad—Warnings to British Subjects

Hi Anna and Bill

I am sure you have heard about the terrible car bombs in Bali where over 200 have been killed including at least 30 Brits and a lot of Australians. They are linking it to Alqueada and the Foreign Office is advising all Brits to stay clear of Indonesia because they have intelligence indicating that there will be more atrocities of this kind. We are not sure whether this area is on your itinerary but if it is, it would seem wise to avoid the whole of this area.

Blake is coming on Friday to stay over night and then coming with us and Grandpa down to celebrate Aunty Millie's 90th birthday on Saturday at

Cullumpton. It should be a big gathering of the Bromley clan, even Uncle Albin from Ireland will be there, so it should be a great occasion catching up with news of those we don't often see.

That's all for now.

Love from Mum and Dad

The news of the bombings in Bali went through the peaceful resorts of Seetanu and Seaflower like a shockwave. Lots of people knew of friends that were travelling in Bali at the time and feared for their safety or were about to fly there and decided to cancel their trips. The next flight on our Round the World ticket is to Singapore. I was hoping to visit some of the family's old haunts in Malaysia, but there are lots of rumours that Alqueada are very active there and that it will be the next target. So we have decided to change our flights and go straight to Australia from Bangkok after we have visited Vietnam and Laos. Bombings and trouble seem to be following us around the world like a bad smell.

* * *

So we arrive safely and uneventfully back in Bangkok on Thursday morning. We head straight for the New Siam Guesthouse behind the temple at the end of Khao San Road. It feels good to be in familiar surroundings.

Bangkok seems busier to me now. Perhaps it is the contrast with our peaceful life on the island, compared to our first impressions after the hecticness of India. People work really long hours here—7am till 10pm, seven days a week is not unusual. How do they have a life outside work? How do they get their laundry done and keep their houses clean? How do they have time for a relationship with their family and friends? How do they manage to stay cheerful and polite to their customers?

We spend our first day rushing about getting our Thailand visas extended, changing our flights to Australia and arranging visas and flights for Vietnam and Laos. It is an exhausting day, but it feels good to get all that sorted out. Now we just have to sit and wait for our visas to come back in time for our flight to Ho Chi Minh next Thursday.

The best part of the day is catching the river-boat down to Sathorn Pier on the way to the immigration office. It is a fast and efficient service which cuts out sitting in traffic jams and is much more scenic. It is incredibly cheap too—8 baht (about 10p) each for a 20 minute journey.

The boat is as crowded as the London tube at rush hour and only stops for around 20 seconds to let a great herd of people off and another herd of people on again. The warning sign for a stop coming up is the guard emitting a series of short blasts on his whistle and then a ramp swings out to connect the boat to the quay. But the river is incredibly choppy, so the ramp is continually parting company from the quay as the boat lurches up and down. Well, if you are told to 'mind the gap' getting off the tube, boy, do you have to mind the gap getting off the boat. Your timing and balance have to be immaculate, if you want to avoid falling over and getting trampled, or worse, falling into the river. We are both very nervous about missing our stop and cling onto our copy of the river map, checking and rechecking which stop is coming up and how many more stops before Sathorn Pier. When our stop is next, we get to the exit way too early, while everyone else on the boat has done this journey many times before and all rush for the exit at the last minute. But somehow we manage to negotiate getting back onto dry land without any adverse events, carried along by the momentum of all the others on their way to Sathorn Pier.

We take a trip on the sky train, which is much like an overland version of the tube. Bill loves it. 'I want to spend a whole day riding about on the sky train!' he says.

Ironically, we find ourselves with a whole week to kill in Bangkok, when time is getting short for the rest of our journey. So Bill might get his wish for a day riding the sky train after all. We are not really Big City people (well, apart from my love of shopping), but we have a lot of general admin to do here, not to mention spending some time on the wedding plans.

* * *

It is Bill's turn to feel tired and out of sorts. He has been very quiet and sad, which is so unusual for him. I hate to see him like this. His brother, Tony, phoned on the mobile last night, which was good as it seemed to cheer him up a bit.

Weather report—autumn is here. The leaves are falling, but the temperatures are not. I find myself feeling envious of all my friends who are e-mailing to complain about the nights drawing in back in Blighty. To be cool at night-time is a wonderful thing.

Bill likes it here at the Siam guesthouse, because all the hotel staff are convinced that he is a movie star. They think he is Brendan Fraser, star of 'The Mummy'. Of course, he has done nothing to disillusion them, and was delighted to pose for a photo with the ladies from reception. He also got mistaken for an Italian footballer, so it's just as well we're going soon before it all goes to his head.

* * *

Time seems to have slipped by incredibly quickly in Bangkok. It all seems to go by in a blur of cruising up and down on the river express boat. We have become really confident about getting on and off the boat, knowing exactly when our stop is coming up and leaving it to the very last moment to scamper off. Bill has had his fill of riding about on the sky train, interspersed liberally with bouts of shopping to keep me happy. Central Bangkok is for the most part a giant shopping centre. Bankokians seem to have based their whole culture on shopping and eating—so we just had to join in. They have warmly embraced Western culture. The giant seven storey Siam Centre houses every kind of retail outlet that would make even an American business development company proud. And if you need refreshment, you can visit a KFC, an Outback Steakhouse, Dunkin Donuts, McDonalds, Starbucks Coffee House or a Pizza Hut. There is not a pad thai noodle in sight.

The only problem with clothes shopping here is that it is not designed to cater for the average Western physique. Thai people are very petite and I cannot find anything in my size. I went into one department store and saw a pair of shoes that I liked. So I asked the assistant if I could try a pair in my size (my feet are considered average in England). She looked shocked and ran off with her hand over her mouth trying to stifle giggles. I thought she had gone to get the shoes for me to try, but instead, she went to tell her colleague what enormous feet I have. They stood pointing and giggling at my feet. One of them went off to tell someone else and soon a small crowd had gathered to laugh at my repulsively large appendages. There was an announcement made on the tannoy. It was in Thai, but I am sure it said, 'Please make your way to the shoe department, where today's special entertainment is the viewing of an English lady with freakishly large feet—you've got to see it to believe it!'

Bangkok is famous for its red light area, Patpong. As well as having tiny little feet, apparently Thai women are very adept at doing all sorts of tricks with their downstairs regions. If you are so inclined, you can pay money to see a lady smoking a cigarette in a way that would never give her lung cancer, amongst other amazing feats. But we did not sample its delights. I had no wish to go there and if Bill did, he did not tell me... and I would not have let him anyway.

Mum is absolutely delighted that we have got our mobile working while we are in Bangkok and is making the most of being able to call us about the wedding, which she is doing on a frequent basis.

'Well, I plucked up courage and spoke to Jean, the organist at St Mary's about Dr Wilson playing at your wedding. She says she is very happy and quite relieved that Dr Wilson is going to play, as she gets very nervous about playing on big occasions,' she said last night.

'Oh, I'm really glad that's worked out without anyone's feelings getting hurt,' I said.

'Oh darling, I've really missed our little chats about the wedding,' said Mum. 'There is still so much to sort out—the reception venue, the caterers, the menu, a band for the reception.'

'Why don't you speak to Rubbery Rachel (my old school friend). She knows absolutely everyone in Herefordshire. She knows lots of caterers and bands and places to hire marquees. I'm sure she will be glad to help,' I suggest. One of the stress factors has been that Mum has set her heart on making the wedding cake, but I don't want a conventional fruitcake because of my wheat allergy. Mum called back again today:—

'Rachel says that it's quite the trend to have a chocolate cake for weddings now and she's got a really good recipe that uses ground almonds instead of flour. And with her contacts in the chocolate industry, she can get me kilos of really good chocolate at cost price. So I think we might have solved that problem now. I'll have a practice run at the recipe before hand. What do you think?' says Mum.

'I think a chocolate cake sounds absolutely perfect, Mum. I'm glad Rachel's put your mind at rest.'

'Yes, she was really helpful. She's given me some contacts for the catering too—people that she has used before that have been very good and reasonably priced. There's a chap called Neil, who catered for Rachel's wedding reception. I've made an appointment for him to come and talk me through his menus.'

'Well done, Mum, that's very efficient of you, but you will hold off the final decision until Bill and I can have a look at the menu, won't you?'

'Oh, well, yes. It's just that you have to book these things in good time or you might miss out on the one you really want . . .' And so the conversation went on.

'I'm so relieved that you feel a bit more relaxed about the wedding plans. I feel terrible that I'm not there to help you more.'

'Well, dear, I've had an idea about that. Harvey and I have always wanted to have a holiday in Australia and we thought that perhaps we could time it so that we can meet you for Christmas in Sydney. How does that sound?' says Mum, saving the biggest piece of news till last.

'Well that sounds absolutely brilliant. I've been feeling pretty homesick lately and it would be so lovely to see you. And we can talk about the wedding plans in person. Wonderful!'

Chapter 9
Vietnam—Sticky Rice Balls

We landed in Ho Chi Minh City (still Saigon to the locals) on 24th October and liked it very much on first impressions. It is the first time my enthusiasm for travelling has returned, since my post-India bout of depression. Bill didn't sleep the night before we left Bangkok, he was so excited. And at the airport he was like a naughty boy on a school outing. In the upstairs restaurant I had to stop him throwing baguettes onto the heads of people walking below.

Before coming here, I had a romantic image of sleepy old Indochina, where we would sit eating croissants in a quiet café by the Mekong, breathing in the heady aroma of coffee mixed with spices, as now and then an elderly Vietnamese lady would saunter slowly by on her bicycle. So it came as quite a surprise to find how hectic it is here. Saigon is a frenetic hive of activity with millions of motorbikes buzzing past in all directions. It is a rapidly developing city with many new high-rise buildings and businesses. There are giant neon signs everywhere advertising computers and mobile phones. Most people are under thirty. Life happens at break-neck speed and many decibels volume. People get up very early and go to bed very late. And the strangest sight?—a taxi hurtling by us with about 50 white ducks with yellow beaks on the roof, all quacking away.

The women here are very careful to keep the sun off their skin, wearing hats and face-masks (which also help against traffic pollution) when they are out and about on their motorbikes. They often wear long gloves to cover their arms when wearing short sleeves. Many of the women still wear the traditional Au Dai dress and it looks very elegant on their petite frames. It consists of a long, closely fitting tunic with a mandarin collar and wrap-front asymmetric fastening over wide-legged trousers in silk or cotton.

Bill says, 'I quite like the women here. I think they're very pretty.' I feel a first twinge of jealousy.

The people at our hotel are incredibly friendly and have made us feel very welcome. The receptionist, An, was almost too friendly. She was admiring my outfit—a green Nehru collared tunic top from India over Thai fisherman's trousers—whilst patting my bottom and playing with my hair. But there was a slight edge to it as well—as if she was making fun of me. I didn't know whether to laugh along with it, or tell her to kindly remove her hands from my posterior.

An information brochure in our hotel room welcomed us to Saigon and suggested some useful phrases in Vietnamese. I hope we don't have to use any of them while we are here:—

> As rude as a bear—hôn nhu gấu
> Smelling as disgusting as cat's excrement—chua nhu cut mèo
> As persistent as a leech (don't we know about that!)—dai nhu dia
> As well behaved as a sheep—ngoan nhu truu
> As smelly as an owl—Hôi nhu cú (not sure I've smelled many owls).

Today we are on a trip to the Mekong Delta. Here, the Mighty Mekong (as Bill always insists I call it) ends its long journey from its source on the Tibetan Plateau, through China, Burma, Thailand, Laos, Cambodia and Vietnam. It has covered over 4,000 kilometres before dividing into nine tributaries that flow into the South China Sea. The delta area is known as Cuu Long, which means, 'The Nine Dragons.' In this area, life for the 25 million people who live here, depends on the river. Every year the river floods and when it recedes, it leaves behind its gift of nutrients. The fertile soil of the delta flood plain can sustain an amazing three crops of rice a year, allowing Vietnam to be the second highest exporter of rice in the world (after Thailand). The river is also richly stocked with fish. Not only is the river the source of nourishment; it also serves as a market place. As well as the fish and rice, lush fruit and vegetables, unique to the area, are traded.

We take a boat from Cai Be, to see the Can Tho floating market, where the local people bargain and exchange goods from their boats. Traditionally, families live on the boats, buying fruits, rice and flowers from local farmers, which are then sold in the floating market. Each boat advertises its wares by means of a long pole, with an example of the goods tied to the end and held aloft.

After the frenetic activity of the market, the boat takes us along shady canals to An Binh island, where we stop for lunch. We cruise along the river, just absorbing the sights and sounds of life on the Mekong. It is like the back waters of Kerala, except that life has a faster pace here in Vietnam, even on the river. Lunch is a feast of fresh vegetables and Mekong fish followed by generous heaps of tropical fruit. Sitting at our table is an Australian couple. We introduce ourselves. Their names are Anthony and Emma and it is the start of a beautiful friendship. They have been travelling for around the same time as us and the rest of their route is likely to coincide with ours, as far as Australia, so we spend a pleasant hour telling travellers tales over lunch. I notice Anthony's appetite is a good match for Bill's. 'Man, this fish is good. It's a bit like the reef fish I've had back home,' he says, polishing off the last of the fish.

After lunch we are encouraged to take a bike ride round the island, to see the orchards and gardens. The only problem being that the bikes are pretty delapidated—Bill's bike has no brakes and the saddle is too high on mine, and can't be adjusted, so we wobble gingerly up and down the sandy path for a few minutes before giving up and going back to wait for the boat.

Back in the boat, we head off to visit some of the cottage industries of the delta area. The first stop is a place where they make rice paper. We all crowd into a wooden hut where a woman is ladling a paste of ground rice cooked up with water from a big metal pot onto a cloth stretched over a fire of burning rice husks. When the paste mixture has solidified enough, she peels it off the cloth and puts it on a drying rack of woven reeds to finish drying in the sun. Inevitably, the paper is round, since this is the easiest shape to make with a sweep of the ladle. I am thinking, 'How are they going to write on that?' So I pipe up and ask the guide, 'Excuse me how do they make the paper square?'

There is a moment when the world seems to pause and go quiet. As soon as the words leave my mouth I realise what a twit I have been. I see Ems and Ant wince and try to stifle giggles. The guide looks at me, with his head on one side and a puzzled look on his face. 'He shrugs his head and says, 'They don't.'

What I hadn't appreciated was that the paper is used to make spring rolls and other Vietnamese delicacies, so obviously they don't write on it and it doesn't need to be square. It is actually a relief when everyone starts laughing—yeah, yeah of course I was joking!

There are several other stops to see local people making things like puffed rice and coconut candy. Everything is done on a very small scale in people's houses. I like the way the candies are wrapped in edible rice paper—very sensible and eco-friendly—but I don't ask any more questions.

We visit the vast market in Vinh Long City. Much of the market is in echoing covered halls where aisle upon aisle of stalls provide every item you could ever wish to buy and many that you wouldn't dream of buying. There are baskets of ducklings, some still hatching out, trays of frogs tied by one leg and busy trying to escape, coils of snakes writhing over each other, turtles, chickens, eels and pigs. The animals seem to sense that death is imminent and are very distressed. The cacophony of noise and smells and chatter combines to make me feel quite queasy and I have to escape outside, where the vibrant array of vegetables, fruits and flowers is more wholesome.

Back in Saigon, we meet our new friends Ant and Ems to have supper at Café 333 on Ðe Tham Street, just around the corner from our hotel, a little gem that we discovered last night. Did I mention how fantastic the Vietnamese food is? Well we thought Thai food was good until we came here. We tuck in with added enthusiasm, having just seen the delta garden where much of this produce has come from. Our new favourites include mini veggie spring rolls, deep fried so they are hot and crispy and then dipped in delicious aromatic sauce; creamy coconut curry called Ca Ry Chay; rice noodle soup full of fresh vegetables and served with piles of herbs like mint and beansprouts, which you can add to make it even more healthy and nutritious; sour soup made with tamarind and served with lots of healthy veg again; light flaky baguettes made with manioc flour, so they're really low in gluten and I can eat them without getting bloated; and the coffee—WOW the coffee! It is the best we've had since we started travelling. They drink it very strong here and freshly filtered at the table through little individual metal filters that sit on top of your cup. Its flavour is so rich and full it almost tastes like chocolate. You can have it black, or white with condensed milk, which makes it taste like Baileys—yum. The Vietnamese call it 'talking coffee' because it takes a while to come through the filter, giving you time for a good old natter. It's a favourite thing for young couples to drink. They can gaze into each others eyes to the sound of the delicious dribble of the coffee coming through. I had noticed that the Vietnamese people seem to get up very early, work very hard and go to bed late. I couldn't understand how they do it until I tried the coffee—it keeps you going for hours. Anyhow, it seems that the crispy spring rolls are a favourite with Anthony and Emma too and we come up with a points scoring system for the quality of all future restaurants, based on the spring rolls. Obviously, the Café 333 spring rolls are the gold standard, scoring a perfect ten.

So we make the most of the talking coffee to get to know our new best friends a bit better. Tall and slim, Ant has a shock of surfy type beach blond hair. We are to find out later that Ant is very particular about his hair and cuts it himself because he doesn't trust anyone else to do it—a fact which Bill finds most bizarre. He has bags of energy and chats away non-stop, with an opinion and a theory about everything. He gets very animated about his favourite topics, leading Bill to nickname him Ants in his Pants. Emma is equally chatty but has to wait for her chance when Ant pauses to draw breath. Emma's trademark is a little beanie sun-hat, which she always wears pulled down low over her eyes. To my mind, the brim is a little too narrow to keep the sun off either your face or your neck. I usually plump for a much wider brim for my own hats, but they tend to wilt in this heat and humidity, making me look faintly ridiculous, while Ems looks very trendy in her slightly impractical chapeau. It is perhaps this air of cool trendyness that gives the impression that Ems would be good in a crisis and I bet she has had to get Ant out of a few scrapes on their travels.

As is the case with most travellers who have been on the road for a long time, they have a deck of cards with them and introduce us to what is to become our favourite way of killing time waiting for buses etc—a game of Shithead. The aim of the game is to get rid of your hand of cards as quickly as possible and there are numerous rules about which card you can put down on which. You can also play a mean attacking game by making your opponent pick up the discarded pile, using certain cards. And at the end, everyone takes great delight in saying to the loser, 'You're a shithead, you're a shithead!'

Originally we thought we would head north from Saigon as quickly as possible, but we began to realise that we needed to hear more about the Vietnam war in order to understand this country. We had both been thinking of our trip to Vietnam purely as a holiday destination and trying to hide from the fact that Vietnam was a war torn country for many years and this fact has really shaped the psyche of the people here. One of the things that is quite striking here is that everyone is so young. Where are all the old people? Was a whole generation wiped out by the war? Do people die very young because of all the toxic things dropped on this country? Apparently the population has more than doubled since 1975, from 36 million to 79 million today. Over 60% of the population are under 30 and 50% under 20 years of age. Imagine that. Imagine Britain peopled by under twenty year olds. Scary thought. The country would just grind to a halt because they would be expecting their mummies to do all the real work and there wouldn't be enough mummies to do everything that needed doing. Whereas here everything seems to be working pretty efficiently and quickly.

So anyway, we are on a trip to visit the Cu Chi tunnels with Emma and Anthony today. Ant isn't feeling too good having had an ongoing stomach bug for a while. By the time we arrive at our destination in the minibus, he is a delightful shade of pale green. Fortunately we have some of our magic ayurvedic tummy medicine and a dose of that manages to get him through the day.

Our guide, Mr Binh (pronounced 'Bean,' as he proudly told us) is very knowledgeable, if a little scary and completely wired, as he chain-smokes his way through about a hundred cigarettes while we are with him. He is old enough to have been through the war and has a thorough knowledge of it, but is ambiguous about his own involvement.

'You can ask any questions you like, but not ask me what I do in war or about personal life,' he says. 'I in the Viet Minh army, that is the Uncle Ho Chi Minh army and I work as the weapons controller.' Later he tells us that he had worked with the American Navy. And he tells us that he has enormous respect for the Viet Cong—the communist revolutionaries. So basically he was a double agent.

So a quick summary of what happened, as far as I understand it:—

It all started way back with the French who took over Vietnam as a colony in the late 18th century. As is quite often the way with colonial powers, they didn't treat the Vietnamese people very well and were deeply resented. War against the French first broke out in 1880.

The most successful resistance against the French was from the communists. The first Marxist group was founded by 'Uncle' Ho Chi Minh in 1925. When World War II ended, Ho Chi Minh, whose Viet Minh forces already controlled large parts of the country, declared Vietnam independent. French efforts to reassert control led to violent confrontation and full-scale war. This led to partitioning of the country into the communist controlled North and the French/anti-communist South in 1954.

In 1960 the Viet Cong was founded to fight against the anti-communist forces in the South. At some stage, the French relinquished control of Saigon to the Americans, who sent their first force of combat troops in 1965. This was triggered by the bombing of the US Embassy by the Viet Cong. There followed ten years of bloody warfare before US-controlled Saigon surrendered to the North Vietnamese Army in April 1975 and the country was reunited.

The Viet Cong operated by gradually infiltrating villages and civilian areas in the US controlled South and then fighting the Americans on their own ground, from within. To achieve this they dug an extensive network of tunnels (about 250km in total) and spent most of the daylight hours underground. The tunnels included field hospitals, weapons factories, kitchens and dining areas, and were so well hidden that although the Americans destroyed vast areas of jungle looking for Viet Cong guerrillas, many of the tunnels remained intact and undiscovered at the end of the war. They enabled the Viet Cong to fight the Americans extremely effectively, despite being bombarded with more than 7 million tonnes of bombs, including the terrible Napalm bombs which incinerated everything in sight and Agent Orange which defoliated and poisoned all the vegetation for hundreds of kilometres for nearly 25 years, not to mention poisoning the local inhabitants and causing terrible birth defects.

The Viet Cong were incredibly resourceful and ingenious—they had an answer for everything. They had tiny tunnels so that their snipers could pop down when the Americans came, run along and pop up behind them to shoot them in the back.

Mr Binh shows us a tiny trapdoor, and demonstrates how a guerrilla would have lowered him—or herself through it into a tunnel below.

'Anyone like to try?' asks Mr Binh. But the tunnel entrance is strictly for Vietnamese hips, and no-one can fit through.

'Viet Cong very tiny people,' says Mr Binh, 'So they can fit in the small tunnels where fat Americans, who drink too much beer and eat too many hamburgers, get stuck.' He throws his head back and laughs at the memory of fat Americans getting stuck.

'You know why the Vietnamese and Chinese eyes slant up and the Western eyes slant down?' he asks. 'It because of the diet. Vietnamese and Chinese eat a lot of the rice which make it hard for you to go to the shit.' He gives us a delightful demonstration using actions to illustrate exactly what he means. 'But Americans eat a lot of the bread and the potatoes, which give you the diarrhoea.' He gives another demonstration. The moderately proportioned American couple in our party, squirm with embarrassment.

After the comedy break, he goes back to telling us about the tunnels. He tells us that the network had three different levels, complete with underground kitchens, hospitals and meeting rooms, in fact everything needed for the Viet Cong to live underground for long periods of time.

'Viet Cong very clever people. They think up many ways to fool Americans. They collect the pieces of American bombs and the weapons, and they make them into the new weapons and the traps to catch the US soldier.' He shows us many vicious looking booby traps.

'They collect other things belonging to Americans and spread them around to confuse the tracker dogs. They also catch the tracker dogs and eat them. They hide the smoke coming from the underground kitchens, and let it out far away from kitchen, so when the American see this, they drop bomb in the wrong place. They put the sandals on the feet backwards and so American tries to follow footprints and thinks Viet Cong going the other way. Very, very clever.'

Further on there are wider tunnel entrances, so we have a go at crawling through about 60 metres of tunnel. I thought it would be great fun, and quite easy. But soon break out it in a profuse sweat from struggling along in the cramped conditions. I emerge at the other end, having been bitten several times by giant evil mosquitoes, feeling claustrophobic and panicky.

It is easy to see why the Americans never infiltrated the tunnels. It must have been pretty grim for the Viet Cong men and women, but with very limited resources, such as ammunition, compared to the American forces, their hide-and-seek tactics were a major factor in their victory. I came away from the trip with a tremendous admiration for the Vietnamese—their ingenuity, their resourcefulness and the way in which they have got their country back on its feet within 25 years, despite tremendous hardship.

As part of the Cu Chi experience, you can pay some money and shoot a few rounds from a kalashnikov or M16 on the firing range. Ant has a go. Mr Binh, who must have done this tour a thousand times, flinches every time he hears a gun go off.

Mr Binh told us that Vietnam was largely closed to trading with the West due to a US embargo that was lifted in 1995 by Bill Clinton. He tells us that within 2 hours of the announcement of the end of the embargo, everyone in Vietnam had a can of Pepsi in their hands (it seems Coca Cola was a little too slow off the mark).

After the Cu Chi tunnel visit, we want to further our education of the country's history, so we go to the war museum. After about 20 minutes of looking at pictures of brutality and seeing a video about the deadly effects of Agent Orange, we come away feeling utterly traumatised.

There is much in the news at the moment about President Bush's intention to bomb Iraq. It makes me really angry. It will solve nothing and cause misery, destruction and the deaths of thousands of innocent civilians.

In the evening we are in need of cheering up and decide on a pleasant stroll down to the river in search of somewhere to have some dinner. But we haven't bargained on such a hair-raising journey, trying to cross the busy roads. The thing about crossing the road in Saigon is that around 95% of the vehicles on the road are motorbikes. The number of people owning motorbikes has mushroomed in the last five years. There are already 2 million motorbikes in Saigon alone, and another 1,000 are registered every day. And they are all ridden by twenty year olds. So the traffic doesn't come at you from two neat lanes going in opposite directions, it comes at you twelve deep and all travelling at differing angles. There is never a gap in the traffic of more than a split second. So it is too much for the brain to compute a safe passage across the road. We stand on the pavement paralysed with fear, as if we are about to attempt to cross a raging river full of crocodiles.

We watch to see how the locals do it. The technique seems to be to step out and just keep walking at a slow steady pace, eyes fixed immovably on the goal of the pavement on the other side. Hesitate for just a moment and you are lost, because you will only confuse the riders of the motorbikes swerving all around you and are sure to cause a pile up. Eventually we pluck up the courage to step out, committing ourselves to certain death. 'Keep going, keep going, eyes straight ahead,' encourages Bill. Somehow, miraculously, we arrive at the other side still alive, breathing heavily and sweating profusely, but with that elated feeling when you know you have just cheated death and can make an arrogant hand gesture at the Grim Reaper.

Trembling from the ordeal and half choked by pollution, we finally arrive at the river, to find that there is only one decent looking riverside restaurant and that is just closing. But there are lots of brightly lit boats in the shape of fish going up and down. They all have restaurants, loud music, lots of customers, many of which are performing karaoke numbers.

Bill says, 'It might be a laugh to have dinner on one of those fish boat things.' So we are about to board, until we see the strained faces of most of the tourists who are all trying to get off. 'Maybe not,' he says. We give up on this disastrous mission and catch a cab back to our hotel. We have dinner again in Café 333.

Sitting in the corner of our café is a sad looking American man, obviously a Vietnam Vet, drowning his sorrows in beer and reliving a past which he cannot resolve or forget. The locals politely ignore him, and once he is drunk enough the barman starts charging him double for each drink. This is a sight to be seen in many of the bars and cafés in Saigon. Although he is a tormented soul, it strikes me as incredibly selfish to do this in the country where he and his colleagues' actions have caused so much misery to the inhabitants.

Gazing onto the street from the café, I observe two phenomena which I do not understand. The first is a number of people, often young lads of around 12, walking about rhythmically clinking a piece of metal with a stick. The other is a young man riding a bicycle and shaking a small stick with cymbals on the end of it. They seem to be advertising some kind of service, but I cannot work out what. On further enquiry, I find out that one service is quite innocent and the other, ahem, not so innocent—it is the second time I've had a red face from asking questions in the last couple of days. Apparently the boys clinking the metal are selling noodle soup from their carts nearby and the man on the bicycle is offering 'massages'—best not to get the two mixed up.

Today we set off for Dalat in the Lang Bien Highlands. We have bought an 'Open Tour' ticket which allows you to stop off at various places en-route to Hanoi in the North. You can stay as long as you like at each stop and then just phone up to book the next leg of your journey. They try to make it sound more attractive by adding in some scenic places that you can stop along the way, but in reality they only stop at the major towns, with the exception of the odd restaurant stop where they get commission for bringing in customers.

We get on the same bus as our Australian friends, Emma and Anthony, thinking that we can go on a few trips with them. Unfortunately, poor Ant is suffering from a bad case of fruity poopy and has to rest up for a while.

The bus drops us off outside the Dreams Hotel, of which we are highly suspicious, but after a quick reccy round town it does seem to be the nicest place and good value at $10 per room including breakfast and free Internet access.

Whilst checking in, we are approached by a couple of characters who run motorbike tours—Tom and Mr Lulu. One of the things we really want to do in Vietnam is to spend some time in the National Park, and cross the Central Highlands. We had a romantic notion of following the old caravan route which crosses this region, joining the ancient Champa capitals of Da Nang with those at Saigon. The route is nearly 500 miles (800 kilometres) long and would take six to eight days to cover. In many places, the roads are in very poor condition and there is still a lot of unexploded ordinance. It seems it is pretty difficult to get off the well-trodden tourist trail here, which mostly follows the coast. So when Mr Lulu describes a tour covering the route we wanted, it seems a perfect way to do it. But we have a lot of reservations. We will be sitting on the back of their bikes—are they safe drivers and can they handle the poor condition of the roads? Can my bottom cope with 6 days on the back of a motorbike on poor roads? It is also a huge chunk of our budget and a lot of our time in Vietnam.

Mr Lulu is quite a pushy salesman, which almost puts us off altogether, so we tell him we want to go away and think about it for a while. We agonise over the decision.

'It could be the adventure of a lifetime,' says Bill.

'On the other hand it could be a terrible waste of time and money,' I say.

'Or worse, it could be dangerous—they could steel all our money and leave us dead in the jungle somewhere,' says Bill.

'Oh, I hadn't thought of that,' I say.

'My gut instinct is to say lets go for it. We may never get the chance again,' says Bill.

'Yes, lets do it! I'm hungry for adventure after spending so much time in touristy places since leaving India. This looks like being our best chance of seeing the 'real Vietnam',' I say.

'Great. Decision made,' says Bill.

So we pay our $280 deposit (50% of the total upfront, which does not include food or accommodation) and go to bed in a state of nervous trepidation.

We are up bright and early and after a breakfast of crusty baguettes and strong coffee, we don our helmets and set off with trembling legs.

Dalat is one of the highest places in Vietnam at about 1500m. Renowned for its verdant rolling valleys, lakes and waterfalls, Dalat is often called 'The City of Eternal Spring.' We have also heard it described as the 'City of Kitsch Gone Mad'. From swan paddleboats to Vietnamese dressed as cowboys, to giant stuffed animals, Dalat has it all. Writing about one of the nearby parks, a friend said, 'Despite the giant cement Adam and Eve sculptures, the vistas and scenery were quite lovely.' So we are not too sad to be heading off so soon without exploring our immediate surroundings.

This morning it is sunny, but pleasantly cool. We board our motorbikes. I sit behind Mr Lulu and Bill sits behind Tom. Having ridden an old Enfield motorbike from Goa across half of India and up into the Himalayas on a previous trip, it is a leap of faith for Bill to put his trust in this stranger. In my case, ignorance is bliss.

On our way out of Dalat we drive through mile upon mile of pine forest. There is a strange, unnatural feeling to this landscape. 'Mr Lulu, are these the trees that you would find naturally here, or has someone planted them?' I ask.

'No Anna, French people like to come on holiday here 100 years ago. They want this place look like France, so they can feel at home, so they plant them. Now government won't let no-one cut them down. Same, same, but different,' he says, laughing at his own joke.

I ponder on how much it must have changed the ecosystem, since nothing else will grow under the pine trees and there is no ground cover for the animals. It feels so sterile. It makes me feel very sad.

We arrive at the Lake of Sighs—a natural lake enlarged by the French and now a holiday spot popular with honeymooners. It is a pretty place, but oh, so unnatural. It is the Dolly Parton of holiday spots. Apparently, it is a 'great place to rent horses and ride the trails around the lake, accompanied by guides dressed as cowboys'. I am starting to feel disheartened. Is this the 'real Vietnam' we paid so much money to come and see?

Our next stop is the Chicken Village, so called because of the giant concrete chicken that towers over it. The village is home to people who are expert weavers and have a co-operative making traditional designs from silk and cotton. The story of the chicken is that there were two star-crossed lovers that wanted to marry. In the tribe's matriarchal society, the woman who wishes to marry has to give a gift to the man's family. This girl was very poor and the dowry demanded by the boy's family was beyond her reach and she was very sad. Finally, the boy's family relented and agreed that they could marry if the girl gave them one chicken. She went away happy to find a chicken in the forest. But sadly she fell sick and died before they could marry. The boy was heartbroken and said that he could not live without her, so he killed himself. And so, the giant concrete chicken was made in memory of the two tragic lovers.

When we arrive, the women from the village all rush out and want to show me their weaving. Mr Lulu warns me not to buy anything, because, 'It is overpriced and not "real"'.

So I just have a look. The women are very sweet. One lady speaks good English. She spends time telling me how they dye and weave the fabric, explaining the meaning of the different designs. Another lady gives me tea whilst we are talking. This is usually a ploy to make you feel obliged to buy something, so when the demonstration is over, I politely decline to buy anything and offer to pay for the tea.

'No problem,' says the lady with a sweet smile as she waves away the money I proffer for the tea.

Perhaps I have made a mistake. The work seems of very high quality and £4 seems a reasonable price for a beautiful hand-woven silk shawl. But it is too late now. We are on our way again.

Back on the bikes and the sun is getting very hot. I am wearing a T-shirt and despite wearing suncream, I can feel my arms burning. My head is being gently boiled inside the helmet.

We stop a few times to see how different crops are grown—ear-shaped mushrooms in dark poly tunnels, tea, coffee, silk worms. Tom is very knowledgeable about the crops and the market in Vietnam.

Vietnam is still a communist country, which seems to have its pros and cons for the people. Perhaps it is the communist ethic that has helped everyone work together to achieve the degree of economic success. I was really surprised to find out that Vietnam is the second highest exporter of coffee in the world, after Brazil, and the fourth highest exporter of rubber.

The communist regime is not completely strict, allowing some private enterprise and largely allowing people to get on with their lives. Everywhere we went, we saw that people had spread coffee beans out to dry on plastic sheets outside there houses. The beans are varying shades, depending how dry they are from green, to orange, through red to brown. So many people are making little bits of money on the side through small crops of coffee. However, the government does set the prices that the farmers get for their crops and then sells them on at a huge profit and they do have a nasty habit of waking everyone up at 5.30am with loudspeaker announcements about birth control and other government propaganda.

We pass a coffee plantation and stop at the tea plantation next door. Bill is amazed. 'So they are growing tea right next door to the field where they are growing coffee? I wouldn't have believed you could do that if I hadn't seen it with my own eyes.'

'Why?' I ask. It has not occurred to me that there is anything unusual in this.

'Well they need completely different growing conditions. They both like a bit of altitude, but coffee likes it really humid while tea likes it cooler and drier.'

'Yes, the coffee here is very good—best in the world, but the tea maybe not highest quality, but still good,' says Tom.

'Well, Vietnam must have a unique climate and environment for them to grow at all like this,' says Bill.

Finally, feeling hot and burnt, we stop for lunch. It is a great relief to sit in the shade and drink iced tea. All morning, the road has been gradually climbing. Now we are sitting high in the hills, with a 180 degree view and a cooling breeze. We have driven away from the manufactured French pine forest and are looking out over hills covered with native jungle. But there are great swathes of bare hillside, which can only support very poor grasses, disfigured by broken tree stumps dotted here and there.

Tom tells us, 'This because of Napalm bombs and Agent Orange. For first 10 years after Americans spray Agent Orange, nothing grows and hillsides are totally bare. After this, grasses start to grow. Now, after 25 years, just a few trees start to grow. Is very, very terrible.'

Bill points at the defoliated hillside, 'These grasses are rubbish—really tough and coarse. Nothing will eat them. I bet even a goat would prefer to chew on a paper bag than tackle that stuff.'

Bill with Tom and Lulu

After lunch we drive higher into the hills. We stop at a remote village of the Mai people. They look very different to the average Vietnamese—taller and darker skinned with longer faces. They could almost be Indian. The village is very poor and people wear nothing but grubby rags. An atmosphere of melancholy hangs over the village. Mr Lulu tells us they used to like to be naked, but now the government makes them wear clothes. Until 10 years ago, they worshipped the spirits of the forest, but recently they have been converted to Christianity by missionaries.

Back in Dalat before we left for the trip, I asked Mr Lulu if we should buy some gifts for the people we were going to visit. He told me to buy sweets and pens and paper for the children, and cigarettes for the adults. I was not happy about the sweets and cigarettes and asked if it would not be better to buy some proper food—rice or tea—if they are poor. He said no. It soon becomes apparent why. Lulu stands in the middle of the village calling out, 'Come and get your sweeties.'

Of course all the children come running. The adults clearly are not interested in talking to us. I can't say I blame them. 'Take a picture, take a picture,' says Lulu, as the children jump up to try and grab the sweets from him.

I feel like a voyeur peeping into these people's lives and don't want a picture to remind me of this. I am having serious second thoughts about this trip.

We are back on the bikes now. The road has deteriorated into a dirt track. It is pretty rough on my backside and I wonder despondently how much further we have to go in these conditions. Now the heavens have opened and I am soon drenched to my knickers. The deeply rutted road has become a river of mud, with knee-deep puddles. It is very slippery and dangerous. We are both pretty scared. The potential for falling off and getting seriously hurt is very high. We cover around 10km, which takes forever in these conditions, all the while, clinging on desperately and praying that we do not have a nasty accident.

Although it is pretty foolhardy of Tom and Lulu to take us on this road in the rainy season, I have to say that I am quite impressed with their driving skills to get us safely through this treacherous section. It's just as well because we really are in the middle of nowhere, with no means of phoning for help. We haven't seen so much as a grass hut since we left the Mai village.

If it is possible, the road seems to have got even worse. Bill looks round at me. 'This is too dangerous to ride. We better get off and walk for a bit.' We trudge along, soaked and plastered in mud, but making faster progress than Tom and Lulu who are now pushing the bikes. Up ahead there is a little wooden hut. A man and a woman come out to look at us. They motion for us to come into their hut to shelter. It is very tempting. Just at this point, Tom and Lulu come round the corner, having freed their motorbikes from the mud, so we don't take them up on their kind offer of hospitality. It is a shame. This is perhaps the first genuine interaction we have had with Vietnamese people who are not involved in the tourist industry. But we are anxious to crack on because we do not want to get stranded in the dark.

Finally we are back on good roads again. Lulu stops at a viewpoint. 'Good place to take picture,' he says. But we look out on a wall of rain, which doesn't make the best photo opportunity.

After another half hour of driving, the rain starts to ease. The sun comes out and we start to dry off. We stop at a village of the Chinh people. They are slightly better off and more cheerful than the Mai people. Some of the children from this village go to school, so we give them pens and paper, which I feel slightly less guilty about than the sweets and cigarettes. The children seem to know the drill well enough. When they saw us coming they shouted, 'Westerners, Westerners,' and gather round excitedly to receive their gifts.

We get back on the bikes and set off. We are travelling through jungle-covered hills, with here and there an isolated bamboo hut and a few fields of crops. One scene etches itself on my mind like a beautiful photo. We are driving through the most gorgeous lush valley. To the right of the road is a wooden house and in front of the house is a pond. Standing thigh deep in the water is a handsome young man, bare-chested, with long dark hair. He is fishing. As we pass, he looks up at me and gives me a radiant smile. He waves and shouts, 'Hello!' I wave and shout back. For a brief moment I daydream about living in such an idyllic place.

We have several more encounters like that with people who obviously rarely see Western tourists riding past on motorbikes. Lots of waving and smiling from people as we pass does much to cheer me up after the mud bath ordeal and the guilt of the candy hand-outs.

Thatched house and paddy field

By the time we arrive at Lak Lake, out destination for the night, it is well after dark. Lulu takes us straight to his mate's shop where he tries to get us to buy some local weaving. It is much inferior to the craft we saw at Chicken Village and about the same price. I feel very annoyed with him for stopping me buying there. I bet he is getting commission here. At least the Chicken village was a co-operative and the whole village would have benefited from the sale.

We are supposed to be staying in a traditional wooden long house of the Hmong people, but something has gone wrong and Lulu says we will be staying in a guesthouse nearby. Far from being disappointed about being deprived of our ethnic experience, I am greatly relieved. I am wet, drenched in mud, chilled and exhausted. All I want to do is have a hot shower, change into clean clothes in the privacy of my own room and eat food that I vaguely recognise. Am I so wrong to want the softness of a sprung bed with sheets, rather than to sleep on the floor under a hand-woven blanket and be lulled to sleep by the snores and farts of the twenty other occupants and the snuffling and aroma of the pot-bellied pigs under the hut? Fortunately, the guesthouse fulfilled all my shallow desires most adequately.

'Bill what do you think of the trip so far? Are you having the time of your life, or are you feeling a bit fed up with it like me? What would you think about cutting the trip short?' I am dreading him saying that he is having the most fantastic time and that he would be terribly disappointed not to continue.

'Well, my arse is hurting and my neck is burnt. We haven't had an accident yet, but we've had a few near ones. And I'm not too impressed with the way Lulu handles the visits to the minority villages. I'd like to give it one more day and then if it doesn't improve, we could bail out and go to Nha Trang on the coast instead of crossing the Central Highlands to Kon Thom.'

'Oh, I'm really glad you feel the same way. That sounds like a good plan.'

We set off back to Lak village and breakfast at a café beside the Lake. There is still a veil of fine mist over the lake, and my eyes are filled with dreamy images of people fishing from dug out canoes, or collecting lake weed to feed to their pot-bellied pigs, which snuffle and scamper among the Hmong tribal long houses of the village. Outside the houses, rice is spread to dry in the sun. There are many little piglets, whose favourite pastime is stealing the rice. The children's job is to chase the piglets off the rice, sending the chickens clucking and squawking away at the same time.

Lulu has arranged a boat ride across the lake to another Hmong village. The boat is driven by 'Mr Crazy Man,' who laughs a lot and wears a ladies hat, trimmed with lace and a big bow. Well, you'd need a sense of humour to get away with that hat.

This morning, Tom has come with us and Lulu stayed behind. The atmosphere is immediately more relaxed without him. Tom has an easy way with people and when we meet the Hmong villagers, they immediately warm to him and therefore to us. He speaks their language and can translate so that we can have a laugh and a joke with them. We meet a family who say that they think we are a very nice couple and hope that we have lots of children. We meet the chief of the village, a very friendly man, who tells us about their culture and way of life. He tells us today is a day of celebration as they have finished bringing in the harvest and it was a good crop this year. We are introduced to three very happy and smiley characters—a father and his two grown up sons. They invite us into their home to drink cang (pronounced 'cung') wine, made from rice and herbs. Their home is a long wooden building on stilts with a thatched roof, much like all the other buildings in the village. We climb a roughly hewn log balanced against the verandah. It has a few notches chopped into it to act as steps.

We step into the dimly lit interior of the house. It is 10.30 am and they are already in full swing celebrating the gathering of the harvest, lovingly patting their full sacks of grain. They proffer a bamboo pot with a long bamboo straw. They tell us that the fermented rice husks are still in the mixture, so you have to make sure that the end of the bamboo is below the flotsam, so you don't get a mouthful of bits. I expected it to be some disgusting brew that you have to swallow down just to be polite, but am pleasantly surprised to find it reminiscent of a very dry Sauvignon Blanc with smokey overtones. I could get quite a liking for it. It certainly seems to have put our three hosts in a happy mood. There is much mutual congratulating going on—we congratulate them on their harvest and they congratulate us on generally being the sort of people they like the look of and are happy to have a drink with.

Tom tells us, 'Cang wine very special. You can drink all day and all night and in the morning no headache and no sick.' I'm not sure I believe him, but I'd like to give it a go.

We leave the village with the feeling that the people here have a pretty good life—living in an idyllic setting next to the lake, making good money from their crops, having a close-knit friendly community and having enough time to spend a day or two partying whenever there is a special occasion. The young people of the community obviously think so too and are keen to uphold their culture rather than abandon it for the big city.

We are back on the bikes now. It is another very hot day and we are getting roasted. We stop in a village to look at the market. There is a mouth-watering array of bright, colourful vegetables, and a special treat in store for Billy. Tom beckons Bill over. 'I think you like this,' he says, gesturing towards a lady who is crouching over a bubbling pot of oil and fishing out deep-fried golden balls. 'Sticky rice balls—try some,' he says buying some from the lady and handing them to Bill.

'What are they like?' I ask.

'Aw, yum,' says Bill in raptures. 'Deep-fried sweet things—need I say more? I think they've got coconut milk in them or something that makes them sweet. They're the Vietnamese equivalent of deep-fried Mars Bars.'

We have lunch in Buon Ma Thuot, the capital of Dak Lak Province and a regional centre for trading Vietnam's great coffee. One positive thing about this trip is that Tom and Lulu really love their food and they certainly know where the good restaurants and cafés are. With their local knowledge, we get to eat in the places where all the locals choose to go and not just the tourists. They introduce us to a staple of the Vietnamese diet, beef noodle soup, known as *pho bo* (pronounced like fur balls without the 'lls'). It is thin and almost clear like consommé, with wafer thin slices of the most tender and juicy beef. It comes with a plate heaped with crisp, fresh leafy green vegetables and herbs.

'What are these?' I ask Lulu.

'Name is *rao wa* which mean "outside vegetables",' says Lulu, picking up a bunch of vegetables with his chopsticks and putting them into his soup. 'You put how many you like in your soup.'

A bowl of *pho bo* feels extremely satisfying and nutritious. 'I love this fur balls. I'm going to have it every day from now on with plenty of outside vegetables,' says Bill.

Bon Ma Thuot was an American base from 1968 to 1972. As we are leaving the centre of town, we pass a striking sculpture commemorating the war. It is a star burst of steel representing the fireballs created by Napalm and a Vietnamese soldier runs from the centre of the incendiary.

We set off again and soon we're travelling through unspoilt countryside, on the way to Dray Sap falls. We had hoped this trip was going to be the Vietnamese equivalent of our Sri Lankan tour with Captain Bandara, but it suddenly strikes me that in all the time we have spent in Vietnam, we haven't seen a single wild animal, not even a squirrel. I ask

Lulu about this. 'Because Agent Orange and because tribe people hunt too much. All animals run over border to Laos and Cambodia,' he says.

We check into a bungalow where we are to stay the night, but just as we are about to go to the falls, there is a tremendous downpour of rain and we decide to delay leaving until the rain stops. On the way, a motorbike passes us with two poor piggies crammed into the smallest of metal crates and strapped to each side of the bike, like a couple of porky panniers. I cannot understand why the pigs seem so docile and are not squealing and struggling, and I cannot imagine how anyone could squeeze a regular pig into such a small space without it complaining greatly. It seems very cruel. Later, Bill tells me that he's heard they blow cannabis up their snouts to get them so dopey.

We park the bikes and have a short walk through jungle to reach the falls. The falls, although not terribly high are still an impressive sight as millions of gallons of water thunder over their wide horseshoe of rock. We sit beside them for a while, mesmerised by the hypnotic power of the water. We are also impressed by Tom's knowledge of the vegetation in the surrounding jungle. While in the army, he learned all the edible plants, so that he could survive in the jungle if necessary. He breaks off a heart shaped leaf and shows us the sap that oozes from the broken stem. 'See, this juice white,' he says. 'No good to eat. Anything with white juice could be poison.'

Back at the bungalow, we both feel tetchy and overheated. I raise the subject of whether to cut the trip short.

'Well today's been a bit better. I enjoyed this morning at the lake and meeting the people in the village, especially those fellas with the cang wine. But I won't be upset if you say you want to bail. My neck is fried and it looks like it's going to be the same everyday—roasted for three quarters of the day and soaked for the other. There's a lot of boys stuff, revving up and overtaking each other between Lulu and Tom which is getting right on my nerves too.'

'Yes, there's something about Lulu that makes me feel faintly queasy. I don't trust him an inch. Tom's nice though—you got the better deal sitting on his motorbike. But tomorrow's going to be the hardest day. We've got a lot more hours of driving and I don't think I've really got the stomach for another four days on the back of a bike.'

'So there it is then—decision made. We bail,' says Bill.

I am still wincing about the amount of money the trip is costing. 'But it's all right because we can use our open tour bus tickets,' I say, trying to comfort myself a little from the blow of the decision—I've always hated admitting defeat.

Bill's looking at his feet and mumbling something.

'What are you trying to tell me Bill?'

'We haven't got the tickets anymore,' he says.

'What? Why not?'

'I gave them away to the nice lady at the Dreams Hotel in Dalat.'

'Oh, you idiot! What on earth did you go and do that for?'

'I told her we would be going on the motorbike tour and she said 'Oh, so you won't need your tickets now. Why don't you give them to me?'

'I bet she did, and she's just gone and sold them on to someone else, and we're going to have to fork out to buy some more, when we've already spent a fortune on this tour. I don't believe how stupid you can be sometimes.'

'Don't shout at me.'

'Well you deserve it for being so silly.'

With that, Bill storms into the bathroom and locks the door, leaving me fuming with no-one to shout at. I try shouting through the bathroom door, but he turns the shower on really fast to drown out the sound of my voice. He is in there for a very long time.

Eventually I start to calm down. I find the leaflet with the bus ticket prices amongst our luggage. When I realise that a ticket from Nha Trang to Hanoi will cost less than £10 pounds, I start to think that it doesn't seem worth falling out with the man I love over such a small amount. But the row is an indicator of how tense, exhausted and overheated we are both feeling. Sensing that my mood has changed, Bill comes out of the bathroom at last.

'You've been a very naughty boy,' I say, giving him a hug.

'I know, I'm sorry.'

'And I'm sorry for shouting at you.'

That night at dinner we break the news to Lulu and Tom. There is a moment's quiet pause as Lulu thinks about what we have just said, then to our relief he says, 'No problem. Tomorrow we take you to Nha Trang.'

Today we take a swift road to Nha Trang on the coast. It is heartbreaking to see that for 20km there is a swathe on either side of this road where the hillsides are still completely defoliated by Agent Orange. Tom tells us that during the war, Buon Ma Thuot was an American base. 'They bring lorries with food and weapons along this road from the coast,' he says. 'They spray Agent Orange so Viet Cong cannot hide in the jungle and ambush lorries.'

To say thank you for the trip and no hard feelings about cutting it short, we offer to take Tom and Lulu out for a meal in the evening. Lulu suggests we go to a seafood restaurant which he knows is good. That is fine with us as we both love seafood. The waiter brings the menu and after a quick glance, Lulu orders lobster—the most expensive thing on the menu. Tom looks embarrassed and orders fish and chips. Before we have even finished our starters, Lulu has turned his back on our table and is chatting to two girls on the next table, trying to sell them a motorbike tour. I guess I can't completely blame him because we did bail early, but it does seem a bit rude. Anyhow, we don't really care as we would much rather talk to Tom, who is looking distinctly uncomfortable about Lulu's behaviour. He tells us he doesn't mind going home early because he is missing his wife and family, as he always does on these trips.

* * *

We are staying at the Sao Mai hotel in Nha Trang. The staff are lovely here and the room rates are very reasonable. Our room is spacious and has air con, which is greatly needed as it is stifling hot here. But apart from that, Nha Trang is not a nice place. It is a big city, with nothing in particular to commend it. We had been looking forward to spending some time on the beach, which is beautiful, but we can't swim here because the monsoon makes the sea too dangerous at this time of the year. The usually blue and beautiful waters are murky and choppy. There aren't that many tourists this time of year, which sends the swarms of sales touts into a feeding frenzy towards us. It makes the beach feel quite threatening. So we take the night bus to Hoi An, where we have arranged to meet up with Ant and Ems.

We arrived in Hoi An early this morning, after a sleepless and uncomfortable night. The bus seats didn't recline and the road was dreadfully pot-holed and bumpy. You would have thought that after 5 months of travelling we would have learnt our lesson by now that night buses are never a good idea.

But I am glad to be here. Hoi An is beautiful—narrow streets wind through a mixture of charming old colonial buildings and ancient Chinese pagoda style houses, set beside the Thu Bon river. The town first rose to prominence as a seaport in the second century AD, when it was the principal port for the Hindu Champa Kingdom. And it enjoyed a second wave of prosperity in the 16th century when a wave of Chinese and Japanese settlers established Hoi An as a port-of-call on the China-India trade route. The homes of the rich Chinese merchants are still perfectly preserved and in many cases still owned by the same families, handed down through the generations.

European merchants soon discovered Hoi An and came from Portugal, Spain, France, Holland and Britain, to buy high quality silk, lacquer, herbal medicines, mother of pearl, porcelain and other exotic merchandise. So Hoi An flourished as one of South East Asia's most important ports until the 19th century when the Thu Bon river silted up and ships could no longer navigate up from the sea. But Hoi An has managed to preserve its reputation as a world class place to buy exotic things and I am looking forward to delving into this shopper's paradise, once the monsoon rain abates.

Well, Hoi An really is the shopper's paradise to beat all shoppers' paradises. The wonderful shops, set among charming architecture are liberally interspersed with cafés serving delicious food and the best coffee to revive you between shopping sprees. And the centre is nice and compact, so that you can walk from one end to the other in less than 15 minutes—well you could if you could manage not to be distracted by row upon row of shops selling the most wonderful colourful shoes, bags, clothes and other delights. Vietnamese silk is a speciality here. It comes in every iridescent jewel shade of purple, pink, green, red, orange, gold, blue and turquoise, that you can imagine. Every other shop is a tailor's shop and you can have exquisite clothes, immaculately tailored to your exact shape and size for unbelievably cheap prices, ready in a matter of hours. And if silk isn't your thing, you can take your pick of any fabric from cashmere to corduroy. A full-length cashmere coat, custom made to your preference, can be yours for as little as $25.

As soon as the rain abated, I got out there, partaking in some major retail therapy. My purchases include an Au Dai in purple shot silk, which I thought would make a beautiful going-away outfit for after the wedding, two beautifully tailored and fitted sun-tops, some gorgeous greeny/blue silk for Mum's wedding outfit, a collection of silk scarves and a silk sleeping bag. Those little silkworms have been busy keeping me supplied.

Bill has been extremely patient in helping me choose the fabric, but we have had to have frequent café stops to keep him going. The food in Hoi An is even more delicious than in the rest of Vietnam and Bill has been happily working his way through the list of local specialities, most of which are dumpling related.

'I like a good dumpling,' says Bill. But an unfortunate side-effect of all this good food is that Bill is beginning to resemble a dumpling, earning him the nickname of 'Billy Tum Tum.'

We are walking down one of the streets in central Hoi An when we spot a couple of characters standing head and shoulders above the crowd of dark heads and pointy straw hats—one blond fluffy bonse and one with a little beanie sun hat pulled low over her eyes. They spot us and yell down the street,

'Hey Guys!'

We rush over and greet them with the usual thing travellers want to know about—'Hi you two, how was your trip here? And where are you staying?'

'Oh man, it absolutely sucked,' says Ant.

'The big bus had apparently broken down, so we had to go the 13 hours in a minibus with six other travellers and the two drivers ... No leg room and very few of those scenic stops that they promise you!' say Ems. 'As usual, we got dropped off at the company hotel. It was 8pm at night and a bit rainy so we just stayed there. But it's a really clean, big room for US$8 with a TV, fridge and a pretty big bathroom.'

'We're hanging to hear about the Highlands trip,' says Ant. 'Why don't we go for a beer and a catch up.' So we step into one of the many lovely cafés on the streets of Hoi An. The boys are soon quaffing ale and reminiscing, but we girls don't want to waste too much valuable shopping time and soon decide to part company and meet up later.

Emma seems to be doing even better than me. She has ordered her entire wardrobe for the coming winter to be tailored for her and shipped back to Australia and Ant has already been measured up for two suits for work back home. 'Anna, have you found the shops that make hand-made shoes yet?' gushes Emma. 'They're dirt cheap and SO cute. I need you to come and help me decide between two different styles.'

'Oh, I love handmade shoe shops—it would be a pleasure. It's so good to have a girl to shop with—boys just don't have the stamina for a really good shopping spree.' And off we happily go.

And the afternoon is to reveal yet further delights of this wonderful town. I am approached by some very persuasive Vietnamese ladies who don't need to twist my arm too much to get me to book an afternoon of pampering involving a hair wash, facial massage and leg wax at Madame Lee's parlour.

The waxing is quite incredible—with a loop of cotton twisted backwards and forwards between her thumb and forefinger, Madame Lee's assistant deftly manages to pluck out all my leg hairs in 10 minutes flat—I am very impressed.

Then I am treated to a hair wash with Madame Lee herself, a very kindly, clucky mother hen kind of lady. First she washes my hair and massages my scalp with soapberry and then conditions it with tamarind and lemon, which smells divine. Then I have my facial treatment and massage, with lots of different stages of cleansers and creams slathered on, massaged in and buffed off. So by the end of it all I am cleansed and buffed to perfection with a face like a shiny red apple and the softest, swingiest hair, smelling like a summer garden. And all this pampering for 40,000 dong (about £2).

I go back to meet Bill and ask him, 'Well, what do you think?'

He tries to say something poetic about my beauty, but stumbles over his words and finishes with, 'You look great. Fancy a snog?'

* * *

Today we hire motorbikes with Emma and Anthony for a visit to the Marble Mountains. While Bill was test-driving the motorbike round the block, I was lured into the tailor's shop across the road from the hotel. The shimmering silks displayed in the window must have hypnotised me and somehow I found myself ordering more clothes. By the time Bill found me, I'd already been measured up for a pair of embroidered trousers and a silk halterneck top. Fortunately he thought it was quite funny and commended me on my sneakiness and the lady in the shop on her swiftness in measuring me and taking the order.

Ngu Hanh Son or the Marble Mountains are limestone hills with marble outcrops which rise from the coastal plain about 24km north of Hoi An. The five mountains are named after the oriental five elements—Kim Son (Mount of Metal), Moc Son (Mount of Wood), Thuy Son (Mount of Water), Hoa Son (Mount of Fire) and Tho Son (Mount of Earth). The local tourist information promises that we will enjoy the serene beauty of the natural caves, 'the native soil of heroes and scholars'. This place has been sacred since the time of the Chams, when grottoes inside the hills were turned into first Hindu and then Buddhist shrines.

It is wonderful just having the freedom to ride through the countryside at our leisure without tour guides or bus timetables. I have with me, my new prized possession—my purple plastic poncho. I purchased it after getting repeatedly soaked on the motorbike tour with Tom and Lulu. Seeing lots of sensible Vietnamese wearing ponchos on motorbikes, I realised I just had to have one. I think my poncho is wonderful—so practical, so easy to fold up and lightweight, such a beautiful colour, so completely waterproof whilst still allowing adequate ventilation. However, Bill and Ant think it is an object worthy only of ridicule. They nickname it Purple Ronnie and laugh at my devotion to it. However, halfway to the Marble Mountains, it empties down with rain, and I am oh so glad of Purple Ronnie.

Ant doesn't have any kind of rain protection at all, so we take shelter in a roadside café. Ems, who has been secretly admiring Purple Ronnie, spots a shop across the road selling plastic macs and insists on going to get one for Ant. 'Oh my God. She's not getting me that pink one,' says Ant, as Ems holds up a candy pink, slightly see-through number with a mischievous grin. 'I'll look like a giant condom.' After a little teasing she gets him a blue one, but I have to say, he still looks like a giant condom—it's the transparency that does it. His poncho doesn't have the lovely opaqueness of Purple Ronnie.

The café is full of local workmen on their morning break. They are all glued to a film about Abba on the telly, but they stop watching to have a good look at us. For some reason they think we are very funny—perhaps it is Ant in that mac.

When the rain stops we head off again and soon we arrive at the village of Hoa Hai, at the base of Marble Mountain. It is Vietnam's version of Mamallapuram, where every shop is full of marble sculptures of everything from tiny Buddhas to enormous oriental lions. A seemingly kind and friendly lady offers to show us the entrance to Marble Mountain, but we soon realise it is just a ploy to get us into her marble shop.

Having run the gauntlet of the marble shop owners and the bolshy old ladies chewing betel nut and trying to sell us incense at an extortionate price, we finally make it into the five Buddha caves. They are very atmospheric, particularly the one containing the huge standing Buddha. Deep inside this natural cavern in the mountain, the temple in the cave is beautiful, peaceful, and blissfully cool. The drapes of the Buddha's robe seem to echo the rock formation in the cave around him.

We decide we do want some incense after all, so Bill is despatched to go and do battle with the incense ladies.

'I don't want to go,' he says sheepishly.

'Why not?'

'Because they look like the three witches from Macbeth, with their stained lips and toothless gums.' We look back and their silhouetted forms against the cave entrance make them look enormous and rather scary.

'Don't be silly, man,' I say, not wanting to go myself.

'Yeah, don't be a pussy, Bill,' says Ant with a snigger.

'I'll go,' says Ems.

'No, it's all right, I'll go,' says Bill, feeling too ashamed to make Ems do what he didn't want to do.

Bill comes back shuddering and muttering, 'I'm going to have bad dreams tonight,' closely followed by one of the three witches, who has taken it upon herself to escort us around the site and show us the correct form of worship at the shrines and how many incense sticks to light at each one—very helpful, but it rather takes away from the serene atmosphere.

There is another cave entrance round the corner, which we almost missed, but I'm so glad we didn't. The cave is vast, almost as if the whole mountain is hollow. The myriad stalactites and stalagmites give the feeling that we are walking through ancient sculpted halls. There are places where you can walk down, down deep. Bill starts to do his demonic laugh and the shrieking of the bats hanging from the ceiling adds to the spooky atmosphere. I wouldn't be surprised if at any moment we hear the stirrings of a monster disturbed from its deep hiding place and have to make a run for it. In another cave you can climb a rickety ladder up the side of the cavern towards a chink of light and peer out of the top of the mountain. This place is called Heaven, and from Heaven we have a wide view of China beach stretching into the distance and a welcome cool breeze.

We finally emerge, having escaped the monster, and go for a walk on the beach. It is vast—the soft, golden sand stretches as far as we can see in both directions. The waves of the South China Sea crash in and Ant gets wistful about surfing back home in Oz.

The sand dunes that border the beach are all planted up by the French with pine trees. They have managed to make a tropical beach on the South China Sea look like the French Atlantic coast—quite spectacular, but so false.

After our bracing walk along the beach, we have all worked up a hunger and go in search of a café with good spring rolls. Back in Hoa Hai, we come across a promising looking café and sit down to a quiet feast. The spring rolls do not disappoint—at a score of eight out of ten they are well above average. The owner is very friendly and speaks good English, so Bill and Ant strike up a conversation with her and learn some new phrases. Ant is much taken with the phrase for 'thank you very much' and keeps repeating it with great gusto and special emphasis on the last two words—'cam ung **zut niew**!'

So these are the useful Vietnamese phrases we've learnt so far:—

Thank you very much—cam ung zut niew
Beef noodle soup—pho bo
Rao wa—outside vegetables
Dog soup—fido pho (just joking)

We are in Hue today. It is an ancient and beautiful city, set on the banks of the Perfume River. It became the country's last imperial capital when the Nguyen dynasty united the country from 1802 to 1945. The city straddles the river—on the north bank stand the walls and moats of the citadel, which used to enclose the palaces, temples and gardens of the Imperial City and within that the innermost Forbidden Purple City; while south of the river is the French colonial quarter, with its villas and tree-shaded streets.

When the last emperor, Bao Dai, abdicated in 1945 with the words, 'I would rather be the citizen of an independent country than an emperor of one that is dominated,' power shifted to Hanoi, and Hue found itself relegated to a small provincial capital.

Tonight we are having dinner with Ant and Ems. They have picked out a recommended restaurant from their guidebook, which other fellow travellers have also raved about. It is a bit of a trek from our hotel, but we set off determinedly in search of good food, fending off the cyclo drivers as we go. When we arrive, we are a little disappointed by the restaurant's scruffy appearance, but the worn out furniture looks as if it has been scrubbed clean, so we decide to give it a go anyway. The restaurant is a family run business; the husband, wife and two daughters all working here and all popping out of the kitchen at regular intervals to check that everything is OK and that we are enjoying our meal. The food is indeed delicious and well worthy of the recommendations it has been given. Amongst other treats, the crispy spring rolls are definitely worth ten out of ten.

Half-way through the meal, I hear a soft thud behind me. Ant looks up and says, 'Ah, the poor little fella just fell off.'

'What was it, a gecko?' I ask.

'No, it was just a little rat. He climbed out of his hole in the wall and was doing really well negotiating his way along that high ledge. It's not even wide enough for a cockroach, let alone a rat. But he ran into trouble when he tried to do a trapeze act, running along that cable,' says Bill. 'He almost made it. He was hanging on by his front claws for a while, but then gravity got the better of him.'

We all just shrug and carry on eating, until after a moment Ems says, 'God we're hardened travellers now, aren't we? I mean no-one even batted an eyelid at a **RAT** falling from the restaurant ceiling!'

Despite its cultural importance, Hue is probably my least favourite city in Vietnam so far. It is full of really aggressive touts, who will not take no for an answer. You only have to stop for 30 seconds to look at the map, and someone has set up a mobile shop next to you and is doing their hardest to make you buy something before you can move on. The pedal rickshaws here are called cyclos and they are the worst. I think they are all slightly mad, so we have renamed them cyclopaths. They stalk you as you walk along. Last night they followed us all the way back from the restaurant—about a 15-minute walk. Today they are getting more sinister. They are starting to physically man-handle Bill and Ant. One of them grabbed Ant's wrist and tried to steal his watch.

The saving grace to Hue has been spending time with Emma and Ant. They both have a great sense of humour and we have laughed our way through most of the difficult situations. We have been exchanging travellers' tales and my favourite one is about the American woman that Ant met. She said to him, 'Oh, so you're a hypochondriac? But that's OK, because so am I!' Ant was outraged when he told us about it, but Ems just smiled and gave us a knowing look. Love him dearly, but we have heard rather more than we'd like to about the antics of Ant's botty since the fruity poopy episode in Dalat.

One of the things to do in Hue, is to visit the tombs and pagodas of the emperors, set along the Perfume River. According to our guidebook, 'one of the most delightful ways to visit the imperial tombs is by boat.' So today we decide to go on such a boat trip. Unfortunately, it was organised by 'Cheat and Smile Tours.' We thought it was suspiciously cheap at $2 a head, which includes lunch, but we're always up for a bargain, as are Ems and Ant.

We arrive at the quayside amongst a throng of tourists and a clamour of voices as it seems there are many other boats doing the same trip today. We find the rep from Cheat and Smile and are ushered onto our vessel for the voyage. There are around twenty other fellow passengers—the usual mixture of Germans, Dutch, Americans and a representation from a few other European countries.

'I don't like the look of the Captain,' says Bill. 'He looks about twelve and he's got a mad crazed look in his eye.' Bill is always very concerned to check out whatever pilot is taking us on any journey.

'I'm sure he'll be fine,' I say and go to find a seat for the journey. These are hard plastic chairs set out untethered on the deck.

'Hope we're not in for a rough ride—these could be a bit tricky,' says Ant, sliding up and down the deck on one of the chairs.

Our vessel has definitely seen many journeys up and down the Perfume River and the engine is belching out diesel fumes onto the deck. I had envisaged a romantic cruise along the Perfume River cooing and gasping in wonder at the beauty of the pagodas and tombs built by the Nguyen emperors, dotted along the misty riverbank. It is not an auspicious start.

In reality the tombs are not actually tombs and they are not dotted along the riverbank, but quite some distance inland, and the tour does not include the entrance fee which, at £3 a go starts to get quite pricey when you add them all up. On top of that, most of them are around 4km from the riverbank and our stop does not give us enough time to walk there, so we have to hire motorbikes each time for another £1.

After the first one, Ems does some calculations and says, 'Do you realise it's going to cost us another $35 each to see all the places we thought were included in this tour—the cheating bastards!'

So we decide not to bother to go and visit anymore that are not free. However, this means hanging around on the riverbank or walking up and down trying to look busy, so as to avoid falling prey to the swarms of touts lining the route.

When we get the free lunch (I know, I know—there's no such thing), I will grudgingly admit that it is relatively tasty, but isn't enough to feed a chicken, which means that after Bill and Ant have attacked the buffet (which they waste no time in doing), there are only scraps left for everyone else. And the drinks laid out with the meal turn out not to be included, a fact they failed to mention till the end when everyone has finished them and then of course they demand a grossly inflated price for them, which is more than the 'free' food is worth.

I have made it sound completely dreadful by focusing on the cheating tour company, but actually the highlight is the boat trip itself. Just gently gliding through the bright red water of the Perfume River, watching life on the riverbanks and on the river itself is fascinating. And swapping jokes with Ant and Ems about what cynical tight-wads we have become is all part of the fun. The other highlight is a very comical French guy on our tour, wearing a Val Doonican style jumper, which seems strangely inappropriate clothing in this heat and humidity. On arriving at one of the pagodas, it is raining heavily and seeing that he does not have a raincoat, a swarm of touts descend on him, trying to sell him an umbrella. But he fends them off with a giant banana leaf, which he then uses to shelter under. He tries to sneak past the man in the ticket booth at the entrance to the pagoda, by camouflaging himself with the banana leaf, but the ticket man does not think it is as funny as we do.

We wake up to a drizzly day, so our plans to hire motorbikes to visit the Bach Ma National Park are shelved in favour of a leisurely day wandering about the intriguingly named Forbidden Purple City, and another chance for me to wear my purple poncho, which is fast becoming a local legend. Despite much asking around, we fail to discover the reason for the citadel's mysterious name, but we have great fun dreaming up possible explanations and making up alternative names, my favourite being the Emperor Purple Ronnie's City of Forbidden Love.

An added bonus to visiting the City of Forbidden Purple Love is that once you have passed through the second wall, you are in an area where no wheeled vehicles are allowed, so we are able to escape the constant barrage from the cyclopaths.

At the heart of old Hue is the Citadel, which houses the Imperial City of the Nguyen dynasty. The Forbidden Purple City was like a citadel within a citadel, protected by a moat. Within that citadel there were extensive grounds containing a spacious palace and within the spacious palace was a vast throne room, decorated in rich red and gold. At the centre of this vast throne room was a raised dais and on the raised dais was a huge golden throne. And on that huge golden throne would sit the tiny little emperor in his voluminous colourful gown. It is a mental image that really makes me chuckle.

I am most impressed with the emperor and princesses gowns—many of which are displayed in glass cases—all exquisitely embroidered with bright-eyed dragons, phoenixes and flowers. And I enjoy the old black and white photos of some of the emperors, priests and courtiers. Ant is particularly enamoured with the emperor's satin platform boots with pointy toes.

We go across the courtyard into another room with a throne on a dais, where we come upon a crowd of people all sitting to watch two Vietnamese girls dressed in replica princess gowns having their photos taken. We sit down thinking there is going to be some kind of traditional dance performance. But we soon realise that anyone can pay some money to dress up as an emperor or a princess and have their photo taken on the throne. I can tell that Ant is just itching to try on those satin boots but he does not want to be the only one to look like an idiot. So he persuades us all to have a go, to the great delight of all the Vietnamese people watching. They nearly fall off their chairs laughing at us. We get the photos back later and yes, we do look pretty funny. Bill does his usual thing of morphing into looking like a local and I swear I can see his eyes getting more oriental by the minute. He is really working his audience, making stern emperor-like faces and pretending to order people about with lots of arm gesturing and pointing. The Vietnamese love it. We decide that it has been much more fun being emperors and princesses in the Forbidden Purple City than it would have been driving through the rain to the national park.

Emperors and Princesses

I found out later that the Forbidden Purple City was used only by the imperial family, and the concubines and eunuchs who served them. It was known as the 'Forbidden City' because anyone else who was caught within its walls would be executed. But I still do not know why it was purple.

It is way way too early in the morning. We have just arrived in Hanoi, after little sleep on the bumpy overnight bus journey from Hue. We just do not learn our lesson, do we? Yes, we are tight wads and did not want to shell out the extra to catch the train. We pass the early morning joggers taking a turn round Hoan Kiem Lake and are deposited by the bus driver in front of Prince Hotel. But clutched in our sweaty little hands is a glossy brochure given to us in Hue, promising large luxurious rooms and a free sumptuous buffet, all for the kingly sum of $9.50. So we shoulder our backpacks and set off in search of this wondrous offer . . .

Do you see that it is taking us a while to get the hang of how things work here in Vietnam?

. . . So we trudge across half of Hanoi with heavy packs, as the sun climbs the sky and the day grows ever hotter. Exhausted, we finally find the Trang An Hotel. And yes, you have guessed it, the brochure is a complete work of fiction. Neither the rooms, nor the buffet bare even a passing resemblance to the photos. It is the darkest, dirtiest, dingiest place we have so far come across in Vietnam. So our search for a more commodious abode begins. We are led a merry dance by the hotel touts, who try to take us to places that are either full, filthy, or extortionately overpriced. Tempers are becoming decidedly frayed. We are taking it in turns to completely lose the plot and to need a pep talk from the other three. Ant is repeating his favourite phrase, *cam ung zut niew* (thank you very much) with such emphasis and sarcasm that it sounds like he is swearing. I think that is what he likes about it.

My turn to lose it comes when we stop to consult a map. I look up seconds later to find that five baguette sellers have materialised out of nowhere. They surround us and stare with waxen smiles and empty eyes, like creatures of the living dead, tugging at my elbow and trying to entice me to purchase their baguettes. They are so sinister, I would no more eat their baguettes than eat my own eyeballs. In a rage brought about by exhaustion, exasperation, and fear, I bellow at them to go away. They look surprised and melt silently away from whence they came. Ems, Bill and Ant stroke my arm and soothe me. 'There, there Anna, the nasty baguette sellers have gone away now.'

Eventually we happen upon the Prince 79 Hotel, a sister hotel to the one we had originally been dropped off at (why, oh why didn't we just check straight in there? We could have been showered, unpacked, breakfasted and sleeping off the journey between clean sheets by now). The hotel is bright and clean and the receptionist says that they will have two double rooms ready by 8am for $8 with private bathrooms and air-con. He will even give us a free breakfast while we wait. I want to kiss him.

So as you can see, our first impressions of Hanoi were not very favourable. Just to add to the trauma of our arrival, in our confusion of traipsing around, we have managed to lose the precious photos of us as emperors and princesses. I foolishly put them in the back of the fictional hotel brochure, to protect their surface, and Emma, in her disgust at the hotel company, threw the brochure away.

As Prof JRR Tolkien so eloquently puts it, 'Now it is a strange thing, but things that are good to have and days that are good to spend are soon told about and not much to listen to; while things that are uncomfortable, palpitating and even gruesome, may make a good tale, and take a deal of telling anyway.' And so it was with the rest of our journey through Vietnam. We had some great times and some real belly laughs, but we also had rather a large share of terrible times and it is those that stick uppermost in my mind and in my throat.

In the Northern part of Vietnam, it seemed that the people grew increasingly cynical and money grabbing, or was it just us becoming more weary and warn down by the scams? Everyone involved in the tourist industry seemed to be out to get their share of the yankee dollar and thought nothing of lying and cheating to part you from it.

To cheer ourselves up, we decide to do something positively cultural in Hanoi and go along to the Water Puppet Show. Whilst queuing to book our tickets we meet a German man leaving the theatre. Bill asks him, 'Did you enjoy the show? And should we get the cheap tickets or is it worth splashing out on the expensive seats?'

'It was rather boring,' says the German man. 'I think the cheap tickets will be quite adequate.'

Fortunately he was wrong about the show being boring, although his comment makes us laugh. It is a genuine delight—very clever and very entertaining. The show is a sequence of scenes created by the farmers of the rice paddies, depicting rural and mythological tales, all set in a pool of water, which acts as the stage. There are dancing dragons with fire crackers issuing from their mouths; a love dance between two phoenixes, who lay an egg which hatches into a baby phoenix; the legend of the magical giant turtle which emerges from the water to claim a sword from the king; ducks diving for fish; farmers playing flutes and riding water buffaloes; unicorns and fairy dances; and children with porcelain arms and legs spinning comically as they swim and play. The accompanying music is played on a traditional single-stringed Vietnamese instrument known as a *dan bau*. It makes a lovely mournful wobbling sound, for the background atmosphere. Bill giggles and whoops all the way through.

Another delight of Hanoi—the Women's Museum. There is, of course, a lot about women's bravery during the war. A photo that summed it up shows a tiny Viet Cong woman leading a huge US soldier that she has captured. Her head comes level with his waist and he is more than double her girth, but it is very clear who is in control as he walks head bowed and shoulders hunched forward.

There is a whole floor devoted to the traditional dress worn by the different ethnic groups. I love the colour, the variety and the craftsmanship of the embroidery. I love the traditional conical Vietnamese hat. Made from palm leaves on a bamboo frame, they are perfect for keeping the head cool, but very lightweight. I find to my delight that there is a whole section devoted to straw hats. They come in many different shapes and designs—some more than a metre across and big enough to shade your whole body let alone your head—fantastic!

So from the assault on our senses that is Hanoi, we long to escape to the quiet of the mountains. We book ourselves on a three-day trip to Sa Pa with our Ozzie mates. We are going to take a trip with Fansipan Tours, which promises that we will, 'Get to know traditional custom and local culture of the Vietnam hill tribe,' which sounds perfect. However, we are persuaded by the staff at our hotel that they can do exactly the same tour for $13 each cheaper. So we fall for it.

Off we set on the night sleeper train to Sa Pa. We are sharing a cabin with Ems and Ant. They are very excited because, despite 10 months of travelling, this is the first time they have ever been on a sleeper train. And I'm afraid we have built their hopes up by telling them the wonders of Rajdhani Express in India. Sadly, it is not up to those standards, but it is OK.

There is a legend known to all Vietnamese people which explains the split between lowlanders and highlanders. It goes like this . . . Long ago, there was a Dragon King who ruled the south of the country. He married Au Co, a beautiful fairy from the north. At first they lived happily together in the mountains of the north where she laid one hundred eggs. The eggs hatched into one hundred boys. But after a while, the Dragon King became sad because he missed his watery lowland home. So he decided to leave and return south with half his sons. These ones became the ancestors of the main ethnic Vietnamese, or Kinh (Viet) people. The fifty sons who were left behind in the mountains became the ancestors of the ethnic minorities, also known as 'Montagnards' or 'hill tribes'.

The mountains remain populated by a mosaic of ethnic groups, each of which have their own history, language, dress, traditions, and way of life. Some of theses groups have several million members, while others have dwindled down to a mere hundred or so members. As if to confirm the Dragon King legend, there are around fifty different ethnic groups in Vietnam, comprising an estimated total of seven million (of a total population of 75 million) which gives Vietnam the richest ethnic make-up of Southeast Asia.

We arrive in the chilly early morning at Lao Cai, a town near the Chinese border, and change onto a minibus bound for Sa Pa. The minibus bumps and winds its way up through the hills. The hillsides are covered in beautifully constructed terraces. The Hmong hill tribes grow rice on these terraces, which are watered continually by channelled mountain streams. The skill of farming this way has been passed down through many generations. It is harvest time and the golden rice grass is awaiting collection.

There is a terrible scar on the landscape created by the road, which is still being carved out of the hillsides by diggers. Everything for 20 metres either side of the road is covered in a film of red dust, thrown up by the traffic piling along the unmettled road and the work of the diggers.

Now and then we pass some of the hill tribes people walking along the side of the road, half choked by the clouds of dust. The Hmong and Red Dzao people are colourfully dressed in indigo outfits embroidered in bright colours and decorated with silver. The women carry large woven baskets on their backs and bare their black-lacquered teeth (a traditional sign of beauty), as a greeting.

After one and a half hours of being jostled in the bus, we arrive tired, sweaty and grungy at the Royal Sapa Hotel. We have a very hurried breakfast and shower before starting our tour at 9.30 am.

Sa Pa, at an altitude of 2,100m, has an alpine feel, reinforced by the style of the buildings, which wouldn't look out of place at a ski resort in the French Alps. The town is a popular holiday destination for the Vietnamese seeking to avoid the heat. Most of the people who live here are ethnic Vietnamese, but during the day many of the local tribes people come into town to do business.

The two dominant tribes around Sapa are the Black Hmong and the Red Dzao. The Hmong and the Dzao people had to occupy the least hospitable land at the highest altitudes because they arrived last into Vietnam. The first Hmong immigrants arrived in North Vietnam from Southern China in the late 18th century. The Hmong made their trek in flight from the Ming Emperor's authority, objecting to the replacement of village chiefs with court-appointed Han Mandarins. The immigration intensified in the 19th century, and continued sporadically until the beginning of the 60s. Once in Vietnam, the Hmong split into several groups, White, Red, Flower, and Black.

The Black Hmong can be identified by their indigo dress and long belts worn wrapped several times around their waists. They wear little black pillbox style hats set far back on their heads. Black Hmong women also decorate themselves with many silver bracelets, silver necklaces and huge hooped silver earrings. One of their more interesting customs is marriage by kidnapping: a young man takes away a young woman with the help of his friends and family. After forcing his wife through the threshold of her home, he informs his new in-laws two days after the kidnap.

Until fairly recently, the Black Hmong from round Sa Pa had little contact with Westerners and were intensely curious about people from such different cultural backgrounds to them. But it did not take them long to see the sales opportunity and they quickly learned to mass produce their crafts, make clothes in larger sizes for the tourists and develop strong arm sales tactics.

The Red Dzao women also wear indigo jackets and culottes, but can be distinguished from the Black Hmong by the huge red turbans they wear to cover their shaved heads and eyebrows. They also embroider the hem of their culottes and elaborate aprons in bright shades of red, yellow and white. There is a local rumour about the Saturday night 'love market', during which the Dzao women take advantage of the 'free love' night granted to them by tradition, and flirt amidst the candlelit market stalls.

We meet our guide. Her name is Mai and she is from the Red Dzao tribe. We walk out of Sa Pa along a jeep track into the hills. It is market day in Sa Pa and I would have liked some time to look round. There are many colourful characters in town today. On the other hand, it is good to get away, having to run the gauntlet of Hmong girls touting their wares and they are some of the most persistent touts we have come across so far.

Our guide, Mai, is a pretty 17 year old, a strange mixture of childlike innocence which alternates with a stern determination and intelligence beyond her years. As is Bill's way, he wants to know all about her and her background and why she decided to be a guide.

'I am only guide from my village,' she tells us. 'I want to be guide because I don't want to spend all my life working in fields. And money is much better—40 dollar a month, but I have to pay 15 dollar for my lodging, because my mother throw me out. She say she no want me to be guide and I no longer her daughter.'

I feel very sad for her. There are several other groups walking our way, each led by a young girl from one of the hill tribes. I wonder how many of them have been thrown out by their families. We join up with a couple of other groups whose guides are obviously Mai's friends, both Black Hmong. One is particularly feisty, teasing us and whistling tunes through bits of grass. She makes a silly hat from a fern that she has picked as we walk. She insists that Ant wears it. She chats to her mates in Hmong and we are sure that she is making fun of us, but as we cannot speak the lingo, we cannot retaliate.

Ant and Mai (right)

As the morning mist lifts over dark green towering peaks, it reveals endless valleys of harvested terraced rice fields. In the distance, rises the peak of Fansipan. At 3,500m it is the highest mountain in Vietnam. But here, lower in the valley, there are clusters of small thatched huts. They are the villages and hamlets populated by the local ethnic minorities. There are bamboo irrigation pipes, there are people pounding rice with a rhythmic thud, dogs play, pigs snuffle about, chickens peck. Men are at work building a new house.

The sun is shining bright, the sky is vividly blue, the air is cool and fresh and the green hills are easy on the eye. I am starting to relax and enjoy myself. We turn off the jeep track and walk through fields of flax and indigo, down into a long valley past the Hmong village of Lao Chai.

We see Hmong women, blue to the elbows dyeing fabric with the indigo that they have grown in the fields nearby. Mai tells us that the fabric is also made from local materials—handwoven from the flax we have seen growing here. It is only the very vivid bright colours that they cannot manufacture here. So they buy bright chemically dyed ribbons and thread from the market to highlight their embroidery and appliqué.

We are met by tiny little snotty-nosed Hmong girls, who must be aged no more than five or six. They are selling tatty little bracelets for 2000 dong (10p). It is the start of a life that will turn them into hardened and persistent sales women. From here on we are followed all the way by people trying to sell us things. Many of their wares are beautifully hand embroidered and I make the mistake of showing a tiny bit of interest. From now on I am mercilessly targeted. Thinking that if I actually buy something they might leave me alone, I buy a bag to carry my water bottle and an embroidered blanket from a dear little girl who seems so grateful for my business. But on the contrary, buying something only makes the others more determined to get some money out of me. I am surrounded by women who pinch me, poke me and mock me because I will not buy their tatty stuff. It is a nightmare. We stop for a picnic under a shelter where an old lady sells cold drinks and more Hmong blankets. She keeps telling me that I should buy another one as hers are much better. They are not.

After lunch we trek to the Dzay village of Ta Van. The Dzay people are much less flamboyant in their dress, wearing simple blouses, skirts and head scarves in pastel colours. I am relieved to find that they do not tout us either. As we walk into the village, we are greeted by small children playing lip instruments. They stare and laugh at us, then run away inside to call to the adults. A small boy, around seven, is sitting astride a water buffalo. He looks tiny compared to the huge animal, but with a string tied to one of its nostrils he rides it with absolute confidence. He smiles at us and calls to us to take a picture.

The homes in the village are wooden huts, surrounded by small vegetable allotments with pens of dark, tiny pigs and skinny chickens running about. There are no machines, no cars and no electricity in the village. I think about how little this lifestyle must have changed since the Middle Ages, despite the complex history of this country. Remembering the hectic traffic, noise, and pollution of Hanoi, the difference is so extraordinary that it is like being in another country.

More useful phrases in Vietnamese:—

Doi kam muir—I don't want to buy anything (we used this one a LOT)
Không cam ung—No thank you (another one we used all the time)
Tam biet—goodbye

The place where we will be staying for the night is the grandest house in the village. It is a timber framed building and (unusually for this part of the world) two storeys high. Our hosts for the night, the diminutive and very friendly Mr and Mrs Cung tell us that it is over 100 years old. We will be staying in comparative luxury—there is a western-style flushing toilet here and even a shower in a cubicle outside. We are shown our beds on the second floor. They are soft and clean with snugly quilts and mosquito nets, far more than I could have hoped for on first impressions of the village.

The other groups that we met along the way are staying in this village too, but we definitely got the best house. We are served drinks at a table in the garden. Dezma and Dougall, a couple who we walked with for a while, stop for a chat. They tell us rather peevishly that they paid twice as much as us for the trip and their house is much more basic.

We spend a very pleasant evening. Our hosts have prepared an absolute feast for us, all cooked over an open fire. Even the gutsy Bill and Ant cannot finish it all. After dinner, Mai teaches us to play a local card game. We call it Messy Waterbuffalo, because despite much explanation by Mai it still seems very complicated. In fact I am almost sure that Mai is just making the rules up as she goes along so that she can win, although she does seem to have a soft spot for Ant and lets him win a couple of hands.

'I win, I win,' she shouts gleefully. 'Bill, you are very stupid. You have good cards but still lose!'

After the card game we sit round gazing into the fire with Mr and Mrs Cung. We want to engage with them and get to know them, but they speak no English and Mai seems reluctant to translate for us. Finally we retire to bed and I sleep extremely snug and sound.

I am awakened by a distraught Bill at 6am. 'We've overslept. Mai didn't wake us. We should have been gone an hour ago. The bus is going to leave without us. Come on, quick.' I jump out of my snugly nest and hastily sling some clothes on, stuffing things into my rucksack as quickly as I can manage in my half asleep state. Ant and Ems are doing the same.

'What happened to that lazy Mai? She must be sleeping off the messy waterbuffalo,' mutters a ruffle-headed Ant as he stumbles about collecting his things.

We rush out, unable to enjoy the beauty of the early morning in the village. We find our jeep driver, who is absolutely furious at us for being an hour late and he treats us to a white-knuckle ride back to Sa Pa along very dangerous roads. Poor Ant who is sitting in the front can see exactly how close we come on several occasions to hitting large rocks and turning over. The rest of us are just hanging on in the back and trying not to look. Bill is particularly nervous about this bad driving.

There is no time for breakfast in Sa Pa. The jeep has to race after the bus which is going to Bac Ha market. Eventually we catch up with it when it stops to pick up more passengers. We climb on board to a frosty reception from the passengers who have had to wait ages for us.

The minibus is old and dilapidated. Exhaust fumes are pouring in. We have a four-hour ride along tortuous roads. After our traumatic start to the day and now being poisoned and thrown about, none of us are feeling too well. It is a miracle no-one throws up.

Finally we arrive at Bac Ha. On the way into town, the land looks drier than around Sa Pa, but the hills are dotted with trees. It is difficult to grow rice at these elevations. The soil is dry and poor. The main crop here used to be opium, but years ago the government stopped people growing it and since then many farmers grow fruit such as plums. The government buys most of the crops, and people earn just enough to live. While there is no official discrimination, the hill tribes remain at the bottom of the economic ladder.

Sunday is market day in Bac Ha, which has the reputation of being one of the most interesting ethnic markets in the whole of South East Asia. It is the occasion for the people of many different tribes to gather in huge crowds to exchange the latest news and gossip, to shop, and to eat a copious lunch. Our guide tells us, 'You have one hour to see market and have lunch. Then back here to get on bus to see Ban Pho village. Then back to Sa Pa.'

We had been told that the drive to Bac Ha would take two and a half hours, not four, and that there would be plenty of time to look round the market and have lunch. One hour hardly seems like plenty of time and we'll be lucky to get any lunch because there are long queues at the only two restaurants. In the afternoon we were supposed to walk to Ban Pho village—a trek of around 6km. The thought of spending all day on that dreadful minibus is not the most appealing thing.

We decide to tackle the guide about this, showing him our type-written programme. He snatches the programme out of Bill's hand and stomps off. We assume that he has gone to find a guide for our trekking, but when we catch up with him, we find that he has just gone for lunch. He looks most perturbed when I find him and ask him what is happening.

'You are disturbing my lunch,' he says huffily.

'Hurry up, man. I've got ethnic minorities to see,' quips Bill (no, not really).

'OK, I make everyone walk to Ban Pho,' he says, waving us away with his hand.

'*Cam ung zut niew!!*' says Ant with feeling. 'Jeez, I can't believe how rude he is. People in the service industry in Oz just wouldn't get away with that kind of behaviour.'

Bac Ha Market

I retrieve the programme and we head off round the market. Bill gets his wish to see ethnic minorities. We are surrounded by a sea of colourful people. It is a visibly festive event and everyone seems excited. There are men on a mission to get drunk or squatting on the ground, smoking hubbly bubbly pipes, or playing cards, or chewing sugar cane. There are stalls with conical heaps of tobacco and the farmers chat with their customers, allowing them a sample pipe before they buy their week's supply of rough shag. A few men ride in on small horses, pre-programmed to get them home safely once they have had their fill of drink. Others arrive on the back of a motorbike, sharing the ride with two other passengers. But most come on foot, from villages as far as 20 kilometres away. The women are here after bargains, or standing with their friends having a good gossip. Even hunched old ladies are determined not to miss the weekly party.

Although there are many different tribes at the market, each with their own traditional dress, it is the Flower Hmong women who stand apart for the vibrancy of their costumes. They wear a number of skirts and underskirts all made with very colourful fabric, a mixture of batik, appliqué and embroidery. Their tops are embroidered with flower motifs, and their heads are covered with tartan scarves starched into elaborate shapes and carefully balanced at a jaunty angle.

Fascinating though it is, I am starting to feel rather unwell after the terrible journey and it being several hours into the day without food or drink passing my lips. It is burning hot, extremely crowded and very jostly. The local people have pointy little elbows and they know how to use them in a retail situation.

There is a livestock section with downcast looking ponies, bony goats, chickens and ducks, but the thing that I am finding really upsetting is that people are doing unspeakable things to cute fluffy puppies and kittens. I see a man who has attached a string handle to the most adorable plump puppy. He carries it like a shopping bag, with its lovely floppy paws hanging down. It has a look on its face that says, 'Ah someone is taking me home to be loved at last. Maybe there will be children to play with too.' But I think that the puppy is sadly mistaken. I am sure he is being taken home to be eaten for dinner.

And the day goes from bad to worse. Our guide is now psychopathically irate. Everyone is tired, hot and suffering from carbon monoxide poisoning and he is marching us through the back streets of Bac Ha, pretending that we are on the way to Ban Pho village.

We get to the edge of town and he says, 'Here is Ban Pho village.' He stands grumpily with his arms folded while people look around in confusion and try to think of something to ask about Ban Pho. It is obvious that this is not Ban Pho and soon we all agree to just give up on it and go back to the bus, for another 4 hours of poisoning on the way back to Sa Pa.

Today we have a pleasant walk with Dza, a 16 year old Hmong girl. She takes us to Cat Cat village and Siu Chai waterfall. Poor Emma is not feeling well at all. She has been sick in the night and is trying to put a brave face on it, but she is virtually collapsing from weakness. It was probably the poisoning we got in the minibus. Ant, who you may have gathered by now, is not your average hard-nosed Ozzie male, is uncharacteristically unsympathetic about Emma's illness. Bill is very concerned and gives her some emergency shiatsu, but it is clear that she will have to go back to the hotel.

'Mate, she's really not well. I think we should take her back,' says Bill to Ant.

'Ah, nah. She'll be right,' says Ant, who is really reluctant to go back.

I have a word with Dza, who says she can get a motorbike to take Emma back when we get to the next village, which is not far. So we help Ems to the village and Dza sorts out a motorbike. 'I'll be fine,' says Ems, weakly. 'You go on and enjoy the rest of the trek, Ant.'

'See, she'll be fine,' says Ant. 'See ya back at the hotel, love,' he says and waves her off on the bike.

We get back to the hotel for a late lunch. Ems is sleeping, but comes down to join us a bit later saying she has thrown up again but feels much better after a sleep.

We spend the afternoon looking round Sa Pa market. I am stalked the whole time by a bald and toothless Red Dzao hag who is trying to sell me her jacket. A couple of times we manage to lose her by ducking and diving between the stalls, but somehow she always manages to find us again. At first I feel really harassed because it has taken the pleasure out of looking round the market, but eventually it turns into a game and Bill and I and the Red Dzao hag are all laughing and chasing each other between the stalls.

Another moment of light relief comes when Ant and Bill find a lady cooking their favourite dish—sticky rice balls. They even have a little song and dance which accompanies finding this favourite delicacy. It goes, 'Sticky rice balls, sticky rice balls, sticky sticky sticky sticky sticky rice balls!' They order the food and perform their little song, with elbows out to the sides and bottoms wiggling. The old lady on the stall next door thinks they are very funny and squirts them with her water pistol. They retaliate by throwing a few sticky rice balls at her. The whole market is in an uproar of laughter and others join in the song and dance. We may have started some kind of tradition here. We will probably come back to Sa Pa in ten years time and find people at the market performing the Sticky Rice Balls song. Well, perhaps not.

In the evening it is time to return to Hanoi and we board the sleeper train at Lao Cai. And just to put the final touch to this most delightful of trips . . .

We find our cabin and pile in throwing our bags on the bunks. 'Oh my God, it stinks of wee in here,' I say, backing out quickly.

'Aw, that's rank, guys. We can't spend a night in here, breathing in someone else's ammonia,' says Ant.

Bill sniffs the air and laughs in disbelief.

'Ew, ew,' says Ems who is still feeling queasy, and rushes out hand over mouth, gagging quietly.

'Well, that just caps it all, doesn't it. This little room where we are to spend the next eight hours of our lives and it stinks of wee. Well done Vietnam,' says Bill. We are all back out in the corridor now, laughing in horror. Bill goes to find a guard. The guard looks at him as if to say, 'What now, idiot tourist?'

'You've got to help us,' says Bill. 'Our cabin, it smells very bad,' he says, holding his nose and saying, 'Poo, poo,' to illustrate. The guard clearly does not believe him, but comes into our cabin anyway. As he steps in and takes his first breath, he visibly recoils, physically assaulted by the stench. He retreats rapidly, his eyes watering. He soon finds the source of the problem—the vent which brings in the 'fresh' air for our air-con system is situated right above the toilets. He remedies the problem by switching the air-con off.

A female guard has joined him to see what all the commotion is about. 'Can we move cabins, please? This one smells very bad,' I ask, hoping the female guard will take pity on us.'

'Very sorry,' she says. 'Train is full. No more cabins. Smell will go now' and walks off hurriedly.

'*Cam ung **zut niew**!!*' says Ant.

We look at each other in dismay. 'I've got some lavender oil—that's a good deodoriser. And we can waft some sarongs around to move the air through quicker,' I suggest. So we waft and sprinkle vigorously for a few minutes. We manage to tone the smell down a notch, and try very hard to make light of the situation, but the smell has permeated the soft furnishings and isn't going away in a hurry. And anytime one of us leaves the cabin, it just serves to renew the horror as the smell hits you afresh on re-entering.

Bonded by mutual adversity, we feel all warm and fuzzy towards Ant and Ems and we know that our time with them is coming to a close.

'Hey, you two, you've got to come to our wedding. If there is any way you could make it to England next June, we would love you to be there,' says Bill.

'Guys, that would be cool. Thanks for inviting us. We've got friends we could visit in London while we're there,' says Ant.

'And loads of my rellies from Mum's side are there too, if Ant didn't mind being dragged round the family. But you're coming to Oz soon aren't you? We must hook up when you're in Sydney. You could stay at my place and we could give you a guided tour of the Northern beaches. It'd be tops,' says Ems.

'Yeah, we'll be your authentic Aussie tour guides. But don't worry, we can do better than Cheat and Smile Tours. It'll be really classy with a picnic and champers included in the price. But Bill, if you're staying at Ems place, which is fantastic, by the way—the locals call it Club Clareville, because it's so posh, with a view of the bay from every room—but watch out for Ems' dad, Brian. He'll challenge you to a game of Bend Arm. He did it to me when I first went round there. And the only rule is—he's got to win.'

'What's Bend Arm?' says Bill.

'Oh, it's his name for arm-wrestling, and I'll tell you, he's bloody strong for an old guy. So it's not just a case of letting him win to keep the peace, 'cos he'll practically break your arm anyway. But you've got to put up a good fight so he doesn't think you're a wuss. Don't get me wrong, he's a top bloke, but he's just got this thing about Bend Arm.'

'Yeah, he's done it to all my boyfriends when he first meets them,' says Ems.

'Well I'll look forward to that,' says Bill with a worried look in his eye.

And if the cabin that smelled of wee was not enough, we arrive back at the hotel (the one that organised our horrendous trip, and the one where we had stored our luggage), to find that the rooms they were supposed to have reserved for us are occupied and the hotel is completely full.

'*Cam ung zut niew!!*' says Ant to the receptionist.

We were going to spend a bit more time in the area, taking a boat trip on Halong Bay, but time is precious now before our flight to Australia. So we have decided not to take the overland route to Laos and have booked a flight straight to Vientiane.

We wave a teary goodbye to Ant and Ems who are off to Thailand to recuperate from the Vietnam experience, with promises to meet up with them in Oz and board our flight for Vientiane.

Chapter 10
Laos—Magical Land of the Nagas

Laos—the land of the mythical water serpent, the naga; the land of a million chickens, after which they have named their currency, the kip; and the land of the all purpose greeting, 'Sábạa-dịi,' which means 'hello', 'how are you', 'I am well' and 'goodbye'. I am highly delighted to be here.

Golden Nagas in Luang Prabang

What a relief it is to arrive in sleepy Vientiane, dozing quietly on the banks of the mighty Mekong River. Laos has only 5 million people, compared to Vietnam's 80 million in roughly the same size country. There are no traffic jams, no tooting horns, no hawkers, no high-rise buildings. The people are gentle, quiet, shy even. I had to tell Bill to tone down the way he speaks to people, as they were all shrinking away from the forceful manner he had adopted in Vietnam.

Vientiane, the capital city is more like a peaceful country town than a teeming metropolis. It is so quiet. The wide streets are filled with shops selling local handicrafts or cafés selling delicious pastries and Laos coffee (almost as good as Vietnamese coffee). Everything is very tasteful. There is none of the usual tat and brashness to be found in other touristy cities. I begin to relax immediately.

Everything in Laos is suffused with magic and spirituality. This is encapsulated for me in the image of the *naga*, or magical water serpent, which is to be found adorning temples and sacred art everywhere. The *naga* is both a symbol of water and its life-giving properties and a protector of the Laos people. It is also a symbol of the ever present Mekong, which snakes its way from North to South of the country and which until relatively recently, was the prime means of travel for the Laos people. An old legend is related of how a *naga* residing in a hole below Vientiane's That Dam Stupa was known to rise up at critical moments and unleash itself upon foreign invaders.

Having had our fill of drinking Beer Lao and watching the sunset over the Mekong in Vientiane, we set off for Vang Vieng. A new express coach service opened a couple of months ago. It proudly announces 'VIP' on the front of the buses. We arrive sleepy-eyed and ruffle-headed at 7 am to catch our bus, to find that we are being filmed for National TV.

I am interviewed by the film crew, who ask me what I think of the coach service and about Laos in general. The interviewer's eyes light up when I say it is the most comfortable coach we have been on in many months of travel and that the service is a very convenient way for us tourists to travel about Laos—so I am sure that bit will get included on the telly!

* * *

According to the date on my watch, Monday 18th November, we have been in Laos for five days now, although I have lost all track of time and my memory of the last three days is very vague.

We stayed three nights in Vang Vieng. On arrival, it looked like a beautiful place—set beside the river amongst green fields with many caves in the limestone mountains. But I did not get to see any of them, as shortly after arriving I succumbed to Dengue Fever, a virus carried by a type of mosquito that is active during the daytime. They call it break-bone fever and I can vouch for the appropriateness of that name. My body was wracked with pain and it felt as if the pain was actually **inside** my bones. For three days I lay on my bed in a nauseous delirium. I felt so weak—even the effort to get out of bed to go to the toilet seemed unbearable.

But once again, Bill's expert healing powers brought me back from the brink. Dengue Fever can be a really serious illness that can lay you out for weeks and even be fatal in some cases. I felt as if I needed to get rid of something that had invaded my body and asked Bill to help. He told me to visualise what the disease looked like and where it was in my body. I saw brown blobs covered in spikes. There was a really big one in my sacrum and smaller ones in my ankles. These corresponded to where I felt the most intense pain. When I described this to Bill, he said that it was exactly as he had pictured it too. Using smudge oil and Reiki symbols, he pulled the invaders out of me and sent them away to be transformed into something less harmful. I started to feel better immediately afterwards—it was miraculous.

After three days, I finally start to regain consciousness. I wake to find Bill at my side. 'How are you feeling now?' he asks.

'Yes, a little better. It feels as if the crisis has passed,' I tell him as the world starts coming back into focus.

'Well, thank goodness for that. You had me really worried there. I thought I was going to have to call the travel insurance company to get you flown home. Do you think you could manage something to eat or drink now? You haven't had anything for days, and I've been out to get your favourite—pineapple and coconut milkshake,' he says holding up a takeaway paper cup with a straw.

'Oh, how brilliant of you. I still feel a bit queasy, but that is the one thing I think I could manage.'

'Good, get it down your neck then. Perhaps later we could venture out and you could have something a bit more substantial. I've discovered an organic restaurant down the road. It's not far and they do brilliant nourishing soups that would do you the world of good.'

* * *

Another bumpy seven-hour bus journey—we are travelling from Vang Vieng to Luang Prabang. The difference this time is that it is daytime, the seats are comfy and the scenery is gorgeous. Peaceful rivers flow through wide valleys, banked by green rice paddies. People in conical palm-straw hats work the fields with fat, dark buffaloes or pound rice outside thatched wooden houses on stilts. All is lush, verdant, pastoral.

Sheer limestone craggy-topped mountains form the sides to the river valleys. They are covered in gravity-defying shrubs and trees that scale their vertical sides. Among their jagged peaks, snake wisps of mist like river dragons.

Now the bus is winding its way higher into the mountains through forests of wild banana and bamboo. The air is getting colder and the mist is thickening about us. We have not seen signs of habitation for many miles now.

Suddenly we round a bend into a village and come to an abrupt stop. The local bus has taken a bend too wide and too fast, colliding with a land-cruiser coming the other way. We all jump off the bus to assess the damage. We cannot get through until a policeman comes to judge whose fault it is and then the vehicles can be moved. Fortunately no-one is seriously hurt and both vehicles are still driveable. But the driver of the land-cruiser is looking shaken and has a bloody hand. We are all secretly relieved that it didn't happen to our bus.

After half an hour, we are on our way again, but our driver is looking worryingly tired and swigging at energy drinks. He has been driving for six hours from Vientiane and has another five to go until we reach Luang Prabang. I was heartened by the sign I had seen at the bus station announcing, 'In the case of unfortunate accidents leading to death or disability, we have to inform you that even though you are a foreigner, you will only be compensated the same as a local Laos person. Separate travel insurance can be obtained from our office.' Let us hope we do not have any such unfortunate accidents, as we omitted to avail ourselves of the separate travel insurance.

At last we arrive safely and gratefully in Luang Prabang. It is already dark and many of the guesthouses are full, so we resort to a rather overpriced one—$8 instead of the usual $5. At least it is clean and quiet.

One illusion I had was that Laos would be less touristy than Thailand or Vietnam. In my imagination, it had become a forgotten, hidden corner of South East Asia that only the most adventurous or cultured people come to—sadly not. The *'falang,'* (meaning white stranger with a big nose), are everywhere. We come in all shapes, sizes, ages and nationalities, from minibus-loads of ageing Norwegian ladies, to young fit feisty Brits on mountain bikes. It seems that everyone knows about this beautiful land already.

I still feel a little wobbly and weak after the Dengue Fever, but I am getting better everyday. It is lovely here—the same slow pace as Vientiane and the same kind, shy people, but in a prettier setting. No high rise buildings, or industrial estates, or shopping malls. It feels like a magical, sacred town. There are beautiful temples everywhere.

We climb the Phou Si, the Holy Hill, in the centre of town to reach That Chomsi, the golden-spired temple at the top. The hill is believed to have once harboured a powerful *naga*. Legend has it that the guardian spirits who founded the city of Luang Prabang, Phu Nyoe and Nya Nyoe, called forth fifteen nagas from the rivers and commanded these water spirits to guard the new city, for which they would receive tribute from the king.

From this vantage point, we have a panoramic view over the Luang Prabang peninsula, created by the confluence of the Mekong and the Nam Khan rivers. It is very green for a city—most of the buildings are hidden amongst the trees—keeping it quiet and shady. And where the city ends, the forest begins, rolling away over the hills into the distance.

As we walk down the other side of the Phou Si, the monks from all over town are beating drums and gongs as a call to prayer. The atmosphere is charged and as we walk past reclining buddhas and golden *nagas*, I feel as though I am part of some ancient ceremony involving everyone in Luang Prabang.

Today we are going on a boat trip to the Pak Ou caves with an old rascal named Mr Nin in his boat, which he proudly calls 007. Neither of us is quite sure what we have let ourselves in for. He approached us in the street to sell us the trip and his grasp of English is very poor. However, that did not inhibit him from chattering away to us. The only intelligible words were 'caves,' 'money, money' and 'whiskey,' interspersed liberally with smiles and chuckles and exclamations of 'oooh!!' with rolling eyes.

'I like him. He's as mad as a badger, but I think we should go with him,' says Bill.

We climb aboard his long-tailed boat, brightly painted red, green and blue with pink curtains. We are greeted by the sweet-faced Mrs Nin, offering us bananas. We had been worried about the river-worthiness of the boat and whether Mr Nin would take us where we wanted to go, but everything is clean, well-kept, ordered. Mr Nin pulls a cord or two and the engine purrs into action like a kitten. He seats himself on his little plastic chair behind the wheel, turns his wrinkled brown face towards us, gives us a mischievous grin and we are off.

There are many other *falang* setting off for the same destination, but **we** have Mr Nin. Navigating the river, picking the best line against the flow, zig-zagging across the water to avoid numerous fishing nets and traps, rocks, sand bars and choppy water, our captain is a consummate boatman.

The boat journey is pure delight. The milk chocolate Mekong slides by. Thick slabs of rich chocolate silt on the riverbanks provide fertile soil for crops of herbs when the river is low. Misty green-clad mountains all around. Bamboo baskets in the water catching catfish.

We arrive at Pak Ou. Many boatloads of *falang* are gathered at the entrance. The caves are full of pixie Buddhas with pointy ears, pointy hats and bulbous noses. Despite the hordes of *falang*, the fairy grotto caves have an other-wordly feel. We light some candles and incense.

Back in Mr Nin's boat, we watch a super streamlined, go-faster striped speedboat roar past like a bright spear slicing through the water. The river valley echoes to the roar of the engine as they pass us. The driver's hair streams back in the G-force. The other occupants are all wearing crash hats and chopping uncomfortably up and down in a shimmer of spray. How much they are missing of this tranquil experience, riding in a boat like that.

'Ooh, not good,' says Bill as they bounce past us. 'I bet their arses will be black and blue by the time they get to their destination, not to mention the cricked necks.'

We arrive at the Hmong village of Hoykhe and are greeted by Mr Vang Cheng Vang, a lovely man who has taught himself many languages and appointed himself ambassador to the village. He shows us round. We meet his daughters, his wife, his son. Everyone smiles and stares curiously.

The village is very poor. The houses are shacks and people are wearing rags. Mr Vang's house is as bare as sticks. His wife, he tells us, is 35, although she looks twenty years older, with her toothless smile and wrinkled face. He tells us how they moved the village down from the mountains eight years ago. He tells us of the malaria problem and says that he is raising money to buy mosquito nets and medicine. Two village members have recently died of malaria. We give him a donation towards the medicine.

He shows us the school. We meet the pretty children and he gives us a lesson in speaking Hmong:—

    Nyoy jong = hello
    Ncai mmus = goodbye
    Na tsang (pronounced 'cho') = thanks
    Koj = you
    Kuv = me

The school has very few facilities and the teacher comes for only two hours per day. But the children play, shout, kick balls, fight and skip the same as anywhere else in the world.

On the way back to the boat, we meet a sprightly 100 year old lady, kicking dogs away. She lives in the chief's house. It is the only stone building in the village and cost £3,000 to build. It is very posh by their standards. The old lady has bright beady eyes and more wrinkles than features, but she can chase chickens away and chase after us, trying to sell us scrappy little bags.

'At least with your 100 year old homemade bag vendor, you have a chance of out-running them,' says Bill, recalling our experiences in Vietnam.

We thank Mr Vang and wish him good luck before heading back to Luang Prabang. On the way back we stop at the whiskey village, where we discover why Mr Nin has been chattering about whiskey and rolling his eyes. It is the home of the famous Lao Lao rice whiskey—a very potent brew.

* * *

In the evening we dress in the finest clothes that we can muster from our travel-worn rucksacks and treat ourselves to a night out at the Royal Theatre. The theatre is in the grounds of the former Royal Palace—a beautiful building with golden finials and mosaics of coloured glass, which glow and sparkle in the evening sun.

We sit on gilded chairs in a large wooden hall with a stage at the front. It is light and airy. The evening starts with the Baci ceremony of prayers and good wishes performed by former singers and musicians from the Royal Palace. There are offerings of food and flowers and all sit with their hands in the prayer position as the priest chants to ask for blessings from the spirits. Then the performers come among us to include us in the ceremony.

A graceful old lady kneels in front of me, gently holding my hand and murmuring words of welcome and good wishes. Then she ties white cords around my wrists to bring blessings into my life. I feel very moved by the tenderness of her gestures and words.

After the ceremony, there are folk songs and dances depicting the Ramayana in glittering costumes, masks and golden headdresses. Bill thinks the dancing girls in the golden headdresses are very beautiful.

Then it is into the garden to see the Hmong people performing traditional dances and music. We are highly entertained by a sprightly old chap, first getting a creditable tune by blowing on a mango leaf and then by performing a whirling dervish dance whilst playing a strange instrument that I can only describe as being a cross between a violin and a set of bagpipes.

There follows a most amazing thing. It is a dance to celebrate the harvest, which would normally have been performed by the tribe's 90 year old shaman. Sadly, he chose to step off this mortal coil the previous week, so the dance was led by his 22 year old daughter.

'Get that,' says Bill. 'He must have been 78 when he fathered her, the old dog, and nothing wrong with his jing by the looks of his healthy daughter.'

Anyhow, whilst the people drum and sing and clap, three huge and heavy earthenware pots are set on a table and each filled with three buckets of water. The shaman's tiny daughter, flanked by two male performers, proceeds to pick up the pot with her **teeth** and dance with it for a full five minutes. And ne'er a drop of sweat marrs her lovely brow.

Afterwards the audience are invited to see how heavy the pot is. Even the strongest men can barely raise it from the table using both arms.

It is said that people often find themselves spending more time than they intended in the enchanting Luang Prabang and this is certainly the case with us, as we have fallen under her spell. We spend more time just wandering aimlessly about or sitting in cafés along the Mekong, watching children playing in the water, shrieking with delight and rolling about on the sandy banks.

We manage a walk to the end of the peninsula. The pace of life is even sleepier there. We wander into the Wat Xieng Thong, which is said to be the most magnificent temple in all Luang Prabang. It is certainly very beautiful and I spend some peaceful moments in contemplation before the flower-bedecked altar. But now the time has finally come for us to reluctantly tear ourselves away and we head North to Luang Namtha.

During the US war against Vietnam, Laos became the most bombed country in the history of the world. At the peak there was the equivalent of a whole planeload of bombs emptied on Laos every 8 minutes round the clock, in an attempt to kill Viet Cong escaping over the border from Vietnam. This went on for ten years. Every year there are still around 200 accidents involving Unexploded Ordinance (UXO), despite the efforts of de-mining organisations. And yet you would hardly know that there had been a war if you hadn't read the guidebook or happened to notice that the flower vases at the altars of some of the temples are made from old bomb casings. Laos people just don't make a big deal of it.

We have heard that the trekking around Luang Namtha is very eco-friendly and well organised and that it is one of the few places where you can walk through pristine forest in the National Park without fear of treading on any UXO left over from the war. And after our terrible trekking experience in Vietnam, we want to be responsible tourists without harming the environment or the local culture.

So here we are in Luang Namtha after a gruelling journey of ten hours on bumpy roads, the first five being on a *sawngthaw*—a truck converted to carry passengers by putting two narrow benches along each side. The sides are left open so that you either get covered in dust if it is dry, or chilled to the bone if it is cold and wet—these conditions alternated on our journey. These are then crammed full of people, chickens, squealing pigs, sacks of rice, you name it, and set off at uncomfortable speeds along the bumpy roads. I thought wistfully of our luxurious journey from Vientiane to Vang Vieng and understood why the Laos people are so proud of their new bus service.

Anyhow, Luang Namtha so far has been worth the journey. Today we are staying at the idyllic and eco-friendly (if overpriced at US$25) Boat Landing Guesthouse, which overlooks the Nam Tha River. The accommodation is in bungalows which are constructed in traditional Laos style from local materials. Each of the timber-framed buildings is raised up on stilts, with walls made from some kind of woven plant fibre and steps up to a large verandah. Hot water and electricity are provided by solar panels.

We spend the day just lounging on the verandah of our bungalow, which is set in a grassy acacia grove, watching the river slip by, reading and recovering from the journey. Children play in the water, men work on their boats or fish for their supper, football and volleyball is played with great skill and dexterity by the locals.

Whilst having dinner in the restaurant here, we get chatting to an English couple, Ollie and Jess, who will be going on the same trek as us. They are both doctors, travelling before getting married and doing VSO work.

'Have you tried the *sa*, here? Oh, you must try it, it's excellent, one of the nicest things I've eaten since we have been away on our travels,' says Jess.

We order it—a local dish made from minced meat with banana flowers, lime juice, mint, basil and other local herbs. She's right—it's gorgeous.

They are both big people, tall and broad—Jess blonde and rosy, Ollie dark with kind eyes. He is very excited about a novel he has just finished reading and enthuses about it to Bill—the Magus by John Fowles. We all chat excitedly about the trek we are about to do.

'I like someone who gets so caught up in the world of the book that they are reading. I do that. I think we are going to get along with Ollie,' says Bill to me later.

We have moved back into town. We could not afford to stay at the Boat Landing for more than a night. Today we hired bikes and cycled to a local waterfall. It was quite wonderful, going down country lanes through peaceful villages surrounded by gorgeous scenery.

Tomorrow we are booked on a three-day trek to visit some Akha villages and walk in the National Park. As we had hoped, it is incredibly well run by UNESCO, to benefit the local tribal people and help conserve the environment and numbers are strictly limited so as not to stress the communities. I am looking forward to it immensely.

Well, we are just back from our three-day trek in the monsoon rainforest and all I can say is that the looking forward to it, was probably the best bit of it. With hindsight, it was a pretty crazy thing to do a mere week after having Dengue Fever, but when I really want to do something, I manage to convince myself that I am indestructible.

As we had hoped, the trek was all those things that I have mentioned—eco-friendly, respectful of the tribal cultures and well-organised. We met our fellow trekkers at the tourist office. Ollie and Jess were kitted from head to toe in brand new Gortex and expensive walking boots.

'Can't be too careful,' joked Ollie. 'Looks like we might get a spot of rain.' Little did we know what we were letting ourselves in for. You see, no matter how well organised something is, there is no accounting for the weather and we were **SO** unlucky with the weather. Fine spots of rain began to dust the windscreen of the minibus as we left Luang Namtha and from then on, it proceeded to precipitate abundantly, day and night for the whole three days of the trek—sometimes mizzly like a net curtain, but more often like rods of water coming out of a high pressure hose. There was not one moment of respite from the ceaseless rain for 60 hours. Perhaps we should have got a clue from the name 'monsoon rainforest'! But having said that, the amount of rain we had is practically unheard of in this part of the world at this time of year.

The effect of the rain was that despite walking through some of the most pristine forest in the world and the most idyllic villages, far away from motor vehicles, electricity, industry, telephones, etc, we trudged along, heads down in silent misery for most of the time. Even Ollie and Jess in their Gortex coats and trousers and their new boots were cold and wet through to the underpants within an hour of setting out. Even my beloved Purple Ronnie poncho could not save me from getting drenched. The rain seemed to seep in from every direction and mingled with the sweat that built up on the uphill sections, so clothing got wet from the inside as well as the outside. And because of the weather all the animals were taking shelter. Not a single bird tweeted in three days.

The paths were soon slick with mud, making the downhill sections really treacherous and the uphill sections even harder work. We had to cross the river in many places, where the only way of getting from one side to the other was by means of a round tree trunk which was as slick as if it had been coated with Vaseline in the wet conditions. The chances of toppling off into the raging torrent below and cutting yourself to pieces on the rocks seemed foolishly high. Whilst the local guides trotted easily across, these obstacles had a terrible effect on us poor *falang*. Grown men trembled at the knees and shuffled nervously across, praying not to disgrace themselves, and Jess, who seemed pretty stalwart in other respects, was reduced to tears in sheer panic.

'Oh, I'm so embarrassed for being such a wimp,' she said once she was safely across.

By some miracle there were no accidents, and each time it became slightly easier as our confidence grew. Even so, there were one or two really difficult ones, with uphill sections, where the guides had to lead us across by the hand like frightened children. It is a blessing that there were no mishaps, because if someone had fallen and sprained an ankle, or broken a bone, or worse, there was no way to get them to medical attention — other than to walk for several hours through difficult terrain.

After what seemed an interminable amount of soggy trudging, finally we started to see signs that we were nearing the village. We passed swidden sites, where slash and burn cultivation is practiced. The remainder of the dry rice crop was growing amongst the charred stumps. There were small conical huts on stilts built to store this season's harvest of rice.

The headman of the village, Asi, who had been guiding us on the trek, was a delightful, smiley man. He trotted lightly through the slippery conditions in a pair of flip-flops. And as we walked he sang traditional Akha songs, which really helped to cheer us on. Nearing the village, Asi stopped several times to relieve his bladder.

'I think he's marking his territory,' said Bill.

We followed Asi into the village, and he led us to the tourist hut, our home for the night. It was the same style as the other buildings in the village—a long, wooden thatched hut on stilts. It was extremely basic, just one big room for us all to share, with very thin walls, but I was just so relieved that the days trek had come to an end and we could get under some shelter. I was feeling awful. There were three things, on top of the rain, that added to my own misery. Firstly, I had a slight sore throat in the morning when we set out, which had developed into a full blown raging fever, cough and runny nose within a few hours of setting out.

Secondly, I had my period, which always makes me feel a little delicate at the best of times, but without even a private place out of the rain and mud to attend to my sanitary arrangements, it seemed an unbearable burden.

And lastly, there were the leeches. Several people got the odd leech bite, but it was my misfortune to hold the record for the highest number of leeches attached to my person at any one time AND the record for having the biggest, scariest, blood-filled monster attached to my leg. The Purple Ronnie seemed to be an absolute magnet for them, as it brushed along the vegetation as I walked and allowed the little bleeders to climb on and attach themselves to my person. When we finally got to the village where we were to stay the night, we went into our hut and I peeled off my sodden trousers to change. I wondered why everyone screamed and pointed to my leg. I looked down and it seemed that there was more leech than leg.

I have to confess that, as it didn't actually hurt, I secretly got some sadistic pleasure out of showing it to some of the most squeamish in the group, which included the head guide, Wundi, who was a bit of a wuss, and was renamed Wendy by Bill forever after that. The main problem with this enormous bite was that it bled profusely for hours, soaking my dry pair of trousers and my bedding with blood.

Having seen the leech on my leg, all the men's reactions were to immediately check their nether parts for leeches. Jess and Ollie were to be found, shortly after this incident, in the corner, Ollie on all fours with his underpants down and Jess with a torch checking his gentleman's region for unwelcome attachments.

So who were the other members of the group with whom we had been thrown into adversity? There was Béard and George, two French friends. George was tall and round of face with smiling eyes. Béard, who was shorter and thin, with a long pointed nose, had something about him that put me in mind of a coyote. The two of them did not stop talking, giggling and laughing for the whole trip.

'They're like two characters from Sesame Street,' whispered Bill.

There was Hannah, a tall graceful American girl with beautiful posture, but an awkward face. Her harshly bobbed hair gave her the profile of a preying mantis. She was a likeable character and kept apologising to us about the American President, George Bush. 'God, he's an idiot. I've got a T-shirt at home that has a picture of him and it says in big letters, 'He's not MY President'. I wish I'd brought it because I don't want people I meet when I'm travelling thinking that I endorse what he's doing to the environment and messing in Iraq.'

Hannah was the only one that was not horrified by the assortment of leeches attached to me. 'Oh, I wish I had a leech,' she said.

'Whatever for? I asked her.

'Well, I'm an entomologist. So I really want to experience one, just to see what it's like,' she replied.

'Here, have one of mine to experience,' I said handing her one that I had managed to free from my person.

'Oh, how cute,' she said, 'It's nibbling my finger. I don't know what made me do it, but I soaked all my clothes in Permethrin before I came away and none of the insects will come near me.'

'Oops, that's a bit unfortunate for someone who likes to study insects, isn't it?' I said. She took it in good humour.

Hannah had a friend with her, Enza, an Israeli PhD student, as timid as a mouse with wide eyes and a smile that did not always reach those eyes. The clothes she had brought were so pathetically inadequate that I took pity and lent her a dry jacket. It happened to be the one I had bought from the Red Dzao hag who chased me round the market in Sa Pa. Ah well, at least it had come in useful in the end.

Our arrival in the village was met with a lovely welcome from all the children calling out 'Sábąa-dįi' and waving at us. Very soon, rosie-cheeked girls in hats wonderfully decorated with silver coins, colourful embroidery and ribbons, and mischievous bright-eyed boys came scampering through the mud to our wooden hut on stilts, laden with fruit and vegetables for our supper. They stood staring at us in wide-eyed wonder for several minutes—we must have made a strange sight all bedraggled and covered in mud.

After a little while, they had gained their confidence and looked shyly around before helping themselves to some of the bananas and more readily edible gifts—the cheeky monkeys. Then out came the bracelets and other trinkets that they had made for sale. We all bought a little something, mainly to give them some pocket money.

Then wood was brought and supper cooked on the fire. Asi, shod only in his flip flops, miraculously managed the whole trek without getting a single leech on him. After attending to a few bits of business in the village, he joined us for dinner and afterwards told us about his village and his culture. His duties as headman included general village welfare, schooling and deciding whether a couple should be permitted to get married. Then he wanted to know about us and his main interest was in our names, countries, ages and whether we were married or not.

Wendy translated, 'He say he very delighted to meet some English people. He saying that it is first time the English people visited here. He say he very pleased you and Bill are couple and ask when you gonna get married and how many children you will have?'

Bill said, 'Wendy, please tell him that we are very honoured to be the first English people to visit his fine village and that we like it very much. Also tell him that we will get married in seven months time when we return to England and that we plan to have lots and lots of children.'

Wendy's translation was greeted with laughter and clapping from Asi, who said, 'Very good, very good, many children, very good.'

Bill asked Wendy, 'Asi seems very young to be the village headman at 30. Could you ask him how that came to be.'

Asi told us that they have a very good form of democracy in this village, where the headman is voted-in for five years by all the villagers. It is obvious that his intelligence and charm had won him this honour at a very early age. He had been instrumental in setting up the trekking to bring extra income to the village and he seemed to welcome the opportunity to learn about other cultures. His main aim for the village was to improve the standard of education for the children and to give them the best opportunities in life.

After dinner, we all turned in for an early night. Our bedding consisted of a thin hard mattress on the floor with a sheet and a blanket for cover. There had been a fire going to cook our food, but as dry wood was in short supply, we were not allowed to sit round it to warm ourselves and it was put out soon after dinner. So we had no means to dry our sodden clothes and it was very cold in the room.

All day as I had trekked, I had been dreaming that there might be a hot cup of tea to warm me on my arrival. Sadly, the dream was only a mirage and there was no cup of hot tea, as was the case for the rest of our trek. So I retired to bed with my cold worsening, feeling chilled to the bone. The thin blanket and hard mattress did nothing to make me more comfortable and I lay awake all night listening to the sound of the pigs and goats shuffling about beneath the hut and the incessant rain beating upon the roof, praying that the sun would come out in the morning.

But in the morning there was no change in the weather. The rain looked set in for the day. Wendy asked us to wait for a while, to see if the rain would ease.

I flopped about, feeling dreadful, coughing and spluttering, with a pounding headache. I was <u>not</u> looking forward to another day's trekking in the rain and another cold and miserable night in the next village. And just to add to this misery, Bill and I were not getting on well with each other.

'You're so grumpy and you just snap at me all the time. I'm beginning to think you don't love me anymore,' he said.

'Well, if I'm snappy it's only because I feel absolutely dreadful and I'm at the end of my tether. How can you think it's because I don't love you?' I replied. In my delicate state, it was all too much for me, and I began to cry, which was highly embarrassing with the rest of the group in the hut pretending not to notice. I felt unloved and unsupported and Bill probably felt the same. It really saddened me that we had reached a point of being unable to help each other in a crisis. In the end we made up and told each other that we still loved one another, which was just as well as it was time to put on our wet clothes and leave.

We finally set off after a cold lunch of slimey vegetables and rice cooked with too much garlic. It was 1.30pm and we really had to push the pace to reach the next village before dark.

Most of us were sorely tempted to go back the way we had come and hitchhike back to Luang Namtha. The thought of another cold night in a village without electricity or enough wood to have a fire to warm ourselves was exceedingly unpleasant. But we weren't sure of the way back and as some of the group wanted to continue, the guide would not let us. So we trekked on.

Physically, I was deteriorating rapidly, but emotionally, I felt a little stronger since my row with Bill had cleared the air and he was now hanging back to keep me company as I lagged behind. Somehow I managed to keep going by just forcing myself to put one foot in front of the other. Eventually we reached the village just as dusk was falling.

That night's welcome by the villagers was a little less warm—their spirits obviously dampened by the weather too. Having removed another enormous leech from my leg, I collapsed in a heap and began to convulse with shivers.

The others resorted to drinking lao lao (the local rice whiskey) to warm and relax themselves, but I abstained, knowing it would make me feel worse. Then it transpired that there were not enough mattresses or blankets to go round. Béard was the unfortunate one who ended up with no mattress and he was getting really obnoxious about it. I tried to suggest that we put all the mattresses together and everyone could squeeze up a bit to make space for him and as someone had a sleeping bag, he could have a blanket too, but in his drunken state he insisted that as Bill and I were a couple, we should share one mattress and a blanket. The mattresses were barely wide enough for one person, let alone two. I wanted to KILL him!

In the end, it made little difference as I was chilled to the bone and spent a sleepless night shivering and feeling wretched, whilst Bill snored drunkenly in my ear, breathing lao lao fumes over me.

The next day dawned cold, cheerless and still raining—none of us could believe our bad luck. The headman of the village was very sweet and wanted to invite us to have tea and lao lao with him in his house, which we did, but all the time we were sitting there in our wet clothes, I was just itching to get on with the trek and get back to a warm dry guesthouse and hot shower.

Eventually we got underway and I knew that I just had to keep myself going for four more hours before I could collapse. It is one of the hardest things I have ever had to do. Most of the time I was just stumbling along like a zombie. It was **SO** slippery after all the rain that I really had to screw up my concentration to stop myself from falling over at every step.

My thoughts swung back and forth between, 'I cannot walk another step,' to 'I have to just get through this.' At one point, it all got too much and I staggered along sobbing to myself. Shortly after that I stopped to rest—I desperately wanted to lie down and go no further.

Bill came up to me and miraculously pulled a chocolate bar out of his pocket. I devoured it greedily and somehow it just gave me enough lift to make the final push back to Luang Namtha.

With something equating to joy (or was it just relief?) in my heart, we reached the guesthouse where we had stored our bags and reserved a room, only to find—horror of horrors—that they had let our room out to someone else. The girl on reception, feigning not to understand, looked at me with an inane smile. If I had had more energy, I think I might have hit her—didn't she understand what I had just been through?

Bill led me quivering away and as luck would have it, the guesthouse next door did have a room. The friendly landlady mothered us like a hen clucking round her chicks. The only downside was that this guesthouse, unlike the other, only had cold water in the bathroom. I desperately needed to wash away three days of mud and warm myself through.

'I'll go and get some hot drinks from the restaurant,' said Bill. I peeled off my filthy sodden clothes, trying to steel myself to get under the cold shower. By the time Bill returned, I still had not been able to do it. As I tried to tell him that I could not bear to pour any more cold water on my body, I broke down in fits of sobs. I couldn't stop crying for several minutes—big noisy, gulping squawks that came rushing involuntarily out of me—three days worth of trying to hold myself together to get through the ordeal all came out in one go.

For the second time, the kind landlady came up trumps, bringing a bucket of piping hot water which she had heated on the fire and so I finally managed to get myself clean, warm and dry. I got into bed early with blankets piled high and slept properly for the first time in three days.

My experience really brings home the reality of how hard life is for the Akha villagers we had just visited. It is all very well for us to play at staying in the village overnight, whilst knowing that we can just go back to civilisation whenever we want. What happens if one of the villagers is seriously ill? It is a three-hour walk to the nearest road even for the fittest individual.

* * *

This morning I still have a heavy cold, but it feels as if the worst of the illness has passed. So we get out of Luang Namtha on the first bus that leaves town in the morning and head back to Luang Prabang. It feels like fleeing back to a safe haven—where the weather is warm and hot showers are the norm, and there is mains electricity instead of having to use a generator for four hours a day as was the case in Luang Namtha. It feels so good to be back—I have developed a real fondness for Luang Prabang.

Anyhow, the next problem is how to get all our filthy sodden washing done and dried in time before we have to leave. Fortunately, the sun shines brightly all afternoon, drying ourselves and our washing out.

After a leisurely breakfast, we book plane tickets from Vientiane to Pakse in Southern Laos. Our time in Laos is running short before we have to get back to Bangkok for our flight to Oz. We have agonised over whether to spend more time in Northern Laos, or to hare down to Southern Laos and to see a few things there. But after our sodden trekking experience, the South won, no contest!

Once our travel plans are sorted, we have time to enjoy LP a bit more. The name Luang Prabang means 'Golden Buddha.' The city is named after a solid gold Buddha, a symbol of Theravada Buddhism, which originated in Sri Lanka. It is 83cm tall and weighs 50kg. The Prabang is believed to possess miraculous powers that safeguard the country in which it is enshrined. It is housed in the Royal Palace and I have been longing to see it, but so far the Royal Palace Museum has been closed each time we pass. But today we finally get to see the museum, and the fabled Prabang, the Golden Buddha.

The Royal Palace Museum is very well preserved and gives a strange glimpse into the way of life of the former royal family, who were in residence as recently as 1975. At this time, the Pathet Lao (the communist resistance) forced King Sissavang Vatthana to abdicate. Two years later, the new communist government allegedly exiled him to a cave in Houa Phan, a journey from which he and his family never returned.

The austere high-ceilinged bedrooms contrast sharply with the ornate throne room full of glittering mosaics. The photos of the king and queen and displays of their clothes are all the more poignant for the sad story of the family's disappearance.

Bill is feeling unwell—I think he is coming down with my cold, whilst I am beginning to perk up. So he goes back to our room for a sleep, whilst I am unleashed on the beautiful shops.

Luang Prabang is full of shops displaying the most gorgeous hand-woven silk wall hangings and scarves. The Laos women all wear wonderful patterned silk wrap-around skirts. So I set about finding myself some good examples of these.

In the evening we have a nostalgic visit to Nazim's Indian restaurant. It is the first time we have been able to bring ourselves to eat Indian food since leaving India. The proprietor is a strange little man with a fat belly who wears a comical felt hat.

'I'm sure it's a lady's hat,' whispers Bill.

The restaurant is packed with *falang*, the food is good and there are several little touches that really make us laugh.

'God, it's so typically Indian here. Everywhere we go in Laos, there is masses of fruit and every other restaurant serves fresh juices and fruit shakes, but what do they have to drink here? Only Coke, Fanta or Sprite, served with a wet glass that you have to wipe dry with a napkin so you don't catch some water-borne disease!' says Bill.

* * *

We get up early and eat noodle soup at the bus station with other sleepy *falang*. The bus journey to Vientiane, which should have taken three or four hours, takes all day because the bus's clutch has given out. The driver just coasts down most of the hills to Vang Vieng, using the brakes and not the gears.

Finally, we arrive in Vientiane, tired and hungry after a long journey and an early start. Bill is still suffering with his cold. But we have to traipse around looking for a guesthouse that isn't either full or swarming with mosquitoes. We eventually settle in desperation for the plush but pricey Douang Deuane. The receptionist entices us in with offers of complimentary breakfasts and free taxis to the airport. The luxurious room with soft mattress, pristine sheets, fluffy towels and . . . joy of all joys . . . a **bathtub** was enough to persuade us we had made the right decision. We haven't come across a bath in many months of travel and Bill sighs with delight at the thought of playing underwater submarines in its foaming depths. He wastes no time in availing himself of its services.

It would have been nice to enjoy our luxury room for longer, but our flight leaves for Pakse at 6.15am so we have to make an early start and reluctantly miss our complimentary breakfast.

By 7.25 am we have landed safely in Pakse, much to our great relief since it was a tiny prop plane and the pilot had to navigate and land by sight, since there is no radar in Laos.

We catch a tuk-tuk from the airport into Pakse and are dismayed to find that it is a pretty dismal town with all the roads dug up—full of dust and mud. Our original idea had been to visit Champasak next, but it seems like a good idea to leave Pakse as quickly as possible.

But first we need food and coffee, since we have had such an early start and are tired and hungry. After breakfast we wander despondently around trying to figure out how to get somewhere more pleasant, when all the travel agencies and money exchanges are shut (it being Sunday).

Eventually we find out where the bus station is. It is quite a way out of town and certainly too far to walk with our luggage. With our last few thousand kip, we have just enough money to get a rickshaw to the bus station and a spur of the moment ticket on a truck headed for Si Phan Don in the far south.

The truck looks pretty ropey and is crammed full of locals and chickens, but it turns out to be surprisingly comfortable and motors at speed down to Si Phan Don in under two hours—a journey we had expected to take at least three or four hours.

It is a fun journey—there is an air of excitement amongst the locals. The following day is going to be a National Holiday and lots of people are going away to visit relatives or friends.

Every time the truck stops to let passengers on or off, there is a rush of local ladies surrounding the truck with strange items on sticks for sale. It is like a macabre puppet show—all the ladies cooing and calling out their sales pitch whilst joggling these sticks up and down at the window, skewered with what looks like barbequed road-kill. Amongst the delicacies on offer are squashed rats and squirrels and even one or two sticks full of fried giant grasshoppers. We decline their kind offers of refreshment, guessing that the copious amount of vomiting emitted by the local passengers might have something to do with their choice of snack.

The scenery and climate are vastly different here from the North. The Mekong River Valley has become wide and flat with grassland and shrubby trees. The air is hot and dry and the sunlight very intense.

The name Si Phan Don means 'Four Thousand Islands.' Here the Mekong is at its widest, being 14km from bank to bank. The mighty river meanders its way around many inhabited islands before plunging over the Khone falls into Cambodia.

Not long after 1pm we are climbing off the ferry onto Don Khong Island. So it has taken us around seven hours to get from North Laos right to the Southern tip of the country — so much speedier than any other journey of any length that we have made so far in Laos.

There is an easy feeling to life on Don Khong. We walk straight off the ferry and find a cheap room in a guesthouse only a few hundred yards from the ferry landing, the Villa Khang Khong. Despite being an island in the middle of the Mekong — a fact I can't quite get my head around — Don Khong has 24 hours electricity, a bank, a post office and plenty of guesthouses and restaurants. Yet it still manages to retain a quaint old-fashioned and very relaxed air to it.

After all our rushing about, we decide to just relax for our first day here, and maybe hire some bicycles to cycle round the island once the sun starts to cool in the afternoon.

I am feeling under the weather again and my ankles and knees are very swollen, so Bill gives me a treatment to see if it will help. Unfortunately it seems to have the effect of moving whatever is left of the Dengue Fever round my body and afterwards I feel exhausted and immobilised on the bed for the rest of the day.

In the evening we chat to a German girl who has organised a boat trip from our guesthouse and we decide to join the trip, which is scheduled for the following morning. One of the highlights of the trip is to be the chance to see rare freshwater dolphins, known as the Irrawaddy dolphin, named after the river in Burma, in which it is also found.

These dolphins hold a unique place in the affection of the Laos people. Known as the *pa kha*, they are the one creature that the Laos will not eat. This is all the more unusual for a people who will normally eat anything that hops, flies, swims or crawls, as we have seen with our own eyes at the truck-side puppet show. Villagers from the Si Phan Don area tell of dolphins saving people from drowning and pulling them from the jaws of crocodiles. They are thought to be reincarnated humans, with a human soul. There is a local folksong, the *Lam Si Phan Don*, which tells of a boatman who is reincarnated as a dolphin after his raft plunges over the Khone falls.

But over the past century, the numbers of these magical creatures has fallen drastically from thousands to little more than 100 today. Gill-net fishing, and across the border in Cambodia, the use of poison, explosives and electricity to catch fish, is largely to blame. But there is still hope in the form of the Laos Community Fisheries and Dolphin Protection Project and the Si Phan Don Wetlands project. Participating fishermen say that they have already seen improvements. There are villagers in the area that even claim that the '*ngeuak*,' the beloved *naga* has returned to Laos waters.

As for the existence of the *naga*, the Laos point to 'proof' that can be seen in a photograph, which we saw in a local restaurant. The photo shows a line of American soldiers displaying a freshly caught deep-water fish that is several metres long. It is a glittering silver colour, with wispy tendrils about its head, almost like a horses mane. It has huge eyes, which seem to look out of the picture with intelligence and an almost smiling expression. On some copies of the photograph, the Laos words '*Nang Phayanak*' *(Lady Naga)* are printed below the scene. Where and when the photo was taken is a mystery, but many Laos believe that the photo depicts a real-life *naga* captured in the Mekong by American soldiers during the second Indochina war.

It is bright and hot by 7 am as we have breakfast before the boat trip. We are both excited by the prospect of seeing elusive dolphins and travelling in the realm of the *naga*.

Our companions for the day are Mr Poumi, the captain of our little boat, Klaus a German policeman, Gilles a French policeman, and Annette and Martina, two German girls who both live in South America.

Mr Poumi leads us to the boat and we meander gently down the Mekong for one and a half hours, watching the islands go by and observing life on the water—fishermen balance on their boats to cast out small nets. We motor past Don Det and get off at Don Khon where we have a very scenic, but very hot walk across the island to its southern tip. Our surroundings are gorgeous—we walk through harvested rice fields and stands of trees—but I feel dizzy and out-of-it, so I have to drag myself along to keep up with the others.

When we reach the tip of the island, we get into tiny dugout canoes and saunter across the water to the Cambodian border. The river landscape changes here. There are trees growing right in the river, almost a water woodland. There are rocky outcrops which we navigate around on our way to Cambodia. There is a border post with the most jolly border guards we have met so far—all sitting around drinking tea and quite happy to have their photos taken as long as you pay them 5,000 kip (34p) for the privilege of setting foot momentarily on Cambodian soil.

Then we get back into the dugouts and sail out to mid-stream which is apparently the best place to encounter the Irrawaddy dolphins. It is 11am, it is blisteringly hot, there are four other boats full of *falang* and no sign of any dolphins. There is too much going on, of course, for them to come. But we wait. People get bored and hot. The sun is boiling our brains.

One by one, the other boats give up, start their motors and head for shore. But our two boats hang on and suddenly everything is quiet again. Now we might have more chance of the shy creatures coming. I have a sudden sense that there are dolphins nearby. 'Over there,' the other boat is full of excited people pointing, but it is too far away for us to see.

Bill gets out his conch and gives it a blow . . . then behind us the sound of air being let out of a blowhole. I swivel round just in time to see the dolphin dive back down into the water. Bill blows another note on the conch and this time a head pops up, looking directly at us as if to say, 'What was that funny noise?'

'Again, again!' we all squeak with excitement—especially the boatman who thinks the conch is a great idea. Bill blows a few more notes and there seem to be three dolphins who are responding to the calls. One is swimming parallel to the boat not more than 20 feet away. It is a beautiful and magical thing. We feel very honoured by their presence and it is definitely worth the sweltering wait. Then as suddenly as they came, I sense them slip away and it is time to leave.

'That was SO magical!' I say to Bill.

'Yes it was. Did you see how they answered the conch?' he says.

'Yes, what a great idea to call them with it,' I say.

Back on Don Khon, we have another hot walk to see the Liphii waterfalls. Here the vast waters of the Mekong rush over a low but turbulent set of falls, spanned by the flimsiest of bamboo bridges used by the fishermen. It is said to be a powerful place of spirits and the fishermen need to be in tune with them, otherwise they would be swept away. I do not pick up on this, feeling rather too hot and bothered to be very sensitive, but Bill says he feels it.

After gazing at the waterfall for a while, we walk back to the restaurant at the top of the island, where the shade and the cold drinks are very welcome. Mr Poumi and the owner of the restaurant are knocking back the lao lao and our captain is so jolly after lunch that he forgets where he left the boat.

Somehow he gets us safely to the mainland and we catch a truck that says, 'Fuck me please' on the front windscreen (I am sure the driver has no idea what it really means). He takes us to see the Khon Papheng waterfalls. These falls are said to be the largest in South East Asia. They are spectacular—a mesmerising roar and charge of water over rock. But time is running short. We have to push back to the boat if we are to get home before dark.

Anna and Bill at the Khon Papheng Falls

We are entertained on the way back by the most fantastic sunset. As the sun sinks behind the Western hills, the Mekong is dyed a myriad of dancing pinks and turquoise. Lone fishermen standing up in their boats to cast their nets are silhouetted in the last of the day's light. Children having their evening bath on the river bank all shout, 'Sábạa-dịi,' with great excitement.

We finally make it safely back to our guesthouse a few minutes after full darkness has fallen, having had a few hairy moments, as the still tipsy Poumi, tried to avoid hitting small islands of vegetation. It has been a completely enchanting day and I am so thrilled to have seen the dolphins.

* * *

Today we are travelling north again to see Champasak, which we missed on the way down. We rise early, eat good noodle soup, drink excellent coffee and then join other *falang* aboard Mr Pon's intergalactic Pakse express. Two hours later, Mr Pon drops us off at the ferry bound for Champasak on the opposite bank of the Mekong. Two huge catamarans circle each other on the river, like vast water birds doing a mating dance. Alongside these are a couple of tiny makeshift things, that look like two dugouts roped together with a couple of planks on top. The owner is trying to get six *falang* + rucksacks +locals + the ubiquitous baskets of chickens onto one of these contraptions, to go all the way to Champasak.

'No thanks, mate, I'm not getting on that thing,' says Bill when approached by the owner of the contraption. 'I'm going to wait to get on the catamaran thing which looks a lot more stable,' he says to me. We leave the other foolhardy *falang* trying to negotiate a price for their risky ride. On the other side of the river, we get a tuk-tuk a short way into Champasak. It is one of Laos' many unique forms of transport—a motorbike with a strange two-seater sidecar attachment, complete with shade canopy. We feel quite silly squeezing onto this with our huge rucksacks, but it gets us to Champasak well before the other *falang* turn up and for the equivalent price. We feel quite smug that we are to get first pick of the accommodation and have not had to risk our bags or our persons toppling into the river.

Champasak turns out to be a sleepy little one-horse town with faded colonial charm. It has a roundabout with a grand fountain (not working) in the centre, but very little else. Its setting on the banks of the Mekong with mountains in the background is delightful. But again, it is stinking hot.

There is only really one decent place to stay—the Kamphoui guesthouse—and we take a lovely clean cool room for a bargain $3 a night. I immediately crash out in the room and sleep soundly for a couple of hours—honestly, I think I have got sleeping sickness.

Our main purpose for staying in Champasak is to visit the pre-Angkor ruins of the Wat Phou temple—Laos' version of Angkor Wat. The temple is set high on a hill to the South of the town and we want to let the midday heat ebb away a little before attempting to visit the temple.

After lunch at the one decent restaurant in Champasak, overlooking the Mekong, we hop into one of the funny looking sidecar contraptions again and head for Wat Phou. The countryside dozes peacefully in the afternoon heat and everything is golden. The mountains in the distance grow closer and one in particular catches our eye because of its unusual shape. This towering peak is known to the locals as 'Mount Penis' and is the setting for Wat Phou.

A long avenue, bordered by carvings of *nagas* and lions, leads to the temple, which is on three levels, progressing up the mountain. As we walk along the avenue, I have weird sensations in my head and stomach. I tell Bill.

'I feel strange too. Perhaps it's built on a ley-line?' says Bill.

We arrive at the temple on the first level. It is made of red-brick with elaborate carvings. It is inhabited by mischievous children who collect the sweet scented blossoms shed by the plumeria trees which line the avenue, and try to sell them to you for hugely inflated prices to leave as offerings.

Bill on the steps to Wat Phou

Then the steep climb begins—up high, narrow and uneven steps to the next level, where Laos ladies sit waiting to sell you incense and intricately woven flower offerings to leave at the foot of the Buddha or on the yoni, the celebration of womanhood, set off to the side of the path.

We climb again to the third level, where many Buddhas sit in the most ancient part of the temple. These carvings have the comical pixie faces which are common in Laos. Many offerings have been left in this place. We add our own with an overwhelming feeling of ancient sacredness.

The ladies selling offerings show us the holy spring that issues from a cave in the mountain. We bathe our hot heads and pray for a blessing. Bill bathes his conch and sounds a note, which echoes round the mountain drawing curious onlookers.

We visit a fairy cave full of tiny pixie Buddhas. I am filled with a feeling of peace and well-being.

We stray from the main temple to find the Crocodile Rock. Some say that this was once a place of human sacrifice. As I walk towards the rock, I reach a point where I feel a sense of loathsome foreboding at the prospect of going any closer. It is almost as if there is an invisible energetic barrier stopping me. I dither about, wondering what to do . . . and in that moment I am bitten by three mosquitoes. Bill, trying to reach the place from another direction is also driven back by mosquitoes. I say a little prayer asking for healing for this place and beat a hasty retreat.

Within a few steps, we are back to the peaceful feeling that surrounds the temple. We look out from our vantage point to a wide view of the plains and the Mekong in the distance. All is golden in the late afternoon light. People sit about with rapt looks on their faces—reluctant to leave this atmospheric place. We stand at the top of the steps that lead back to the mundane world from this magical plane and I feel great resistance to embark on our return journey.

Eventually we descend the steep steps and find our 'jumbo' driver watching a romantic film in the café. We buy him a drink and watch the end of the film together—they all live happily ever after—before he drives us back to Champasak in a dream-like state. It is not until we reach the guesthouse that I realise that, despite the intense heat and the steep climb, I feel energised by the whole experience, which is such a contrast to how ill I have been feeling lately.

* * *

We leave Champasak on the 6.30am converted truck-thing that serves as a bus and head for Pakse. At Pakse bus station we change onto a packed coach and head for Salavan on the Bolaven plateau.

We are going to a resort called Tadlo, where we have heard that you can go trekking to nearby villages of various weird and wonderful ethnic cultures, or take elephant rides, as the local people have a long time tradition of training elephants. We have also heard that the resort is in a beautiful setting next to a waterfall on the Se Set River.

We were certainly not disappointed by the setting, beside a green-banked river, with the roar of the falls to lull us to sleep. We booked ourselves into a luxurious $12 a night bungalow with a view of the falls, and there we remained for the final two and a half days of our stay in Laos. I was once again hit by the exhaustion which has been dogging me ever since I had Dengue Fever, and spent most of the time sleeping or lolling about.

I felt depressed and weepy, wondering if this lethargy will ever end and beginning to tell myself that I must be a hypochondriac. Bill thinks I do not love him or fancy him anymore. But that is not the case. I feel so disconnected from myself that it is hard to connect with someone else. He means the world to me, but I cannot deal with his passion at the moment, as I have no passion left inside me, only sadness.

I do not know where this sadness comes from, but it may be that I am sensing the sadness of the people in this land. Unlike the Vietnamese, I have never heard the Laos people complain about the war or moan about its devastating after effects, but I still sense it, hidden under the surface.

* * *

Tonight is our last night in Asia. Tomorrow we fly to Australia for Christmas. My parents will be waiting for us at Sydney airport. I am so looking forward to it.

We are back in Bangkok now and I have been starting to feel better ever since we got here—maybe a combination of better food, easier transportation and the good that resting and sleeping for two days did me.

It was strange leaving Laos. I loved the country and the people and the experiences we had there and yet I had such a difficult time there, almost from the start. And when it was time to leave, the contrast between the modes of transport before and after the border were so marked. On the Laos side, we were crammed into an open-sided truck which struggled along at 30 mph in the baking heat, covering us with dust. I was squashed cheek by jowl with a young Laos girl, who continuously stuffed her face with a series of messy spring rolls and smelly fish sauce, bread rolls, fruit and drinks which dripped everywhere. About half of the food went in her mouth and the rest over me. And I was living in mortal fear that she would throw up at any moment—a common occurrence on these bumpy journeys.

The truck stop was about half a mile from the actual immigration control, so we had to shoulder our packs and trudge through blazing sun to get out of the country.

Whilst on the Thai side of the border, we were met at passport control by a young man with a sunny smile who arranged an air-conditioned taxi to take us all the way to the train station at Ubon Ratchathani, where we caught a luxury overnight sleeper train into Bangkok—so easy!

Many people do not like Bangkok because it is a big, busy, polluted city, but for me it was such a relief after feeling so unwell. This is our third time here now and we know how everything works. We know where to get a good hotel room, we know which are the best restaurants, we know how to get around town. Everything is easy, clean, efficient. I would not have missed our experiences for the world, but my goodness, I am glad to be back in Bangkok now.

'Anna, do you think your health is up to travelling in South America?' asks Bill.

'Well, the answer is I don't really know, but I'm hoping that three easy weeks in Australia will fix me up well enough to cope. I've been looking forward to seeing those countries ever since we started talking about coming on this trip, and I would be **SO** disappointed to get all this way and then miss them,' I reply.

'Well I hope you are right, but if you're not feeling better after a couple of weeks in Oz, we should go home. It's not worth ruining your health,' says Bill.

I am sad to be leaving Asia and there is a big part of me that is looking forward to next time—travelling in Laos with more time and a clean bill of health is one of my dearest wishes, but I guess that will not be for a few years to come.

Chapter 11
Australia—Hawkeye learns to bodysurf

Well, here we are in Australia. I have been looking forward to this as a little holiday, between the onslaught of Asia and South America. The culture, the sense of humour, the food, the cars that drive on the left hand side of the road—it is just like England, but with better weather. The familiarity of it all is so wonderful, so stress-free. One of the things that really strikes me is just how **clean** everything is. It is all sparkling new and clean, almost sterile, even compared to Bangkok, which was a lot cleaner than India.

We are to be met at the airport by my parents. They have already been here for a few days, visiting relatives near Melbourne. It will be a chance for Bill to get to know the future in-laws a little better.

We arrive at Sydney airport and wait for my parents to come and pick us up. It is so lovely to be picked up—it feels like coming home. We go to the airport café and sample new coffee and new money.

Bill says, 'I'm a bit nervous about seeing your Mum and Dad. I don't know them very well and suddenly we're going to be spending a lot of time with them. I hope they think I've been looking after their daughter on our travels.'

'Don't worry. You'll be fine. They'll love you as much as I do once they get to know you.'

Mum and Dad are late—we hope everything is OK. Mum arrives looking hassled after navigating the Sydney rush hour traffic. We have more coffee and wait for Dad who is parking the car.

'I better just tell you while he's not here, that he hasn't been very well,' says Mum. He had a bit of a turn and had to go to the doctors.'

'Oh no. What happened?' Bill and I chime together.

'Well, we hired a car straight from the airport when we arrived and we set off to Melbourne to visit my cousin Elizabeth and her husband,

Edwin. It was rather a long drive through the mountains and when we stopped to have a picnic lunch he had a dizzy spell.'

'So you arrived after a 24 hour flight, with jetlag and coming from the cold of December in England to the heat of Australia in high summer, and then you got straight in a car and drove for 550 miles through the mountains? I'm not surprised he had a dizzy spell. He must be knackered,' I say.

'Yes, I know, you can't tell him. He just wants to make the most of his time on holiday. I had to drive back from Elizabeth's.'

Dad arrives, looking tired but quite well, apologising for being a bit late. It is wonderful to see them both. It makes me realise how homesick I have been.

We were expecting to stay with a family friend in Sydney for a few days, but Mum and Dad still have the hire car and have planned a trip up the East coast for a few days.

'I don't mind sharing the driving,' says Bill. 'Why don't we get my name put on the documents while we're near the car hire office?'

'Oh, yes, that's a very good idea,' says Mum, giving Bill a knowing look.

We are both hanging with jetlag after a 10 hour flight through the night with no sleep and a change of time zone, but Dad is taking the first stint at driving, so for now there is nothing to do but sit in the back of the car and snooze or gaze out of the window as the landscape slides by.

We set off immediately up Highway One towards Byron Bay. We are in an air-conditioned rental car on a slick tarmac road, travelling at 100 kilometres per hour. Dad comments, 'It's rather a bumpy road, don't you think?' Bill and I fall about laughing and say that it seems like luxury after spending seven months in Asia.

Mum and Dad are very excited to see us, chattering away, wanting to tell us all the news from having seven months apart. Bill is trying valiantly to keep his eyes open and make polite conversation, but I cannot stay awake a moment longer and slump unconscious against the window.

We stop at Avoca Beach for lunch. The bright sun, reflecting off the crashing surf as it rolls onto the golden sand dazzles my eyes—a sensation somewhere between pleasure and pain. There is just enough breeze to keep us from overheating. It is the kind of perfect weather that makes you feel glad to be alive. We have delicious fish and chips for lunch—it has been a few months since we have sampled such fare and it is great.

We continue our journey up Highway One, which now turns inland and runs through miles of eucalypt forest and bush. Australia is experiencing its worst drought in twenty years and everything here is still black and smouldering after recent bush fires. Many of the road signs are twisted and blackened by the heat.

Our destination for the night is Nelson Bay and so we head off the highway and out along the Port Stephens peninsula. The landscape changes to rolling green farmland with fat glossy horses in the fields and shops advertising local produce everywhere—a rural idyll.

We choose our accommodation, the Dutchies Motel, mainly for its wonderful setting with its own private beach and because after a long journey, we want to settle in quickly. But Bill and I are in shock at the price of $180 (about £60) for a small suite with one double bed and a sofa-bed. It seems like a small fortune compared to the prices we got used to in Asia.

We want to make the most of it here and dash straight down to the beach for a swim, where we have our next shock—the water is freezing! How can this be? We are British and used to swimming in the Atlantic in the most inclement of weather. So to find the Australian sea cold seems ironic. It must be that those warm waters in the Gulf of Thailand have turned us into delicate flowers.

After hot showers to warm our bones, we wander into town along a coastal path for supper. Our path is surrounded by trees ablaze with the red, green and blue of parrots chattering in the sunset and the intoxicating smell of eucalyptus.

We find a restaurant by the marina and the waiter comes to take our order for drinks. Bill introduces Dad to the delights of Victoria Bitter (VB). Dad says in a West Country accent, 'Aarp, it goes down nice when you're a bit dry,' and winks at Bill. It is the start of a beautiful friendship.

'We're going to have to watch those two,' says Mum. 'I predict that they're going to be getting up to mischief.'

We order steak and a bottle of red wine. It is the first alcohol I have had for months and I must say it goes down splendidly, as does the steak. There is an air of relaxed contentedness at the table. We have all arrived safely together and everything is going well.

'Right you two,' says Mum. 'Now I've got a captive audience, this holiday's a good chance to finalise some of the wedding plans. The thing that I'd like to sort out is the reception. We need to decide on the venue, the sort of food you want and whether you want a band or not?'

'Well, we'd really love to have the reception in a marquee in the garden of your house. Do you think that's possible?' I ask.

'I'm not sure our garden would be big enough for a marquee for 200 people,' says Mum.

'What? Two hundred people? I thought we'd agreed to limit the numbers to 120 guests,' I say.

'Yes we agreed to limit the official invites for the church service and the main meal to 120, but I've invited some of the locals to the evening do. I thought we could have a light buffet for the extra guests at around 8pm.'

'So you've invited 80 locals? Do we know any of them?' I ask.

'Oh, yes, or you'll have heard me talk about them. They're all very nice and it will bring the community together,' says Mum.

'Well, OK if you're happy to pay for all the extra food. Any chance we could have a marquee in the meadow next to the house?' I ask.

'I might be able to persuade the lady who owns it. She owes us a favour since her sheep got through the fence into our garden and ate all my vegetables,' says Dad.

'So what about the food?' asks Mum.

'We'd like traditional English — local Herefordshire beef followed by strawberries and cream,' Bill and I chorus together.

'OK, that sounds nice,' says Mum. 'Rachel has given me the name of a caterer who does that sort of thing very well.'

'And what sort of band do you want?' asks Dad.

'How about a ceilidh band,' says Bill. 'A bit of 'Swing your partner by the hand' is always good for breaking the ice.'

'Oh good, I know a very good band that played at your Aunty Chris' birthday party.'

'Well, it's all decided then. That was easy,' says Bill.

'Yes that's put my mind at rest a bit,' says Mum.

'Mum, thank you so much for doing all this organising while we're away,' I say.

'Yes, you're an absolute star, Hazel. May I drink to your health,' says Bill raising his glass. Mum blushes a little and raises her glass back to him.

On the way back, we see our first possums, silhouetted in the trees against the gathering dark. I know most of the Aussies see them as pests, but they are beautiful to me.

We sleep very well despite the sagging camp-bed. It has been a very full day following a ten-hour overnight flight with no sleep.

Dad likes to get up early and get on with the day, but I find it difficult to drag my eyes open at 7.30am as he is laying the table for breakfast about two metres from my head.

We like it here and decide to stay for another night. Dad goes to re-book and has to do battle with the money grabbing old bag who owns the motel. She tells Dad that the girl who booked us in last night undercharged and that if we want to stay, we will have to pay more. Dad gives her a polite version of, 'Well, you can stick that where the sun don't shine. We're leaving,' and stomps off, guessing rightly that she would back down if he called her bluff. Sure enough the room phone rings a few minutes later and she graciously offers for us to stay another night for the same price. We are all secretly glad that it was Dad who dealt with her—he likes a challenge!

With tonight's accommodation sorted, we walk to the top of Tomaree Head for a view of the coastline. It is hot and tiring even at 10.30am, especially for Mum who struggles up valiantly despite arthritic knees. But it is definitely worth it for the view—a 360 degree panorama of waves crashing onto dramatic headlands, sand spits, long sandy beaches, sheltered coves and eucalypt-covered hills.

Then it is a quick whizz back to the pier to catch the ferry across the bay to the Tea Gardens. We have been told by the tourist officer that taking the ferry is the best way to see the dolphins in Nelson Bay and there is no need to take a special tour.

As we wait to catch the ferry, my eye is caught by a lady who is about to board the boat for the dolphin tour. She is just like an enormous round ball in a voluminous flowery cotton dress, with little arms and legs sticking out of the sides. I try to stop myself from gawping—it is just that overweight people are such a rarity in Asia. But Dad has noticed too. He nudges Bill with his elbow and raises his eyebrows with a wry smile.

The ferry arrives and we climb aboard. There is a good stiff breeze and the ferry chops through the water, the sunshine sparkling off the waves. We all crane our necks over the side, hoping to spot the dolphins, but no luck this time. I find myself wishing I had got on the dolphin tour with the round flowery lady. We arrive at Tea Gardens, our bags of swimming gear clutched in our hands, but are disappointed to find there is no beach and little else to do. With a name like Tea Gardens, I had expected a pretty, quaint little place, but actually it is rather dull.

'Well let's have some lunch and catch the next ferry back then,' says Mum.

'Good plan,' says Bill.

'Look. There's a Chinese restaurant with an all you can eat buffet for $9,' says Dad. Being thrifty pensioners, Mum and Dad are partial to a cheap all you can eat buffet and so is Bill, for that matter. So we have lunch at the Chinese restaurant. Unfortunately the food seems mediocre when you have had several months of eating authentic Asian food and it is a relief when I spot the ferry coming back in to dock.

We all dash over to the landing stage and the ferry lady is surprised to see us back so soon.

'We were very disappointed not to see any dolphins on the way over and we didn't realise there is no beach here, so we thought we'd head back early,' says Mum.

'I'm sorry to hear that. Let's see if we can find some dolphins for you on the way back,' says the ferry lady. To everyone's great delight, she spots some about five minutes into the journey. Everyone on board gives a big cheer and the captain switches off the engine so we can watch them for a while. A couple of the bolder ones accompany us back to Nelson Bay, surfing the bow wave alongside the ferry and providing perfect photo opportunities.

So we go back to Dutchman's Cove, the private beach at our motel, and have our swim there. Then its hot showers again and into town for a fish and chip supper. The pre-dinner VB is becoming a bit of a ritual for Dad and Bill. They both start saying, 'Aarp,' and we all know what is coming next. They are like two naughty little boys together, always giggling at something and winking at each other about private jokes.

The fish and chip supper is something else. Mum, Dad and I sit at a table outside the café, while Bill goes in to order. He comes out struggling under the weight of an enormous paper parcel, which he deposits on the table and proceeds to unwrap, taking over the whole table. He unveils a giant mountain of golden, crispy chips, topped by four of the most perfectly formed pieces of battered fish. Mum cannot quite believe her eyes. We all tuck in with gusto.

'Oh, by the way, Anna, Grandpa has really been enjoying your e-mails. Dad prints them off and takes them over to Dulas whenever he visits. Grandpa reads them avidly and says things like, 'Oh yes, I remember that place,' or 'Oh, how wonderful—they did go there.' It's been a real tonic for him. I'm afraid he's getting really frail now. He has to use a frame to get round the garden at Dulas, but he's still enjoying his birdwatching,' says Mum after she has had her fill of fish and chips.

'Yes, he's given several talks and slideshows to the other residents,' says Dad.

'Oh, that's great. But I hope he showed them the interesting ones like Peru and not the Galapagos Islands where all the birds are camouflaged against the rocks,' I say.

'I don't suppose it would make much difference anyway,' says Mum. 'I think most of the residents would probably fall asleep whatever he showed them.'

'Oh, Mum, don't be rotten.'

'Well it's true.'

* * *

Harvey and Hazel with sleepy koala

Up bright and early again—we set off for the Tiligerry Peninsula in search of koalas. In the visitors' information office, a very cuddly-looking, hairy man, much like a koala himself, tells us where we might spot the little darlings.

So we spend a happy morning looking for wild koalas at the delightfully named Lemon Tree Passage, a strip of eucalypt woodland next to the river. Well, perhaps 'wild' is not quite the right word for koalas—they are pretty sleepy most of the time, although we did see one stretch its furry little leg out for a while, before dozing off again.

Dad is the first to see one, gaining himself a new nickname—Hawkeye Harvey. He is very excited. 'These binoculars are really powerful,' he says. 'I can see right inside his furry little ears.' The koala rouses himself from sleep, yawns and stretches. Then attempts to climb a little higher in the tree. He wobbles, nearly falling out of the tree, then thinks better of it and settles back down for another snooze in exactly the same spot.

A bit further on, we spot another doing much the same. It really is no wonder they have not been very successful at colonising the world. A very slow, sleepy animal that lives in trees, but is a bit clumsy and not very good at climbing, and only eats poisonous eucalyptus leaves is not going to thrive in many environments.

Eventually we are beaten into submission by the relentless onslaught of mosquitoes. We rename the place Monster Mosquito Passage after even the leathery-skinned Hawkeye is covered in itchy welts.

'They don't seem to be biting me,' says Hawkeye, oblivious to the fact that there is one on his arm drawing a fat drop of blood.

'What's that then?' I say, pointing it out. 'Ooh and there are several biting through the back of your shirt and one on your neck.'

'Oh, yes. Now you mention it, my neck is a bit itchy,' says Dad.

After a bad cup of coffee in a café where an old timer is playing the guitar and singing quaint songs, we head off on the next leg of our adventure. We drive through miles and miles of monotonous eucalypt forest. Dad is at the wheel again. He has done so many of this sort of long road trip in his life that he gets into a certain zone and just gets on with it. Mum and he have a little drill about the supply of sweeties—Mum knows exactly when to pop the next one in his mouth to keep him going. The other thing he does is to find things along the way to amuse himself, like crossing the occasional creek with a strange name. He swears he saw one called Smelly Bottom Creek.

We stop for afternoon tea at Crescent Head—another dramatic bit of coastline with great surf—a very popular spot for Aussies on holiday. There are lots of wooden cabins and the place is crowded with families here for the weekend. We all set off enthusiastically through the dunes heading for the beach. It has been hot and sticky in the car so we quickly change into swimmers and race into the sea. But the sea is rougher than we had bargained for. First Mum is beaten back by the rip tide.

'It's a bit tough on my knees,' she says. 'I think I'll go back and read the paper on the beach.'

Then I get trashed in the waves, finally managing to get upright long enough to discover that my bikini bottoms are full of sand and hanging down almost to my knees—highly embarrassing. I look over to see Bill valiantly trying to teach Hawkeye how to body surf, but they are both getting trashed too.

'Get ready for the wave, Hawkeye,' shouts Bill above the roar of the surf. 'Arms up and go for it. Uh-oh, too late' . . . as Dad is tossed about like a piece of flotsam, rolling over and over till he finally manages to stand up with hair in his eyes and water up his nose. I tell Bill I am going back and ask him to keep an eye on Dad. He has absolutely no concept that he is 65 and might need to take it a bit easy sometimes. He still thinks he is 20 and invincible.

Sadly we do not have time to explore the other beautiful beaches in the area, as recommended in an e-mail from Ems and Ant. I had been quite looking forward to seeing Delicate Nobby. So after a restorative cup of tea, we drive on to Nambucca, where we find rooms in the Blue Dolphin Motel and have supper in a Thai restaurant.

On the road early again. It is still rather a long way to Byron. Our first stop is for coffee at the Big Banana in Coff's Harbour. The 'Moderately Sized Banana' or the 'Considerably Over-hyped, Over-priced and Rather Disappointing Banana' might have been more appropriate names for the aforementioned fruit, but hey, it is as good a place as any to stop for coffee. In fact, Hawkeye and Bill have their first Australian iced-coffee experience here. These are huge things full of ice cream and covered in piles of whipped cream and chocolate sauce. They are both grinning like little boys whilst eating them. And I am sure I heard the occasional contented 'aarp' too.

Later we find Mum in the Banana Souvenir Shop. She is slightly glassy-eyed and buying enormous quantities of furry little animals and postcards of koalas.

'What do you think of this one for Esther and Ben?' she says holding up a hideous furry banana thing that has space to slide in a photo.

We all wince and say, 'Ooh, no!' in unison.

'Step away from the banana merchandise, Hazel,' says Bill taking her by the arm. She is drooling slightly and has to be led gently away.

We have another stop for a posh lunch at a café in Lennox Head, which overlooks the beach. Seafood and salad accompanied by a glass of crisp chardonnay. Umm that is what I have been missing. It is very windy and we watch the kite surfers doing tricks and amazing feats, jumping 30 feet into the air.

I have fond memories of spending time in Byron whilst staying with a friend at Possum Creek a few years ago. So I am really quite over-excited about getting there, and also anxious that the others will like it as much as I did. But isn't it always the way that whenever you build up your expectations too much, you are setting yourself up to be disappointed?

We finally arrive in Byron around 3pm, to find that the world and his wife has decided to come for the Christmas holidays. All the hotels are full. We grow more and more despondent trying to find somewhere affordable to stay. Knowing that I have been here before, everyone looks to me for a solution. But I am as stumped as the rest, since I did not actually stay in town last time.

We decide to head back down the coast and see if we can find somewhere in a less trendy place. On the way out of Byron, we stumble on the Sunseeker's Motel and find a very nice apartment with two double rooms for $140 between the four of us. It has the added bonus of a comfy lounge room and a big telly, so the boys settle down to watch the cricket with calls of, 'aarp' and 'pscht' sounds as the ubiquitous VB bottles are cracked open.

The cricket match is England versus Australia in (coincidentally) the VB Series at the Melbourne Cricket Ground. But after the initial excitement, Hawkeye and Bill watch with growing despair as 'McGrath flew like a pigeon to remove Shah,' and 'Brett Lee finished England off by bowling James Anderson and James Kirtley'. The final result is another comprehensive victory to Australia.

To add insult to injury, this is on top of the recent loss of the Ashes series, mere days ago in Perth. England has now lost eight series in a row against the old enemy, and Bill and Hawkeye are in mourning at the seeming demise of our glorious game.

By the evening, we are starting to get hungry again, but after the high emotions of the afternoon, we are all a little tired and grumpy. This is not a good start for finding something to eat in a crowded, strange town. We wander from pillar to post, unable to make a decision, until we finally stumble into the Orgasmic Café, where the kindly Israeli owner takes us under his wing and tells us what to have. We end up with a delicious Mediterranean platter and chicken schnitzels. Gradually, as the food goes down, the senses of humour return and the evening ends pleasantly.

After feeling so jaded yesterday, we have a later than usual start, but head off to Cape Byron by about 10am. Named by Captain Cook after the poet Byron's grandfather, Cape Byron is the most easterly point of Australia where a great limb of land juts out into the Pacific Ocean. It is possible to stand at its tip on a clear day and if you squint hard enough, you can just make out Northern Chile in the distance. Well, in my imagination I can anyway.

As we walk up the Cape, the sun is bright and all the colours are intense. There is a strong breeze to keep us cool, but I can feel my skin rapidly burning to a crisp despite the suncream and hat. The weather and the intense colours are really invigorating—my senses are saturated with blues, greens and golds and the smell of the sea air.

Hawkeye, living up to his name, spots a pod of dolphins fishing off Tallow Beach. It is wonderful watching them from our vantage point above. We walk right out to the most easterly tip, just passed the lighthouse, and there we see four more dolphins playfully jumping and surfing the waves in the turquoise waters below. We also see several loggerhead turtles majestically gliding along—just coming up momentarily for air before disappearing deep beneath the waves again for several minutes.

Hazel, Hawkeye and Bill at Clark's Beach

The heat and strength of the sun finally drives us off the Cape and we seek a shady spot on Clarks Beach. We go for a cooling swim. It is glorious jumping about in the waves, which are just big enough to be exciting, but not so powerful that we get trashed all the time like yesterday. Hawkeye's bodysurfing lessons continue and he seems to be coming along nicely.

Lunch at the Pass Café is a perfect end to a perfect morning—delicious fish burgers and Caesar salad washed down with a really good coffee, whilst watching a brush turkey and a huge frill-necked lizard. My skin has that pleasant tingling feeling from the morning's sun and wave jumping.

After lunch the girls part company from the boys for a couple of hours. Mum and I park Bill and Hawkeye in a shady spot on the Main Beach, while we have a leave-pass to go Christmas shopping. We are both bedazzled by the array of wonderful goodies in the shops.

'So cheap compared to the UK,' says Mum.

'Such good quality compared to Asia, and clothes that actually fit me,' I say. So it is a race against the clock to see who can get the most shopping done before our time is up. We return to find Bill and Dad looking quite content and being serenaded by two old hippies playing guitars and singing Bob Dylan songs—a typical Byron scene.

For supper we treat ourselves to delicious blue-eyed cod at a little bistro just off the main beach.

Bill and I have booked to go sea kayaking, hoping to get a little closer to the dolphins we had seen the day before. We have an early start and it is already blisteringly hot, so we cover up as much as possible and smother high factor sun cream on all the exposed bits.

Our guides are nice enough chaps—big and brawny from their active lifestyle and quite handsome—but they have a goggle-eyed entourage of single women, all flirting and vying for their attention, so it is difficult to build up any kind of rapport with them.

They make us sign a shark attack disclaimer. 'Is this serious?' I ask.

'Well you never can be too careful on the ocean,' says the head guide. 'But it's years since anyone was hurt by a shark.' A few days later we are told the full story by Ant. Eight years ago, there was a horrific accident in the very spot where we are about to go paddling around in blissful ignorance.

The story goes that there had been a group of divers waiting in the water to get back into their boat. The group included a honeymooning couple. To their horror, they looked down to see a Great White Shark circling below them and deciding which one of them to pick off. Then the shark skyrocketed towards the woman. The brave husband saved his new wife by pushing her out of the way, only to be killed himself, as the shark munched out his whole middle section.

Anyhow, back to our sea kayaking trip, thankfully we did not know about that tragic incident, and we are lucky that the sea is pretty calm today. Bill and I share a kayak and after a slight scary moment as we are launched through the surf, we soon get the hang of it. There is a great sense of freedom being out on the open water and Cape Byron looks stunning in the dazzling light.

Today, it seems that our timing is off and we are not lucky enough to see the dolphins, despite going to the exact same spot where we had seen them yesterday from above. As we pull into Little Wategos Beach for a cuppa, the last guide spots them, but by the time we have relaunched, they are gone.

It is great fun riding the surf back onto Clarks beach. That is, until we get rammed from behind by two idiotic women.

'Get out the way,' says one of them, shoving us with her paddle and capsizing our canoe. Then they paddle off without even asking if we are OK. I get trapped under the canoe for what feels like forever, as it rolls about in the surf. I feel really freaked out by this, fearing that I might drown. Eventually Bill manages to get me out from under the canoe. But we cannot get back into the boat, which keeps being overturned by the waves.

'This is no good. We'll never get it upright again. The waves are too strong. We'll have to swim in, and drag the boat and the paddles,' says Bill.

I try to swim and drag the boat at the same time, but the waves are crashing over me and I am severely hampered by my life-jacket which is not on tight enough and is floating up round my ears and threatening to drown me.

Eventually, one of the guides tears himself away from his harem and comes out to help us. Back on dry land, I am really angry, frightened and shaking. The thing that really makes me angry is that having endangered our lives, the two women do not even ask us if we are OK, let alone apologise—they are far too busy flirting with the guides. Is this a cultural difference, or have we just had an unfortunate run in with two particularly rude individuals? I know that if it had happened the other way round, I would have done everything I could to try to help the other person.

Anyhow, Mum and Dad are waiting for us and we go to lunch. I start to tell Mum and Dad about our ordeal and burst into tears, trembling and shivering despite the strong sunshine. Bill puts his arms round me and Mum asks Dad to fetch a strong cup of coffee with lots of sugar.

'What would you like for lunch, love?' asks Mum.

'I want chippies,' I say nuggling into Bill. 'And maybe a cheeseburger would make me feel better. And some chocolate ice-cream.'

'Then that's what you shall have,' says Mum. 'Poor thing, do you remember when you were three years old and we were sailing on Shearwater Lake? The rudder snapped and the dinghy capsized, trapping you underneath. You couldn't swim then. I had to dive under and drag you out and then pull you to shore under one arm and drag the dinghy with the other. It was Easter and freezing cold. Afterwards, we had to wrap you in blankets and feed you hot-cross buns.'

'Oh yes. I'd forgotten about that, but it was a similar feeling being trapped under the canoe.' After a good moan and a spot of lunch I feel much better.

After lunch we get straight in the car and head for the town of Dorrigo. Mum wants to see some of the Australian hinterland and to see how people live away from the coast. Close to the town of Dorrigo, is an area of outstanding natural beauty, the Dorrigo National Park. It is a World Heritage rainforest, and Mum suggests this would make an interesting contrast to the beach culture we have been experiencing so far. It turns out to be one of the best bits of the trip.

En-route to Dorrigo, we pick up a leaflet listing some accommodation in the area and phone ahead to book ourselves into a self-catering cottage, Wyldefel Gardens.

We have a beautiful drive through green rolling countryside with herds of dairy cattle munching contentedly all around us. We pass through the pleasant looking town of Bellingen, full of Victorian houses, craft shops and a creamery to process the milk coming in from the rich pasturelands. The air grows cooler as the road climbs towards the Dorrigo plateau.

Just outside Dorrigo we turn left along Rocky Creek Road towards our cottage. But the road seems to be going nowhere and has soon turned into a dirt track. We begin to worry that we have taken a wrong turn and are about to go back, when a smiley man in a pick-up truck stops.

'Goodday! Where you headed?' he asks.

'We're looking for Wyldefel Gardens. I don't suppose you know where it is?' says Dad.

'Yep. Aw'm goin that way meself. Follow me,' he says. We follow him for seven kilometres along this dirt track without another house in sight.

'P'raps he's a mad axeman luring us to our doom,' says Bill, winking at Hawkeye.

'Oh, Bill, don't say that,' I say.

'It's all right. I can see the sign for Wyldefel Gardens,' says Mum as the man in the pick-up waves goodbye to us.

Our genial host for the night, Bobby is waiting at the gate for us. She greets us with, 'I know you're just gonna love it here,' and she's not wrong. To our utter amazement, the modest description of our accommodation in the leaflet does not do it any justice. It is a palatial country home, tastefully decorated and very well equipped. It is set amongst three acres of lush and well kept gardens with a deck looking out onto the green and fertile hills.

Bobby lets us raid her raspberry patch and brings us homemade meringues and clotted cream to go with them. She supplies us with vast amounts of food for our breakfast—bacon, eggs, sausages, bread, milk, tea, coffee, cereals, orange juice and homemade marmalade. She tells us to make ourselves at home and goes back to her house across the way. We certainly do. All this for the princely sum of A$140 per night (£47) between four people. We have arrived in paradise.

It is most refreshing to have breakfast in the garden amongst the jacaranda trees, breathing in the musky scent of their purple flowers and being entertained by the song of wild birds, whilst looking out over the view towards the hills.

Today we are to visit the Dorrigo National Park, but first we spend some time in the Rainforest Centre learning about the ecosystem and the flora and fauna of the area. This is an experience in itself, where the comprehensive information is illustrated interactively, complete with the sounds of the birds you are likely to encounter and a model of a rainforest pool full of diving duck-billed platypus.

We learn that Dorrigo National Park lies on the remains of the Ebor Volcano. Under the heavy annual rainfall, the lava from Ebor weathered to form the impressive escarpment and rich soils around Dorrigo.

The tablelands of Eastern Australia were once decidedly cooler and supported alpine flora. But for the last 17,000 years, the continent of Australia has been heating up and the alpine flora has all but disappeared from the lower tablelands. Today, most of the Australian landscape is dominated by dry forests and woodlands dominated by eucalyptus. The broad-leafed rainforests typical of the Dorrigo National Park and the native animals which are dependent on them now only occur in fire and drought resistant refuges, such as along the Great Escarpment. For example, a relic of the cooler climates is the Antarctic beech which is to be found here. Other examples of the rainforest species are the Dorrigo plum, the pink cherry, the monkey nut and the brown tamarind.

Within 200 years of European settlement, extensive clearing and burning of the rainforest in New South Wales had reduced its area by half. Fortunately, the area of the Dorrigo National Park managed to escape some of the worst ravages of the loggers because of its isolation and difficulty of access.

'Did you know that Dorrigo was the first National Park in Australia and one of the first in the world?' says Bill. 'And the ironic thing is that it was set up with private money, which had been made from logging.'

The park has a rich native fauna. Thirty species of native mammals live here, the largest of which is the swamp wallaby. Other furry inhabitants include the long-nosed potoroo, our friend the sleepy koala, the dingo and several species of possums and gliders. I am excited to learn that both of the Australian monotremes, the echidna and the platypus, live in the park. These strange creatures, kind of a cross between a mammal and a reptile, that lay eggs but suckle their young, are only to be found in Australia. But the rarest inhabitant of the park, classed as a threatened species, is the red-legged pademelon, which we are very keen to see.

Most of the park's mammals are nocturnal, and so the most observable animals are the birds. The forest is a rich habitat for ground dwelling birds that feed on the abundant life within the leaf litter. These include the lyrebird, brush turkey, whipbird, logrunner and noisy pitta, as well as the smaller yellow-throated and white-browed scrub wrens.

The treetops are home to a different set of birds — the wompoo fruit dove, king parrots, green catbirds and the satin and regent bowerbirds. The park is home to three species of owl — the powerful owl, the masked owl and the sooty owl all of which are obviously more likely to be seen at night.

The dense undergrowth of the park is also home to many elusive reptiles including the mythical sounding southern angle headed dragon.

And so we learn that this is a very special place. Mum has chosen a real gem to visit, being both a rare example of pristine rainforest but at the same time highly accessible to us tourists.

With our appetites for nature thoroughly whetted, we embark on the Skywalk, which allows you to walk out over the forest canopy to look down on the treetops and gives you a fantastic view across the valley to distant mountains.

As we stand contemplating the wonders of nature at the end of the Skywalk, an Australian woman joins us. She then proclaims loudly, 'Well, bugger me, that's me mobile going off.' She proceeds to answer it and have a loud and lengthy conversation — 'Aw'm in the rainforest. Well, s'pose it's OK . . . blah, blah, blah . . .' She then turns to her companion. 'What's that ya say, Granny? Ya don't like it 'ere? Oh, well let's go then.'

We all breathe a huge sigh of relief and go back to contemplating nature and listening to the sounds of the forest.

Now it is time to experience the rainforest at ground level. We set off along the Wonga Walk amongst buttressed trunks, palms, thick woody vines, orchids and ferns. We pass majestic soapy box trees, booyong, strangler figs, the perilous giant stinging tree and giant yellow carrabeens, their enormous trunks supporting giant crowns way up in the sky. Deep in the forest, there is a feeling of extreme ancientness.

'These are the biggest trees I have ever seen,' says Bill in raptures. There are glossy black regent bowerbirds sitting in the bushes and tiny wrens scrubbling about in the undergrowth. We are accompanied by the raucous call of the satinbird, the bizarre sound of the catbird, which sounds exactly like a mewling cat, and the whipbird, which sounds, funnily enough, exactly like someone cracking a whip.

Our final destination is the Crystal Shower Waterfall, where you can walk behind the cascading water into a cool mossy green space. Hawkeye is much taken with this place and wants to have his photo taken looking out from behind the water. But although he can see us, we cannot see him behind the streaming torrent, so it will have to live on only in his memory.

Our destination reached, everyone's thoughts turn to the subject of lunch. Before we set out, Mum had been eyeing up the fare in the Canopy Café. And now, looking at her watch, is concerned that we might not make it back before the café shuts. So us younguns are despatched as the vanguard to secure provisions, whilst Mum and Dad bring up the rear. We need not have worried, for spurred on by the goal of a tasty lunch, Mum makes it back in record time, nearly trampling us in the rush to get to the counter.

We have our lunch, looking out at the scenic backdrop of the rainforest, where Hawkeye, true to form, spots the elusive red-legged pademelon grazing amongst the undergrowth. It is much like a tiny kangaroo with a pointy and very twitchy, whiskery nose and bright beady black eyes.

After lunch, Bill drives us to the romantic sounding Never Never picnic area, because we thought there was another lookout point there. When we arrive, Bill looks round to find he has a car full of well-fed, snoozy, Bromleys. In fact, Hawkeye is getting a bit of shut-eye.

'Shall we get out and have a bit of a walk?' says Bill.

'Is there a lookout place here?' Mum murmurs sleepily from the back. 'No? Well perhaps you could just take us home now.' So we never got out at the Never Never picnic spot.

We return to our wonderful country haven, where lovely kind Bill cooks us roasted organic veggies to go with the last of Bobby's bacon, and we wash it down with a bottle of Browns Bin 61. Yum. Bill has scored top marks with Mum, being able to do all the manly things and cook a decent meal.

* * *

Our time in the idyllic country haven has sadly come to an end. My favourite part of staying in Wyldefel Gardens has been wandering about the secluded gardens in my nightie first thing in the morning and being able to make myself a cup of tea whenever I want. I felt so at home here that after only two nights, I feel the most refreshed I have been for months.

But it is now time to set off back to Sydney. We decide to try to make it back in one day, as we have had such a leisurely pace until now, and we need to get the rental car back the following day. So after brief stops for coffee, lunch and afternoon pies for Bill, we arrive at Barbara's house in St Ives, in the northern suburbs of Sydney at 6.30pm. So our little road trip is over. It has been a lot of fun and a good bonding experience for Bill and my parents, who are firm friends now.

Barbara is my cousin's wife's Mum and she has kindly said that we can stay here over Christmas. She is just back from a Serbian celebration — which marks the date when the family first converted to Christianity. Barbara is of Scottish descent, but her late husband George was a Serb and she still has many friends in that community.

This morning Barbara set off to stay with her son for the Christmas break, kindly giving us the keys and the run of her house whilst she is away. We return the rental car, and feeling a little bereft, set off into the teaming metropolis of Sydney on foot. We find St Leonards Station and buy a Sydney Daytripper ticket, which rather wonderfully allows you to use any form of public transport — ferries, buses, trains and metro — as much as you want for a day. I have seen Sydney Harbour before, but I am still excited as we trundle across the Harbour Bridge to see the white sails of the Opera House seeming to float in the water of the harbour. And if I am excited, Bill, Mum and Dad are ecstatic.

So we head for Circular Quay and get lots of tourist information to help us plan the day. 'What does everyone feel like doing?' I ask.

'We just want to ride backwards and forwards across the harbour on the ferry,' chime Mum and Dad together.

'I want to go to the aquarium to see all the sharks,' says Bill.

'Great, we can do both,' I say.

So we set off in a ferry for the aquarium at Darling Harbour. It is great fun. We get to see some real platypus, like the ones we know exist at Dorrigo. Other highlights include the graceful little seahorses, lovely weedy sea dragons and an endearing Maori wrasse. He is the size of a Shetland pony, with big plump lips and he keeps swimming up to the glass to stare at me with a very human-looking eye. We watch the playful Australian fur seals from the side of the pool and then go downstairs to where you can view their tank from underneath through a glass wall.

'It's not often that you get to see the furry underbelly of a seal as it swims by. I quite enjoyed that,' says Bill. Walking on through a see-through tunnel surrounded by giant wrays and sharks of all species—leopard, tiger, nurse and reef—is an unnerving but fascinating experience and Bill's favourite bit.

There are some wonderfully colourful giant prawns and crayfish, but I am shocked to find myself drooling into their tanks and thinking how delicious they would be sautéed lightly in some garlic butter.

After lunch at the aquarium, we decide to make the most of our daytripper ticket with a ride up the Paramatta River. The journey itself is pleasant enough, with good views of the harbour, but Paramatta itself is very hot and rather disappointing, especially as we have missed the last boat home and have to walk a long way in the searing heat to catch the train back.

When we eventually get back to Pymble station, we cannot find the buses back to Barbara's and have to walk for another one and a half hours to get home after a long and tiring day. To make matters worse, Dad cuts his foot badly on a razor sharp piece of grass. Only in Australia, could the grass be so dangerous! We try to get a taxi, but there are none to be had by phone or flagging down. It seems in this suburb, everyone has a car, and no-one is foolish enough to try to walk. We feel very lost without the rental car.

We finally stumble into St Ives, exhausted and hungry and to our great delight find a Thai restaurant to revive our flagging energy levels. I get to eat the giant juicy prawns in garlic butter that I had been dreaming of. Bill tries out the Thai that he has learnt to say 'hello' and 'thank you' to the waitress,

'Sawàt-dii,' says Bill and, 'Khàwp khun khráp.' She looks very surprised but highly delighted to hear her language.

* * *

Back in Vietnam, we had told Ant and Ems of our plans to be in St Ives. Coincidentally, they live not far away and are now back from their travels. We have kept in touch via e-mail and today they are coming to take us on a tour of their favourite places around Sydney. The doorbell rings and we open it to find one blond tousle-haired person and another darker one wearing a little sun hat pulled low over her eyes. They look very at home in their native environment.

'Hi guys!' they chorus.

'Congratulations!!!! You guys have won a trip to the Northern Beaches with your fantastic Aussie tour guides, Ems and Ant,' says Ems.

'Yes we're here to help you claim your special prize,' says Ant.

I feel very torn that we are not spending every moment with Mum and Dad before they go back, but it is the only chance we will get to see Ems and Ant, and who knows when we will see them again after this.

They give us a whistle-stop tour of their favourite Northern beaches—lots of golden sand, crashing waves and bright sunshine. We walk to the edge of a cliff and look down on a little cove where the surf crashes onto the sand.

'Now this is my absolute favourite beach,' says Ant. 'The surf is awesome here. Come on let's get down there.' He leads the way onto a narrow ledge that clings to the side of the cliff. 'It's a bit tricky but I'm sure you'll manage,' he says, practically running along the tiny ledge.

I go more cautiously using one hand to steady myself against the rock face and eyeing the hundred feet drop down onto the rocks below nervously. I am starting to get vertigo. We get to a place where the ledge runs out and there is a frayed old piece of rope hanging over the edge.

'Ya have to drop down onto that little platform below,' says Ant. 'But it's cool 'cos you can steady yourself using the rope. I'll go first so you can see how it's done,' he says lowering himself over the edge.

I peer over to see him dangling from the end of the rope, then letting go and dropping another few feet onto the tiny platform, which is still at least 70 feet above the beach. Ems goes next and lands safely on the platform.

'I'm not sure I can do this,' I whisper to Bill.

'Don't try it if you're not sure,' says Bill. 'It's a bit necky, but I've got to have a go,' he says not wanting to lose face. Bill's years of tree surgery have served him well and he makes it down safely.

I start to lower myself over the edge, clinging onto the rope. There is a strong wind blowing me sideways and I cannot get the image out of my head of me toppling over when I land on the platform and plunging to my death on the rocks below. 'Sorry guys, I can't do it. You go on and I'll sit here and wait for you.'

'Oh, OK then,' says Ant looking surprised. He probably thinks I am a wuss, because Ems can do it, but she is a tougher girl than me and

I am not ashamed to admit it. They disappear for a while and then I see them running about on the beach chucking stones into the sea. When they come back I realise that I definitely made the right choice. They have to leap up from the platform, to catch hold of the end of the rope scrambling madly with their legs up the side of the cliff and hauling hand over hand to get up. I know my arms would not have been strong enough to do that.

We buy a picnic from a local deli, including Aussie champers and jumbo prawns with a pot of garlic mayo for dipping. I am really getting my wish after the aquarium. We have lunch at Palm Beach and have a great time reminiscing about Vietnam and comparing notes on Laos, which already seems like an age ago.

'Wasn't it cool in Laos? For the first few days I kept expecting them to grab us and hassle us, but they didn't. It was such a nice change after Vietnam,' says Ems.

'Yeah loads of people we met asked if the Vietnamese are as hassling as the Thais and we literally laughed out loud in their faces! The Thais just don't hassle in comparison. We thought 'Ahhhh, they will soon find out themselves . . . "says Ant. 'D'you remember the tour we took to see the ethnic minorities? I still can't get over how rude that tour guide was—'You are disturbing my lunch'—very funny!'

'Yeah and the wee-smelling cabin on the way back,' says Bill.

'Ew, yeah, disgusting,' says Ems, laughing with a horrified look on her face.

Wild Animals and Wedding Outfits   Chapter 11: Australia

Ems and Ant, our authentic Aussie tour guides

After lunch they take us on a walk to their favourite look out spot near the lighthouse. It is blisteringly hot, but very windy and the champers has gone straight to my head. I wobble my way up giggling inanely.

We have a short swim/jump in the waves at Newport Beach and then back to Em's palatial house at Clareville, known to the locals as 'Club Clareville'. Em's Mum and Dad designed it themselves. It is in a prime spot looking out over Pittwater—many yachts floating on a deep blue harbour with tree-clad hills in the distance. There is a mouth-watering view from every room and from the pool and hot spa in the front garden.

We lounge in the hot spa for ages, chatting with Em's Dad, Brian, who looks like Ollie Reid and is a larger than life character. He tells us how he met Maggie, Em's Mum, on a boat from England to Australia. Em's Mum is what is known as a '£10 Pom,' owing to the cheapness of her emigration ticket. Brian apparently first chatted up Maggie's best friend who said, 'Brian, I like you very much, but I think you would be much better suited to my friend Maggie.' Such a great line, I can think of a few situations where that would have been really useful for me!

For supper, we have a takeaway curry with far too much wine and lots of jollity. I think if you were a teetotaller at Club Clareville, you would probably go thirsty. Wine and beer is in plentiful supply, but a cup of tea is rather more scarce.

The subject turns to music and whether there is any decent stuff around these days or whether only the old stuff is any good. Brian goes to put on an album and the sounds of Neil Diamond fill the room. 'Well what do you think of that, eh? It doesn't get much better than that, does it?' says Brian.

'Well, obviously he's got a good voice, but I'm afraid he just doesn't butter my muffin,' says Bill who is a bit drunk and does not realise that he is challenging Brian's manhood.

And then the moment comes that Bill has been dreading. 'Harumph,' says Brian, 'Anyone for a spot of Bend Arm? How about you Bill?'

'Oh, Brian, leave the poor chap alone,' says Maggie. 'Anyone for more wine?' And Maggie deftly moves the subject matter on and saves Bill from certain pain and perhaps a broken arm.

We awake to the smell of a cooked breakfast on the go. We are both feeling a bit delicate this morning, after too much wine last night. We go down to the kitchen to find Brian cooking mountains of bacon, sausages and egg.

'Come on, get that down you. It'll set you up for the day,' he says handing us generously loaded plates and mugs of coffee. Ant and Ems come to join us. Breakfast on the terrace, breathing in the fresh sea air does wonders for restoring us. And when Brian suggests a tour of Pittwater in his little 'runaround' motorboat, to see where the wealthy and elite of Sydney live, it seems the perfect way to spend a morning.

'Check out the launching machine,' whispers Ant, as Brian leads us into what looks like a garden shed perched over the water. Inside the shed, everyone gets into the boat which is suspended above the water by the launching machine. Brian proceeds to lower us rather jerkily and ungracefully into the water by means of a remote control—great fun!

Our first stop is the Royal Yacht Club because Brian needs to fill up with petrol. He also wants to show us Spartacus, his yacht in which he won a race the previous day.

Then we sail off to the Basin, a sheltered spot for a swim, and are given a run down on who owns which fancy house and how much it cost. These range from business tycoons to Hollywood film stars. One of the houses recently sold for A$22 million—a lot of money by any standards.

As well as motorised boat launches, some people also have motorised 'inclinators'—essentially a little cubicle which transports you from your posh house down the slope to your boat without having to walk down any nasty tiring steps—very comical and extremely lazy.

After our swim, I am delighted to make use of one of the best ideas I have seen in ages. Captain Cappuccino has a little boat from which he can serve you proper espresso coffee or ice-creams right on the water. You just hail him over and he sails right up to your boat to deliver your delicious beverage. How very civilised.

We have lunch back at Club Clareville looking out over Pittwater and then play pool in Brian's games room till it is time to return to Barbara's. It is sad saying farewell to our travelling buddies. Who knows when we will see them again?

* * *

This is to be our last full day with Mum and Dad before they return home to spend Christmas with my elder sister, Jennie, and her family. So we spend the morning relaxing and chatting at Barbara's before heading to our favourite part of town—the harbour. We have a splendid lunch at Wolfies in front of the Rocks with a view of the Opera House—delicious food, stunning view, good company—perfect.

After lunch we split up into the usual twosomes—the girls for shopping, the boys for sightseeing. Mum and I are after a few last minute Christmas presents, but we are disappointed to find the Rocks is mostly full of tourist tat and we do not know which part of town the regular Sydneysiders shop in.

We take a ferry to Watson's Bay for an early supper. It is famous for Doyles Seafood Restaurant and the sunset views looking back over the harbour towards the centre of the city. After our initial shock at the prices, we decide that we will splash out for our last night together and it is well worth it. The food is fantastic. Bill and I both have the seafood platter and Mum and Dad have Atlantic salmon, all cooked to perfection. The sunset does not disappoint either. The sun is a huge amber ball flanked by red clouds and mist, sinking behind the brightly lit skyscrapers of central Sydney and dying the sails of the Opera house pink—marvellous!

* * *

It is Christmas Eve and time for us to wave a sad farewell to Mum and Dad. Spending time with them has helped to dispel my homesickness and it now feels like we are on the home run of our journey. It has been good to see Bill getting to know them better and wonderful that he has developed such a bond with the old rascal, Hawkeye.

We catch a taxi with them into the airport and have a final lunch together. Eating copious amounts seems to have been a bit of a theme of the holiday and Bill is starting to look like your typical brawny Aussie boy.

I feel really sad as we wave them off at the departure lounge and it is with a huge sense of anticlimax that we catch the train back into town. We want to buy each other some treats for Christmas day and we have now discovered where all the department stores are. But the city is heaving with last minute Christmas shoppers and it turns into a stressful ordeal.

Finally we give up on the idea and go back to St Ives. The house seems cold and empty now everyone has gone. We crack open a bottle of bubbly to try and get ourselves more in the Christmas spirit and sit out in the garden in the gathering dusk. There are lots of horrid cockroaches scurrying about until suddenly, whoosh!! An owl comes silently out of the dark, grabs one and flies off. Hurray for the owl! Two more cockroaches meet their death the same way. Each time the owl comes so silently that we are not aware of it until it is right in front of us.

A joint e-mail from our two best mates only adds to the wistful feeling of homesickness. They write:—

Dear Bill and Anna,

What a difference a year makes! Who would have thought that we would be sending out joint Christmas messages? But it's true the old Virgo is organising me into such respectable practices and the cards are even going into the post on time!!

From your sunny vantage point you may have forgotten what an English Christmas is like, but so as not to disappoint you, it hasn't changed. We've had a week of chill north easterlies zipping off the North Sea, some crisp clear beautiful days mixed in with days when it hardly seems to get light before it's dusk again. In fact December has been pretty reasonable after a very wet and windy November.

Winter Flowering Cherries are starting to brighten the days and the weather has been such that we are coming across the odd optimistic specimen, like the Hazel that had its catkins out and buds swelling to burst at the end of November!! Really there is a lot of stuff out that shouldn't be and a lot of trees that have forgotten to drop their leaves. Odd but it seems to be the norm now.

Just to keep you in touch Bill—Brian is causing mayhem on the Archers—not able to choose between his wife and the mother of his secret child!! If I could remember all the names you'd be really excited but I can't and I don't get to hear it often enough to make it interesting for you.

The Premiership is jolly exciting too, 10 points between the top ten teams, of which Leeds are not one in fact they are struggling to stay out of the relegation zone. A revival is expected soon but El Tel has not made the best of starts at Elland Road. Liverpool are contriving to give up the lead they had at the top, while Arsenal and Man U are stepping into ominous form. Chelsea surprisingly are close behind and even managing to win away from home on cold Saturday afternoons. Amazing the effect Global Warming is having on the world.

You will be brought up to speed on the cricket news by just about every Aussie you meet, so I won't even bother to go down that route. But when they give you some stick, just mention the rugby!! We were bloody awesome!! Well bloody lucky, but it looked good—don't think we will be so fortunate in the World Cup.

Life at home has been busy. I'll let Karn give you all the girlie details. We haven't done much DIY lately, but the place looks great, which doesn't help motivate me to get on with all the jobs. Right, it's daylight so it must be time to go to work.

Have a great Christmas and a splendid New Year.

Love Abava

What!!!! THE OLD VIRGO!!!!!!! This is what I have to put up with, living with a young upstart. He's off to work now, armed with Christmas presents, so I've got a quiet moment to write this. He's spent the last 2 days in full Christmas spirit, doing the rounds of all his ladies and friends, and giving out cards and presents like a jolly, bald, checked-shirted Father Christmas without a beard, who drives a battered old car instead of a sleigh!

MERRY CHRISTMAS! Hope this finds you relaxed and happy and enjoying the Christmas heat of Aussie. You must be so thrilled to see your parents Anna, and catch up with home—have a wonderful time.

And we both want to thank you for the bag of coffee all the way from Vietnam, and your card—it's so exciting to get parcels from these remote far-out places. The coffee will have to wait to be sampled in our new kitchen, could be our celebratory cup of coffee when it's all finished and fitted out with a coffee grinder etc. In fact you'll probably be back by then, you could join us!!

Really looking forward to spending Christmas with Abava—our first Christmas together—with both my family and his. Yes, what a year it's been. Abava was wide-awake and chatting at 5 o'clock this morning (bastard!) about how we were going to celebrate the New Year. We decided that nothing could beat the extraordinary time we had last year on the beach in the icy wonderland of the moonlit Gower Peninsula, with you guys, so we decided to have a quiet, cosy time at home this year.

So, it seems to have been a year of great change and excitement—for a lot of people, not just us. Wonder what next year will bring—the year of the sheep. Doesn't sound quite so exciting, but perhaps we need a quiet year to make up for all the changes and upheavals.

Well my dears, I must get on with my day. Whatever you're doing, have the most fantastic Christmas and New Year.

Loads of love to you both,

Karn XXXXXXXXXXXXXXXXXXX

Christmas Day

We do our best to have a romantic morning, despite feeling very homesick. We eat chocolate in bed and open our presents from each other and the presents that Mum and Dad brought. Bill has bought me some Issay Miyake perfume and it feels like the height of indulgence after spending so many weeks feeling really skanky, whilst travelling round Asia. I know it will be a godsend in South America too. He has also bought me a beautiful Tibetan necklace that I had admired in Darjeeling, and had no idea that he had sneaked back to get it. It came from the same shop where he got his conch and it feels like a very special thing. It even has a secret compartment for concealing precious things. I love it. Clever Billy.

We had imagined Christmas in Australia to be blazing hot and everyone goes to the beach for a barbie. But it is just our luck that it is cold, overcast and threatening to rain any moment. At least this makes us feel at home.

Barbara's daughter Alexe picks us up for Christmas lunch at her place. She is one of those terribly organised people who manages to look after her six children and also have loads of other people round for Christmas—much respect to her.

It is all a bit chaotic and difficult to relax in the company of so many people that we do not know and I find myself wishing that we did not have to 'do' Christmas at all. There is a good deal of Pommie bashing over lunch, especially about the cricket, which is rather a sore point and I can feel Bill bristling and having to sit on his hands.

After lunch it begins to rain in earnest and there are lots of jokes about us Poms bringing the weather with us. It is pretty ironic, since Australia was in the middle of its worst drought for 20 years. So hey, we have done them a favour. Since a swim is not very inviting in this weather, Alexe's husband, Guy, puts on the *Fellowship of the Rings* DVD, and we spend a pleasant afternoon wrapped up in Middle Earth and all its characters.

Boxing Day

Today, we pack our stuff and head for Melbourne. Our intention is to use it as a base to explore Victoria and the South coast until our flight leaves for Chile on 6th January. As the plane is coming in to land, I am shocked at the sight of miles of brown, dry fields everywhere. The effects of the drought are very evident here in Victoria.

We catch the shuttle bus into Spencer Street Station and then get a taxi to St Kilda's, a suburb of Melbourne set along the shores of Port Phillip Bay. The hostel we had intended to stay in is grotty and overpriced for a tiny room, so we tramp around for ages looking for somewhere better. It is the same story everywhere—full up and overcharging because of the Christmas holidays.

We finally manage to find a nice motel on Fitzroy Street with a room free and we bargain the manager down to $80 a night. We book it for two nights thinking that we will be able to find somewhere cheaper and quieter for the rest of our stay. Fitzroy Street is really happening—lots of trendy restaurants, bars, shops and trams rattling past on their way into town—a great place for a night out, but not so restful to stay here. In its favour, it leads down to the sea and has a bright fresh feel to it with the breeze coming in from the ocean.

After a spot of lunch, we catch the tram into the centre of Melbourne. It is my first tram experience and I have to say I think it is a marvellous way to travel about a city.

Melbourne centre is a pleasant mixture of arty and modern next to the original Victorian buildings such as the Flinders Street Station, and the trams give it a romantic feel.

The new Lord of the Rings film, *The Two Towers* has just been released and having refreshed our memories of *The Fellowship* on Christmas Day, we are eager to see it. But it is fully booked and we have to settle for the new Harry Potter film—a poor substitute in my eyes.

* * *

England is playing Australia again in a 5-day Test Match at the Melbourne Cricket Ground. And guess what? They are losing badly. However, this fact does not seem to dampen the spirits of the Barmy Army who are here in full force, supporting the England side no matter what the score.

Micky Jay, writing for the Australian spoof sports website, *The Bladder*, tells us that, 'Barmy Army song leader, Alfred Smyth-Rockbottom says that everywhere they go, people want to know who they are and where they come from. They also want to know why they are at the cricket and admitting that they are English.'

One of the Australians' tactics is of general mockery and name-calling to humiliate their opponents. Known as 'mental disintegration' it involves suggesting, for example, that England's James Kirtley runs like a girl. Steve Harmison tries to retaliate by asking Shane Warne why he is so fat, to which Warne replies, 'Because every time I sleep with your wife, she gives me a biscuit.'

Well, the mental disintegration tactic seems to be working like a dream. By now Bill has got to the point of not being able to watch any more matches or even to check the score, so traumatised is he by England's ongoing defeats. He has even taken to faking an Aussie accent in public so as to avoid any more taunts.

The presence of so many cricket fans in town, combined with the Christmas and New Year holidays means that we cannot find anywhere to stay. We cannot even extend our stay at our current motel, because it is fully booked. So in a mild panic we phone Elizabeth Savery, Mum's cousin, and arrange to stay with her near Wangaratta, in rural Victoria. We had intended to visit them after New Year, but fortunately they are kind enough to have us a bit sooner because of the accommodation problems.

Crisis averted, we walk down to the beach and along St Kilda's pier. The sun is bright and there is a fresh sea breeze. I cannot wait to get in the ocean.

'Come on in, it's really invigorating,' I shout to Bill, who is sitting on the beach looking a bit sorry for himself. 'The waves are just the right size for jumping without getting trashed.'

'Sorry, I don't fancy it. The wind's too cold,' says Bill.

I am amazed—Bill not get in the sea? 'But you're usually such a water babe,' I say. 'I hope you're not sickening for something.'

After lunch we head into town to see *The Two Towers*. We enter the Crown Casino complex where we have booked tickets to see the film. The place is huge. There are hundreds of people milling about. There are row upon row of cash machines, and there are row upon row of slot machines. There are many people moving their money from the first type of machine to the second. The people that designed this place are experts at parting us from our cash.

Bill and I are, I am afraid rather geeky Lord of the Rings fans and we have both been looking forward to seeing the latest in Peter Jackson's trilogy for a very long time. There is a buzz of eager anticipation in the theatre. We guess that the other people in the audience who have made it to the second day of screening are just as excited as we are. We are all here to lose ourselves for the next three hours in Tolkien's world. The task of the ringbearer weighs heavy on our hearts. The Riders of Rohan are magnificent. Aragorn is thigh-tremblingly heroic. Gandalf the White is even better than Gandalf the Grey. Gollum is cunningly tricksy and the little hobbitses are so valiant. And all set against the stunning backdrop of New Zealand scenery, with Howard Shore's haunting sound track.

Unfortunately, I have made a fatal error of judgement. Whilst in the queue for tickets, I was seduced by the signs advertising a pack of free Lord of the Rings playing cards being given away with every giant carton of Coca Cola. The thought of being able to gaze upon Aragorn's handsome face every time we play cards to while away the time waiting for buses, or on long train journeys, very quickly had me parting with my cash and staggering to my seat under the weight of the enormous bucket of Coca Cola I had just purchased. For those of you who have not seen the film (I am sure there must be someone, although I cannot for the life of me understand why) it is over three hours long. So you can begin to imagine how unwise it was for me, in my already heightened state of excitement, to purchase and drink such a large quantity of caffeinated beverage. About halfway through the film, I begin to squirm uncomfortably in my seat. By three quarters of the way through I have my legs firmly crossed and am sweating with the effort to hold on. With ten minutes to go, I can bear it no longer and make a dash for the loo. What a fool I feel when I return to find that I have missed the crucial moment of the whole film, the climax of the Helm's Deep battle—damn! And the irony of it is I do not even like Coca Cola. And to add insult to injury, there are no pictures of Aragorn on the playing cards.

* * *

We go to the Post Office and post lots of stuff home, to lighten the load of our rucksacks. Then we go shopping. We discover a whole street of outdoor activity shops and go mad stocking up on new equipment for our travels, including Gortex jackets and merino wool thermals to keep us warm and dry in the Andes. We have immediately managed to refill the space we had made in our rucksacks.

We squeeze in a short visit to the Botanical Gardens—always a favourite destination for Bill—before we have to head to the station for our train to Wangaratta. But it is really too hot to enjoy them very much.

The train to Wang is also very hot. I am really quite surprised that it is not air-conditioned. We sit opposite a very amply proportioned young lady, who has obviously eaten more than her fair share of pies. She looks as if someone has accidentally over-inflated her and she is spilling out of her rather inadequate clothing in all directions, much to the delight of her amorous boyfriend. I spend most of the journey trying to avert my gaze and look out of the window at mile upon mile of brown, sere, drought ravaged land. It is early evening by the time we arrive in roasting Wang, which is still a sweaty 40 degrees Celsius. We have a wonderful welcome from Elizabeth and her husband Edwin, whose car and house are thankfully much cooler than the rest of the surroundings.

Elizabeth has cooked us a delicious roast beef dinner, which is accompanied by copious amounts of wine and we all get quite hammered. The sparkling Shiraz is a particular favourite.

We get up rather late with a tad of a hangover, to much teasing from Edwin. Elizabeth shows us her garden and the wedding catering business which all looks like jolly hard work. I am impressed at how she keeps her garden looking so lush in such dry conditions. She is a woman with abundant drive and energy.

At coffee time their neighbour Geoff comes in for a chat. He is the archetypal Australian farmer—as hard as nails, but with a great sense of humour. He has a lot of stock and is lamenting how dry the land is.

'At least A'wm better off than some of the other farmers round 'ere. Aw've got a river running through me land an aw use it for irrigation and for the stock to 'ave a drink. Some of the fellas aw know are goin out of business because they 'ave to buy water in an' it's costing 'em a fortune,' says Geoff.

It seems that this land is just not able to support such intensive grazing and it is in danger of being turned into desert.

Elizabeth kindly lends us her car to see some of the local sights. We drive to Beechworth, a very attractive town which was built during the gold rush of Victorian times. We spend ages in the Burke Memorial Museum, fascinated by the way of life of the early pioneers—very tough people by all accounts. The museum takes its name from the hapless explorer, Robert O'Hara Burke who was the Superintendent of Police in Beechworth during the early days of the gold rush, before he set off on his historic but ill-fated trek to reach the North coast with William Wills in 1860.

Woolshed Falls, now a popular picnic area, was once the site of a major alluvial gold field, which yielded over 85,000 kg of gold in 14 years. The most famous story of the gold prospectors is of 'Johnson's claim' at Woolshed in 1856. He found so much gold that he had a pair of gold horseshoes smelted. His friend was to be a candidate for a seat in local parliament to represent the miners. So Johnson shod his friend's horse in gold and he rode into town in style for the election, which he won.

It is said that there is still gold in them there hills if you know where to look, because occasionally, small pieces of gold are found in the rivers, but it seems that most of the wealth has now gone.

As well as gold, this area was once rich in gems. The largest on display was a very beautiful sapphire. Bill's favourite exhibit was a crystal with water inside it—very rare apparently.

We fall into conversation with the woman who runs the museum and she tells us about a lady who has a collection of gems found locally, so we call in to visit her on the way back. A tiny white-haired old lady greets us and welcomes us into her bungalow. Her name is Mrs Goldsworthy, which seems very appropriate for a lady whose husband used to be a gold miner. She is a real enthusiast on the subject of mineralogy. We have hours of fun chatting to her while she proudly shows us her collection.

On the way back, we drive down a dirt track through the bush. It is late afternoon and everything is golden and beautiful. We follow a small creek through the eucalypt forest. Suddenly we catch sight of our first real live wild kangaroo. We are very excited. A little further on we come across a very large black kangaroo, which stops and watchs us for a while before hopping off. I feel there is something special about this animal. I have since asked about black kangaroos and looked in books, only to be told that there is no such thing and it must have been a wallaby, but I know that it was too big for a wallaby. It was at least five feet tall. Perhaps it was a colour mutation? To me it was a mythical creature.

Back on the main road another miracle is happening—storm clouds are gathering and the first fat spots of rain begin to hit the windscreen. Soon it is a veritable downpour. We really laugh.

'That's typical,' says Bill, 'First we have a rainy Australian Christmas and now we've brought rain to drought stricken Victoria!'

Back at Elizabeth's a small crowd has gathered for another enormous dinner. David, Elizabeth's brother and his wife Diana are there, as are Elizabeths' son Julian and his wife Ceryl. Another boozy feast ensues with much jollity.

David and Diana very kindly lend us their car so we can explore the nearby National Parks. We decide to visit Mount Buffalo National Park, which is a huge rocky plateau where the granite has been sculpted into fantastically shaped boulders and tors by the action of heat, wind, water, ice and plants. I am looking forward to getting out into nature once more.

It is still drizzly and overcast as we head for Mount Buffalo. As we drive, the landscape becomes increasingly green as the road begins a gradual climb into the mountains. We pass wineries, orchards, fruit farms and dairy farms in this lush landscape so different from Wang. We finally wind our way up Mount Buffalo and arrive at The Chalet.

It is still raining when we arrive, so we sit drinking coffee in The Chalet, waiting for the worst of it to pass. We shall have our first chance to try out our new Gortex jackets. It is a very strange sensation, sitting here. It reminds me so much of cosy wooden cafés at ski resorts in Europe, coming in from the cold for a hot drink. It is not something I had ever envisaged experiencing in Australia.

We study a leaflet which illustrates lots of treks through the bush to wonderful vistas across the valleys. So when the rain finally eases off, we set out in search of the intriguing sounding Underground River. We walk amongst the snow gums for half an hour or so and come upon a place where dark rocks are heaped one on top of each other and there is a sound of rushing water coming from beneath them. We climb through a gap in the rocks into a cramped underground cavern, and there is the river, dark and ominous. It is a very spooky place, full of spiders. As Australian spiders have a fearsome reputation for their toxicity, we do not hang around for long. The spooky theme continues as our walk takes us to a view point named 'Haunted Gorge.'

We climb up out of the gorge, coming across lots of roo poo, but none of the actual creatures who made the deposit. We step out onto a sun-warmed granite plateau where the smell of lemon myrtle and eucalyptus is intoxicating. We walk amongst strange shaped rocks and tortuously sculpted eucalypts whose bark is striped in shades of cream and ochre. I dreamily imagine the forms of animals and faces in the rocks as if in some mystical far off time these creatures once walked the earth until some sudden cataclysmic force froze them forever in this shape.

All along our path there are brightly coloured wildflowers—pinks, purples, yellows. Bill is fascinated by the bright yellow lichens covering the rocks, which he tells me must be hundreds of years old.

Our circular walk takes us back to the Chalet for lunch, before we set off for a different part of the mountain. We visit The Monolith, a giant granite boulder balanced impossibly on the edge of a precipice. It puts me in mind of Logan's Rock in Cornwall and I have a pang of homesickness.

There is a rickety, rusty ladder, up the side of the rock. It has been there for around 150 years and there are photos of Victorian day-trippers happily scaling the rock. The Park authorities have warned people not to use the ladder and I am happy to comply. But Bill, who has a penchant for climbing things, looks around to check that no-one is coming, before scaling the ladder. As he climbs, he disappears from my view, until a tiny face appears, peering at me from the top of the vast boulder. He looks so far away. And it looks so unsafe. I wish he would come down.

I hold my breath until Bill is back on safe ground. He tells me that as he stood on the top of the Monolith he suddenly feared that with his extra weight unbalancing it, the rock might choose this moment to topple off its precipice into the valley below, taking him with it to his death. Fortunately it did not and I can breath again.

Now we head for the very peak of Mount Buffalo, known as The Horn. We climb to the top and are rewarded with a fantastic 360 degree view of the Alpine National Park—miles upon miles of forest covered hills, with the euphoric vapour of eucalypt wafting up to us.

We are joined by an elderly, but fit looking Australian man. We fall into conversation about travelling. He tells us that he has just come back from South America and enthuses about the five day trek from Cusco to Machu Picchu. He tells us that he had great difficulty with the altitude, but despite that, it was the highlight of his trip. It is good to get excited about the next phase of our journey, which is looming ever closer and filling me with apprehension.

Finally, we leave Mount Buffalo, driving across a spur of hills to Mount Beauty, where we find a room in the Bogong Moth Motel.

New Year's Eve

During the night I wake up needing the loo, and feeling disorientated, I grope about looking for the bathroom. I feel what I think is the shower curtain and assuming that I must have walked straight through the open door of the bathroom, I exclaim, 'Oh, here I am!'

Bill hears me rustling about and switches on the light to reveal that I have actually climbed into the wardrobe and am feeling my coat rather than the shower curtain. We both fall about laughing and cannot get to sleep for ages because we keep bursting into giggles again. Bill has only to say, 'Oh, here I am!' to send us off into fits. It is to become a bit of a catch phrase for the rest of the holiday.

In the morning, we set off for the ski resort village of Falls Creek, intending to repeat our lovely walking experience of yesterday. As we drive along, the weather gets progressively worse. The rain lashes down and the wind buffets the car from side to side. After seven months in hot climes, it seems like the middle of winter to us.

The weather is so inclement, that when we arrive at the tourist office in Falls Creek and enquire of the lady behind the counter what fun things there might be to do in the area, she replies, 'Well, lets face it, its about as much fun as cat's wee out there, so you'd be better off visiting a couple of wineries on the Gourmet Trail!' We have to agree with her.

So after thawing out in a café, we follow the 'Gourmet Trail' through Oxley and Milawa, where there are cheese factories, berry farms and wineries. It is when we stop at the Oxley Cheese Factory that I have my second toilet-related incident of the day. I wander off to the Ladies while Bill looks around. They are just building a new toilet block and I unwittingly go into one that is not yet finished. Everything seems to be in order except that, once inside, the door is a very snug fit and there is no handle to pull it open. I try everything to open the door, breaking my fingernails and getting into a complete panic before squeaking plaintively for help.

Eventually someone hears me and manages to shoulder the door open, to find me rather shaken and very embarrassed inside. I rejoin Bill and relate to him what has just happened. 'Oh, here I am!' he quips, but it does not seem so funny this time and I have kind of lost my enthusiasm for the Gourmet Trail.

Elizabeth has arranged for us to spend New Year at Julian and Ceryl's with some of their friends. It is very kind of them all to entertain us, but what I really want to do is just to snuggle up for a quiet night with Bill. But we think we may as well join in the party spirit and both drink far too much bubbly Shiraz.

New Year's Day

We greet the New Year by watching Red Dwarf videos and nursing hangovers. When we have all recovered sufficiently, Julian drives us into Glenrowan for the Ned Kelly experience. The town is full of museums, shows and tacky souvenir shops, dedicated to this small town horse thief who murdered a couple of policemen and was finally captured in a shoot out a hundred years ago. He is an unlikely character to celebrate as a hero. The more I find out about him, the less I like him. It strikes me that not a lot can have happened in Glenrowan in the last 100 years if they are still talking about Ned Kelly.

*   *   *

Back in Melbourne once more, we have booked ourselves into a motel called the Quest on Redan in St Kilda's. Now that the cricket and the New Year is over, we finally managed to find ourselves some quiet and affordable accommodation and we intend to guard it jealously for the rest of the time we have left in Australia. We have managed to secure ourselves a studio apartment complete with kitchen and dining area for the bargain price of $65 per night. The staff running the motel made us feel very welcome and it is becoming a bit of a home from home, with the added luxury of being able to make our own meals.

We have three days left before flying to South America and neither of us really feel ready for it. We have lots we need to organise, such as getting Bill a yellow fever jab, catching up with our e-mails and the small matter of learning some Spanish before launching ourselves on a continent where we have heard that very few people speak English.

I would have loved to see more of the area round Melbourne, but time and budgets are running out. We try unsuccessfully to postpone our flight, but everything is booked up till the 14th February. So there is nothing for it, but to get on with our chores and brace ourselves for the culture shock of South America. I have to keep reminding myself that it has been my dream ever since I was a little girl to see such things as Machu Picchu, llamas and the Amazon.

* * *

In the end, Melbourne proved to be the tonic we needed. We ate well, we slept well, we jumped in the waves at St Kildas beach and we both felt much stronger and more able to deal with the rigours of new and unfamiliar countries by the time we flew out to Santiago on 6th January.

So far on our travels we have always just pitched up at a place, trusting that we will be able to find a hotel easily when we arrive. But I do not want to take that risk in Santiago. I do not want to get stranded in the wrong part of town at some strange hour of the night. So I go online and book us a room for the first night in a nice little hotel in a safe part of town. Farewell Australia. South America, here we come.

Chapter 12
Chile—Pisco Sours and Seeing Stars

So our South American adventure begins. Another continent to discover. One more step closer to home and towards the end of our journey. After a cushy time in Australia, recharging our batteries and expanding our waistlines, we set off for South America with some trepidation. Neither of us has any previous experience of the continent and we have heard many scary tales of misadventures in this part of the world. My secret fears are that we will be robbed by bandits or kidnapped by drug barons. But as a wise man once told me, 'The difference between excitement and fear is a few deep breaths,' and this is potentially the most exciting leg of our journey.

We leave Melbourne at 9am on 6th January and fly via Auckland to Santiago in Chile—a 17-hour journey. We arrive in Santiago and as we walk through the airport Bill finds a clock and says, 'OK, I'm going to set my watch to local time. It's now 3pm on 6th January.'

'No, it must be the seventh today. We can't have travelled for 17 hours and it still be the sixth,' I say.

'Well this clock definitely says the sixth. Let's find another one to double check,' says Bill. The next clock says exactly the same. 'Oh, you know what's happened?' says Bill. 'We've crossed the International Date Line. So it's still Monday 6th here.'

'Oh my God! I've booked our hotel room for the seventh. We'll just have to hope they've got space for us tonight.'

We catch a shuttle bus to the hotel. From the outside it does not look inviting. It is very small and there are bars on the windows. The street is hot and dusty and the hotel door is locked. The shuttle bus driver sneers at the place, before driving off, leaving us standing in the street beside our luggage. I have a few moments trepidation at the idea of having to wander round a strange and potentially dangerous city in our jetlagged and disorientated state trying to find another hotel. Then the door opens to reveal . . . a peaceful oasis inside. And fortunately our congenial hosts at the Rio Amazonas Hotel have another room free.

Relieved and exhausted, I crawl gratefully into bed. I wake several hours later to find that Bill has already been out for an adventure, acquainted himself with Chilean beer and made a new friend called Walter, who has given him free tickets to the opera.

Our hotel is a nineteenth century colonial-style house decorated in warm Mediterranean colours, with carved wooden doors and spacious high-ceilinged rooms. There is an interior courtyard and a garden, as well as a cosy living room and a dining room. Our kindly hosts play jazz or classical music in the communal areas, speak immaculate English and serve delicious homemade breakfasts. The other guests are an eclectic bunch, including Uncle Jack an eccentric old American sailor and two English girls, Anne and Sylvej, with whom we cry with laughter comparing horror stories about travelling in India.

So our introduction to Chile has so far exploded my preconceived ideas about the country. Everyone we have met so far is easygoing, incredibly friendly, well read and very cultured. Having been so worried about how difficult things were going to be in South America, I could not have been more pleasantly surprised by Chile.

On this first night, as Bill and I lie wide-eyed and jetlagged, everything starts to shake. At first I think that the hotel must be near a train station or on the flight path to the airport. But the shaking grows more vigorous.

'My God, I think it's an earthquake,' says Bill.

'Oh yes, I think you're right,' I say.

In our ignorance, we have no idea how bad it might be or what we should do, so we just lie there in wonder. Fortunately it is not a serious one and nothing breaks or falls on us, but it is a curious feeling all the same.

* * *

Feels like we have had this day already! I had not realised that jetlag could be so bad—lying wide starey-eyed all night and then feeling like death in the morning. My eyes—dry, sore and bloodshot—feel as if someone has given them a light rub down with sandpaper. So we do not do much on our first day in Chile, except wander about Barrio Brasil, the area round our hotel, looking for nice cafés and absorbing the atmosphere. Come to think of it, that is what we normally do in a new country—so nothing new there then.

The city was founded in 1541 by Pedro de Valdivia, whose job it was to extend the Spanish colony south from the Inca territory in Peru and northern Chile, which had already been conquered by Francisco Pizarro. Valdivia chose a good spot here, where the Mapocho and the Maipo rivers flow down from the Andes. But I am still surprised at how European Santiago feels. We could be in any Spanish city—good shops, colonial architecture and a Metro. But Santiago does have something more—it is romantic, sexy, poetic, cultured, vibrant. It is a shock to us that the people are genuinely friendly, without wanting any of our money. We have got used to having to defend ourselves in Asia against the onslaught of people trying to sell you things. So when we stop to consult a map and a man approaches us, it is a really pleasant surprise that he is merely offering to give us directions.

At lunchtime we wander into the tiny but charming Café Brasil in a shady square just round the corner from our hotel. As our grasp of Spanish is very rudimentary, gleaned entirely from reading a phrasebook on the flight from Australia, the rotund and smiling owner helps us decipher the menu. He points to each dish in turn, saying, 'moo' or 'oink' or 'cluck, cluck,' accompanied by the appropriate action—wings flapping, etc.

The next day, feeling a little more together, we venture into town for a day of culture. Highlights include the chalky-red Iglesia San Francisco, a 450 year old Franciscan church with a wonderfully cool and peaceful interior, which is a pleasant contrast with the heat and busyness outside. There are many beautiful carvings and paintings and a touch of Arab influence. Our other favourite, the Museo des Artes Pre-Colombino, chronicles 4,500 years of pre-Columbian civilisation. It is a treasure trove of fantastic artefacts from the cultures that existed before the arrival of the Spanish—different styles of pottery from watering cans to women giving birth, from big fat cat pots to tall wooden grave guardians. It is a feast of colour, shape and texture and transports us to a magical world of lost ancient civilisations.

At lunchtime we make our way to the Plaza de Armas, full of trees and sculptures and surrounded by big austere buildings. On one side of the plaza is the Paseo Ahumada. We wander through this shopping mall looking for somewhere suitable to eat. Progress is slow, as we make our way through the noisy throng of shoppers, business people, street vendors and ice cream stalls. The favourite thing for a Santiagoan's lunch seems to be a thing called a *'completo'* —a hotdog with all the trimmings as far as I can make out. People are queuing at the fast food stalls and coming away with their giant *completos* heaped high with cheese, onion rings, mustard and ketchup. But we do not fancy hotdogs and eventually we find a diner with people eating tasty looking food, where we are once again warmly delighted by the friendliness of the local people. We are having difficulty ordering. I have a sudden twinge of guilt—Grandpa Bromley would never have found himself at such a loss for language skills. We are saved by a man on the next table who speaks good English. He explains the menu to us and tells us what is good here. By the end of the conversation, he has given us his telephone number and told us if we ever have any problems or need a place to stay, just to call him.

On the way back to the hotel, we catch the Metro to buy tickets for our first adventure out of Santiago. It is clean, modern and efficient and delivers us back to Santa Ana station near our hotel without mishap.

* * *

We catch the Tur-bus from Santiago to La Serena, seven hours north. The modern bus station is spotlessly clean and there are little shops and cafés selling everything you might need for your journey. We sit on stylish chrome bar stools and drink café latte from posh glass cups while we are waiting for our bus.

'I can't quite believe the luxury of this bus, after all the terrible journeys we've had in Asia. These seats are so big and squidgy and comfy,' says Bill, bouncing up and down. 'And there's even legroom.'

'Yes, and did you know that *semi-cama* means you can recline them right back and there are supports that come out for your legs,' I say, pulling the lever to demonstrate.

'Wow! There are even headphones and a movie,' says Bill.

'Yes, and here comes the conductor serving drinks. And there's roast chicken and rice on the menu for lunch. There's even a toilet,' I say.

'It's more like being on an aeroplane than a bus and the road is as smooth as silk—my backside is breathing a sigh of relief,' says Bill.

After an hour we are away from the urban sprawl of Santiago. We drive through dry barren hills with the occasional splash of green on their lower slopes where vines are growing. This is one of the main wine-making areas and relies on irrigation from the water flowing down from the Andes. There are occasional smallholdings growing vegetables with handsome-looking horses and foals grazing the meadows. Now the highway follows the coast and the sea is in view to our left for most of the journey.

We arrive in La Serena, a pretty colonial coastal town, feeling comfortable and rested. We find ourselves a very nice room for $15 a night at the Hotel Soberania, and set off into town exploring. La Serena was founded in 1543 as a trade link between Santiago and Lima. In the centre of town there is a wide plaza, a big clock tower and a 400 year old church, the Iglesia San Francisco, with its baroque façade, but La Serena has a modern feel to it. Everything is very clean and there are department stores and shops selling cameras and other electronic equipment. With its setting on the coast and a long sandy beach, it is a favourite holiday destination for Chileans. There are lots of travel agents and before long, we have booked ourselves on a tour to the Mamalluca observatory later that night and have just enough time to have dinner before being picked up for the tour.

'I hadn't realised until now that Chile is famous for its observatories,' says Bill looking at the brochure. 'I'm really looking forward to this. I like a bit of star gazing.'

'Yes, apparently the skies are so clear because the atmosphere is really dry. And there's very little light pollution because the population is so sparse in the mountains.'

We climb aboard the minibus and set off into the Valle d'Elqui. It is dark and the moon is less than half full, yet even so, the mountains surrounding us seem to be alive and glowing. I feel an intense sense of excitement at the prospect of learning about the stars and the planets.

When we step off the bus, high in the mountains, I am astonished by the myriad of stars in the sky. Everything is **so** clear, it is possible to see two other galaxies with the naked eye that I have never seen before. They are the Clouds of Magellan, two satellite galaxies of our Milky Way visible to the unaided eye at a distance of 180,000,000 light years away.

Our guide, Louis, clearly loves his subject and enthuses about all the things he shows us. He points out the Southern Cross to us, something we Northern hemispherians have never seen before. He shows us how to find the South Pole. He teaches us how to recognise various constellations like Taurus and Sirius. But most wonderful of all, he sets up a Smith-Cassegrain telescope with a 30 cm lens for us all to have a look at some of the constellations and planets. Through it, we can see the planets and stars in more detail than I ever thought possible. We see the rings of Saturn. We see Jupiter rising over the hills and focus in to see its stripes and moons. We see the nebulus in Orion's belt, except that Orion appears to be upside down to us. We see myriad clusters of twinkling stars that to the naked eye appear as only one star. It is mind-blowingly wonderful.

I say to Louis at the end of the night, 'Louis, you have shown us Saturn, you have shown us Jupiter, you have shown us Alpha Centaurus and you have shown us Sirius. But there is one thing I am sad about—you didn't show us Uranus!' Boom, boom! Well, I didn't really say that, but Bill and I giggle childishly about that joke for ages.

Later that night, I awake to hear Bill rustling about and muttering that he cannot find the handle. I switch on the light to find him spread-eagled across the bedroom wall looking unsuccessfully for the bathroom door which is on the opposite side of the room. 'Oh here I am!' I say to tease him. So it is now 2:1 on the toilet mishap episodes.

After a long and tiring day yesterday (finally in bed at 3am), we have a late start today. We book ourselves on more tours. There's so much to do round here. I also find time for one of my favourite pastimes—shoe shopping. La Serena is a girl's idea of heaven—shoe shops by the dozen and all with '*Liquidacions*' (Spanish for sale). However, for all La Serena's wonderful shopping opportunities, it seems to be lacking in good places to eat and part of the problem is that we do not understand the menus. An example of this is one restaurant that had attempted to translate its food into English. Here are some examples of the dishes which we did not fancy trying:—

Menu entry in Spanish	**Translated as:**
Erizos y salsa verde	Hedgehogs green sauce
Machas y verde	Male and green
Tomate relleno	Padded tomato
Papas salteadas	Fried Popes

* * *

Today, we set off on a tour of Fray Jorge National Park accompanied by Maria our English-speaking guide. So far, the locals have been very tolerant of our abysmally poor Spanish and we have been getting by with whole conversations consisting largely of elaborate hand gestures and pointing a lot. But with the prospect of an educational tour, we thought we might learn more from someone who could speak good English.

Fray Jorge National Park has a special microclimate created by the sea mist called the Camanchaca, which allows temperate forest to exist despite practically zero rainfall. Have I mentioned how dry Northern Chile is? No? Well, it's **really, really** dry. In a normal year, there will be

60 days out of 364 when there is rain. But over these 60 days, they will be lucky to receive a total of 7cm of rain.

One of the huge advantages of this phenomenon for me is that there are **NO** mosquitoes. I cannot begin to explain how much that fact delights me after months of being plagued by them round Asia and Australia. On the other hand, it is not so great for the Chilean vegetation. Most of the landscape we have driven through is very arid. About the only thing that grows here unaided is a spiky cactus called *cardon*. One interesting fact about the cacti in Chile is that the fruits always grow on the North side of the plant. So if you ever get lost in a desert, just look for some cactus fruits and you will be home and dry (if you pardon the pun!).

As we drive into Fray Jorge through this arid landscape, we begin to climb higher and to get nearer the coast. In the distance, the phenomenon of the Camanchaca is perfectly illustrated where a cloud of sea mist bathes the seaward side of a high ridge and just in that place, there is dense green vegetation, living off the mist as it rises up the ridge and condenses.

Apparently the Camanchaca allows the cloud forest to collect the equivalent of 1200mm of water a year—nearly 20 times the amount that normally falls in Northern Chile. It is quite weird to suddenly go from dry dusty plains to a damp forest with huge trees dripping with water. We disembark from the minibus and walk amongst the olivillo, the myrtle and the canelo (cinnamon tree) with its beautiful white flowers, sacred to the Mapuche Indians.

Bill's horticultural knowledge allows him to communicate with the park ranger in the common language of the plants and flowers, despite his lack of Spanish. The ranger shows him a special herb known as *chachacoma*, which is reputed to be a cure for altitude sickness.

'This might be really useful when we're in the Andes,' says Bill.

'Yes, let's get some. Maria, do they sell this is La Serena?' I ask.

'Yes, I think you should be able to get it from the pharmacy, no problem,' she says.

After the tour of the cloud forest, the descent back into the semi arid sector of the park is a sharp contrast in flora and fauna. We are lucky enough to see the beautiful Chilean fox, the *sorro*, and we are also treated to sightings of the *aguilucho* (eagle) and the *pavo* (wild turkey).

After lunch, our tour promises to take us to the Enchanted Valley, *the Valle del Encanto*, where 'petroglyphs, pictographs and characteristic mortars ground into the rock, whisper of days long gone when the Indians of the El Molle culture inhabited this beautiful valley of gargantuan boulders and murmuring streams'.

No-one really knows the meaning of these strange rock markings, left 3,000 years ago, but it seems that this valley was very special to the El Molle people. One unusual feature is that there are natural springs of freshwater in this area—something that must have been very precious to the people that lived in such an otherwise dry area. Some of the figures seem to indicate where the water springs from. Others show ceremonial figures wearing headdresses—perhaps giving thanks to the water spirits. Still others show masses and masses of four-legged animals, perhaps representing a count of the guanacos in the area, or maybe a ceremony to ask for success in hunting.

On the way back to La Serena, we tell Maria of our difficulty in finding good food, so she tells us about some local delicacies to look out for. These include:

Humitas—made from corn shoots or alfalfa
Cazuela—a type of casserole made with chicken or beef and vegetables
Porotos Granados—bean stew
Empanadas—Chile's version of a Cornish pasty (Bill's personal favourite)
Pastel de choclo—minced beef pie topped with mashed sweetcorn.

That evening we go in search of some of these delicious things and in the process have one of the most embarrassing incidents of the trip. Maria told us that some of the best restaurants are above the market, an area that we have not yet explored. So we go to check them out.

Somewhere along the way, I have managed to pick up a bad dose of the 'Fruity Loopy'. When we get to the market, I realise that the Fruity Loopy is upon me, so I have to find a toilet pretty quickly. We are approached by one of the waiters touting for business for his restaurant. I tell him that I need to find the toilets first.

He says, 'No problem. There is toilet in my fine restaurant.' He is most insistent and as my need is urgent, we follow him upstairs. I dash into the loo, which I find to my horror is only separated from the restaurant by the flimsiest of partitions—more of a saloon door than an effective barrier against untoward sounds and smells, of which there are plenty. I try to muffle the explosive sound of pebble-dashing and stifle my cries of agony, but am spectacular in my failure to achieve either. Meanwhile, poor Bill is sitting in the otherwise empty restaurant trying to distract the waiter from what is going on in the toilet, without actually ordering any food.

Eventually I manage to clean myself up enough to venture back out into the restaurant, closely followed by the awful pong and Bill and I make a hasty and excruciatingly embarrassing exit.

* * *

One difficult decision that we had to make about our travels was not to go to the south of Chile. It sounded amazing with its glaciers and the wildlife that lives so close to the Antarctic. But it is in the opposite direction to the way we want to go, namely Bolivia and Peru, so we decided that we would have to save that trip for another time. So, to get a tiny taste of what it may be like in the South, we booked ourselves on a tour to Isla Damas, which is in the Pinguino de Humboldt National Park, where the unusually cold Humboldt current allows wildlife from much colder climes to thrive.

We drive north from La Serena through ever drier desert. There are lots of vultures sitting about waiting for the next thing to die. There are slate-coloured slag heaps, from the copper mines. We pass through one town that apparently lives entirely on goats—there is an overpowering smell emanating from hundreds of them in a huge corral. Further on we come to a town where they have managed to grow olives in this dry, dusty desert, and the olive trade is the only thing keeping the place alive.

Finally we come to the little port town of Punta de Choros, where everything is painted in bright colours, making it look like Toy Town. An icy wind blows off the sea and huge waves chop ominously at the pier.

'Blimey, that's a very tiny boat that they propose to take out in such a big sea!' says Bill. It takes them three attempts to get the boat close enough to the pier in order to lash it to the side so that we can all get on. Even then, it is lunging violently up and down and you have to take your courage in both hands to jump on.

To our dismay, about a mile out of port, the motor of our little boat stops, leaving us to be tossed about amid the huge waves. I look back at the land, saying, 'Bill, do you reckon we could swim back before we totally seize up from hypothermia?'

'I'm not sure, but if the captain doesn't get the boat going again soon, we might have to find out,' says Bill.

The captain takes out the spark plugs, gives them a bit of a clean and to our huge relief, manages to start the motor again. The swell of the sea gets bigger and bigger. Behind me are the sounds of a German man filling a carrier bag with vomit, whilst his insensitive wife chomps into a large ham and cheese baguette. When she offers him a bite, his head dives once again into the plastic bag.

'I think that answer was 'No,' then!' says Bill heaving slightly in sympathy.

But soon the many wildlife sightings help to distract me from my fears. We see Humboldt penguins swimming in the sea and climbing the rocks of Choros Island. We come across a huge colony of noisy gannets and watch them diving like spears into the sea. There are red beaked sea duck and everywhere the pungent smell of guano.

As we sail past a solitary rock, suddenly a huge face peeps round the corner—it is an enormous male fur seal guarding his two wives and baby seal. Further on, a very relaxed elephant seal waves its flipper at us from the beach of Choros Island.

More seals and penguins watch us from high up on the rocks. There is the smell of seal piss and the barks of seals as they fight each other for territory. Now some of them are swimming around the boat—so much more swift and elegant in the water than their lolloping movements on land.

We leave Choros Island behind and head for Damas Island. Suddenly a pod of bottle-nose dolphins surrounds us, jumping and spinning in the air. There are other boats which have stopped to watch and everyone cheers whenever the dolphins jump. The dolphins are responding to the cheers and really playing to their audience. They give us a wonderful show lasting several minutes before they decide it is time to move on.

We stop at Isla Damas and go ashore—a strange landscape of pebbles and squat clumps of red flowers, brightly coloured lichens and seaweed like sculptures. It is very cold but there are people lying on the beach in swimsuits and bathing, determined to have a good time on their holiday. The scene is like a typical chilly British summer day in Porthcawl.

On the way back to Punta Choros, we encounter another huge pod of dolphins. When they see our boat, some of them break away from the main pod and come to swim alongside us. When they jump out of the water, they are so close we can almost touch them. Sometimes they jump right in front of us, then dive under the boat. Their beautiful smiley faces are only two or three feet away from us when they do this. I am completely enchanted.

Back in Punta Choros we have a late fishy lunch before heading back to La Serena. Everyone sleeps on the coach—worn out by all the excitement. Occasionally I wake to see the colours of the desert hills bathed in the afternoon sun—miles upon miles of emptiness except for a lone person riding a horse and a group of donkeys grazing.

Off again, this time on the public bus along the Valle d'Elqui to Pisco Elqui, home of the famous 'Pisco' drink, a regional brandy made of Quebranta or Muscat grapes. People wax lyrical about the Valle d'Elqui, saying that it has very special energy. The Lonely Janet guidebook describes Pisco as somewhere 'it's hard not to relax.' So we are very keen to see this special place and spend a couple of relaxing days there after all the rushing about.

The valley is indeed beautiful—a lush green stripe set between brown arid mountains, with the glacial blue River Elqui tumbling through it, straight off the Andes. Every square inch of the valley floor is used for some kind of crop—mostly avocados, papayas and the grapes used to make the Pisco drink.

A few kilometres inland from La Serena, the Puclaro Dam has stoppered the River Elqui and created a vast lake of turquoise blue. It looks strange to see such a huge amount of water lapping at the foot of the bare mountains.

A little further on, we pass through the picturesque town of Vicuña, where the bus stops outside a restaurant serving fresh empanadas. Bill cannot resist the smell of freshly baked pies and finds himself drawn zombie-like to buy not one, but two of the delicious fragrant pastries. He merrily devours the first pie and all is well, but when he starts tucking into the second, it looks as if he might have bitten off more than he can chew. Sure enough, halfway through the second pie, it squirts hot red staining juice all down the front of his favourite new shirt—a Christmas present from Byron Bay. It is a case of instant karma, as if God was pointing a finger and saying, 'Billy, one empanada is quite enough.'

The bus winds on through the beautiful Elqui Valley and then starts to climb up towards Pisco. As we leave the valley floor, the scenery becomes hotter, drier, dustier. We arrive in Pisco, to find a quaint, sleepy, typically colonial town based around a church and central plaza.

We book into the Hotel Pisco, just off the main square, which is a charming old-fashioned building of adobe with wooden balconies. It has a great restaurant where we have coffee and are serenaded by a man playing a harp. There are big sleeping dogs everywhere and the feeling of not much to do. So far, it seems the perfect place to relax for a couple of days.

Back in our room, Billy attempts to wash the empanada stain from his shirt. To his horror, he only succeeds in bleaching a big patch where he has used cheap washing powder neat on the stain. He hangs it sadly from our balcony to dry. A little later, it is returned to us by one of the hotel staff who looks most distressed and tells us it is full of *espinas*. It seems that the ill-fated shirt had blown out of the window and landed on a cactus.

'She told me my shirt was full of *penis*,' says Bill looking forlornly at his shirt.

'I think you misheard, darling. *Espinas* is Spanish for spikes,' I tell him.

After mourning his shirt for a while, Bill recounts his dream of last night to me. In the dream he was living in Chew Magna, a sleepy little town in Somerset, and happened to bump into Gandalf in the town square. They fell into conversation and Gandalf tried to persuade him to buy some homemade jam, made by his wife. Hmm, I wonder what all that means?

After an afternoon nap, Bill says, 'I've just had another dream. There were cakes on special offer — two for the price of one.' Well, there seems to be a bit of a theme developing here. Bill seems to be displaying all the symptoms of phantom pre-menstrual tension. He is clumsy, a bit sensitive and grouchy, bloated tummy, craving sweet food and baked things and he has got lower backache!

Later, we go for a walk to explore our surroundings. The town of Pisco begins to sour on me very quickly. It is a dusty ghost town full of drunks lying about everywhere cradling half-empty bottles of Pisco. There is also a bit of an 'alternative' scene, no doubt attracted by the claims of the place having special 'energy'. Lots of people with smelly dreadlocks and tasteless ethnic clothing sit around thinking they are really cool and playing the didgeridoo badly.

'Ooh, that's what I call a didgeridont,' says Bill wincing at the lack of musicality of one player.

Pisco is one of those places where there really is nothing to do, but instead of being relaxed, everyone is either going slightly mad with boredom or drinking themselves into oblivion. The edginess of the place is reflected in the town's dogs who bark all through the night. Add to that, the fact that there are a couple of infuriating smelly hippies playing the drums (again very badly) in the town square for hours on end, and you will see why we did not get much sleep.

The drummers were accompanied by a dwarf who was collecting money. He asked Bill for money. 'No — it's crap,' replied Bill. 'I'll give you money if you make it stop.' At that the dwarf gave a maniacal laugh and ran away.

After a bad night's sleep, we high-tail it out of Pisco on the first bus leaving town. Ironically, Pisco is beautiful and peaceful in the early morning, when all the drunks have crawled away, the drumming has stopped and the dogs have run out of things to bark at. The air is fresh and cool and the sky is bright and blue over golden majestic mountains. What a shame it is not like that all the time.

We catch the bus back as far as Vicuña, which has a much more normal feel to it. It is just a happy little town where people get on with their everyday lives. We have a welcome rest and catch up on last night's missed sleep.

In the evening, we sample our first Pisco Sours. We cannot leave the valley without seeing what all the fuss is about. It seems that an Englishman, Elliot Stubb, is to blame for the birth of the Pisco Sour. He opened a bar in Iquique, Peru in 1872 and experimented with many aperitifs and drinks. His favourite ingredient was the limon de pica, a small lime grown in the area. One day, Stubb mixed pisco with his most valued ingredient, the lime, and added a good dose of sugar. Fascinated by the delicious result, he made it the specialty of the house, and called it 'sour' because of the acid touch which the lime gives it.

We sit in a grand café just off the main square in Vicuña sampling one of Mr Stubb's cocktails. They are actually very pleasant tasting, but exceedingly strong. My tongue goes numb within a few mouthfuls. We both become very giggly and start talking gibberish—and that is before we have even got halfway down the glass. But the most fortunate thing is that the effects wear off quickly and we are almost back to normal by the time we have walked (or wobbled) back to our guesthouse.

Once more back on the bus to La Serena, where we book a ticket on the night-bus to San Pedro de Atacama, an oasis town in the middle of the Atacama Desert, and reputedly the driest place on the planet.

Meanwhile, we have a whole day to kill before our bus leaves and we manage to fill it very nicely with shopping, internetting, sitting about in cafés and visiting the wonderful Archaeological Museum of La Serena. It is beautifully laid out and gives a really good grasp of how the different indigenous groups have developed over the years, with great examples of their art. Some of these groups were the Diaguitas and El Molle. They are well known for their pottery decorated with drawings of great precision, decorated in black, red and white. This museum has the most complete archaeological library of Chile. The piéce de résistance of the museum is an original statue from Easter Island, strikingly displayed in a room of its own.

Eventually it is time to board the night bus for our 14 hour journey to San Pedro. We have booked semi-cama seats, which have loads of leg room and recline right back, so we manage to get quite a bit of sleep before being woken the next morning. Breakfast is provided—half a cup of black coffee and a small wafer biscuit. It is very welcome, but woefully inadequate.

The journey from then on seems interminable. Miles and miles and miles of arid desert slide by the window. Not a speck, not a molecule of water is to be had. There is not even enough moisture to support cacti. There is nothing to see except a few roadside graves and a dust devil. Very occasionally there is an isolated house in the middle of nowhere and I wonder how anyone could live in a place like that. Although devoid of water, the area is rich in minerals such as copper, lithium, borax and iodine. We go through one mining town where **everything** is covered in a thick layer of dust. The whole place gives me a feeling of utter desolation.

After 14 hours, we finally arrive in San Pedro at around 4.30pm feeling terrible, having had nothing to eat since the meagre rations at 6am.

'For once, I really hope we get touted by someone who owns a nice guesthouse at the bus stop because I don't have the energy to tramp round to find a place to stay,' says Bill.

'No, me neither,' I reply.

Fortunately, our prayers are answered and a very nice man from Mama Tierra's guesthouse loads us into his jeep and takes us to his lovely clean place with a comfy room for C$4,000 (£3.50) each. It turns out to be the best budget accommodation in town.

San Pedro is a little greener than the rest of the surroundings due to the presence of a small river flowing off the Andes. But it still seems like the driest, dustiest place in the world. And when I say dry, you can actually feel the moisture being sucked out of you—a bizarre feeling for one who comes from damp old Blighty. Water does not quench your thirst in such a place, when your mouth is full of dust. Apparently, in the nearby town of Calama, it has never rained in living history. After arranging our things, we wander into town.

'Blimey, they're optimistic—putting gutters on the roofs of their houses in a place so dry! Either that or the builders conned them out of a bit of extra cash for something unnecessary,' says Bill.

The town is full of gringos. We are shocked at how expensive the restaurants are—even by Chilean standards, which in general is much more pricy than we got used to in Asia. But we are famished and tired, and way past shopping around for the best deal, so we go into the first decent looking place we find. The food is very good—but then it ought to have been for £15 for quite meagre portions.

After our food, we wander about town and bump into a very jolly German girl, who we met on our tour of Isla Damas. I suspect that her jollity is due to copious consumption of the pisco sours. But she is compus mentis enough to tell us which is the best travel agency to go on a trip across the Altiplano and the Bolivian salt flats, the Salar de Uyuni. And for that I will be eternally grateful to her. We immediately go to book our tour and to book a tour of the Valle de la Luna. Then we go home and sink gratefully into bed.

In the morning, we visit the archaeological museum. It is very good at giving a picture of how this dry, dusty area was first inhabited and how the people survived. But it is full of mummies which give the place a creepy feeling. The dead should be allowed to rest in peace where they are buried, and not put on display in a glass museum case.

In the afternoon we go on our tour to the Valle de la Luna. But first we spend a very pleasant hour or two in the Valley of Death. The valley is full of weird rock formations and enormous sand dunes climbing into the sky on either side of the path. And everything is **so** dry. Bill tries to climb one of the dunes but comes back complaining that the sand is burning his feet and the dust is burning his lungs. Perhaps that is why it is called the Valley of Death.

Next stop is our final destination, the Valle de la Lune, where everything is covered in salt and looks as if it has had a fine dusting of snow, which has been frozen overnight. There are dozens more strange rock formations. Such an alien landscape I find hard to comprehend. We climb up the mother of all sand dunes and wait for the sunset when, we have been told, the colours will be at their best. Call me an old cynic if you like, but in our year of travels we have seen many breathtaking sunsets and I am afraid that this one seems like a bit of a damp squib by comparison. I find myself feeling eager to get home and have some supper (it is 9pm by now).

Chapter 13
Bolivia—No Hay Anaconda
(And We Couldn't Find the Tapir Either)

So after a very brief but thoroughly enjoyable 12 days in Chile, we set off on a trip that will take us from the Chilean Atacama up onto the Bolivian Altiplano, reaching dizzying heights of over 5,000 metres.

We climb aboard a minibus with a dozen other gringos and head for our first stop—to clear Chilean immigration at the Police station. Everything goes smoothly and soon we are heading for a high pass (4,000m) on the Chilean/Argentinean/Bolivian border.

Our guide, Emilio, stops the bus and asks if anyone is suffering from altitude sickness. So far so good—everyone is feeling fine. Emilio points out a volcano, Volcan Lincancabur, which rises to over 5,000m on our left and the strange amber coloured shiny tufts of grass that cover its slopes. He calls them *amarillo* and says that they support llamas and vicuñas. The rocky face of Volcan Lincancubur is striped pink and blue, whilst wispy clouds trail from it and I wonder whether it is completely extinct?

Well, it is to be the week of strange alien landscapes. For a person that comes from the green rolling hills of England, I struggle to find a vocabulary to describe what I see. For three days we travel through the most incredible scenery, the like of which I have never seen anywhere else in the world.

Now we are travelling through an area where there is no vegetation—just rocks and red mountains. Bright turquoise rocks are scattered here and there. I keep doing double takes, because I cannot quite believe what I am seeing.

We arrive at the Bolivian border post and entrance to the Parc Nacional Eduardo Avaros, where jolly border guards ask, 'Que pasa, Anna?' and change our Chilean pesos to Bolivianos.

'Imagine having a job like this—so far away from civilisation. It would be great to work in such a peaceful place. No wonder they're all so jolly,' says Bill.

From the border, it is a short drive to Laguna Blanca, full of chalk. The pinks and blues of the mountains surrounding this lake are reflected perfectly in its milky waters. Sprinkle the scene with three species of pink flamingos that feed on the micro-algae in the lake, and set it against a backdrop of dazzling azure sky—it is impossibly beautiful.

Anna and Bill on The Route of Jewels

We stop for a while to take breakfast by the lake and to get to know our fellow gringos a little better. Damien and Dan are English and travelling with a Kiwi, Ashley. They are all tall, handsome and very cool. Whenever we stop they play hacky-sack. There are two Argentineans—Mario and Loco (Mad)—I never find out his real name. We have a brief but friendly chat about football and amiably decide that the Argentinean and English football teams are even now. There are two French girls who are also very cool. They have a habit of standing on top of rocks looking picturesque and practising Kung Fu.

From now on, we will travel in 4WD jeeps, the cool boys and girls and the Argentineans in one jeep together. Our jeep consists of Miriam, a French girl with good language skills, but a bit uptight; Mikkel, a friendly

Danish guy; Jens and Volkmar, two large and jovial, but very sunburnt and peeling Germans.

Our driver is Emilio. He has the typical dark-skinned, hawk-nosed look of the Bolivians, except that he is quite tall. He is a solid, dependable character who gives the impression of immense strength. I am very thankful that he has these qualities, for our lives and our well-being are in his hands for the next three days of our adventure. We will be travelling in an environment where there is no habitation, on unmapped dirt tracks. I am sure we would not survive more than a few hours without Captain Emilio at the helm.

There is a third jeep driven by a new driver. I get the impression that Emilio and the driver of the cool jeep have given him the oddballs of the group.

After breakfast we set off for Laguna Verde, full of magnesium and arsenic, but no flamingos. It is the colour of a swimming pool and set strikingly in front of Volcan Lincancabur. The sun bakes down on our heads as we wander over the white crusts of magnesium and arsenic to the water's edge, which steams and bubbles.

The effect of the altitude (we are at 4,500m) combines with the coca tea I had for breakfast and perhaps the toxic fumes coming off the lake, to make me feel a little mad—giggly and light-headed.

Vicuñas

Back in the jeep, now we are driving through bare, dramatic landscape. Two elegant vicuñas skitter away from the road. What do they find to eat and drink in this barren land? Weird wind-eroded rocks in the Salvador Dali Desert look like herds of grazing mastodons.

We stop at some thermal pools. They look most uninviting and smell like a bad eggy fart. Sleety rain is coming down and an icy wind blows through us. Despite this, the Argentineans strip to their underwear and climb in. Everyone else makes do with rolling up their trousers and having a warm footbath.

As Loco emerges from Termas de Polques, he finds a golden ring next to the pool. He holds it aloft, but no-one claims it. The ring bears markings in a strange language that none can understand. From that moment forward he is known as 'Loco the Ringbearer.' He is on a quest to find Volcan Ollague, the last active volcano in Bolivia, and to cast the ring into its smoking chasm. None but he can bear the burden.

Back in the jeep, the landscape slides by, a blur of colour—ochre, amber, terracotta, slate, duck egg blue, salmon and Herefordshire pink. Now vapour is rising all around us from underground thermals—a million will-o-the-wisps.

We have climbed to 4,900m and step out to visit the thermal mud geysers, which smell like the breath of Satan and plop and fart huge glops of mud high into the air. We have to watch our step here—it would be easy to get burnt by a flying mud glop or plunge through the thin crust into a scalding bath of foul smelling liquid. It really is like the landscape of Mordor.

The altitude is starting to weigh me down now. I retreat to the jeep exhausted. Bill hands me a few cubes of chocolate. As I eat, I find that I am miraculously revived. We drive through a shower of sleet and hail. Out of nowhere swoops a huge black and white bird of prey. What kind of creature has it found to hunt in this desolate land?

A break in the hailstorm gives us a brief glimpse of Lago Colorado in the distance—deep blue, pale blue, terracotta and gold, lit by a burst of sunlight amongst the mountains. I am feeling very sleepy and overwhelmed by the strange beauty of it all. I desperately want to close my eyes, but cannot bear to miss a thing.

We arrive at the hostel where we are to stay the night. It is scenically located on the shores of Lago Colorado, but it is absolutely grim. It is freezing cold as the sleet beats down, finding its way in through the roof in several places. The beds are all ancient and rickety with sagging mattresses and wobbly, creaking legs. Some are wet from the leaking roof. The sheets have not been changed in recent history and the blankets smell of wee. The toilets are indescribable. But it is the only building we have seen since we stopped for breakfast.

Emilio apologises for the state of the beds, but says that the hostel down the road, which is slightly better, is *occupado*. We have the feeling he is under orders to get us to stay here.

I want to explore my surroundings—I want to walk by the lake and look at the flamingos. I want to look out for vicuñas and viscachas (rabbits with long tails). But the bitter wind, the sleet and the onset of altitude sickness drive me back into the hostel.

Altitude sickness is like the hangover from hell—blinding headache and nausea combine with fatigue, irritability and complete over-sensitivity to any stressing factor—the Hostel Grim seems like a prison. I desperately want to lie down but cannot bring myself to climb between the wee-smelling blankets.

'We've got some of that *chachacoma*—the herb we saw in the Fray Jorge Park. It's supposed to be a cure for altitude sickness. I could make it into some tea for you. We'll soon find out if it works,' says Bill with a look of concern on his face. He goes to the kitchen and asks for a mug of hot water. The kindly woman, guessing what it is for, ladles in a couple of spoonfuls of sugar.

I sit, ogre-like, cradling my brew and growling at anyone who leaves the door open to let in the icy breeze on my aching back. But a miracle happens. Sip by sip of the sweet perfumed brew, I start to feel better. By about halfway down the cup I am able to smile and laugh. The sun comes out.

'Bill you're my saviour,' I say, resting my head against his arm. I crawl sleepily into the pungent bunk and drift into oblivion for an hour.

After an early supper, I crawl back into bed for an early night. I am not feeling very sociable and it has been a BIG day!

I awake to crystal clear sky and bright dazzling sun. The rain of last night has fallen as snow on the mountain tops but it is warm at altiplano level now. Despite much snoring and farting in the dormitory last night, mainly from the two large Germans, I got a good night's sleep and am feeling much better today.

We are away in the jeep by 8am. I am relieved to leave behind the smelly, leaky, creaky, pooey, toilet place that has the audacity to call itself a hostel. We cross miles of flat red land flanked in the distance by the snow-capped mountains. Here and there, small groups of vicuñas graze on their imperceptible fodder.

We stop at Arbol de Piedra, a place where the wind and ice have eroded rocks into trees, cobras and other fantastical shapes. Ashley bounds about like a big red setter looking for games to play. Dan and Damien join him in another game of hacky-sack. We all run about like children. Some climb the rocks. The spirit of this place, the Desierta de Siloli, is very strong. It makes me feel small.

'Look, there are tiny little plants among the sand and rocks,' says Bill. 'I'm amazed that anything can grow here.'

'Oh, so that is what the vicuñas are feeding on,' I reply. They are the ultimate survivors. Emilio tells us that they cannot be domesticated like llamas because they are too wild, and it is very difficult to hunt them because they have a sixth sense about people's intentions towards them and are gone in a flash if they sense danger.

Back in the jeep we pass low, rounded rocks covered in domed clumps of moss. This is a favourite place of viscachas, but none grace us with their presence today. We arrive at Laguna Honda—the pink lake, covered in pink flamingos, reflecting snow-capped mountains. The beauty of it brings me close to tears. The rocks seem to be changing colour in front of my eyes from brown to turquoise and the clouds are the colour of rainbows. They call it *La Ruta de los Joyas*, the Route of Jewels. It is aptly named.

We wander down to the lakeside to watch the flamingos feeding. Heads upside down in the water, their long necks in an exaggerated arc, they swish their beaks from side to side to filter out the algae that they feed on. One takes flight and it is only then that I realise just how big they are. The sky darkens for an instant as the huge wingspan of the incongruously pink bird blots out the sun for a second and then it passes us, neck outstretched.

Once more in the jeep, Volcan Ollague looms into view. It rises 1,000m above us to 6,000m (18,000 feet). Emilio is playing an Abba tape in Spanish—*'Dame, dame, dame amor esta noche* (give me, give me, give me a man after midnight),' accompanies our dramatic view of the vapour issuing from the volcano.

We stop for lunch beside a landscape of pink undulating rock—these were the last spewings of Volcan Ollague. Loco the Ringbearer contemplates his goal in the distance. Here and there the rocks are dotted with huge mound forming succulents known as *quenoa*. They exude a sticky aromatic sap which helps them against the freezing temperatures at night-time. They remind me of the green blobby monster on Dr Who. At least I do not have to hide behind the sofa from these ones.

After lunch, we reach the edge of the salt flats. The road is waterlogged and very treacherous. There is a big danger that we might get stuck. We stop at Chiguana, where bored young soldiers check our passports. They are staged in an old fort that looks as though it has been renovated by the Telly Tubbies—it is full of dome shaped buildings covered in child-like impressions of a camouflage pattern.

A storm that has been threatening in the distance since lunchtime is chasing us across the plain. Lightning strikes Volcan Ollague and thunder booms towards us. If the storm catches up with us, it will make the roads even more perilous.

We have driven perhaps a kilometre from Chiguana, but the other two jeeps are not with us. Emilio turns back to find them—it is too dangerous to travel alone. Halfway back to Chiguana, we meet up with the cool jeep. Emilio chats to the other driver; the discussion gets quite heated. Miriam listens in and translates for us. It seems that the new driver has decided to take a different route. In the distance we see him speeding across the plain at 90 degrees from the direction we have been taking. Emilio proclaims that he is an idiot because the route that he has taken, although shorter, is much more dangerous. The two drivers discuss whether to go after him. The cool jeep driver wants to vamoose—he says the other driver has gone too far to catch him and that we risk getting stuck if we follow him. Emilio clearly feels guilty about leaving him, but we continue on our chosen route.

The road is deeply rutted and full of puddles. We are jostled from side-to-side. Bill and I, who sit higher in the rear seats, hit the roof several times as the jeep bucks up and down over the ruts. It is an uncomfortable journey.

A little further on, to my amazement, I see someone riding a bicycle across the plains. Where might he be going in this desolate, God-forsaken place and how on earth is he managing to stay on a bicycle, when we are being tossed about like dolls?

A while later, we see a big herd of llamas with dogs and llama herders—the first signs of civilisation and normal everyday life since leaving San Pedro. A little further still we see people sitting outside a few stone cottages and crops of quinoa nearby. It must be a hard life up here.

The lightning and thunder is catching up with us. It will not be long before the storm is upon us. There is an added danger now—we are dangerously low on petrol.

Across the plain in front of us run two huge birds which Emilio names as Niandu. We find out later that they are American Emus.

We finally reach the village of San Juan as the storm hits us. The village women put their hands over their ears and hurry their children to shelter. Emilio gets out to use the telephone and a bolt of lightning narrowly misses him. He is reluctant to go further because of the petrol situation and the storm, so he enquires about accommodation for us. We all look about in dismay—it is about as grim as the previous night.

We stop for a cup of tea. Emilio is trying to delay the decision until the storm blows over, because he needs to get permission from head office for us to stay here and it is too dangerous to use the telephones right now because of the lightning. There is the added problem that the driver of the third jeep has not been seen and he should have arrived by now if he has not got stuck.

By the time we have finished our tea, Emilio has made the decision to crack on. There is no petrol to be found in San Juan and the other jeep is also running low, so we are only delaying the problem by staying the night. We set off again, even though there is still no sign of the third jeep. We limp to the next village, but to our dismay, there is still no petrol to be had. We set off again. Emilio has a look of grim determination on his face. The low petrol light is now full on and the gauge needle is thumping against the bottom of the dial. We are all praying and willing the jeep on.

We make it to the next village. This place is almost a town by comparison but still desperately isolated. We have heard rumours of the strikes and road blocks set up by the coca campesinos and are wondering whether they have stopped supplies getting through. Emilio starts making enquiries about town. Finally he finds someone who can direct us to a man who has some petrol for sale.

We pull up at the address—it is just a tiny house. An old man answers the door and we wait with baited breath as Emilio asks about petrol. 'Si, hay gasoline,' is the reply and we all breathe a huge sigh of relief.

It is not far to our stop for the night—a tiny village on the edge of the Salar de Uyuni—the biggest and highest salt lake in the world. The hostel is like heaven compared to last night. It is clean and warm, with new beds and firm mattresses. Each room of six beds has its own bathroom with a proper flushing toilet and a shower.

In my delight at arriving here, I forget for a while the fate of the poor people in the other jeep, which still has not arrived. There is a hum of contentment in the air. People are buying beers and chocolate from the bar; the cool gang have started a ping pong tournament; smells of delicious cooking waft from the dining room. Ashley bounds about, a huge grin on his face and keeps saying, 'It's SO nice here, isn't it?'

We have a good supper of soup, roast chicken and vegetables, served by the stalwart Emilio. I can see that he is tired and strained after a long, tough day's driving, but he is still smiling and joking with us.

At 9pm the third jeep finally arrives. Its passengers are exhausted and furious with their driver—but at least they are safe. I can see the relief on Emilio's face—no need to send out a rescue party after such a long day.

After dinner we relax around the table with a few beers telling funny stories. Jens and Volkmar are a hilarious double act, telling us of their adventures in Columbia, where on their first night they were desperately trying to find a hotel before nightfall.

'Vee had been vorned zat it ees very dangerous to be outside after dark,' says Jens. 'So vee choose a hotel from zee guidebook und vee knock on zee door. Zee manager greets us srue a small flap in zee door, und he sinks vee are very strange gringos ven vee ask if he has vun room vee can share. But vee show him our money und he lets us in. In zee morning vee realise zat it ees a 'hotel off luff' because all zee uzzer rooms are filled viz old ugly men und beautiful young vimen.'

'Now vee understand vie zee manager sinks vee are so strange staying in a room togezzer!' says Volkmar.

We take it turns to tell jokes, but Miriam is having difficulty getting the jokes. 'Miriam, I thought you were a linguist,' says Bill.

'I am,' she protests. 'I understand zee words, but I do not understand why zay are funnay.'

'Ah, perhaps it's your sense of humour that's the problem,' says Bill. Mikkel nods and winks at us. 'I always thought it was the Germans that are supposed to have no sense of humour, not the French, but Jens and Volkmar here are very funny.

'But I <u>have</u> got a sense of humour,' she protests.

'How about this joke then, Miriam, with a French flavour especially for you,' says Bill. 'There was an English dog and a French cat and they decided to have a race to swim the Channel. The dog was called 'One Two Three' and the cat was called 'Un Deux Trois.' So who do you think won the race?'

'Well, zee French cat of course,' says Miriam.

'No, it was the dog actually. And do you know why?' asks Bill.

'Non,' says Miriam.

'Because Un Deux Trois quatre cinq,' says Bill. Jens, Volkmar and Mikkel all roar with laughter, while Miriam just looks confused.

'But eet is not funnay,' wails Miriam.

I awake at 5am, to see a beautiful sunrise over the Salar de Uyuni. There is only one hot shower in the building and I make the most of my early rising to be the first to use it. I **have** to wash the wee smell out of my hair. The shower feels divine.

Before breakfast, Bill and I have time for a wander around the small village in which we have spent the night. Apart from the modern hotel, everything has a feeling of ancient decrepitude. Toothless, wrinkly old ladies in voluminous skirts and hats set at a jaunty angle croak 'Buena dias' as we pass. There is a quaint little church. The village square is full of chickens. There are more dogs than humans in this place. After a turn around the square, we return to the hotel for breakfast.

We are in the jeep driving across the salt lake. A hard salt crust is covered with a skim of about four inches of **very** salty water. The sky is clear and the sunlight is dazzling at this altitude. Everything is white. Spray from the wheels sparkles past the window, lit by the bright sun. Ahead I cannot make out the horizon. The sky and the lake are both white—one merges with the other. To each side, mountains reflected in the lake seem like islands floating in the sky. I wonder how Emilio can navigate in these conditions.

Speeding across the Salar de Uyuni

Ahead of us, the loco jeep has stopped. Everyone is on the roof waving at us. It looks so weird; they are on a jeep island floating in a milky sky. We pass them and the romantic illusion is shattered as Loco drops his shorts and bares his hairy arse to us.

After the giggling has subsided, Emilio tells us some amazing facts about the salt lake. It is 12,000 square kilometres in area—roughly 120 kilometres from east to west and 100 kilometres north to south. The solidified layer of salt is over 100 metres deep. It used to be a sea until movements in the earth's crust raised it 3,660 metres into the air. That makes it the highest and biggest salt lake in the world.

Now in the distance the mountain Tunapa looms, snow clad, out of the clouds at over 5,000m. We have an hour's drive through the blinding whiteness till our first stop. I am very thankful of my newly purchased polarised sunglasses. Behind us the other jeep still follows with the locos on the roof. They must be getting burnt to a crisp.

Just when I thought the landscape could not get any weirder, we come upon a coral island in the middle of the salt lake covered in 12 metre high cacti. Isla Pescadores was once a coral outcrop at the bottom of the sea that became the Salar de Uyuni. Could there ever be more of a contrast of extremes? In the middle of this great sterile inert vastness, suddenly there is an island which supports life.

The locos climb down from their jeep top. They look pretty comical—their hair and clothes stiff and grey with salt, their eyes bleary and their skin burnt red and crispy.

The cacti are ancient, some over 1200 years old. They all have character, like a crowd of people standing to attention. Sitting at the top of Isla Pescadores gives me a weird sensation that I am at the bottom of the sea, even though I am 4,000m up in the air.

We have lunch, whilst the jeeps need some maintenance. They are thick with a crust of salt from the spray. The moving parts—windows, door locks, etc will cease to function if not hosed off. Emilio has protected the engine by stuffing it full of twigs before we set off. It seemed a bizarre thing to do at the time, but it seems to work.

We meet three Argentinean girls. They are in tears. Their jeep got stuck in the middle of the Salar last night and they had to walk to the island through the salt, abandoning their luggage and not knowing how they will get home. No-one seems willing to help them—they do not want the responsibility. We are very thankful for the driving and preparatory skills of Emilio who has got us here safely so far. By the end of lunchtime, I am relieved to hear that the driver of the Argentinean girls has got their jeep going again.

We stand on the shore and look out towards Dan and Damien a few hundred feet away. They look as if they are walking on water.

Mikkel and Miriam have taken a turn in the rear seats of the jeep, after Bill and I did it for the past two days, getting the tops of our heads bruised against the jeep roof over the rough terrain yesterday. Mikkel has been moaning constantly even though the trip across the Salar has been as smooth as silk.

'Would you like to take a turn in the back?' he asks Jens and Volkmar.

'No, vee vould not,' is the emphatic reply as Jens and Volkmar climb into the most spacious seats in the front.

Another two hours in the jeep and we reach the Hotel Playa Blanca — where everything is made of salt — the walls, the beds, the chairs, the tables. It is a novel idea, but what a bleak place. Bill peeps his head in to have a look and is shouted at by an angry man who says he must buy something if he wants to look. More jeep maintenance gives time for a game of hacky-sack. Jens wanders about barefoot, his feet crusted with salt.

Back in the jeep for the last push across the Salar, we are greeted by the bizarre sight of someone bicycling past us. Is it the phantom cyclist we saw yesterday on the altiplano? It is the first sign that we are nearing civilisation. We arrive at a village on the far side of the lake. A woman makes a fire to dry the salt. A child stands holding a kitten. A few stalls sell drinks and primitive little effigies of llamas made from salt.

This adventure is over and Emilio seems very relieved that we have made it here safely. It has been the most amazing three days of the whole of our eight months of travel. It feels as if I have been in a dream for the last three days and suddenly we are back in reality. We bid farewell to Emilio in the Colque Tours office in the rather dismal Bolivian town of Uyuni. There is a sense of urgency to get somewhere else — Uyuni is not somewhere to spend a lot of time. There are also stories of the coca campesinos blocking the roads in demonstrations and heavy rain flooding the roads. We have a window of opportunity to leave before things may get worse and we could find ourselves stranded.

I consult the guidebook and chat to our fellow altiplano veterans. 'Bill, it looks like we have two choices — we can go to Oruro by train and then a short journey to La Paz. That's the quickest way, but the least interesting. Or we can take a seven hour bus journey to Potosí, leaving at 7pm tonight. The disadvantage of that is that we will be arriving at 2am in a strange town. What do you think?' I ask him.

'Oh God, I don't know. What's everyone else doing?' says Bill

'Well, the Argentineans and Dan, Damien and Ashley are all going to Oruro, and everyone else from our jeep is going to Potosí.'

'I don't want to miss out on seeing the middle part of Bolivia, but that journey sounds horrendous. It's going to be difficult finding a hotel in the middle of the night,' says Bill.

'Yes, it is, isn't it? But I suppose it won't be so bad if there's a gang of us and the hostels must be used to people arriving on the bus in the middle of the night,' I say.

'You're right. OK, let's do that then. Potosí here we come. Let's grab something to eat before the bus goes,' says Bill.

I am relieved to see the Argentinean girls, who had been stranded on the island, have made it to Uyuni. We buy a few snacks and head for the bus station. We board the bus with our jeep gang and climb in amongst the locals, the old folks and children. I feel nervous, because we have not got the hang of Bolivia yet and it is very different from Chile. So far, we have had Captain Emilio to hold our hands through the difficult bits.

The bus bumps its way through the inky blackness of the night. It adds to the mystery of where we are going. The journey goes pretty smoothly, except for the lady who is being copiously sick out of the bus window at frequent intervals and filling the bus with bad smells. We arrive on schedule at 2 am in Potosí and all six of us manage to squeeze in a taxi—the two large Germans crow-barred, one on top of the other, into the front passenger seat is very funny. We get out at Hostal Santa Maria to be greeted by a sleepy old lady who says yes, she does have a double room with private bathroom and hot water for 90B (about £7). Bill and I take it, but the others decide it is too expensive and drive on in search of something else. We sink gratefully into bed at 2.45am.

Potosí is the highest city in the whole world, a very picturesque colonial town set at a breathless 4,070 metres. It was built in this inhospitable place by the Spanish conquistadors for one purpose—silver mining. It is said to be in the shadow of a cursed mountain, Cerro Rico (Rich Mountain).

We awake at 9am, very chilly, and make good use of our *baño* with *agua caliente,* taking long, hot showers. The nights are bitter at this altitude.

We venture into town in search of breakfast, laundry and money changing. We puff our way up a steep hill and it is a shock to step out into the crowded market square after so many days in the wilderness. The sun is very bright and beats hotly on our heads. I soon feel very disorientated and ratty because of the altitude. We are in a strange town full of strange looking people making lots of noise and selling things I do not understand. Wide-beamed ladies wearing long pleated skirts and bowler hats at a jaunty angle carry their babies and their shopping on their backs wrapped in woollen shawls. There are tiny shoeshine boys who should be at school. Old men with bent backs, perhaps from a life in the mines, hold out wizened hands for spare change.

I do not know whether it is the late night or the high altitude or the fact that we have not had breakfast yet, but we both have a bit of a sense of humour failure and finally give up on finding the laundry and head for the nearest café. Much revived with some fuel inside us, we manage to find a cashpoint and supply ourselves with enough bolivianos to feel secure for a few days.

We spend the rest of the day trying to get our heads round Bolivian culture. The people seem quite dour and serious by contrast to the friendly Chileans. We wonder whether living at this altitude has a bad effect on one's sense of humour. The local women are like something left over from another era. They still wear costumes inspired at the time of the Spanish—huge voluminous skirts that swing behind them as they walk and billowing aprons above wrinkly woollen stockings. They wear their long black hair in two plaits, topped by the jaunty bowler hat. The babies are very cute, with round copper coloured cheeks and huge round dark eyes.

'It makes me feel broody,' says Bill catching the eye of a baby peeping from its snug wrap on its mother's back.

In 1544, an Indian named Diego Huallpa discovered silver in the Cerro Rico of Potosí, the greatest seam ever discovered. From that moment, Bolivia's fate was sealed. Over the next 200 years, everything in Bolivia was geared by the Spanish towards extracting the maximum out of this rich vein of precious metal. So Potosí is a city built up on the wealth of silver mining. It is very photogenic, with a beautiful town square and lots of colonial buildings, but there is an unhappy feeling to the place. There are many shops stocked full of expensive goods such as TVs and stereos. There are many restaurants and karaoke bars—plenty to spend your money on—but there is obviously a lot of poverty too. Many people are begging and there is a lot of child labour. It is sad to see eight, nine and ten year old boys touting for the micro buses until very late at night.

Potosí was once the largest city in the Americas, rivalling contemporary London and Madrid in size. Whole towns were founded with the sole purpose of supplying Potosí with goods traded from other parts of the Spanish empire or to transport silver back to Spain. The wealth and size of the city came with a price. The price was the lives of the indigenous and African miners forced into the service of the mine. The system of obligatory labour commanded that indigenous communities send one seventh of its work force to the mines. There were up to 13,500 miners in the mines at one time, many of them spending weeks at a time underground. The vast majority of these miners did not survive to return to their homes. People still work in the mines today.

Casa de Moneda is now a museum but was once the mint that made much of the currency for the entire Spanish colonial empire. The amount of silver taken from Potosí is mind-boggling—16 million kilograms arrived in Seville between 1545 and 1660. But the irony is that most of this wealth was squandered in futile religious wars or wasted by extravagant noblemen and clergy. Most of it ended up in the coffers of Flemish, German or English bankers.

In the evening we go into an Internet café and find Jens and Volkmar drinking copious quantities of beer. They have been to see the mines and tell us of the very difficult conditions there.

'Vee had to go crouching und crawling srue leettle tunnels to see zee miners vorking by hand just as zay did hundreds of years ago. Zair are men off 25 years old who look like zay are old men und zee air is so bad zat I start to cough so bad zat I sink I cannot breeze, even zo I am normally very hellsy,' says Jens.

'Vee bought presents for zee miners—cigarettes, coca leaves und zee dynamite. Zay like zis very much und gave us zee demonstration vis zee dynamite. Vee votched a miner who had been vurking for several hours viz a hammer und chisel. He lights zee fuse und vee run down zee dark tunnel und around zee corner. Und zen KABOOOM! Vee feel zee shock in zee whole body,' says Volkmar.

They order more beer. It is as if they want to drown out the experience they have just had. After another drink, the conversation lightens up and they go back to telling funny stories. Bill joins in with the beer drinking and tries to catch up, but the Germans' capacity for hoovering down beer is phenomenal.

Mikkel and Miriam arrive and the atmosphere changes again. Miriam has a snide dig about us paying too much for our hotel, but at least we did not have to drive around for half the night in search of something cheaper and then have a row with the taxi driver about not paying him extra for driving them about, which is what we hear that they did. It is such a typical niggardly attitude held by many travellers, to put yourself through all that stress and insult the local person you are dealing with all to save yourself the equivalent of £1. I do not know how Mikkel puts up with her.

She also has a dig about us not going to see the mines. I had a fairly good idea that it would be awful, which Jens' experience confirms, and we did not see how our going there would help the people living with those conditions. Anyhow, everyone breathes a sigh of relief when Mikkel and Miriam leave to catch the night bus to Tupiza.

We go into town early for breakfast and to buy bus tickets for Sucre, the official capital of Bolivia. We go into a travel agency for advice about the strikes to hear that there have been roadblocks last night but that the 1pm bus is still leaving, so we go ahead and buy our tickets.

Later we see a newspaper article describing the blocks last night, but saying the situation is under control today. The headline, *Los campesinos son agresivo*, (the farmers are angry) is not very encouraging. Despite the ominous signs, I have a strong feeling that we will be OK and that we are meant to go today.

So we get on the bus and the first hour of the journey goes without a hitch. The road drops down from the dizzying heights of Potosí to travel through lush farmland. Then we come to a town where there is a big demonstration. The road through town is blocked off with many stones and there is a large crowd gathered at the roadside. An angry campesino is shouting his protests, whilst a soldier shouts to appeal for calm. A queue of buses and trucks line up waiting to get through. The atmosphere is charged with emotion and everyone on the bus is very tense. Then suddenly the bypass is open and we race through. Twice more, we are held up by roadblocks. The second time they charge us 50 centavos (about 4p) per passenger to get through.

It seems that what they are protesting about is that the government, under pressure from the US, is telling them to rip up and destroy all their crops of coca leaves. Coca has been their main source of income and part of their culture for thousands of years. They have not been given any alternative source of income, so it is little wonder they are angry. The US government says that coca is bad for American people because it is refined into cocaine. The campesinos say it is not their fault if people in the US want to make cocaine. The unrefined leaves are used here to make harmless maté tea, which is such a part of Andean life and is a cure for altitude sickness and many other ailments, without side effects.

With around an hour of the journey to go, I start to get awful stomach cramps and ominous rumblings in my lower regions. I know that this is a prelude to a monumental fruity loopy episode and quickly stuff down an Imodium, hoping to stem the tide long enough for us to get into Sucre without any embarrassing stains or smells occurring. Unfortunately, the Imodium is too little too late and the last hour of the journey seems the longest hour of my life. Every bump in the road threatens to end in disaster. It is agony holding on.

'OK we need a drill worked out for when the bus arrives,' says Bill. 'Get ready to jump off the bus and get to the nearest loo and I'll hang back and look after the luggage.'

I sit poised with toilet roll and wet wipes in hand. The bus seems to take forever and ever winding and jolting through the suburbs of Sucre, whilst I sit sweating and praying. We have an almost disastrous false alarm when the bus stops at a suburban office and I jump out demanding directions to the toilet, only to be told that this is not the main bus station and there is no toilet. With a supreme effort, I gather myself together and clenching my buttocks in desperation, get back on the bus.

Time seems to slow almost to a standstill. Seconds crawl by interminably. But at last, at long long last, we arrive at the bus station and I leap off the bus, barging and trampling sales touts of various descriptions aside in my haste to get to the baños. Phew, made it just in time.

We hop in a taxi and head for our chosen guest house. Sucre looks like a pleasant, sunny town with plenty of colonial charm and nice cafés. Its whitewashed colonial buildings are organised in a grid of narrow streets mirroring the Andalusian culture on which it was based, and earning Sucre the nickname of 'La Ciudad Blanca' (The White City).

Sucre was founded by Pedro de Anzures, Marques de Campo Redondo, in 1538, as a result of mining activities in the area. Nestled at the foot of the twin hills of Churuquella and Sika Sika, Sucre lies at an altitude of 2,800m, but this seems positively low after our recent experiences in Potosí and on the Altiplano. As the constitutional capital of Bolivia, Sucre is the seat of the Supreme Court (Corte Suprema de Justicia) and remains the seat of the Catholic church in Bolivia and there are numerous convents and churches.

Our first choice of hostels is full, but the receptionist kindly directs us to a place up the road. There we meet the lovely Señora Ruth who is delighted to let us stay in a double room which is part of an apartment with kitchen, bathroom and living/dining room area. It is perfect as we intend to stay for a few days and take a Spanish course. We go to the supermarket and buy provisions for the next few days. It feels really nice to be able to cook for ourselves. We make ourselves right at home and it is a pleasant end to a very stressful day.

* * *

Sucre seems like a pleasant enough place to spend a few days and I have heard that it has a good language school. I have been feeling bad that my Spanish is not good enough to converse with the locals unless they speak good English and that is less common here than in Chile. We spend most of the day finding out about language courses. The main language school is very impressive and well organised. It will cost $80 each for 4 days of lessons, with the next course starting in 4 days time.

* * *

It is a dull overcast day. I feel miserable and depressed for no apparent reason. Bill gives me a shiatsu treatment and I sleep for 2 hours. Finally, I drag myself out of the flat at around 3pm. We go for a walk in Simon Bolivar Park, which is sadly neglected, in need of a good bit of weeding and tender loving care.

In the evening we do some budgeting and realise that we will have very little money and time left if we stay to do the language course.

'Bill, do you realise it's only five weeks till we're due to fly home and there's still so much that I want to see,' I say.

'I know. It's crap that we didn't learn more Spanish before we came, but I don't want to miss out on a trip to the Amazon jungle and to see Machu Picchu,' says Bill.

'No, me neither. I've dreamed of seeing those two places for years and I don't want to run out of money or time to see them. Then there's Lake Titikaka—we can't go home without spending time there. I'm worried about the cost of finding another flight home too.' Our current round-the-world ticket means getting to Dallas for our homeward flight. 'Now that we don't have time to do anything in the US, it's going to be expensive and inconvenient to get to Dallas,' I say.

'That settles it then—we ditch the language course and crack on. And we need to book a cheap flight home direct from Peru,' says Bill.

'Agreed,' I say.

* * *

We spend the morning searching the web for cheap flights and e-mailing companies to ask for help. We have lunch at the Joyride café where lots of tourists hang out and hear tales from other travellers of what a terrible time people have had getting from Potosí to Sucre. The campesinos have been throwing stones through the bus windows and the journey, which should take three hours, is now taking nine. This is all rather worrying and it sounds like going back that way is not an option now.

After lunch, partially as a way of distracting ourselves from the worrying developments, we go on a tour in the Dino Truck to a disused quarry where dinosaur footprints have been discovered. The truck departs from the main town square and we are alarmed at the build up of policemen and soldiers in the square as we leave.

Putting that to the back of my mind, the tour is excellent. We have a very comical but informative guide, named Javier, who re-enacts dinosaur life using plastic children's models by way of an introduction and does wonderful impressions of each kind of dinosaur to illustrate the different footprints.

It seems that millions of years ago, this was a wide area of soft mud that solidified into rock, and now, imprinted in the walls of the quarry, is the poignant evidence of life at the time of the dinosaurs. In one place the footprints of a small herbivore are intercepted by a megaraptor. After a slight scuffle, the megaraptor walked on alone . . .

We see prints of the tricerotops, a creature somewhat like a giant three horned rhino, whose knock-kneed, pigeon-toed gait is demonstrated beautifully by Javier. There is a long trail of a mummy and baby brontosaurus walking along side-by-side (aah!) and a scrap between a velocoraptor and a stegocaurus. Javier has a soft spot for Bill, insisting on calling him Willy. He invites him to help re-enact the fight, with Bill playing the role of the velocoraptor. It is very funny and I am delighted to say that Bill's velocoraptor clearly wins the fight. I do not think Javier was quite ready for the enthusiasm and gusto which Bill brought to his performance.

Javier tells us the story of the beliefs of the Roman Catholic Church when dinosaur bones were first found. It goes as follows:

Layman: 'Bishop, what kind of bones are these?'
Bishop: 'Why they are dragons bones, of course.'
Layman: 'And where are the dragons now?'
Bishop: 'Well, they were too big to fit on Noah's Ark, so they all died in the great flood.'

When we arrive back in town, the main square is blocked off because of the demonstrations. As we are dropped off near the textile museum, Arte Indigena, we decide to take our minds off the trouble for a bit longer by looking at some beautiful indigenous weavings.

Rather than being just a museum, Arte Indigena is actively encouraging the local people to rediscover their traditional crafts, which have been dying out. They are also working to promote awareness of these crafts and helping people to earn a good living from their art.

The proprietor explains to us how the weaving techniques and forms of dress evolved among different ethnic groups. They have projects working with two groups—the Jalq'a group whose weaving style is chaotic and depicts mythical creatures in red and black; and the Tarabuco group whose weaving style is much more ordered and symmetrical, based in reality with a wider variety of more subtle colours.

The traditional cloth worn by the women is an *asqu*. It used to be a large piece of weaving used to cover the whole body like a toga. With the coming of the Spanish, the indigenous people were told to cover up their legs, arms and shoulders, so they started wearing other clothing to cover themselves and the *asqu* was reduced in size and used only as a wrap from waist to knee. The men wear an *unku*, which is a poncho-like tunic, but sewn up at the sides. Men, who had stopped weaving altogether, have been encouraged to take up the art again.

There are weaving demonstrations and displays showing how the designs have changed over the years. It is a feast for the senses. I love the colours and forms and patterns. It makes me long to be able to weave and to create such beautiful things.

The weaving is done in a ceremonial way, asking the spirits for help and inspiration. The women cleanse their materials using the smoke from incense and give offerings before starting work. They also go to the 'Virgins' for inspiration. These are special rocks that are reputed to have spiritual powers. For example, someone has heard the rock crying or speaking. The stones are painted and dressed up like a woman. The Virgin of Chatakila is an important sanctuary at the summit of a mountain. It is a bizarre example of how the Roman Catholic faith has been blended with the old indigenous beliefs.

Another strange hangover from the time of the conquistadors is that some groups of indigenous people have adopted a decorated style of hat, which in shape, closely resembles an old Spanish helmet.

After the museum, we go to the bus station to try to book some tickets for La Paz. We are told there will be no buses on Sunday, but that they will be running again on Monday. So with our exit tickets booked and our minds satiated with beautiful colours and designs, we return to the flat for a quiet evening.

We have a lovely leisurely morning, doing washing and lazing about, knowing that nothing much is open in Sucre on Sundays.

We have lunch at the Kaypichu Culture Café, on San Alberto Street. The café specialises in vegetarian food and regional delicacies. I have my first experience of *api*. It is a delicious hot drink made from corn and honey. It is a rich, nourishing deep red colour which comes naturally from the purple coloured corn.

On the way back to the flat, we bump into Rob, a fellow traveller we have chatted to several times before. He tells us of the worsening situation with the *campesinos*.

'Did you hear that a policeman was shot and killed in Sucre on Friday? It was in retaliation for a *campesino* who was killed by the police in Tarabuco,' says Rob.

'Oh my God, no,' says Bill.

'That was the day that I wasn't feeling well and didn't want to leave the flat,' I say.

'Well, it's a good job you didn't. I got caught in the square when the police let off tear gas and they tried to confiscate my camera. I was really scared, so I just grabbed my camera and ran as fast as I could all the way back to my guesthouse. They didn't try to follow me.'

'Sounds like you had a lucky escape,' says Bill. We've got bus tickets for La Paz booked for tomorrow but it doesn't look as if the buses will be running at this rate.'

'No, I think you're right, there. Your best bet would be to fly to La Paz. The airport is still running at the moment. I think you should get to a travel agent and book a ticket as soon as possible. I've got a flight booked for tomorrow,' says Rob.

'Well thanks for the advice and good luck with your journey,' says Bill.

So we head off to find a travel agent. Unfortunately, being Sunday evening, everything is now closed. We go to see Señora Ruth and her daughter, who speaks good English. As it happens, her daughter is flying to La Paz in the morning and kindly offers to phone the airport to see if there are any tickets left on the same flight. We spend the evening packing our bags in readiness for a quick get away.

Señora Ruth and her daughter call to see us in the morning. There are no tickets left on the flight today, but space is available for tomorrow. We thank them profusely and rush into town to get tickets.

As we enter the square, we can hear a marching band playing a mournful tune. It is the funeral procession for the policeman who was killed in the riots. We stand and pay our respects as the procession marches solemnly by. As the relatives pass us, I feel a huge wave of grief wash over us. We are both very moved and have to choke back the tears, even though we have never met the man.

We book our flight tickets and feel greatly relieved to be finally, definitely leaving. Some unexplained urge makes us go into the natural history museum. We have just finished looking at a bizarre collection of moth eaten and badly stuffed animals, when the curator slams and bolts the front doors and whisks us upstairs, on the pretence of showing us a collection of art and treasures from the colonial period. Bill looks out of the window and says, 'I've just seen policemen letting off tear gas and people running away with their eyes streaming and hankies over their mouths.'

We politely pretend to be interested in the shabby collection of chairs, paintings and chandeliers, but soon the tear gas has even penetrated into the rooms where we are standing. It stings my eyes and the back of my throat. Everyone stops pretending that nothing is wrong and covers their mouths and eyes.

After a few minutes the gas has dispersed enough to move on. We get out of the square as quickly as possible, but I am amazed to see that things are returning to normal already — the old men have resumed their usual seats on the benches, people are out shopping and children are running about.

We stop in at the market en-route to the flat to get last minute provisions. It is good to spend time around the cheerful stallholders, where everything is business as usual. We even buy some coca leaves from a very smiley man.

In the evening, I start to feel unwell. I cannot digest my supper and my stomach is very bloated. I progressively feel worse until I start vomiting. I get little sleep and have to get up twice more to vomit in the night.

* * *

Finally, the time has come for us to leave and I am desperately relieved. But I feel so dizzy, weak and nauseous, that I can barely stand up.

'I'm worried that you're not well enough to travel,' says Bill. 'Do you think we should change the flights till tomorrow?'

'Oh, no. I don't think I could bear to spend another day here. This may be our last chance to get out.'

Fortunately, I do not have to do much. We have already packed most of our gear and we have a car picking us up to go to the airport. It is only an hour's flight to La Paz.

Because of my zombie-like state, Bill has to take charge of everything. He has to get me and all our luggage into the car, through customs, onto the plane and off the other end, into a taxi and find a hotel room in a strange city—all this with a very limited knowledge of Spanish. I do not know how he manages it, because I am completely out of it, but he does. He truly is my knight in shining armour.

All I remember of the whole journey is a desperate desire to lie horizontally in a peaceful place. I have a vague recollection that it was a supreme effort to walk from the plane through baggage handling and out to the taxi and another vague memory of my first view of La Paz nestled in its bowl high up in the air.

As soon as we get into the hotel room, I crawl fully clothed into bed and sleep for the next 16 hours waking very occasionally to have a sip of water or to be fed a bit of yoghurt by Sir Bill.

After one of his forays into town, Bill comes back with his leg bleeding profusely and I ask him what happened. 'I was rammed into by a man pushing a sack-truck. I went sprawling onto the ground and cut my leg. No-one bothered to stop and help me.'

First impressions of La Paz—not good.

Finally, the world swims back into view. 'I feel much better today,' I tell Bill, 'Although I still feel pretty wobbly and as if someone has thumped me hard in the chest. D'you know, I think the bad vibes in Sucre got to me. It was as if my body was absorbing all the grief and anguish that was going on there.' I give a little shudder at the thought of it.

'Yes, you are a sensitive little flower. I wish you could find a way to shut it out a bit,' says Bill.

'Thank God it didn't get you as well or we would never have got out of there. You are my knight in shining armour you know.'

'Well, thank you very much—it's all part of a hero's duties, but it was pretty tough getting you and all our luggage here safely.

So we venture out into the city together. Here we are in the highest capital city in the world at 3,600 metres. We are just about used to the altitude now, and La Paz seems a doddle compared to Potosí at over 4,000 metres and the altiplano at over 4,500m. All the same, La Paz is an ugly, dirty place and the people have that weighed-down look that we first encountered in Potosí. The streets are lined with market stalls manned by women with jaunty hats and sour faces. Some do not even bother with a table and display their goods in piles on the ground. Most of the stalls sell food or clothing, but one or two bizarrely seem to supply everything you might need to get a party going, such as helium-filled balloons, streamers and tooters. The traffic is busy, noisy, smelly.

We visit some travel agencies to see what the chances of travelling about in Northern Bolivia are. My fear is that the protests from the campesinos will prevent us from getting to the places we really want to go. To our delight, there does not seem to be a problem around here and so all our plans to visit Lake Titikaka and to go to the Amazon jungle are still feasible.

'Cor, it's such a relief to hear that. At one point I thought we might have to chuck it all in and fly straight home,' says Bill.

'I'd have been devastated if we'd had to do that. These are all the places I've wanted to see more than any others in our whole travels,' I say.

To my added delight, we receive an e-mail from Journey Latin America saying they have found us some cheap flights from Lima in Peru straight to the UK. These will cost us less than having to go from Lima to Dallas to pick up the last leg of our Round the World ticket. Suddenly everything is coming together for us. We do some calculations and we have £31 a day and 35 days of travel left. The countdown to our return begins. So we book tours to Tiahuanaco and to the jungle and spend the rest of the day in excited anticipation.

There's an e-mail from Mum and Dad too:—

Hi Anna and Bill

We have just received your e-mail telling us you now hope to return around the 5th March. Of course you can stay with us till your house is free, and it might help with some of the wedding plans.

I don't remember thanking you for the beautiful blue Vietnamese silk you sent for my mother-of-the-bride outfit and the turquoise pendant you gave me for Christmas—I've been looking at designs and collecting pictures of necklines, sleeves etc.

Dad spoke to Reg Burgoyne when playing golf last Wednesday and the next day an appointment was made for Peter Burgoyne to come and measure up the site for a marquee. They were delighted with the site and have drawn up a plan for kitchen, bar and band and a loo vehicle not far away. I don't think we need a dance floor for a ceilidh—people might fall off! And there is a choice of colours for linings, which we'll have to decide on when you get back.

Grandpa Bromley has been ill from overdosing on Senacot when having to be given heavy duty painkillers for his back. He is well on the mend now having had quite a few visitors and will have an X-ray on his back on Feb 10th.

Lots of love
Mum and Dad, H and H

Poor Grandpa — It is a relief to hear he is on the mend again. So that is it now, the marquee is booked for the reception. Not much left to organise — ha, ha! I e-mail Karn to let her know of our return. She replies: —

'Wow! Home so soon! Just think—only 5 weeks left before we sit round the kitchen table getting drunk and catching up on a year's worth of adventures! Can't wait! Lots of love to both of you, Karn XXXXXXXXXXXXXXX'

* * *

Having pretty much emptied my system, my appetite is now back with a vengeance. Bill calls me the Come-back Kid because of my trait of being at death's door one day and chomping happily into a hearty repast the next. I must say that La Paz is not over supplied with attractive or hygienic-looking places to eat, so we were really pleased to stumble upon the all-you-can-eat buffet breakfast at the Tambo Colonial Hotel. It really set us up for our trip to Tiahuanaco.

Tiahuanaco is another one of those places that has captured my imagination for many a year. There is so much mystery surrounding the age and origins of this place. I have wanted to see the Gateway of the Sun with my own eyes from the first time I heard about it.

We are picked up in a minibus by our guide, Wilson. He is a nice enough chap, but certainly not an expert on his subject. I find myself frustrated with the holes in his knowledge. Anyhow this is what he told us as we drove out of the city: —

At the height of its power, Tiahuanaco was not just a city, but a state, which stretched from Peru through Bolivia, Argentina and Chile. Its capital was the site which we are about to see in Northern Bolivia, currently 12 miles south of the shores of Lake Titikaka.

Today the Aymara Indians are the descendents of the people of Tiahuanaco, and they make up most of the population of modern day Bolivia. Tiahuanaco pre-dates the Incan times. The descendents of the Incas are the Quechuas, who form the majority of modern day Peru.

We drive out of La Paz and across a high plateau surrounded by rounded hills. Stone cottages are dotted here and there. Many are derelict. People are herding sheep and cattle. There are crops of quinoa and some barley. There are many donkeys — a legacy of the Spanish.

We cross a high pass, El Mirador, at 4,028m. We are flanked by wayside flowers of purple, white and pink. On the other side of the pass, the scenery is much the same, but the houses are different. Instead of stone, here the Hansel and Gretel houses are all made of pink adobe with thatched roofs.

There is a feeling of being left behind in time — a feeling of ancient decrepitude. I have had this feeling a few times in Bolivia — the women who still wear the voluminous skirts imposed on them by the Spanish in the 16th century; the indigenous people who wear hats like conquistadors' helmets; the wrinkly old Indian ladies who beg in the town squares and look just like the mummies of ancient people you see in the museums — these are not people who change their clothes with the latest fashions.

We turn off the road towards the site of Tiahuanaco. We can see a low mound in the distance, where the seven-tiered temple once stood. But first we visit the museum. Having set off late because we had to wait for one of the other passengers, we are hurried through the museum which houses most of the special finds and artefacts from this site. I am rather upset by this. Having wanted to see this place for so long, I would like to spend a lot more time savouring these things.

The first thing we are shown is the huge statue known as Pachamama, which once stood as the sentinel silhouetted through the Gate of the Sun. It is a great shame that they moved it. It is the figure of a male priest wearing a crown and holding strange ritual objects with its hands in a very specific configuration — one facing in and one facing out. The given knowledge is that this represents giving and taking and that the ritual objects represent political and spiritual power. It is thought to be from between 0-70 AD, dated by the layers of ceramics found in the soil strata around it. It is also thought to represent a calendar, as below its elaborately decorated belt are 365 circles, which are presumed to represent days.

However, all this can be taken with a huge pinch of salt because there are so many anomalies in this thinking. For a start, to name such a clearly male statue 'Pachamama' and say that it represents Mother Earth is ludicrous even to a lay person like myself. There is nothing feminine about it. It is angular and masculine. Also, from halfway down its shins, the carving is eroded away by what looks like water. How then is it possible to decide there are exactly 365 circular markings that represent the days? The experts also have no idea why the statue has been eroded in this way. And the interpretation of the hand gestures and ritual objects? It seems like pure guesswork.

The next thing we are shown is a stone pillar carving said to be from the Chirapa culture of 2000 BC. In the centre is a frog, which represents fertility. The spirallic shapes seem to form a step cross, which is said to represent the Southern Cross constellation and is also a form of calendar. The spirallic motives remind me very much of Celtic designs that I have seen at home.

We are told that the people of this area were among the first in South America to use stone to create large permanent buildings. The builders of Tiahuanaco were very skilled. They used huge blocks of stone, the largest of which weighed a colossal 132 tons. In order to keep their tolerances tight, they had plumb lines and spirit levels and certain stones they used as templates to ensure that they got angles like 90° correct. The huge stone slabs were held together at the back using pieces of bronze shaped like the letter H.

One of the weirdest exhibits in the museum is of some skulls of the priests from Tiahuanaco. They are strangely elongated at the back of the head, having been bound onto a board as babies. This exaggerated head shape was supposed to denote nobility and intelligence.

'I wonder what that did to their brain function?' speculates Bill. 'Perhaps they had met some aliens and were trying to copy them.'

Throughout Tiahuanaco, there are repeating symbols in the sculpture. The puma, the condor and the llama all feature heavily. The puma and condor are said to represent power.

They had wonderful carved bowls with calendars round the rims. They would fill them with water and use them as mirrors to reflect the night sky and to study the stars.

Throughout the whole site, there are channels that brought water from Lake Titikaka to surround different parts of the temples. (Perhaps this might have something to do with the water erosion round the feet of the 'Pachamama' statue?). The Temple of the Sun also collected rainwater and then channelled this sacred water towards the agricultural plots that lie not far away. One amazing fact—most of the altiplano reaches sub-zero temperatures during the winter, except the terraced plots adjacent to the

Temple of the Sun, which have their own special micro-climate and never fall below zero.

The Temple of the Sun is described as a solar watch. It marks the equinoxes and the solstices. In its original position, the sun shone through the archway in the Gate of the Sun on 21st March each year. It is such a shame that the Gate of the Sun has been moved, as has the 'Pachamama' which would have been framed in the sunshine pouring through the gate at this time.

The collapse of Tiahuanaco was said to be in 1200 AD, when the level of Lake Titikaka receded, causing drought and crop failure, at which time the city was abandoned. But it has not been properly explained how Tiahuanaco was once a port on the edge of Lake Titikaka and yet the lake is now 12 miles away. What happened to cause the lake to move 12 miles in 800 years? Perhaps Tiahuanaco is much older than the archaeologists suggest.

The structure known as the Puma Punka is the remains of a great wharf and a massive, four-part, now collapsed building. One of the construction blocks from which the pier was built weighs an estimated 440 tons and several other blocks are between 100 and 150 tons. The quarry for these giant blocks was on the western shore of Titikaka. There is no known technology in the ancient Andean world that could have transported stones of such massive weight and size. The Andean people of 500 AD, with their simple reed boats, could not have moved them. Even today, with modern advances in engineering and mathematics, we would struggle to make such a structure. How did they move such gigantic stones and what was their purpose?

So now we go outside to visit the site itself. The low mound we saw as we approached in the minibus was once a seven-tiered pyramid, known as the Akapana, and sometimes called the Sacred Mountain of Tiahuanaco. Measuring some 200 meters along its side and nearly 17 meters tall, it is much eroded and was destroyed by the Spanish who thought there might be gold inside. The Akapana is precisely aligned to the cardinal directions. Each of the seven levels is constructed with beautifully cut and precisely joined blocks that were once faced with panels covered with metal plaques, carvings, and paintings. In the centre of the Akapana's flat summit is a small, sunken courtyard laid out in the form of a square superimposed over a perfect cross. This courtyard is also orientated to the cardinal directions. Recent excavations of this courtyard, the interior of the pyramid, and the grounds beneath it have revealed a sophisticated system of interlinked channels. These channels brought water collected on the summit down through the seven levels, to exit below ground, merging into a subterranean system underneath the pyramid, which then flowed into Lake Titikaka.

As we walk beside Akapana, looking at the remains of the stone walls that were the channels to receive water from Lake Titikaka, I have a sudden strange flashback to a dream in which I was navigating these channels in a reed canoe. Just then, Wilson starts telling us how they used to transport things from Lake Titikaka to here in reed canoes. How weird!

In ancient times, the whole ceremonial core of Tiahuanaco, comprising the Akapana pyramid, the Kalasasaya platform (The Temple of the Sun), the Subterranean temple, and the Puma Punku, was surrounded by an immense artificial moat. The purpose of the water was thought to be to create pools in the temples to act as mirrors to study astronomy, in the same way as the beautiful calendar bowls. I imagine for a moment, the Temple of the Sun flooded with water and the reflection of the sun, pouring through the Gate of the Sun and silhouetting the Pachamama at the spring equinox. It must have been very beautiful.

Perhaps it was intended to create the image of the city as an island, mirroring the Isla del Sol, the sacred island of Lake Titikaka, the mythological site of world creation and human emergence. The original name of Tiahuanaco was Taypikala, meaning 'the stone in the centre.' Does this signify that the city was thought of not only as the political capital of the state, but also as the central point of the universe?

We walk on through the site. There is a strong feeling of life and fertility here. Wild guinea pigs scamper about everywhere and there are masses of birds. The grass growing at the base of the Temple of the Sun is a vibrant green—quite different from everywhere else—and there are masses of flowers in a myriad of different colours.

We are told that there were seven temples throughout this valley, but that this site has the best-preserved remains. It is said that the population in the valley at that time was around 6,000—far more than there are today.

Wilson shows us the Subterranean Temple. It is a very weird structure. In the centre is a red sandstone statue of a bearded figure—quite out of keeping with the style of carving from the rest of the site. It is said to be older, from the Chirapa culture of 2,000 BC. There are many stone faces protruding from the walls of the sunken temple. They are all different and the experts say they represent people from different races. It seems that no-one really knows what they are for. Another interesting fact—llama wool and coca leaves have been found in archaeological digs of ancient

Egypt, showing that there was contact between the continents long before the accepted time that the different cultures met.

At last I finally get to see the magnificent Gate of the Sun. It is vast, carved from one gigantic piece of granite. It is covered in strange symbols and carvings, among them a figure wearing a headdress of sunrays and holding strange objects in his hands. It is said to be the god Viracocha. He guards the gateway to the heavens.

There is more apparent calendar symbology. There are 24 symbols on each side of Viracocha. Do these represent 24 hours? There are 52 important decorations altogether—52 weeks? There are four trumpeters. Do these represent the four seasons? It is all conjecture that the people of the culture that built this site used numbers from the Gregorian calendar, which was introduced much later.

The two pairs of back-to-back trumpeters, when viewed from a distance, also look distinctly like elephant heads. Is this more evidence that South America had contact with Africa at that time? Or is it evidence that Tiahuanaco is far, far older than the accepted wisdom. Perhaps it dates from thousands of years earlier when a species of elephant roamed the land in this part of South America? There are other strange looking animals, one something like a hippo—another prehistoric animal that lived in South America thousands of years ago, but has since died out.

The conventional theory assumes that the civilisation that built Tiahuanaco began around 600 BC and fell into decline sometime soon after 1000 AD. But this site seems to have been designed and crafted by a people with an artistic, scientific and philosophic style which is distinctly different from other pre-Columbian cultures.

There is one last wonderful thing to relate about Tiahuanaco, and that is to describe the granite loudspeakers. They are slabs of granite built into the walls of the Temple of the Sun with an ear-shaped hole in them. When you speak from the outside, it allows your voice to be amplified into the temple. We tried them out, and they really work. It is said that this was for pilgrims to make their requests to the priests inside.

Our visit to Tiahuanaco was fascinating, but it left me with more questions than answers. Was Tiahuanaco built by some unknown sophisticated culture back in the mists of time? Was there any factual reality behind the many Andean myths of great cataclysms and enormous floods in ancient times, and were the people of this ancient culture wiped out by this natural disaster? Was it this natural disaster that separated the port of Tiahuanaco from Lake Titikaka by 12 miles? Tiahuanaco is the source of many creation myths. Here is the myth of Viracocha[1]:—

Long ago in a forgotten time, the world experienced a terrible storm with tremendous floods. The lands were plunged into a period of absolute darkness and frigid cold, and humankind was nearly eradicated. Some time after the deluge, the creator god Viracocha arose from the depths of Lake Titikaka. Journeying first to the island of Titikaka (now called Isla del Sol or the Island of the Sun), Viracocha commanded the sun, moon, and stars to rise. Next going to Tiahuanaco (Taypikala, 'the rock in the center'), Viracocha fashioned new men and women out of stones and, sending them to the four quarters, began the repopulation of the world. With various helpers, Viracocha then travelled from Tiahuanaco, bringing civilization and peace wherever he went. Known by other names including Kon Tiki and Tunupa, he was said to have been a bearded, blue-eyed, white man of large stature. A teacher and a healer, a miracle worker and an astronomer, Viracocha is also credited with introducing agriculture, writing, and metallurgy.

The mystery of Tiahuanaco stems from the alignment of its structures, because a study of astronomy indicates that it was built far earlier than any other archaeological site in all of South America.

Arthur Posnansky, a German-Bolivian scholar, studied Tiahuanaco for almost fifty years. Living at the ruins and intimately familiar with them, he noticed dozens of things that could not be explained by the conventional archaeological theory or did not fit with the accepted chronology. For example, the enormous blocks of stone that no known pre-Columbian culture had the technology to fashion or transport. And the orientation of these structures, in relation to each other and to the stars above, indicated to him that the people who built Tiahuanaco had a highly sophisticated knowledge of astronomy, geomancy and mathematics.

Posnansky had conducted precise surveys of all the principal structures of Tiahuanaco. The Kalasasaya, meaning 'the standing pillars,' is a rectangular enclosure measuring about 450 feet by 400 feet structure, with a series of vertical stone pillars and aligned east to west. Using his measurements of the lines of sight along these stone pillars, the orientation of the Kalasasaya, and the purposely-intended deviations from the cardinal points, Posnansky was able to show that the alignment of the structure was based upon an astronomical principle called the obliquity of the ecliptic.

---

[1] Taken from www.sacredsites.com/americas/bolivia/tiahuanaco.html by Martin Gray

The tilt of the obliquity changes very slowly over great periods of time, but in a highly consistent way. By calculating the tilt of the obliquity with which the Kalasasaya was aligned, Posnansky was then able to calculate the date of the initial construction of the Kalasasaya and this dated Tiahuanaco to 15,000 BC. This date was later confirmed by a team of four leading astronomers from various prestigious universities in Germany.

This initial construction date, vastly older than previously accepted, was ridiculed by mainstream archaeologists and prehistorians. But there are other mysteries that seem to confirm the great antiquity of the site. The ancient myths from throughout the Andean region that tell of Tiahuanaco's founding and use in a pre-flood time, followed by its destruction by devastating floods, seemed to be verified by scientific evidence that proves a cataclysmic flood did indeed occur some twelve thousand years ago. Utensils, tools, and the fragments of human skeletons are mixed in with the deepest layers of the flood alluvia, indicating human use of the site prior to the great flood.

But what caused these floods? There is evidence of several events that could be a possible cause. These include comets and continent-shifting earthquakes that impacted human civilisation in prehistoric times. Scientists have suggested possible causes for the great cataclysms such as the cosmic object of 9600 BC which passed close to the earth and caused the phenomena of crustal displacement, and the seven comet impacts of 7460 BC.

Other evidence is there in the strange carvings of bearded, non-Andean people that are found around the site and the sculptural and iconographic details that are so different from any other pre-Colombian civilisation. And then there is the evidence of the Puma Punka being a port, which is now 12 miles away from Lake Titikaka.

Posnansky, and other writers such as Graham Hancock, Zecharia Sitchin and Ivar Zapp, have suggested that these findings and the astronomical alignments of the site, strongly point to an original Tiahuanaco civilisation which flourished many thousands of years before the period assumed by conventional archaeologists. Rather than rising and falling during the two millennia around the time of Christ, Tiahuanaco may have existed during the vastly older time of the last Ice Age, some 15,000 to 20,000 years ago. So Tiahuanaco may be a surviving fragment of a long lost civilisation. But who were the people of this lost civilization? We will probably never know.

* * *

Today is a day spent doing what we do best—that is wandering about, just absorbing the sights, sounds and goings on of La Paz. A little shopping for souvenirs is punctuated by copious amounts of sitting in cafés watching the world go by. La Paz has many museums, churches and other places of interest, but I am still so full up with our visit to Tiahuanaco that I cannot take in any more culture for a while.

We take a wander through the Mercado Negro (black market) and the Mercado de Brujos (witches market) both of which are rather unpleasant for different reasons. The Negro is very hassly and I have my bottom touched up by a local. I cannot quite decide whether he is an incompetent pickpocket or a pervert.

The Witches Market is crowded with stalls selling dried llama foetuses, and other unmentionable objects for use in rituals to bring good luck, fertility, etc. The dried goods are accompanied by a heady aroma, which is pretty stomach churning. But there is at least one character who is enjoying the Witches Market rather more than me—a naughty young puppy has sneaked his way in amongst the dried foetuses and is having a lovely time licking away at them, unbeknown to the stallholder.

The highlight of the day is shopping for hand-woven traditional ponchos. We have been inspired by our trip around Arte Indigena in Sucre. We shop around until we find a local woman who is very knowledgeable about the provenance of her merchandise. She talks us through the history and significance of all the ponchos in her shop. We choose two antique ceremonial ponchos from Potosí. Bill's has a black background with purple, cream and green stripes. Mine is mostly green with cream, pink and orange stripes. The wool is heavy and coarse—just right for keeping out the weather and designed to last for years.

Tomorrow we fly to the Amazon jungle. We both spend the evening getting very excited.

'We're about to see amazing things that we've only ever seen on the telly before. We're going to see giant trees, jaguars, tapirs, monkeys, anacondas, caimans and loads of amazing exotic plants,' says Bill.

'Yes, how brilliant is that? I'm really looking forward to it and I'm very excited,' I say.

'Me, too,' says Bill, grinning broadly.

Today we are setting off for a six-day trip into the Amazon jungle. We were due to fly out at 7am, but we got a belated message to say that the flight has been delayed due to heavy rain last night soaking the grass runway in

Rurrenabaque. We will have to wait for the sun to dry everything out—well I guess that is the problem with trying to go in the rainy season.

We spend the morning hanging about, drinking coffee and e-mailing until eventually it is time to go for our rescheduled flight at the military base where the military airline, TAM (Transporte Aéreo Militar) is based.

We arrive at the airport only to find that the flight is delayed for a further 1½ hours. I get the distinct feeling that the delays have nothing to do with the weather and rather more to do with the whims and inefficiency of TAM.

At last we board the plane. 'Oh, my God. This is more like a dilapidated old Indian bus than something that's going to carry us safely through the skies to the Amazon jungle,' says Bill. We walk past a pile of luggage, ours included, to get to our seats which are tattered and saggy.

I point to the other passengers who are crossing themselves and praying before take-off. 'Do they know something we don't?' I say. The airhostess, dressed in combat trousers and a military bomber jacket, hands each passenger a bag of peanuts, a can of Coke and a pair of cotton earplugs. Bill and I look at each other bemusedly, until the engines start up and the ferocious din makes the need for the earplugs blatantly clear.

I am not usually a nervous flier, but the whole journey is such a juddery and noisy experience that it really highlights the fact that we are an awful long way up in the air and the safety of our lives is in the hands of the so far not very efficient TAM.

'That air hostess has got her eye on me,' says Bill. 'If we crash in the jungle I bet she's thinking that she's going to eat me first.' I believe that the scenery en-route was exceptionally beautiful and dramatic, but as Billy had nabbed the window seat and his excited little face filled most of the window for most of the flight, I will have to take his word for it. Now and again I did catch a few glimpses of the craggy snow-covered Andes as we left La Paz and later miles of forest covered hills, broken up by the snaking paths of brown muddy rivers.

We are very relieved to arrive at Rurrenabaque in one piece. Stepping off the plane onto the grass runway is like entering another world. The heat and humidity of tropical Rurrenabaque with its banana and coconut trees at an altitude of 100m is a sharp contrast to the chilly and dizzying height of La Paz at 3500m.

The first sight that greets our eyes as we drive into town is a large furry monster riding a motorbike down the high street. Bill is doubled up laughing. 'I've seen it all now!' he says. The motorbike-riding monster is followed by an enormous chicken and several people in Llama costumes dancing down the street. 'Woah, this seems like a pretty lively town,' says Bill. 'Bit of a contrast to all the serious people in La Paz.'

'I think there must be some kind of festival going on,' I say.

'Great! I'm liking it here already,' says Bill.

After checking in at the Hostal Beni, we sit by the River Beni, drinking lemon juice and eating delicious river fish. 'This reminds me of sitting by the Mekong drinking Beer Laos in Vientiane,' says Bill.

'It's gorgeous here, isn't it?' I say as we watch the sun sinking over the horizon. In the streets outside, the festival to celebrate the founding of Rurrenabaque is starting to gain momentum.

'Sounds like the party's really getting started out there. Shall we join them?' I say.

'Yeah, let's,' says Bill jumping to his feet. We spend the rest of the evening listening to the bands and watching the whirl of colour as people dance by.

Our long awaited adventure in the Amazon jungle is about to begin. Another one of my long held dreams is about to come true. Every wildlife programme, every David Attenborough documentary about this area, has served to fuel my imagination and my desire to see the flora and fauna of this part of the world with my own eyes. To say I am excited is the understatement of all time. And if I am excited, Billy can hardly contain himself. We arrive at the Inca Land Tours office with very high expectations.

We are about to spend three days in the Pampas, an area of swampy grassland, followed by three days in the jungle proper. The reason for this arrangement is that although the Pampas is less beautiful than the jungle, the wildlife is more plentiful and we are more likely to see the animals because of the better visibility. After our magical encounter with the river dolphins of Laos, I am particularly excited about seeing the pink river dolphins in this area.

There are to be six on our tour—a couple of young pups from Australia, straight out of school named Sebastian and Nicky, and a very nice English couple, Edward and Clare.

Having bolted our breakfasts to get to the Inca Land Tour office in time, we have to wait around for 1½ hours while the jeep is prepared for our journey. Anyhow, this gives us a bit of time to get to know our fellow travellers a little better.

Ed and Clare are quintessentially English, well mannered and well spoken. They are wearing white cotton shirts and khaki cotton trousers. Clare's hat has something of the pith helmet about it and Ed's shirt is a pristine pin-tucked dress shirt. They look like the sahib and memsahib about to go for an expedition in the bush. They really are keeping the side up for Blighty. They both have a great sense of humour and Ed and Bill share the same repertoire of 'interesting facts' and silly songs. We like them immediately.

The Australian pups, though very enterprising for their age, are already irritating me. They have the gauche selfishness of teenagers and the attitude of having something to prove. But I guess we were probably just like that when we were teenagers, long, long ago.

Eventually the jeep is ready. We meet our guide, René, and we climb eagerly aboard. It is about a two hour drive to Santa Rosa along hot dusty dirt tracks past many farmsteads. We are to board the boat here for a trip along the Rio Yacuma, which will bring us to our camp in the Pampas. But first, we have lunch in a pretty unhygienic looking restaurant where the chicken oozes blood and the toilets are unspeakably awful. They are enough to turn your stomach if the chicken has not already done so. Ed comes back from the loo with a look of disgust on his face, saying, 'Only the maggots are having a good time in there!'

From the restaurant it is a short drive to the boat landing, where our welcoming party is waiting—thousands upon thousands of mosquitoes. To the locals we must make an amusing sight—flapping, swatting, spraying—but nothing seems to deter the evil creatures.

It starts to rain, not a good thing when you are about to have a three hour trip in an open-top boat and it seems to drive the mozzies into even more of a biting frenzy. We all help to load the boat with the provisions for the next few days—boxes of food, our luggage and drums of water. René fetches an outboard motor from a shed and fixes it to the boat. We climb on board and the mozzies hitch a ride with us, feeding all the way. Clothing does not seem to deter them—legs under thick canvas trousers are a particular delicacy for them. I foolishly think that with my Purple Ronnie poncho wrapped around my legs I am safe, but they manage to get in and make a handsome meal of the delicate area at the backs of my knees.

The boat ride should have been a scenic opportunity to view the animals in the forest along the tree-lined banks of the Río Yacuma, but as it is raining, all the animals are sheltering—as are the mosquitoes, under my poncho. So the three hour boat trip is filled with the drone of the boat motor, the splash of water, the occasional screech of a bird and the buzz of the mosquitoes. Visibility is severely hampered by the veil of rain that seems to hem us into the boat.

Finally, nearing the camp, we round a bend in the river to be greeted by excited squeaking. René stops the boat and gets out some bananas. The squeaking reaches a crescendo and materialises into tiny little capuchin monkeys, who surge down the branches of a tree overhanging the water and hold out their hands for fruit. They are adorable—like little elves with expressive faces. It is a welcome moment of distraction from the onslaught of the mosquitoes.

We arrive at the camp to be greeted by—yes, you have guessed it—thousands more mosquitoes. It is beginning to drive us all slightly mad. The camp consists of two simple wooden buildings, one for dining and one for sleeping, a shed with a compost toilet and the cook's kitchen, set amongst scrubby jungle. The walls of the two larger buildings are made of wooden planking from floor to waist height and are open to the elements from waist height to the roof, but covered in netting to keep out the mosquitoes. This would have been a very sensible arrangement except for the fact that there are huge gaps between the planking, allowing the accursed creatures to come and go as freely as they do outside.

Clare gets out her red plastic fly swat. 'Do you know, this is the one thing that my mother insisted I bring. I thought she was mad at the time, but I'm so glad I brought it now,' she says running about like a demented thing, swatting away with great relish.

It is at this point that we discover the real reason that Clare and Ed are dressed like the sahib and memsahib and the reason that they seem to be troubled slightly less than us by the mosquitoes.

'We were forewarned about the mozzies by some of our friends back in England who are veterans of the Pampas,' says Ed. 'So we bought some secondhand clothes in Rurrenabaque, and doused them liberally with permethrin before we set off. I think this dress-shirt is rather fetching, don't you? One has to keep the standards up, even in the jungle, don't you think?'

'Yes, we spent ages trying to dream up the perfect mosquito defense outfit. We came up with the idea that a beekeeper's outfit was pretty close,' says Clare.

'That gives me an idea,' I say, going to fetch our old mosquito net. 'We could cut this up and fashion it into veils that drape from our hats.'

Fortunately there is enough to kit out all six of us. We look hilarious—but who cares, if it keeps the little mozzie bastards at bay. The veil draped around Clare's pith helmet really completes the memsahib look.

Another group arrives back from a trip looking for anacondas, bearing tales of how much worse the mosquitoes are in the swamps and congratulating us on our ingenuity in making the veils. They tell us we are really going to need them. They kindly inform us of another delight which awaits us tonight—the bed bugs. We all go into the dormitory and eye the scabby mattresses with distaste.

Our cook, Mabel, is the only cheerful looking person. Her cooking hut is filled with wood smoke—the only mozzie-free zone in the camp. I note that her bed is in there too—smart woman. Anyhow, enough about mosquitoes. Suffice it to say that it took all of our reserves of humour to deal with them—thank goodness for the company of Clare and Ed.

The highlight of the evening is a nighttime boat journey in search of alligators. It is fun speeding along the river in virtual darkness, fresh breeze in our faces, searching the banks with torches for the red eyes of the alligators. Fireflies twinkle around us like stars. René must know the river very well to be able to navigate in darkness.

René pulls the boat to the riverbank and makes a sudden grab over the side. He hauls a baby alligator into the boat for us to look at. It is a two year old, measuring about two feet in length, but I note how carefully René holds its jaw shut. He tells us that several guides have lost fingers trying to catch the baby alligators. I am not that fond of reptiles, but I feel quite sorry for this little creature. It looks stressed and frightened, and I wonder how many other times it has been caught to show to tourists.

René and the baby alligator

Then it is back to our scabby bunks for an uncomfortable night of scratching accompanied by the strange eerie noises of the jungle. I am woken a couple of times by what sounds to me like a big cat yowling—it sends shivers of excitement and fear down my spine.

This morning finds us irrationally cheerful, especially given the impending ordeal that awaits us. We don our face nets and set off into the Pampas in search of the giant anaconda, cheered on by the other group.

It is a short trip by boat across the river to where the vast flat expanse of Pampas awaits us. Grassland stretches out to the next horizon, broken only by the occasional copse of scrubby bushes. It was once a sea and every year it floods, making swampy, slightly salty terrain. Small streams cross the land in places and there are stands of grass ten feet high dotted here and there. In some places it is farmed—campesinos graze cattle and sheep—but not in this area.

After five hours of tramping through stinking mosquito-infested swamps, being alternately rained on and then baked by the sun, we are less cheerful than when we set out. We have failed to find even a sniff of a snake. At one point we have to wade thigh-deep through the gruesomely odiferous swamp. It is tough going, the thick, stinking mud sucking at your feet with every step and threatening to relieve you of your boots. Seb forgot his facemask and tried to make light of it saying how dumb they look, but I think he is regretting it now as the mosquitoes feast on his face. He is tall and spindly, with that awkward gait of a teenager and seems to be having the most trouble with the swampy conditions.

'He's got a woman's legs!' jokes Ed in a silly accent, trying to lift the mood.

But it is me who manages to topple sideways and immerse myself in swamp up to my armpits, which is most unpleasant. I can tell that everyone is dying to laugh but are politely refraining because they think I am upset, so I break the tension by giggling, at which point the others gratefully roar with laughter.

Ed, who had been walking directly behind me at the time says, 'Anna, I do apologise for laughing, but that was a piece of classic slapstick. It was the most fun I've had all day! I particularly liked the way it seemed to happen in slow motion. You listed to one side a bit and said, 'Uh oh, I'm going.' Then you tried to take another step and said, 'I'm definitely going.' And then you waved your little arms in the air and let out a plaintive cry, something like, 'Whoa, oohuhooh!!' and in you went. Unfortunately I was too far behind you to get there in time to save you.'

I look round at him, 'Edward, thank you so much. It's the thought that counts,' I say, giving him a little bow.

Anna, shortly before the unfortunate incident

Reaching an area of slightly drier land amongst the swamp, René motions for us to wait there and disappears. He is gone for ages. At first we joke about him being eaten by a caiman, but as the minutes tick by, a tangible fear grows amongst the group that something really bad has happened to him.

'What if he doesn't come back at all?' asks Clare.

'Can anyone remember the way back to the boat?' asks Bill.

The general consensus is that no-one has the foggiest idea how to get back to the boat and spending a night out here is a very unpleasant prospect.

Half an hour later, René finally reappears, having given up on the idea of finding a snake with the words, *'No Hay Anaconda.'* Much relieved, we gratefully trudge back, weak with fatigue and hunger. It is crazy to think that we are actually paying to be put through this ordeal.

After a late lunch, we go for a boat ride in search of capybaras. The weather has cleared up and now it is a beautiful sunny afternoon. It is really pleasant clipping along in the boat with the sunshine and river breeze. The good weather has brought the animals out. There are turtles sunning themselves on logs and howler monkeys in the trees. There are masses of birds including pairs of birds of paradise, which look like colourful chickens and hiss at us in a most unfriendly way as we pass; huge birds known as the 'condor of the pampas,' which look far too large and ungainly to be perched in the tops of trees, and whose flight is wobbly and precarious; vultures everywhere; pretty yellow darters; kingfishers; and many others. This is definitely the best way to see the Pampas.

With Ed, Clare and René in search of capybaras

As we pass the next camp along from us, Ed spots a huge alligator. As he points it out, it is disconcerting to see that it is coming right for us. Even more disconcerting is that, rather than take evasive action René is heading towards the alligator. He pulls over to the shore and gets out to feed the beast on leftover rice. We all think he is very brave, or perhaps foolhardy, as he gives it a friendly pat on the head.

The main aim of the trip is to see some capybaras and as we round the next bend in the river we are lucky enough to see a whole family of them. They are large ginger rodents with very little brain, rather like giant guinea pigs, as big as a sheep. They have little flickery ears and whiskery noses.

'I want to give them a big squeeze and scrubble them behind their ears,' says Bill.

'Ooh, yes, me too,' says Clare. 'They are so adorable.'

Later that afternoon when we return to camp, Ed and Seb go piranha fishing, whilst the rest of us sit about chatting and drinking tea. Nicky, quiet from the start is now barely saying a word. We ask if she is OK—'just tired' is her reply, scratching away at her bites. Seb and Ed return—the piranha fishing was about as successful as the anaconda hunting and the only thing they caught was an old boot.

Ed and Bill, announcing that they feel rather skanky on account of the absence of showers or other washing facilities at the camp, decide to brave the non-piranha infested waters for a swim. Much more of a danger than the piranhas is exposing one's skin to the ubiquitous mosquitoes. I decide I would much rather remain skanky than to expose my flesh to the hordes of bloodsuckers. The boys' technique for minimising this risk is to get into their beds under their mosquito nets and strip to their undies before making a mad dash for the water.

'Why don't you all just shit-off,' shouts Ed in the general direction of the mosquitoes as he launches himself out from under the protection of the net.

The water flows very fast and they have to swim hard to stop being dragged downstream. There is much splashing and shrieking like girlies. 'I can feel strange creatures nibbling at me under the water,' says Bill.

'Let's hope it's not one of those *candirus*—a most unsociable fish, said to inhabit these waters,' says Ed. 'It's rumoured to swim up your gentleman's parts and get lodged their owing to its backwards facing barbs. Then you'll need a very painful operation to remove it.'

'Oh really? I think I've had enough swimming for today,' says Bill rushing to the shore.

After supper, René gives us a talk about all the animals that live in the Pampas, kindly translated by Sebastian, who speaks very good Spanish. The capybaras live in small family groups of four to nine individuals. They are herbivores and do no harm to anyone. But they are the prey for everyone else—the alligators, the jaguars, anacondas and the eagles. It is a hard life being a capybara. Only one in twenty of the young make it past the first year of life.

The alligators are smaller than caimans (crocodiles), but can still grow up to four metres long and the one we saw today must have been nearing that limit. They are not usually aggressive to humans, unless they are defending their young, but all the same I would not want to get close enough to test that theory. The mothers are very protective of their young until they are a year old, when they are left to fend for themselves.

Then there are the caimans—enormous creatures which can grow up to six metres in length. They are reputed to be much more aggressive than alligators, with enormous heads and huge powerful jaws—veritable dragons left over from pre-historic times. We saw one lurking in the shadows at the edge of the river on one of our boat journeys. It was only a medium sized one, but even so, its black head was about two feet long and it put the fear of God into me.

René tells us a story about the area of Pampas where earlier today we had been traipsing around in blissful ignorance searching for anacondas. A year or two ago, the water was much higher than it is this year and the Pampas was about a foot deep in water. One of the guides disturbed a huge mother caiman and to protect her young she chased him. Understandably, he ran as fast as he could back towards the boat. But the knee-deep water was a severe hindrance to him—unlike the caiman, who was in her element. So she caught up with him just as he reached the river's edge. She snapped at him and bit through his calf muscle, but fortunately she did not get a good hold on him, otherwise she would have dragged him down and rolled him over and over until he drowned. As it was, he escaped with his life, but it took three months for his leg to heal. In my opinion, another good reason not to go anaconda hunting.

René goes on to tell us about the big cats in the jungle. This is the most exciting part for me, as I am fascinated by the big cats of the world. So far on our journey, despite coming close to tigers and leopards, we have not seen any in the flesh and I have a burning desire to see one this time.

Here in the Bolivian Pampas and jungle, there are three kinds of cat—jaguars, panthers and ocelots. The biggest and most powerful are the jaguars. They are consummate hunters and will prey on anything from a monkey to a dolphin. In fact, René tells us that he has seen many dolphins with the scars of great claw marks on their backs from close encounters with jaguars.

Unbeknown to us at the time, there is also a jaguar whose territory covers the area where we foolishly searched for anacondas. It is said that jaguars can smell fear in your footprints and if you are alone will stalk you and attack from behind. René relates the story of a group of tourists last year who were on the snake hunt. A girl in the group decided that she had

had enough and set off on her own to return to the boat. On her way back she got lost and climbed a tree to get a better look at her surroundings.

Fortunately for the girl, the others found a snake quickly and set off back to the boat. On their way, they came across two sets of footprints—those of the girl, and those of the large jaguar that was stalking her. They hurried to find her and, because there was a big group of them, managed to scare the jaguar away.

We all look at each other aghast. I think that, on balance, I probably would have given the anaconda hunting a miss if I had known about these two stories before setting off.

It seems there is also another jaguar who lives very close to the other Inca Tours camp, about a mile away. At this time of year, ie the low season, they do not use the camp because Mabel is scared to stay there on her own and who can blame her?

'I heard strange roaring sounds in the night. I'm sure it was the jaguar,' says Ed.

'So did I and I'm thinking that a mile isn't very far away,' I reply. We grimace at each other.

With these cheerful tales rattling around in our minds, we prepare for bed. Going to the toilet is a rather scary experience. We are all imagining jaguars lurking in the bushes, attracted by the strong pong of fear in our footsteps, waiting to pounce on us with our trousers down.

On my way back to the dining area, I hear strange noises coming from the direction of the river. They are like an animal exhaling air and in my heightened state of nervousness I convince myself it must be the jaguar. But it seems that it was a pod of dolphins swimming by and I really wish that I had overcome my fear to go and watch them.

So we all retire to bed and eventually I manage to calm my overactive imagination enough to fall asleep.

I awake to the unpleasant prospect of putting on my stinking clothes, which have festered nicely overnight after their dip in the swamp. It is to be our final day in the Pampas and I am glad. The sun is bright and hot, which on the plus side is driving the mosquitoes away, but on the downside is making the many existing bites itch like crazy.

Poor Seb, after his fit of teenage bravado in not wearing his face net yesterday, is regretting it now. His face is so covered in bites that there is not a spare millimetre of skin that does not have a nasty bump on it. He looks like a monster from a B-movie and must be in extreme discomfort. Bill has also managed to get a couple of bites on his eyelids, which have swollen up, giving the impression that someone gave him a severe beating in the night. Nicky sits quietly cowed and Clare is scratching her badly bitten hands until they bleed. Only Ed, who somehow seems to have avoided the worst onslaughts of these evil creatures, is his usual cheerful self. I am not the only one who is glad to be leaving the Pampas today.

It is to be a day spent mostly in the boat and it is pleasant to speed along with the cool river breeze blowing the mosquitoes away. The bright sun has brought out the wildlife again. There are many monkeys in the trees, turtles sun themselves on logs, before plopping into the water at our approach. Birds of Paradise hiss at us. Alligators lurk in the shadows of the bank. It seems a good omen for the main quarry of the day—to see the pink river dolphins.

Whenever we come to a deep pool in the river, René slows the boat to a crawl and knocks on the bottom to attract the dolphins. He does this several times, but so far we are out of luck. Then we come to a place where the river is extra wide, at the confluence of two rivers. In the centre of the river is an island of rushes and René parks the boat with its nose in the rushes and switches off the engine. Once more he knocks on the bottom of the boat. This time Bill gets out his conch and blows a couple of long notes on it. Then, just as with the Irrawaddy dolphins in Laos, they come. Only two or three, but they have answered the call of the conch and we are delighted. We hear them letting out air through their blowholes—the same sound I heard near the camp—and we briefly see their backs before they dive down again, but that is all. They have evolved away from their ocean going cousins. They are paler in colour, hence the 'pink' fable, with longer snouts and poor eyesight because the water is muddy and opaque. They do not have a marked dorsal fin, so it is really difficult to get a clear view of them in the murky water. Instead we **feel** their presence as they circle around and beneath us, these elusive and mysterious creatures. After a while they leave us and we return to camp, feeling that we have probably seen as much as anybody ever sees of them here.

Just as in Laos, the locals say that they are the humans' friend and whenever you see dolphins it is safe to swim. They chase away the piranhas and scare away alligators by ramming into their sides. On the way back to camp we are lucky enough to see some more capybaras and further on the big caiman lurking in the shadows.

After an early lunch we pack our things and return by boat to Santa Rosa—more sunshine, more wildlife—the Pampas is much more appealing by boat and when the sun is out to drive the mozzies away.

When we reach the boat landing, there is no sign of the jeep to take us back to Rurrenabaque. There is, however, a lonely and incongruously located establishment known as the Pink Dolphin Karaoke Bar, so we pile in on account of it having good mosquito netting and cold drinks. Apart from ourselves, there are only two other customers and all goes deathly quiet for a moment when we enter.

The proprietor—a very large jolly man—breaks the strained atmosphere by welcoming us and offering to put on a video showing a huge (8 metre) anaconda which was caught in this area. Well, this is the closest we are likely to get to see one, so we accept his invitation. And there it is—a vast creature which takes eight men to pick it up. And there is René too, looking very fetching in nothing but a pair of pink shiny shorts. Apparently they were going to take it to the zoo, but I was glad to hear that it managed to escape—so it is still out there somewhere.

We think we hear our jeep coming and all pile outside—we are really eager to get back to Rurrenabaque to get showered and change into clean clothes. It is not our jeep, but another, delivering a couple more hapless gringos, completely innocent of the fate that awaits them. We waste no time in filling them in on the horrors of the mozzie hell—they have only to take a look at Seb's hideously distorted face to believe us—and we solemnly hand them our face nets and wish them luck.

Just then, our attention is drawn by the sounds of loud and raucous singing issuing from the Pink Dolphin. We cannot resist peeping back in and are greeted by the surreal sight of the large proprietor, naked to the waist, strutting about with his trousers slung low under his ample belly. He is singing with great gusto and drama to entertain his two friends with Tom Jones' 'Delilah'. What his performance lacks in tunefulness it makes up for in raw emotion and sincerity. We all laugh—this man's talent for entertaining is sadly wasted in such an out-of-the-way spot.

Finally, our jeep arrives and we thankfully climb aboard, dreaming about the hot steaming showers in Rurre. The jeep driver seems to be in a bit of a hurry too. He races over the stoney, bumpy road at breakneck speed. Several times the vehicle takes off into the air over extra large humps, causing cricked backs and a tyre blowout.

Standing at the side of the road waiting for the tyre to be changed, we are overcome by a feeling of warmth towards our companions engendered by the sense of togetherness after going through the Pampas ordeal together.

'We're getting married in June. Will you be back in England by then? Come to our wedding. We'd be greatly honoured if you would come. It's in a beautiful part of the world, in Herefordshire, just a couple of miles from Hay-on-Wye,' says Bill to Ed and Clare.

'Oh I know Hay-on-Wye. It's gorgeous round there. Oh, we'd love to come, wouldn't we Ed?' says Clare.

'Yes, definitely. It's a date. Thank you, it's an honour to be asked,' says Ed.

'Great that's settled then,' says Bill.

Everyone falls quiet for a moment before Ed says, 'Ah, good old Blighty,' and we all give a collective sigh of sweet homesickness as we think of England—Herefordshire in early Summer has to be one of the most beautiful places on the planet. And there is the added bonus that it is mosquito-free.

After a quick tyre change, we are on our way again, and soon back in Rurre where the festival and the rodeo are still in full swing. We check back in to the Hostal Beni, where the smiley-eyed proprietor has saved us a room. I cannot begin to explain how blissful it is to get into the shower. I stay in for ages, scrubbing every inch of mosquito repellent, suncream, grime, mud and swamp stink off my body.

I have stupidly only brought one pair of trekking trousers —everything else is in storage in La Paz. The thought of wearing them for another 3 days in the jungle is unbearable, so I have to give them a quick scrub and hang them out to dry.

We meet up with Clare and Ed for dinner and have a very funny evening, de-briefing all the horrors of the trip and comparing other notes about our travels. They have just come south through Peru, which is next on our agenda, so they give us lots of good tips about places to stay and places to avoid.

Ed tells us lots of libellous stories about famous people—there was the rather ugly overweight actress who got drunk at a dinner party at their house and made a pass at his Mum, and there was the BBC newsreader/political interviewer who played ping pong with his Dad and made a complete arse of himself because he was so competitive and such a bad loser.

'God, one of my pet hates is people who boast about how cheap the amazing hotel they stayed in supposedly was. We've come across so many of them on our travels,' says Ed.

'Yeah, they're the same sort of people who will tell you that they went everywhere getting lifts for free from local people, and how they ended up in a really remote area where no-one has ever seen white people before, and there just so happened to be the most amazing ten day ceremony starting and they were asked to be the guest of honour and ended up being made the chief of the tribe. I call it travel lies,' says Bill. Everyone laughs and agrees that we have all met someone like that.

It is **really** sad to part company with them at the end of the evening. We are about to launch ourselves into the jungle and we will not even have them for moral support, as they are going with another tour group. We find out that their camp is not far from ours and we arrange a sign to let them know that we are close—Bill will blow the conch and Ed will answer with his bird impression.

* * *

I awake feeling tired and apprehensive about the prospect of a further three days of heat and nasty biting insects in the jungle. Bill has got a pooey bum and I feel as if my system has been poisoned by all the bites. So we are both in a bit of a grumpy mood. After breakfast and a quick whizz round the second-hand shops, to replace our still sopping clothes with ones that we do not mind wrecking, we head for the Inca Land Tours office.

En-route we have an argument about whether we really want to go or not. But neither of us wants to be the one to pull the plug, knowing this is our one chance to see the Amazon jungle—something we have both dreamed about for so long. So despite our misgivings, we agree that we can put up with another three days of discomfort to fulfil this part of the dream.

So we are off again. This time it is just the two of us. René and Mabel are to be our personal guide and cook for the three days and it all feels quite cosy. I have already grown really fond of René and Mabel. Our whole journey is to be by boat, first along the Rio Beni and then branching off along the Rio Tuichi, where the camp is situated. We stop to buy tickets which will allow us to enter the Madidi National Park.

The rain hammers down for most of the journey. Our little open-topped boat is fighting against the fast current. On either side of the river are brown muddy cliffs topped with trees which come right to the edge. I sit silently contemplating whether we have made a huge mistake in coming. A soggy-looking Bill looks round at me. 'It's not looking good so far,' he says glumly.

But there is one thing I feel quite smug about. I fare rather better than the others in the rain. I am very thankful that I have remembered to pack my Purple Ronnie poncho. Not only does it completely cover me, but also the bag of newly purchased secondhand clothes that I nurse on my lap—I am not about to repeat the experience of having to wear clothes sodden with stinking swamp water for three days. I love my poncho and it was well worth all the abuse that I have had hurled at it since I bought it in Vietnam several months ago. Poor Bill and everyone else in the boat get soaked to their underpants.

When we arrive at the camp, the rain, thank goodness, has abated. We scale the steep muddy bank with the help of some slippery steps cut in. It is tricky carrying our heavy packs. We are greeted by Eric, an American, and two Swiss girls, who had been part of the other group we met in the Pampas. They are on the last day of their jungle tour and I am very eager to find out how they have got on. Eric seems quite happy, but the two girls do nothing but moan—'It's so hot here, but it rains all the time and nothing ever dries out. We haven't seen any animals. The food is terrible . . . . etc, etc.'

At first I buy into it and seriously think about asking René if we can cut the trip short. But then I remember that they had been moaning constantly on the Pampas trip too. My most pressing concern was: 'Are there many mosquitoes in the jungle?' To my great relief, the answer is, 'No, there are hardly any here.' Thank goodness for that—I can stand anything except mosquitoes.

Then Eric comes over and says in a conspiratorial whisper, 'Don't listen to them. They never stop moaning. I love the jungle. I've had a great time here and it's much better than the Pampas.' There is a marked change in René too. In the Pampas he had seemed stressed and wore a permanent frown. But as soon as we arrived here his face broke into a radiant smile. He kicked off his shoes and ran about singing and whistling. He seems to be blossoming in the verdant jungle.

Once the others leave, the whole atmosphere changes. We make the dormitory our own. It seems much cleaner—no flea bitten mattresses here, only bamboo cots with carry mats.

I think there might be another reason for René's good mood.

'Ai, ai,' says Bill. 'I don't know whether you've noticed, but there seems to be love blossoming between René and Mabel. I bet they are glad to be away from being teased by the other guides and cooks.'

'Yes, I spotted that too. They are very sweet together.'

After lunch, René tells us to get ready for our first walk in the jungle. A story told me by my Hungarian friend, Erika, makes my number one priority to wear my hat.

When I first told Erika about our travel plans, she said, 'Oh darlink, do be careful in zee jungle. I have a friend who just came back from zare . . . ven I met him from zee plane he voz varing zis seelly baseball cap.

And I said, 'Darlink take off ziss seelly hat so I can kiss you properly.'

But he said, 'No, Erika, I can't. It is to cover up zee bacon I have on my head.'

And I said, 'Vie have you got bacon on your head, darlink?'

And he said, 'Because in zee jungle zare are zese creatures zat live in zee trees and zay drop onto your head as you pass by and burrow into your scalp. And zee only vay you can get zem out is to put bacon on your head so zat zay vill burrow into zee bacon instead of your head.'

'So darlink, promise me you vill **allvays** vare a hat in zee jungle,' said Erika to me.

Just walking in the lush green forest is wonderful. We walk in silence most of the time. A hushed awe has descended upon us and we do not want to disturb the animals. The silence heightens the feeling of the spirit of the forest, La Selva. It feels friendly and welcoming.

René points to the tree canopy. 'Howler monkeys,' he says. High in a tree we spot them. They are a vivid foxy rust colour against the lush green, and they are looking back at us as curiously as we are looking at them.

Deeper into La Selva, we hear animal sounds. 'Pig,' says René but they catch our scent and run off before we can catch a glimpse of them.

There is an amazing variety of ants of all colours and sizes, from the Paulo Diablo (red fire ants), to lines of black ants with cut pieces of leaf on their backs which look impossibly large for their little bodies to carry. The scariest ones are the giant Buna ants, which are over an inch long. René points at them and says, 'Much much pain for three hours.' Hearing this, we think he is a little foolhardy to go barefoot, but he has the eyes of a hawk and always manages to avoid them.

We come to a tree bearing small orange fruits. René shins deftly up and throws some fruit down into Bill's hat.

'*Achachairu*'—lychee of the Selva. *Muy bien*,' says René biting into one. And he is right—they are absolutely delicious.

A little further on we come to a giant tree. It is a huge cathedral of a tree, with its vast buttresses spreading out in all directions to support its great height. It is covered in a climber, which René clambers up and swings about like a monkey. He is like a different person here in the Selva—much less inhibited. But the sad thing is that the climber is a parasite and will eventually kill this magnificent tree.

We hear a macaw squawking in the tree canopy, but it is too high for us to see. It is a whole different ecosystem up there.

Next we spot a tortoise ambling along. René wants to show it to us, so we try to head him off by taking a circular detour. But to our great surprise, when we get there he is nowhere to be seen. Later we spot him heading off in the distance. I am amazed that tortoises can move so fast. Whilst on the track of the tortoise, we hear a snort and a crashing in the undergrowth. It is a tapir, but again, it is gone before we catch a glimpse of it.

On the way back we hear, but do not see a toucan, high above us in the tree canopy. So it is a walk full of near misses. But it is good to know that the animals are out there and that the jungle is so full of life.

We return to a feast prepared for us by the lovely Mabel and have a little free time before going on a night-time walk.

Night has fallen and we are creeping through the jungle. It is intensely dark and very scary. There are many *bunas* and poisonous spiders to avoid and we walk in a state of nervous tension. Some of the spiders have constructed huge webs across the pathway and we have to duck under so as not to disturb them. This is very nerve-wracking as I am not sure which ones are poisonous and am living in dread of feeling a tickle as something furry drops down the back of my neck.

Twice we hear a deep whirring sound and ask René what it is. The answer, 'Vampire bats,' is not what we wanted to hear.

René shines his torch on a tree and we see a tiny snake—brown striped with a black zigzag down its back. René wags his finger and says, 'No touch. *Muy toxico* (very poisonous).' I keep my distance, but it strikes me that you would have to be seriously unlucky to get close enough to be bitten by this little creature, whose head is only about half an inch across.

Bill keeps saying, 'It's SO dark.' It is nighttime after all, but I know what he means. There is a totality and a density to the darkness that is unusual and adds to the scariness of encountering all these dangerous creatures.

We both sleep soundly, falling asleep to the strange sounds of the forest and waking to another beautiful day. I feel glad to be alive and so glad that we did not cancel because of our experience in the Pampas.

After breakfast, we set off for a long walk towards some watering holes where we might have a chance of seeing some of the larger animals. We see more really vast trees—giants of the forest. Bill is in raptures.

As we walk, we hear the eerie sound of the howler monkeys rising and falling. The sound fills the whole forest. Eventually we find the tree where the noise is coming from. It sounded like a hundred monkeys all warbling together and yet we are astonished to find that a sole male was responsible for all that noise. And he does not look as if he feels guilty about it at all. We stare at him and he stares at us. He seems particularly fascinated by my hat. It has already been a source of great amusement for Edward, so perhaps the monkey thinks it looks rather comical too. But hey, it is better than having to put bacon on your head.

Apparently howler monkeys always make lots of noise at dawn, but if you hear them later in the day, it is a sign that it is about to rain. In this case, the monkey is absolutely right and it is not long before the first fat rain drops start to fall. But we are having too much of a good time to let a bit of rain deter us.

Poor Bill has been suffering from a runny bum, so when René shows us a tree that is a good cure for diarrhoea, we collect some of its bark to use later.

We come to some more vines hanging from the trees and Bill has a great time swinging about with René. But the noise startles another animal, which goes crashing off through the undergrowth—our second close encounter with a tapir.

By now we are nearing the watering hole. We can hear and smell wild pigs—phew, it is like bad B.O. We quietly stalk them. Finally we get near the herd and are just in time to see the last stripy piglet racing after his family into the undergrowth.

It is now time to head back for camp and we walk through an area of the forest where I have a really strong feeling of being watched—maybe the elusive tapir again, or a jaguar?

A little further on and there is another crashing sound in the undergrowth. Bill sees a deer, but René and I are not quite quick enough.

Back at the camp, we are really grateful for the huge lunch that Mabel has prepared, having worked up quite an appetite on our long walk. She also makes the bark we collected into a tea for Bill.

After a short siesta, René shows us how to make jewellery from things that grow in La Selva. We have a very creative afternoon making rings cut from big nutshells and René shows us how to polish them to a deep shine on a stone. We make pendants from slices of a woody fruit and thread them onto strings made by plaiting thin strips of the *hippy happa* palm. The ring that René is making is to be a love token for Mabel.

We hear the sound of a boat going down the river and René beckons us to the riverbank just in time to see Ed and Clare on their way back to Rurre. We call and wave frantically, but the noise of their outboard motor must have drowned out our voices. We return to our jewellery making. 'I wonder what kind of time they've had in the jungle?' I say to Bill.

'I hope they had a good time, but I wish they could be with us now,' says Bill.

Later we go for another walk to the banks of a small river, which is a tributary to the Tuichi. We pass a whole ant community on the move. Workers carry the eggs and bigger guard ants flank them, protecting their precious cargo. We see the tracks of a family of capybaras in the soft mud at the river bank—there is no mistaking their three-toed footprints—but our timing is wrong and they have already moved on when we get there.

That night after supper, it is story time. René delights in telling us lots of spooky stories about strange spirits in the jungle and people being attacked by devil monkeys with red eyes—a strikingly similar tale to the one told us by Bushman Bandara in Sri Lanka.

René speaks no English, but understands a little, so his stories are translated from Spanish, very badly by me for Bill's benefit. Sometimes it takes me two or three goes to get the meaning . . .

'And then he smelled honey,' I translate.

'Non, non,' says René.

'And then he smelled shit,' I try again.

'Non, non,' says René.

'Oh, you mean, 'then he became afraid."

'Si, si!'

The eeriest story is that of a hunter who lived in the forest a few years ago, before it had been made into a national park. This man was such a successful hunter and killed so many animals that he actually exported them by boat out of the jungle and sold them at the market in Rurrenabaque.

One day he was sitting on the banks of the very river we had visited that day, smoking a cigarette. On the riverbank in the distance he saw a tapir. It was thin and poor-looking and the hunter considered that it was not worth killing for meat, so he ignored it at first.

But the tapir came closer and closer and then started to run towards him. He thought it was going to attack him, so he raised his rifle and fired at it from close range. To his fear and consternation it disappeared right in front of his eyes. He dropped his rifle and ran back to his camp, feeling that he was being pursued all the time by the tapir.

He reached the camp, shouting, 'Help, help, the tapir's going to get me.' But no-one else saw the mysterious tapir. That night he fell into a fever and in his delirium, he kept shouting about the tapir. His friends took him to the hospital at Rurrenabaque, but they could not cure his fever.

The man's father knew a shaman and asked him to help his son. The shaman performed a ceremony to try to cure the man, but he came back saying, 'It is too late. The guardian spirit of the animals in the forest has taken its revenge on this man for killing so many animals.' Shortly after this, the man died.

So the mystery of the elusive tapir deepens for us. This story seems to explain why René was reluctant to pursue the two tapirs that we heard in the forest. We know that before he became a guide, René had been a hunter and perhaps he was scared that the spirit tapir would get him too.

Just before we retire to bed, he takes us to a tree and shines a torch to show us a big hairy tarantula munching on a large green bug. The spider has big round black eyes and an expression which seems to say, 'Can't a spider get a little peace around here, when he's trying to enjoy a light snack of an evening?' The disconcerting thing is that the tree is right next to where we had been sitting to make the jewellery earlier in the day.

So once again, René has managed to make us feel all spooked at bedtime. We accompany each other to the toilet out of fright and retire to bed trying not to think of all the spooky things in the jungle which might get us.

Another big walk after breakfast—we should be very fit after this trip. We set off through the dense greenness past more giant trees, poisonous trees, trees with roots which grow out from 3 metres above the ground and look like giant spiders, ferns, bamboos and shrubs all add to the profusion of plant life. René shows us lots more medicinal plants—to cure cancer, to cure rheumatism, to cure heart disease—the Selva is a huge natural pharmacy. René asks Bill how he is feeling after the herbal tea. 'Oh, loads better,' he says. 'It's worked wonders for my stomache.'

He even shows us a vine which can be cut and drinkable water pours out of the end. It tastes slightly bitter, but very refreshing and it seems to give me new energy.

We come across a beautiful iridescent blue cicada that has just hatched out of its old skin. It looks and sounds as if it were made of metal, like a clockwork toy bug.

We hear howler monkeys in the distance. Perhaps it will rain again. Further on, we come to a special tree, where a very nasty creature lives. It looks like a giant furry moth, camouflaged very well to blend in with the tree bark. René reassures us that they are quite placid during the day, but at night they will land on you and inject acid into you. If you do not immediately drink water, you will die. On hearing that, we feel that we have seen quite enough of these bizarre creatures and move on quickly.

As we are nearing our camp, a beautiful sight greets my eyes. A shaft of sunlight beams down in front of the kitchen tent and in and out of this light dance a cloud of huge iridescent blue butterflies. René sings out a love song for Mabel and she steps out smiling into this fluttering cloud. All the colours are so vivid, it seems like something out of a fairytale.

But at lunchtime, our cosy little world is interrupted by the arrival of another boat, bringing Brian, an English guy who is just about to spend three days on his own with René and Mabel. I feel a tinge of regret that our magical time is nearly over.

As Brian's Spanish is practically non-existent, and neither René nor Mabel speak English, we feel duty bound to give him a brief lesson—*muy toxico* = very poisonous; *pellegroso* = dangerous; *Buna* = three hours of intense pain. The rest he will have to work out for himself.

In the afternoon we are going to risk life and limb to watch parrots from a cliff top, but it is worth it. Many times over our three days we have heard the parrots chatting high above in the tree tops, but it is virtually impossible to see them because of the height of the tree canopy. So we take a boat to the other side of the river and climb a steep and dangerous cliff, clinging onto precarious looking vines to help ourselves up.

At the top, we are rewarded with a panoramic view over the Selva. There is a fresh breeze which makes a pleasant change from the steamy heat of the jungle. The parrots are nesting in the muddy cliff and flying in and out of their nests several metres below us. It is a relaxing way to spend the afternoon, watching the bright blue, red and green parrots flying back and forth and shouting to each other across the forest. They seem to be having conversations with each other, gossiping about all the goings on in the Selva.

'I wonder what they are talking about?' says Bill. 'Hey amigo, you should try the fruit on that one. It is delicioso!'

The way back is even more daunting than the way up. You have to kind of abseil your way down, trusting that the vines are not going to part company with the crumbling cliff face and send you hurtling to your doom in the valley below.

In some places, it is very hard to see your next foothold because of overhanging rocks obscuring your view. At one stage, René comes back to help me over a particularly tricky bit. Unfortunately, one of the rocks he tells me to put my foot on gives way and I crash into the rock face, letting out a squawk of pain.

Somehow I manage to still cling on and despite a cracked knee and grazed arm, I am able to shakily continue my way down on jelly legs.

'Anna, are you all right? Please tell me you're not dead. Please tell me you haven't been smashed to pieces on the rocks,' shouts Bill. My squawk and the crashing rocks have given Bill a fright as he cannot see me and feared the worst for several moments, until I can shout to him that I am OK.

To make matters worse, it starts to pour with rain, making things even more slippery and treacherous. I am very relieved to get to the bottom and would not recommend the experience to anyone with a dicky ticker.

After that last bit of death defying adventure, our jungle trip is finally over and we board the boat for Rurrenabaque, bidding farewell to René and Mabel who have looked after us so well for these past six days.

One and a half hours later, we arrive in Rurre, wet, tired and filthy. So it is back once more to Hostal Beni for a giant scrub up. We pop into the Inca Land Tours office just to check that all is well with our flight in the morning. Although we have had a fantastic time, we are both desperate to get back to climes where there are no biting insects and its cool enough to need a blanket at night. We are reassured that all is well and told to be at the office at 9 am the following day for our flight with Amazonas.

Feeling content, we head for a drink at a nearby café, where I discover to my utter delight that they serve *achachairu* smoothies — now my new favourite drink.

Over breakfast we notice that there is an Amazonas office just across the street from us. As the weather is looking a little ominous, we pop in to see if the flight is OK. The friendly and helpful man tells us that there is no flight this morning and that the afternoon flight is already full and our names are not on the list.

We storm round to the Inca Land Tours office to demand to know what is going on. The lazy and apathetic woman in the office looks a bit guilty when we say there is no morning flight and our names are not on the list for the already full afternoon flight, all of which she would have known had she actually bothered to try to book us onto the flight.

She asks us to wait five minutes and rushes off. On reflection 'rushes' is perhaps too strong a word for her sloth-like amble. She returns to tell us that we are now booked on the TAM flight at 4.30pm. So, placated a little, we wander off, wondering what we are going to do with ourselves for the rest of the day, having already checked out of our hostel.

The other problem is that we are starting to run out of Bolivianos, having given some money to the Australians who had under budgeted, and there is nowhere to take any more out. There is no bank in Rurre, which really surprises me, as it is such an epicentre for the surrounding region and a base for anyone who wants to visit the jungle and the Pampas.

So we hang about making a cup of coffee last a long time and reading till it is time to meet the woman from ILT for the TAM flight. At the TAM office we are greeted with the exasperating news that the TAM flight is cancelled because of heavy rain in Riberalto, where the plane is coming from. To add insult to injury, we hear that the Amazonas flight which we should have been on, if not for the ineptitude of the ILT woman, has taken off as scheduled. We will have to stay another night, but we do not have enough money to pay for a hotel room or even to buy food.

I am livid. The ILT woman just shrugs her shoulders. I lose my rag and start shouting at her. I cannot believe her incompetence. We have checked at least three times whether they had booked us on an outbound flight—when we first arrived in Rurre, when we got back from the Pampas and again yesterday afternoon. Each time she told us everything was fine, when actually she had done nothing about it. The look on her face says, 'Do you think I give a sh*t?' Clearly she does not, and that has been the problem all along. She makes no suggestion as to our lack of money or place to stay for the night. I guess I was really foolish to think that a supposedly reputable company might offer to lend us some money or even put us up for the night at their expense, since it was entirely her fault.

A kindly Swiss girl overhears our conversation and says that she knows of a shop that will change dollars. Fortunately, Billy has a secret stash of dollars for just such an emergency. So all is not lost and we will not have to spend the night on the street after all.

When I have calmed down we manage to change some money and find another place to stay. We are loath to go back to the Hostal Beni, having had a bit of a row at check out time, because the usual proprietor was not there and the surly woman who was filling in for him tried to charge us more than we had paid before, saying the prices had gone up. I am sure she intended to pocket the extra.

So things are starting to turn a bit ugly in Rurre. But on the plus side, the new place we are staying in has a beautiful garden and a place to do our laundry, so we set to scrubbing our filthy clothes.

After supper, we retire for an early night feeling pretty pooped. But there is to be no rest for us—it is Saturday night and the disco just down the road starts up with loud pumping music and a very annoying DJ who loves the sound of his voice and talks over the top of all the music. This goes on till about 4am after which we finally get a couple of hours of fitful sleep before at last it is time to get on a flight back to La Paz.

Over breakfast we are dismayed to see a fine drizzle coming down. The prospect of more delays is terribly depressing. But in the TAM office they are bright and positive that the flight will go today—we do not even bother consulting the ILT woman anymore as we cannot believe anything she tells us. In the end we have to re-route via Reyes which has a better runway but means an hour's bone-shaking ride on a battered old bus, but I do not care—at least we are on our way.

The plane taxis down to the end of a grass runway, turns and then gathers momentum and we finally take off at great speed and tumultuous noise. The flight goes pretty smoothly until we descend towards La Paz. Where suddenly there is no noise and we seem to be drifting down towards the city.

'Oh my God,' says Bill. 'I think the engines have cut out.' For a brief moment we contemplate our mortality, until we can hear the engine noise and start to breath again.

After our first inauspicious arrival in La Paz, this time it feels good to be back. We have had so many days of roughing it, that we decide to treat ourselves and check into a posh hotel. So we splash out $25 a night at the Naira Hotel on Sagarnaga and it is worth every penny—crisp white bed linen, a carpeted room, a proper mattress, a really good and spotless bathroom with a powerful **hot** shower (most of them dribble and are lukewarm), fluffy towels and a laundry service. We waste no time in handing over our by now festering laundry, which has not dried after our last scrubbing.

We have a big sleep to catch up on the disco-disturbed night and spend the rest of the day pottering about, checking e-mails, drinking really good coffee and revelling in the clean and insect free environment. There is an e-mail from Mum and Dad. It reads:—

Hi Anna and Bill

Thanks for the epistle—what experiences! Look forward to photos.

We took the marquee plans up to your Aunty Maureen's at the weekend. Aunty Chris came too. Have amended them according to advice from my two sisters. This saved nearly £400. We are now looking into catering, getting 3 sample menus and comparing prices etc. Will leave final choice until you come (if possible). I have sent deposit and plan to the Ceilidh Band people and will firm up times with them when you're back.

Not long now. Lots of love

M and D.

Having completely ignored most of the cultural sights on our previous visits to La Paz, we thought we would do something a bit touristy today. 'Hey, shall we go to the zoo? I know it's a bit ironic, having just spent a week in the wilds of the Amazon but I really want to see some of those mysterious animals with my own eyes. I mean, what does a tapir actually look like?' I say to Bill.

'Yes, me too. It sounds like a great idea. I would love to see a jaguar,' he says.

The zoo is 10 km out of town and it is a different kind of adventure trying to find the right micro (minibus) to catch and figure out which stop to get off at. But the journey goes pretty smoothly and we arrive just in time for the feeding of the carnivores. The first enclosure houses three one-year-old jaguar cubs. Even at this age, their hunting instinct is very strong. The three of them are stalking a dog, who is fortunate to be on the other side of the bars. Then one of them stalks Bill, staring him down with eyes that bore into your soul, saying, 'I'm going to get you, and then I'm going to eat you.'.

'My God that was scary—that is no cute kitty,' says Bill. 'Even though I know he's behind bars and can't really get me, it brings up this primal fear about being eaten.'

There is another enclosure which houses two adults. We see the keeper disappear into the back of the sleeping quarters with a wheelbarrow full of meat. Then we hear the most blood curdling snarls and growls and roars, that make the hairs on the back of my neck stand up. It sounds as if the keeper is being torn limb from limb. A huge powerful male comes running out with a bloody carcass, which it proceeds to devour at top speed, still uttering those terrifying snarls and slavering sounds. We are much relieved to see the keeper emerge unharmed from the enclosure.

In the enclosure next door to this is a beautiful puma, which in isolation I am sure would have looked quite magnificent. It is not hard to see why pumas are sacred to the Incas. But even this wild creature is terrified of the sounds made by the jaguars. 'Just imagine how we would've felt if we'd really come across one in the Pampas?' Bill says.

'I think my trousers would've been soiled with rather more than swamp water,' I say.

There are several other cute and furry animals including an ocelot who rolls coquettishly on his back for us and looks for all the world just like a large tabby pussycat. But the other two animals we had hoped to see in the wild elude us once more. We cannot find the anaconda's enclosure and although we see the tapir's enclosure from a distance, when we get there it is mysteriously empty . . .

Today our main task is to catch the bus to Copacabana on the shores of Lake Titikaka. It seems that we are leaving La Paz just in time. We were wondering about the build-up of police with tear gas and riot gear as we looked out of the taxi window bound for the bus station. We find out later that a demonstration about a new tax got out of hand and ended in a full-scale battle between the police and the army. A riot with petrol bombing and looting ensued.

I am very glad to be four hours drive away and close to the border with Peru. I have heard it said that, *'Sooner or later the traveller in South America may happen upon a revolution, and especially should he choose to spend much time in Bolivia, where the government is chronically so fractured and unstable that it can scarcely be called a government at all.'* These words were written over forty years ago, by Peter Matthiessen in his book, *The Cloud Forest*. It seems that in all that time, nothing much has changed.

It is a four-hour drive from La Paz to Copacabana. The bus climbs and climbs up out of the bowl filled with the sprawl of smoggy La Paz. Eventually after many stops to pick up more people, the bus, groaning under the weight of passengers, crests the edge of the bowl and we drive out into open countryside. There are small farms dotted here and there and white-tipped mountains in the distance. We have to cross a bit of Lake Titikaka on a ferry. It is very exciting to be finally seeing the fabled lake with my own eyes. The water is a sharp shade of turquoise and it smells like the sea. There are waves beating against the shore, just like the sea. Lake Titikaka is vast—175km long by 50km wide, and very deep at 275m. It looks very inviting for a swim, but at an altitude of 4,000m, its waters are freezing all year round. Just like the sea, it even has its own species of seahorse. Its icy depths are home to other strange creatures such as the giant tricolour frog, discovered by Jacques Cousteau. The frog is more than 20 inches long and apparently never comes to the surface. I would not mind betting there are many other strange and mysterious things yet to be discovered that lurk in the depths of the lake. Perhaps it even has its own version of the Loch Ness Monster.

Copacabana is delightful—a rather eccentric town dominated by a vast Moorish-style cathedral dedicated to the Virgin of the Candelaria, or the Dark Lady of the Lake, depending whether you are Roman Catholic or prefer the indigenous religion. This icon was sculpted by the son of the last Incan Emperor and the story goes that when she was finished and installed in the cathedral, healing miracles began to happen. She certainly seems to hold a strange power.

'I could swear that her eyes are following me round the room,' says Bill with a slight shudder when we visit the church.

There are many strange traditions in Copacabana, such as taking your new car, truck or bus to the cathedral to have it blessed by the priest and christened by dousing it in beer, wine or whatever other alcohol you can afford. There is also the festival where people buy miniature versions of the things that they want for the coming year eg a mini house, car, TV, baby etc, etc, as good luck charms to make their wishes come true.

The setting of the town beside the turquoise lake amongst the mountains is quite stunning. There is a holiday feel. Pedalos are pulled up on the beach and tour boats go in and out. Dogs sniff about and Bolivian ladies sit and survey the scene. There are lots of gringos wandering around. We find ourselves a room in a reasonable hotel with fantastic views of the lake and have a pleasant supper of fish from the lake, blissfully unaware of the rioting we have just left behind.

In the late afternoon we climb the Cerro Calvario, the hill north of town, which at 3,966m is lung-splittingly difficult. But we are rewarded at the top with a breathtaking view over the town and the lake just as the sun is going down. We also build up good appetites for scoffing delicious steak in creamy pepper sauce at La Orilla restaurant just up the road from our hotel.

The high altitude seems to have been having a bad effect on our spirits. I have felt quite irrationally depressed and miserable, despite the glorious setting and Bill says he feels the same. But the walk to higher altitude seems to have a good effect as it gets the blood pumping round and we both feel more cheerful afterwards, especially when our bellies are full of yummy food.

Isla del Sol in the middle of Lake Titikaka is a sacred island, steeped in Inca mythology. Legend has it that it is the birthplace of Manco Capac, the first Inca and his sister/wife Mama Huaca. The Incas believe that these two gods rose from the rock on the island called Titikaka or 'rock of the puma.' Legend also tells that it was here that the bearded white god, Viracocha, made his mystical appearance.

So we set off with packed lunches gripped in our sweaty paws to board the Titikaka Tours boat bound for the island. The boat crawls along at a snails pace and it feels as if we will never get there.

Rain clouds gather and black twisters whirl down out of the clouds onto the mountains surrounding the lake. 'Wow! Look at that,' says Bill, who is very fond of a twister.

I am afraid it might be a wet, miserable walk across the island, but after a brief squall, which turns the waters of the lake choppy and rocks the boat from side to side, the sun comes out once again.

After a brief introduction from the obnoxious boatman, which roughly translates as, 'Most of you gringos understand nothing because you can't speak Spanish,' we get off the snail boat onto dry land.

There are many ancient ruins on the island from the Inca period, from the earlier time of Tiahuanaco and even before that. It is a steep walk up to the first site through a village where people tend crops, where donkeys and sheep graze, where flowers grow in pretty gardens, where pigs root around, where all seems peaceful and idyllic.

At the first site, there is a sacred stone and an altar where ceremonies are still held to celebrate the solstice on 21st June and nearby crops of corn are turned into chicha, the sacred drink of the gods.

Another steep walk takes us to the major ruins of the Incas. It is here that you can see the rock shaped like a puma's head—that is if the light is just right, and if you squint at it and have a very good imagination.

The ruins themselves are a network of rooms made from straight rectangular blocks, set beautifully above a gently curving bay of turquoise waters lapping at a beach. The island reminds me of somewhere in the Mediterranean, with its stony hillsides and stands of eucalypts, which could be mistaken for olive trees at a distance.

After the ruins, we set off for an 11km hike along the spine of the island. The air is very clear and the sun is cruelly bright and blistering as we puff our way up onto the ridge. The lake is already at 3,820 metres and we feel every metre that we rise above this. But once we are on the ridge, the path is relatively easy and gives us panoramic views of the island and the lake. All is peaceful and quiet, apart from the busyness of a few dung beetles and the hum of the crickets.

About halfway along the ridge, we pass another little village set scenically around a horseshoe bay of turquoise water. There are three communities on the island—Challapampa in the north, Challa, the town we have just passed and Yumani in the South. Three thousand lucky people live in this idyllic place, where there are no cars, just donkeys, llamas and sheep.

A little further on, a man sells drinks and sweets from an isolated hut, so we stop and eat our packed lunches. We buy a coke from the man, but regret trying to drink something fizzy at this altitude as it gives us both hiccups.

After lunch, it is a long roller coaster track to the other end of the island with the bright sun blistering our skins, despite liberal applications of suncream, sunglasses and hats, so we are relieved to meet a couple going the other way who tell us that we are not far from Yumani.

The first sign of civilisation is a couple of charming and comical local boys with a llama that they have decorated with balloons around its neck. They want us to give them money to pose for a picture. We think they are very enterprising, so we do.

Finally we arrive in Yumani and wind our way through the village, before walking down the enchanting Escalera del Inca (stairway of the Incas), surrounded by shady trees and greenery with a stream of crystal water running beside it. There is something very magical about this place after walking for so many kilometres along the barren ridge.

We have a delicious and well-earned cup of tea at the bottom of the stairs before boarding the boat for home, and crawling back at a snail's pace.

Reed boat on Lake Titikaka

In the evening the wind gets up and a really big storm blows in. We have managed to settle ourselves snugly by the fire in La Orilla, drinking red wine and eating more of their lovely steak before the full force of the storm lashes down all around us. Signs blow over, doors blow open, Bolivian ladies' hats blow off, making them chase them down the road, rain lashes down and thunder and lightning split all around us.

'Wow, that's pretty spectacular,' says Bill as a fork of lightning cracks across the sky. 'It's a good job that it didn't hit us while we were still on that boat. So, tomorrow we say goodbye to Bolivia and start the last leg of the journey in Peru, eh?'

'Yes. Lots of great things to see in Peru, but only three weeks till we're home,' I say.

Chapter 14
Peru—Gringos in the Sacred Valley

From Copacabana we travel by bus across the border into Peru. The route follows the edge of the lake and we have one of the smoothest border crossings we have experienced so far—just get off the bus, get your passport stamped, change some money from Bolivianos to Peruvian sol and away we go. Over the border in Peru, nothing much has changed. The scenery is the same, the houses look the same, the people look the same. The only difference seems to be a subtle change in the shape of the ladies' hats. Rather than the bowler shaped Bolivian hats, the Peruvian hats are taller with a waisted middle.

Our destination is Puno, another town on the shores of Lake Titikaka. But unlike Copacabana, Puno is anything but delightful. It is sprawling and stinking, dumping its sewage into the lake and creating a thick layer of green scum on its surface. The only reason to stay in Puno is to take another boat trip to visit more of the islands on the Peruvian side, which we organise for tomorrow.

The whole atmosphere in Puno makes me feel uneasy. It is not a good first impression of Peru. Because of the dodgy atmosphere, we decide to book into a posh hotel, which is a little above our budget. Bill manages to barter them down to half the asking price and it is well worth it to have a relatively warm room, with a good mattress and a bathroom with a fantastic shower.

After a grotty and overpriced meal in town, we head for an early night, only to be kept awake by the last night celebrations of the Fiesta of the Virgen de la Candelaria. Bloody locals—how dare they celebrate when we are trying to sleep!!

We set off for the docks to catch our boat for a two-day trip visiting the Uros' islands, Amantani and Taquile. We are relieved to find that the boat is rather more luxurious than the snail that took us to Isla del Sol—comfy seats, a good engine and even a *baño*! Our guide, José, is also much friendlier and speaks good English.

Our fellow passengers are a jolly crew and everyone seems particularly excited about the trip. We get chatting to one character—a young Irishman called Connor. An instantly likeable chap, he is gifted with the charm of the Irish and loves a good craic. He has been on his travels for several months and has just come from the carnival in Rio. It is clear that he has been causing mayhem along the way and probably breaking a few hearts too, with his twinkling blue eyes, rosy cheeks and fair hair.

The boat pulls through the stagnant, green waters of Puno. They lift and swell around us like a gelatinous carpet. It feels good to sail clear of them into the cleaner waters of the rest of the lake. Here there are extensive reed beds.

The first stop on the boat trip is to visit the bizarre phenomenon of the floating islands of the Uros people. The islands are made by piling cut reeds on top of an already growing patch of reeds. The growing reeds float, so the islands are movable and many islands move location every few months, pulled by motorboats.

The story goes that many years ago the Uros people took to the lake to escape persecution by first the Incas and then the Spanish. They created floating islands from tortora reeds and proceeded to create a way of life based entirely on these strange islands. Many years later, no longer persecuted by anyone, they still choose to live on these islands which are like spongy waterbeds. Everything gets very damp and many of them suffer terribly from arthritis as a result. It is a mad, mad idea—each to their own!

The people are different now, the last full blood Uros died 43 years ago and now the islands are populated by Aymaras and Quechuas—45 islands housing 2,500 families. So is it just a way of earning money from tourists? José tells us that 60% of the people make a living from tourism and the other 40% from hunting lake birds and fishing.

As our boat nears the island, we are met by a Uros Islander, paddling a long canoe made from bundles of tortora reeds lashed together. Each end of the canoe comes to a long point, which curves upwards, giving it the appearance of a Viking long boat. José tells us that these boats take two men two months to build. They only last about a year before they have to be scrapped and a new one made. He invites anyone who fancies a go on this mode of transport to get on the canoe for the last bit of the journey to the island. The canoe feels surprisingly stable as we get on board and our ferryman manoeuvres us quickly and deftly to the island using a wooden paddle.

Walking on the island is a strange and slightly unsettling experience. The surface is spongy underfoot, necessitating a giant-stepped moonwalking gait. Connor, who is tall and rather gangly, looks particularly funny on his way across the island.

'Look at him,' laughs Bill, 'He's all legs and arms and blarney.'

'Ah, you're not looking so stylish yourself, there William,' retorts Connor.

In this world of reeds **everything** is made of reeds. Not only the island and the boats are made of reeds, but also the dwelling huts and all their furniture are made of reeds. The beds, the chairs, the tables, the shelves, the baskets and other containers—all made of reeds. People are even eating the reeds. There is a full sized village hall, which doubles as a church, and a watchtower made of reeds. And if walking on the island is slightly unsettling, climbing the tower gives me the complete heeby geebies.

So after that mad experience, we set off again across the beautiful azure lake in bright sunshine to the island of Amantani, where we are to spend the night. We are greeted by the locals, all dressed in colourful traditional clothes. The women wear bright voluminous woollen skirts and white blouses embroidered with birds and flowers. They wear a dark shawl over their head and shoulders, also embroidered with bright flowers. With their rosy cheeks and sparkling dark eyes, they remind me of the Flower Hmong people of Northern Vietnam, except that they are wider. Bill has a theory why this should be. 'At these altitudes, you need big lungs and with big lungs you get broad backs,' he says.

The headman of the island decides who will stay where. He calls out the name of each islander, and they step forward to claim their tourist. We are to stay with Lucilla, a tiny little lady with a big smile. She beetles off in front of us, leading the way to her house at high speed up the hill, spinning wool with great skill as she goes. Flick, goes her wrist every few seconds, launching a wooden spindle in a spinning arc to bounce onto the ground and then back up into her hand. At the same time, she is teasing unspun wool from a scarf-wrapped bundle at her waist, which miraculously twists itself into yarn under the momentum of the spindle, and then coils itself neatly onto the stem of the spindle. We puff and pant behind her, trying hard to keep up—this island is even higher than Isla del Sol.

Amantani is very beautiful—green hills and fields edged by stone walls, a little like rural Wales, but in bright sunshine and set about by the turquoise water of the lake, with the snow-capped Andes in the distance. The people live in pretty stone cottages, usually set around a courtyard. There are abundant crops growing right up to the doorsteps—maize, barley, potatoes, beans—and masses of wildflowers. There are no cars, no roads and all the electricity is solar powered. Everything is clean, green, fresh—a little island paradise.

Lucilla's house is very pretty, with passion fruit growing round the windows and sheep bleating in the corral at the back. We step through a low archway and into a cobbled courtyard. The buildings to our right were built in the time of the Incas, we are told. We are led up stone steps on the side of the building and a tiny door in front of us leads into our home for the night. I had been expecting very basic conditions, as we had experienced in Laos, so I am pleasantly surprised to find a bright, clean, freshly painted room with a polished wooden floor and new looking beds with fresh linen and hand-woven blankets. Lucilla makes us a delicious lunch of quinoa soup with fried cheese and local potatoes. She is a very good cook.

After lunch we all puff our way further up the hill to the football stadium. Yes, that is right, a football stadium. Another mad idea—to play football at 4,000m. I can hardly stagger up the hill without feeling like my lungs are going to explode. The thought of trying to run about seems sheer lunacy. But there are several takers amongst our group, including Bill and Connor, and the locals jump at the chance of having someone new to play.

It is an exciting, goal-filled game, with the tourists acquitting themselves well despite the lung-splitting altitude. Bill is one of the heroes, scoring a spectacular goal, as he slides full length across the ground to reach a pass from his new friend Connor Feet of Fire. This is matched in skill by a very fit old local gentleman, looking dapper in waistcoat and trilby, who dances his way lightly round three opponents before slotting the ball past the rather rotund tourist goalie. And the final result—the locals kindly let the tourists stop before they all expire, when the score is Amantanis 3, Tourists 3.

When everyone has got their breath back, there is even more uphill walking to do, to the top of the mountain in the middle of the island—the highest point at the centre of Lake Titikaka at 4,100m. Our procession is accompanied by a host of little boys playing panpipes and drums. On top of this mountain is a temple to Pachatata, the Earth Father, which is still in regular use. Every year the Amantanis make offerings of 3 coca leaves to Pachatata and Pachamama, the Earth Mother, on 21st January. The island is supposed to have special geomagnetic properties and it certainly feels like an enchanted place. José tells us that if you walk three times round the perimeter of the temple, holding your most longed-for desire in your mind and your heart, your wish will come true within one year. So Bill and I walk hand-in-hand round the temple, making our prayers for our future life together. It feels very magical. Then in a dream-like state, we sit on some stone steps and watch the most dazzling sunset through an archway of the Inca ruins. It is unspeakably beautiful to watch the myriad of colours in the sky reflected in the lake and bathing the hillside with light.

Just before the light has completely gone, we set off back down the mountain, and in front of us rises a huge full moon casting a silver pathway across the lake. It seems like an auspicious night to be making wishes.

After supper, there is more fun in store. Lucilla and her husband, Pedro, dress Bill and I up in local costumes—colourful poncho and pointy hat with earflaps for Bill and a huge billowy woollen skirt and embroidered top for me. Then they take us on a moonlit walk to the village hall where lots of other colourfully dressed people have gathered for an evening of madness and mayhem. In our costumes, it is now harder to tell Amantanis and Gringos apart.

With Lucilla and Pedro at the local shindig

'May I say how lovely you are looking tonight,' says Connor, taking my hand.

'Oi, Mr Irish charm,' says Bill. 'Hands off my lady.'

'Ah, no harm meant. Let me buy a drink for our goal-scorer. Will you take a beer with me?' says Connor and the two new buddies head for the bar.

Bill buys a beer for Pedro and a coke for Lucilla, who smile politely and gratefully accept them. But he has made a *faux pas*. A little later, I spot Lucilla giving her coke away to a child and sipping from Pedro's beer. I mention it to Bill and he quickly remedies the situation, buying two more beers. Lucilla rewards him with a beaming smile.

A band of young local men start up a melody, which begins with a few slow bars and quickly builds into a chaotic frenzy. Everyone's nerves disappear as we are grabbed by the locals and flung onto the dance floor. Resistance is futile, as your hands are clasped by strong working hands and you are spun about, jigged up and down and generally hurled round the dance floor. The heavy woollen costumes and the vigorous dancing make it necessary for frequent mass exoduses from the hall to get some air and cool off outside.

There is much hilarity about the different ways in which people have chosen to wear their outfits. A particular source of amusement is the different methods of wearing one's earflaps—down flat to the head, or sticking straight out to the sides, or for the best effect one of each. Connor and Bill spend a long time just pointing and laughing at each other.

Then it is back into the fray to be jigged up and down and whirled about again, giggling helplessly all the while. I have not had so much fun in years.

Eventually it is time to head for bed and we have another beautiful walk back to the house under the moon and stars. We collapse into bed and sleep deep and sweet till morning. It is so peaceful—not a single sound to disturb us.

The next day we wave a sad goodbye to Lucilla's family and Amantani, before boarding the boat for one more island—Taquile. It is another clear day and the sun is bright, but the waters of the lake are choppier today and a large American lady is very seasick.

We have a steep climb of 500 steps onto the path that will take us to the main square. We pass terraced fields and men tending stock. There are donkeys here and there. Taquile is equally as beautiful as Amantani, but the people are rather more shy than the friendly exuberant characters on Amantani. They have a very distinct culture and way of dressing. It is as if they have been isolated for hundreds of years and time has stood still for them. They still dress in the style of the Spanish from Catalan of the 16th century, who first brought them to this island to work for them.

The women wear full stiff skirts in bright shades of orange or hot pink. Their skirts end just below the knee, revealing hard knotted calves the colour of burnished copper, from climbing up and down the steep slopes. They wear knitted jumpers in similar bright jewel colours. Their waists are cinched with embroidered cummerbunds, and over their heads and shoulders they wear dark woollen shawls. The men wear dark trousers and beautiful white shirts with billowing sleeves. Their outfits are finished off with brightly embroidered cummerbunds and waistcoats, in shades of red, white, cerise, blue and black.

The most unique thing about Taquile is that EVERYONE knits, from the smallest child to the oldest man, they are to be seen either sitting or standing in groups, knitting needles and wool in hand, clicking away. And the purpose of all this knitting? They all wear hats that identify their place in the social structure. For example, the married men wear colourful hats with a long red tail section, whereas single men have a white tail section. So, everyone knows where they stand . . . unless of course, some naughty man decides to wear the wrong kind of hat . . .

Although many of the Taquiles are illiterate, life is peaceful and ordered on the island. There are strict codes of behaviour and everyone adheres to the philosophy: 'Don't lie, don't steal, don't be lazy and always help your neighbour.' They have set prices for everything, and work in co-operatives. Crime is non-existent in Taquile. Who needs university degrees when you can live in such peace and contentment?

We wander about the town square looking at the crafts in the co-operative shop, then have a coffee at the nearby café, before taking a long hot walk to the other end of the island. At every turn we have a stunning new vista across the lake—through cross-topped stone archways, past little churches, past quaint cottages. The heat and the dazzling sunshine make me wonder how the locals manage in their heavy woollen clothing. Eventually we arrive at a restaurant where we have a lunch of trout from the lake. It is a relief to sit inside the shade of the restaurant because at this altitude, the sun has an incredible intensity, that no amount of high factor suncream seems to protect against. And the light reflecting off the lake means that wearing a wide-brimmed hat makes no difference, since it just bounces up under your chin. I feel as if about three layers of skin have been blistered away. After lunch we get back into the boat and set off back to Puno.

After spending time in such idyllic places, Puno seems even more grim and we waste no time in booking a bus to Cusco. Even our luxury hotel seems cold and unwelcoming.

After another appalling supper, we retire early to bed. I wake in the middle of the night having had a nightmare that my skin is crawling with little insects. Ever since Rurrenabaque, I have been finding little bites on my legs and lower torso. At first I thought it was a few mosquito bites that were still flaring up, but it is too long ago now for that to be the case. Then I started blaming it on bed bugs in Copacabana—it was rather a scabby old bed, but here in this luxurious hotel—it couldn't be, could it? Maybe I brought the bugs with me—maybe they are in my clothes. Euw, yuch, what a horrible thought.

With a fresh change of clothes and my body covered in lavender oil to quell the itching, we board the bus for Cusco. (I eventually track the itching problem down to a pair of second-hand trousers I had bought in Rurrenabaque, which subsequently became known as 'The Haunted Trousers.' Fortunately, the problem had not spread to any of my other clothes, and having the trousers washed very hot seemed to cure the problem.) Meanwhile, on the giant bus with comfy reclining seats bound for Cusco, I am very happy to be leaving Puno behind, but wistful about leaving the beautiful Lake Titikaka, which was everything I hoped it would be—beautiful, magical, eccentric and lots of fun.

The bus turns away from the lakeside, past fields of corn to bleak altiplano and herds of alpacas. The snow-tipped mountains seem very close. Then we start to come down a few hundred metres. Here the landscape is greener, kinder. Sparkling rivers run by and there is a feeling of abundance.

All goes smoothly during the journey except for an incident when a local woman boards the bus in Juliaca. She is carrying a heavy bundle and I absentmindedly wonder what is in it. I am soon to find out when she sits down in the aisle next to us and unwraps it. A foul stench issues from a pile of animal carcasses inside, which she proceeds to carve up and sell to the locals on the bus. The stench is so strong that I have to open the window and cover my nose with a scarf to stop myself from vomiting.

'How can people eat that stuff?—it's rotten!' I exclaim to Bill, who has his jumper pulled up over his face.

'Thank God for that,' he finally says when she gets off. But it takes several miles with the windows open for the vile smell to blow out.

By around 4pm, we are coming into the outskirts of Cusco. It has a very different atmosphere to the other Peruvian towns we have been through so far. It is full of ancient Inca stone walls made of huge stone blocks fitted neatly together, and Spanish colonial buildings built on Inca foundations, which are practically indestructible and have withstood many earthquakes.

There is a huge plaza in the centre of town—the Plaza de Armas—and narrow cobbled streets leading away from it. We take a taxi to the San Blas area on recommendation from Ed and Clare. San Blas is known as the Artists' District. In Incan times it was one of the most important districts of Cusco. Known as T'oqo-kachi, meaning salt hollow, it was inhabited by the Quechuan nobility.

It is beautiful—colonial buildings, narrow streets winding up steep gradients, a small plaza with a pretty church and lots of craft shops and restaurants, but very quiet and peaceful. Bill finds us a lovely room in Hostal Marani, a colonial building set around a courtyard with wooden balconies. He has to do some hard bargaining to get the price down to something we can afford, but it is worth it. Everything is functional, beautifully laid out, clean, newly painted. The bed has crisp linen, there are clean fluffy towels and the shower is powerful and hot. Many people have told us that it is hard not to stay longer than you planned in Cusco because it is so lovely. I can tell I am going to like it here immediately.

The twelve-sided stone at the Palace of Inca Roca, Cusco

Cusco, the capital of the Incan empire before the arrival of the conquistadors 500 years ago, seemed to be the perfect base for us to visit lots of Inca sites including the famed Machu Picchu. It is a good job that there is plenty to see locally because we have been holed up here in the mountains for the last five days, by rain and thunder; rain, rain and more rain; endless sitting in cafés to shelter from the rain. I feel utter, utter frustration and boredom at being hemmed in by the rain and unable to venture far to see all the Incan sites in the Sacred Valley, especially because we are getting so close to the end of our travels.

At the height of the Incan empire, Cusco was home to 15,000 people and was linked to the rest of the kingdom, known as the Tawantinsuyo, by impressive royal roads known as the Qhapaq Ñan. They were magnificent walkways, hundreds of leagues in length, with magical floating sections along the edges of cliffs and tunnels through solid rock, all achieved by a civilisation that had not invented the wheel, discovered steel and did not use any large working animals such as the horse. Integral to the communication system were the *chasquis*, or long distance runners who carried messages and goods to the four corners of the Tawantinsuyo. Because of its central importance, the Incas thought of Cusco as the navel of the world. The central square of Cusco, now the Plaza de Armas, was known in Incan times as the Huancaypata. It is the exact centre of the empire and was the place where the most important religious and military ceremonies were held.

The area around Cusco was populated long before the Incas and some of the Incan architecture is built on the foundations of earlier cultures. For example the Qorikancha, the famed Temple of the Sun, is thought to be built on the foundations of a Killki sun temple, from around 700-800 AD. But it was Pachacutec, who became leader of the Incas in 1438, that conceived the design of central Cusco in the shape of a Puma. The zigzag walls of the nearby fort, Sacsayhuaman, form the sharp teeth and head of the animal. Its heart was in the ceremonial square, the Huancaypata. The Qorikancha lies where the cat's reproductive organs would have been. Pachacutec had the rivers Saphi and Tulumayo turned into canals and the puma's tail lies at the junction of these two rivers.

Atahualpa, the last of the Incan emperors was captured en route to Cusco by the conquistadors, under the leadership of Francisco Pizarro. The conquistadors were astonished at the beauty of Cusco, with its remarkable stonework and all the precious metals and gemstones which adorned the temples. They wasted no time in looting and destroying it, after first holding Atahualpa to ransom and then garrotting him.

The conquistadors made it their mission to obliterate the 'pagan' Inca culture and 'civilise' the Indians, but Cusco is testament to the tenacity of the indigenous culture and is a strange mixture of Inca, superimposed by Spanish Catholicism. The architecture is a typical example of this. The cathedral on Plaza de Armas is made in part from stones hauled from the nearby fortress of Sacsayhuamán and was built on the foundations of the palace of Inca Viracocha.

The cathedral took a whole century to build. It is home to the biggest bell on the continent. Made from a ton of gold, silver and bronze, presumably looted from the Incas, it can be heard over 40km away. Inside the cathedral, the fusion of cultures continues, with a giant painting of the twelve disciples eating roasted guinea pig (a local delicacy) at the last supper and a sculpture of Christ made out of black llama skin.

We have spent the last three days dashing between the downpours, visiting lots of museums and colonial churches, and on top of the oddities in the cathedral, we have enjoyed looking at giant paintings of religious art with bearded ladies; beautiful colonial houses and courtyards again built on Inca foundations; coats of arms mixing Spanish and Inca symbolism — lions and eagles with condors, snakes and suns; the house of Garcilaso de la Vega, a mixed-race historian who described Cusco in great detail in his book 'The Royal Commentaries,' at a time before the Spanish had managed to obliterate almost every trace of Incan culture; photos of the devastation of the 1950s earthquake; little gold objects from the Qorikancha in the museum — all that is left after the Spanish robbed the golden temple and filled their churches with gold (or sent it home to Spain).

The Qorikancha (the Golden Palace) was the Sun Temple of the Incas and once stood in the space occupied today by the Santo Domingo Catholic Church. It was the most important religious complex of the vast Incan Society. It represented the world's centre in the Inca's vision of the cosmos. According to Inca history, it was the first Inca, Manco Capac who built the original temple. But, it was the ninth Inca, Pachacutec who reconstructed, enlarged, improved and modernised it from 1438 onwards. The quality of the building was said to have been extraordinary. The blocks of polished grey basalt fitted perfectly together with hidden joints tied together with H-shaped bronze clamps to protect the building from earthquake damage. The walls taper from bottom to top to form an almost pyramidal shape, another feature designed to withstand seismic activity. As proof of the ingenuity of its design, the building was still standing after the two huge earthquakes in 1650 and 1950 had flattened most of the Spanish buildings.

The four walls, every doorway and even the wooden ceiling of the Qorikancha were completely covered in gold. Spanish chronicles describe the astonishment of the Europeans when they saw the Qorikancha's courtyard filled with life-sized gold and silver statues of llamas, pumas, trees, flowers and butterflies. The main altar had an image of the Sun God in gold—a round face encircled with rays and flames. The gold Sun God was so huge that it covered the whole temple front from wall to wall. The windows were constructed so that the sun would cast a dazzling reflection of golden light off the precious metals inside. When the treasures were looted and distributed among the conquerors, by casting of lots, this huge golden piece went to Mancio Sierra de Leguisamo, an inveterate gambler who lost it during one night playing dice, the event from which the famous saying 'bet the sun before dawn' was coined.

In the Andean Cosmogony it was considered that the Moon or Mamakilla was the Sun's wife. The Moon Temple was located on the eastern side of the Solar Temple. Unfortunately it was almost completely destroyed in order to build the Catholic Church. Sheets of silver completely covered its walls, and as in the Sun Temple, there was a giant image of the Moon made of silver in the centre of the temple.

In this vast complex there were five water fountains, in which flowed clean water transported through underground channels. The source of the water was kept completely secret. The fountains had religious significance, as water was another deity in the Andean religion. The fountains were also adorned with precious metals, with golden spillways, and large gold and silver jars. In colonial times the water fountains were destroyed. Garcilaso de la Vega says that he saw just one of them—the last one was used by the Dominican monks to irrigate their vegetable garden. In 1975, an archaeological dig located one of the five original fountains and water still flows through its finely carved channels.

When the Inca houses and palaces were given away during the Spanish invasion, the Qorikancha was given to Juan Pizarro who donated it to the Dominican Order headed by the first bishop of Cusco City, Fray Vicente Valverde. He immediately ordered the construction of a church and convent over the most important Incan Temple, demolishing it almost completely. That church was destroyed by the earthquake of 1650. The present-day structure was built in 1780. In 1950 another violent earthquake destroyed a large part of the convent and church as well as its tower uncovering many Incan structures and the interior area of the Solar Round Building. By that time a strong indigenous movement suggested the relocation of the church and recovery of the Sun Temple, but it is a pity that the Catholic Church still did not allow the ruins of the major Tawantinsuyo's sanctuary to be cleared.

Everywhere you go in Cusco there are pictures of Machu Picchu and because of this overkill and the great expense to get there, set against our dwindling budget, and the terrible weather, we almost decided not to bother going. But you cannot really come all this way and not go ... so we have been avidly following the weather forecast on the Internet and we are finally taking our chance to go. The Inca trail which leads to Machu Picchu is closed at the moment because of the bad weather. I am secretly relieved, having feared another experience like trekking in the monsoon rainforests of Laos, but I think Bill is rather disappointed.

We get up at 5am to catch the 'backpacker train'. It is not raining so far, but it is misty and overcast. It rained heavily in the night and water is running in streams at the side of the track. The train finally pulls away, only to reverse back towards the station. Back and forth, back and forth the train goes. Actually it is zig-zagging its way up and out of Cusco, because the gradient is too steep to climb in one go. I watch the Plaza de Armas grow smaller in the distance. We have probably passed it four or five times. At last we crest the brow of the hill and we are on our way out of town. It has taken us almost an hour to get this far.

It is still early and I sleep a little, although my head is being thrown from side to side with the motion of the train on the rickety tracks. The girl in the seat opposite is very drowsy too. She is making a feeble attempt to write her journal, but cannot keep her eyes open long enough to write more than one word at a time before her head nods, her eyes close and her pen slides across the page. At one point her head falls so far forward that she is in danger of poking herself in the eye with her pen. Nevertheless, she forces her eyes open and tries again and again, only to be defeated by sleep. Now she is dribbling on the page and smudging her ink. Bill and I try not to giggle.

Out of the window, I watch the landscape sliding by. We are in a green and fertile valley filled with crops of corn, potatoes, flowers, flocks of sheep, donkeys, cows and adobe houses dotted here and there.

The train's route follows the Rio Vilcanota along the Sacred Valley. It starts life as a vigorous babbling brook, but grows in girth, volume and speed as we pass along the valley, until it becomes the Rio Urubamba—a raging torrent full of red/brown mud which jumps and surges four or five feet into the air as it hits rocks in its path. It will eventually feed into the mighty Amazon. All around, the mountains reach into the sky, snow-capped at first, but increasingly green as we near Machu Picchu. The vegetation changes from the alpine conditions of Cusco to the sub-tropical of Machu Picchu, which is just on the edge of the Amazon basin. Nearing Machu Picchu, the scenery has changed again. Sheer cliffs rise up around us and somehow, tropical vegetation manages to cling to their sides. The roar of the Urubamba is deafening.

Amongst all this beauty is set the foul pustule that is Agua Calientes, the dormitory town that serves Machu Picchu. It epitomises all the worst that mankind can do to nature — sprawling new buildings going up everywhere, workmen banging and hammering, squalid rotten looking half-finished shacks, the stink of rubbish and bad sanitation, shops selling tourist tat crowding in upon themselves and us, vendors of this tat and bad restaurants plaguing your every step, loud thumping music issuing from every building and competing with each other to create a horrendous din etc, etc — you get the picture.

Faced with all this, I have a sudden crisis of despondency at the prospect of having to stay the night here. I whinge at Bill, pleading with him to let us see the site today and go straight home.

'You are joking, aren't you?' says Bill. 'That would mean that we would only have one and a half hours to see the site before we had to catch the train back to Cusco. We haven't spent all this money and effort to get here just to go back in one and a half hours, have we? It'll be years before we get the chance again. Don't worry, I'll find us somewhere decent to stay the night and then maybe you'll start enjoying yourself.'

I come to my senses and agree it seems a terrible waste to go home today. So my hero Bill once again pulls off the trick that he is getting very good at — he walks into one of the best hotels in town and manages to get us a room for the night for $15. At least we can stay in a little comfort and style in this dreadful place.

We are planning to get up early the following morning and walk up to Machu Picchu, to arrive just as it opens and before the day-tripping hordes arrive. So we check out the route that we will have to take. We have a pleasant walk alongside the river and then round a corner and see it in front of us — a magnificent peak towering green, sheer and very, very high — we decide to catch the bus! It is not only the prospect of the hard toil to get up there, but half the day will be gone and we will miss the quiet early morning slot.

'I had the best night's sleep in ages,' I tell Bill, having a good stretch.

'Yeah, so did I. It must be the lower altitude,' Bill says. We are up bright and early to catch the first bus at 6.30am. 'I think we're going to be lucky with the weather — it's misty but looks fine,' he says looking out of the hotel window.

We board the bus with a real feeling of excitement and wind our way slowly up the steep slope. 'Woah, look at those hairpins,' says Bill looking from his usual vantage point of the window seat at the vertiginous drop to the valley floor, as the coach heaves itself round the next extreme corner.

As the coach drops us off, everything is shrouded in mist, which adds to the mysteriousness of the site. We walk with no clear idea of where we are going, but make our way in the general direction of a place known as *The Caretaker of the Funerary Hut*, or so we think. The few other visitors on the bus with us seem to have disappeared in the opposite direction. We pass steep terraces and stone huts with thatched roofs—the rest of the site is closed to us by the mist.

Suddenly in front of us looms an important looking staircase with terraces on either side and a group of llamas peering down on us through the mist. 'This looks like an interesting path to follow,' says Bill.

'Yes, let's see where it goes,' I say. The stairs go up and up and up. We seem to be leaving the site and walking out into the cloud forest and high up the mountain over-looking the city of Machu Picchu. A strange quiet mood has overtaken us and we walk in silence, soaking in the atmosphere of the place.

As we climb higher through the cloud forest, we pass brilliant red orchids, green flowered orchids, clumps of wild purple lupins and pink begonias. All is peaceful, quiet, tranquil. The mist drips from the vegetation all around us. I do not know where we are going, but it is lovely anyway.

After a while, I realise we must be climbing the mountain behind the site, the 'Machu Picchu' or 'old peak' from which the city takes its name.

We get to a look out point and stop to catch our breath. When I turn round to look back at the way we have come, the clouds suddenly part to reveal below us a city of ordered stone buildings built into the natural surroundings, golden in the early morning sunshine.

We get the most wonderful views across to other mountains all around, vast sheer cliff faces with trees somehow clinging to them. Below us Machu Picchu—a city built on the only flat area around, this atop hundreds of constructed agricultural terraces on the sheer sides of the mountain and curling almost full circle around the bottom of this mountain is the raging River Urubamba.

I am overwhelmed by a sense of enormous well-being—a feeling of oneness with the place, with myself and with Bill. I do not want to leave. To think that we have come all this way to see the ruined city and the first thing we did was to turn our backs and walk away from it, seems strange. But I feel so happy here amongst the dewy forest with the splendid view of the ruins nestled amongst the mountain peaks. Somehow visiting the site itself seems almost irrelevant.

But we go back anyway and we are not disappointed. There is a wonderful atmosphere here. Sometimes the hype about a place can lead to disappointment in seeing the reality and I have been concerned that this would be the case. But the feeling of tranquillity and happiness stays with me as I wander about the site.

The city is full of symbolism—from the air the whole site looks like a condor with its wings spread, the opposite mountain is a giant puma curled around the city to protect it and half the city looks like a caiman which has crawled up from the River Urubamba and is basking on the rocks.

Walking around the site itself I am struck by the elaborate stone work—giant stones, weighing 50 tons or more, fitting together perfectly with their neighbours in a stone wall jigsaw puzzle, and not a gap big enough to slide a piece of paper between them. There are streets of small houses fitting perfectly into the natural rocks; a watering system fed by natural springs, with channels cut out of beautifully dressed stones; temples, palaces, baths and an observatory; and all hidden up here on top of a mountain half-way to the sky.

We make our way to see the most important shrine, the Intihuatana, meaning 'Hitching Post of the Sun.' As we step onto the stone platform of the shrine, Bill says, 'Wow, what a fantastic view you get from here. You can see all the way round—360 degrees. Look at those amazing mountains,' he says, spinning around to take it all in. 'This must have been the perfect place for the Inca's ceremonies.' At the centre of the platform is a stone, shaped in a way that seems to mimic the distinctive shape of Huayna Picchu, (meaning 'young peak'), the conical mountain which forms the backdrop to the city ruins. 'So this is the actual hitching post,' says Bill. 'I wonder how they did it?'

The Intihuatana at Machu Picchu has been shown to be a precise indicator of the two equinoxes and other important astrological events. At midday on the two equinoxes, March 21st and September 21st, the sun stands directly above the pillar, creating no shadow at all. At this precise moment, the 'sun sits with all his might upon the pillar' and is for a moment 'tied' to the rock. At this time, the Incas would have held ceremonies to commune with the power of the sun by tying it to the stone.

The Intihuatana is also aligned with the Pumasillo (the Puma's claw), the most sacred mountain of the western Vilcabamba range. At sunset on December the 21st, the summer solstice of the southern hemisphere, the sun sinks behind the mountain's peak, as viewed from the shrine.

'Bill, did you know that there is a legend which says that if a sensitive person touches their forehead to the stone, the Intihuatana can open their vision to the spirit world? These stones were thought of as really sacred by the Incas. They believed that if the Intihuatana stone was broken, that the spirit of the place would die or leave. The Spanish searched out and destroyed all the Intihuatana stones that they could find. Luckily, they never found this one,' I tell him.

The sacred rock is roped off from the public, presumably to stop people clambering on it and damaging it. By now the site is full of tourists and official guides. So Bill and I feel too self-conscious to try our luck with the stone.

At Machu Picchu every feature or construction appears to be planned and aligned with purpose, leaving nothing to chance. The Incas held many of the surrounding mountain peaks as sacred. The four cardinal directions from the Intihuatana platform all align with sacred mountains. The main gate frames your view on the Huayna Picchu Mountain as you enter and on the Machu Picchu peak as you leave the city.

Just outside the main gate, where several important routes converge on the city, there is a plaza with a stone shrine shaped to mirror Cerro Yanatin, a mountain aligned with this place. This may have been a ritual welcoming and leaving place similar to one just outside Cusco. Another example is the unusual D-shaped building, known as the Torrean, which also contains a sacred carved huaca stone. The eastern window of the building gives a view of the Pleiades constellation, which was worshipped by the Incas, rising into the sky in the early morning during late May and early June.

These features could only have been planned and built by people who had detailed knowledge of the movement of the celestial bodies, such as the location of the sunrise, and the symbolic meaning of the mountains. Were they trying to create an earthly mirror of the cosmos?

Some say the Incas built Machu Picchu as a sacred city, which they kept secret from the Spanish invaders. The Inca people certainly used Machu Picchu and built hundreds of stone structures from the early 1400s. The mountaintop sanctuary fell into disuse and was abandoned some forty years after the Spanish took Cusco in 1533. Although they suspected its existence, the Spanish never found Machu Picchu and the city remained untouched and undiscovered until Hiram Bingham, a Yale archaeologist, explored it in 1911.

Although mainstream archaeologists attribute Machu Picchu to the Incas, legends and myths indicate that Machu Picchu was revered as a sacred place from a far earlier time. In many places, Bill and I notice that there seems to be two distinct phases of construction, some within the same building. Many of the constructions have a lower layer of the magnificent giant jigsaw puzzle blocks, which look as if they have been melted and squidged together. On top of this is a much cruder layer made with smaller stones. Perhaps the Incas built on top of what was left by some long forgotten people. No-one really knows, but whatever the truth, it is certainly a very magical place and I am very glad that we finally made the effort to get here.

Back in Cusco, we return to our lovely temporary home at Hostal Marani, where we are welcomed by the cheery housekeeper and pick up our key, to find that our bags have already been put in our room for us.

* * *

Another beautiful day and I feel extraordinarily happy—so different to the boredom and frustration I was experiencing before visiting Machu Picchu, when we were hemmed in by the rain.

Both of us feel absolutely wasted, almost as if we had done the four day Inca trail trek, rather than the lazy bus ride up there. But with that physical tiredness, I feel at peace with myself, as if I have been washed, wrung out and hung up to dry, all clean in the sun.

We spend the day pottering about, visiting favourite cafés and doing chores, like picking up Bill's hat from the Sunset Cinema Café, where he left it by mistake a week ago. I did not hold out much hope that he would get it back after all this time, but luckily the lady who runs the place has a soft spot for him. Apparently someone tried to walk off with it, but she recognised that it did not belong to him and saved it for Bill. It is so strange—everyone else tells horrendous stories of getting robbed and mugged in Peru (particularly in Cusco) but we meet kind ladies that look after our belongings for us! Perhaps it is because of all the prayers we have said along the way and that I know our families are saying for us. I like to think so.

We have a few more days before having to make our way to Lima for our flight home. So we vow to make the most of the good weather, to see some of the other Inca sites near Cusco, having been so impressed with Machu Picchu. We set off to the travel agents to book a couple of tours to explore more of the ruins.

Our first trip is a day's ride on horseback through the Sacred Valley. We thought we would do it in style and so we dress in our colourful stripy ponchos, bought in La Paz and finish the look with neckerchiefs, wide-brimmed hats and sunglasses. When the travel agent comes to pick us up, he gives us a look that says, 'Oh, we've got a right pair here.'

We are met at the stable by our guide for the day, Antonio, a good-natured young lad, who takes our strange garb in his stride and is soon laughing and joking with Bill. It is Bill's first time on top of a horse, so we ask Antonio to choose a *muy tranquilo* horse and Capa Blanco (White Head) certainly fits this description. In fact this gentle white creature needs much coaxing to lift his head from munching grass long enough to actually go anywhere. But by the end of the day, a firm friendship has been forged between Bill and his trusty steed. My horse, Bella, is decidedly nippier, but I am glad to say a well-behaved little darling.

From the stables it is a 3km ride to Qenko, the first Inca site on our journey. The sun is shining as we cross the flat grassy land dotted by whitewashed houses with terracotta tiled roofs. Our outlandish dress style seems to give the locals a laugh as we pass—at least we hope that is what they are laughing at.

We arrive at Qenko and dismount.

'What is this place?' Bill asks Antonio.

'Is Temple for the Moon,' replies Antonio. 'When you walk in the tunnel you see hole where the moon shine in.'

Antonio looks after Bella and Capa Blanca whilst Bill and I go clambering about the site, carved into the side of a hill. The name Qenko means labyrinth and the network of holes, tunnels and galleries is very inviting to explore. Inside the biggest underground chamber there is an altar and ceremonial carvings. A hole in the roof would let the full moon shine in on the altar. The site was said to be used for funeral rituals. The earthy smell and the sound of dripping water add to the distinctly spooky atmosphere in the chamber, which is just big enough for Bill to stand upright in. We make our way back out into the sunshine and walk over to the amphitheatre, opposite the entrance. It is a great elliptical wall with 19 entrances that appear to be wide seats or thrones. There is a five metre high monolith, which the locals say looks like the ubiquitous puma, but you really have to use your imagination to see it.

Another group of Gringos on horseback arrive and we decide it is time to move on. Amongst this group is a French woman, who clearly thinks she is the best horse rider in the world. She is yanking hard on her poor horse's reins, whilst telling everyone else in her group how to ride. She dismounts and her horse immediately makes a break for freedom.

'Can't say I blame it,' says Bill.

'I take Bella?' Antonio asks me.

'Si, si,' I reply.

He leaps onto her back and chases down the runaway horse. Antonio deftly catches it from Bella's back and they lead it back to the group. It comes meekly enough until it spots its tormentor and tries to make another dash. But the guides manage to keep hold of it and Antonio returns Bella to me. She is the heroine of the day and I feel proud to ride her.

'I don't think Capa Blanca quite has the turn of speed to catch runaways,' says Bill, gently trying to urge him to stop eating for a minute and start on our way.

We turn off the road and up through a steep field where two farmers are rounding up some llamas on horseback. They smile and wave at us. The Frenchwoman's horse takes this distraction as an opportunity to head off in the opposite direction again and she has no control to bring it back. Her guide has to go and rescue her again.

A 3km ride brings us to Puca Pucara, a red sandstone fortress, built to guard the entrance to the Sacred Valley. On a promontory higher than the rest of the surrounding land, it is located at a strategic point along the road to the *Antisuyo* (the jungle part of the Inca empire). It served as a checkpoint and an administrative centre. We dismount and wander about exploring its terraces, stairways, tunnels and towers, marvelling at the Inca stone craftsmanship which has produced these sharp straight walls from hundreds of irregular blocks.

Back on the road again, another kilometre brings us to Tambomachay, sacred bathing place of the Inca rulers and the royal women. Bill stands looking aghast at the gigantic blocks of dressed stone, twice his height, which have been slotted together to form enormous terraces, stairways and channels for the cascading water. It is a hydraulic engineering marvel with an aqueduct system that still feeds a series of showers.

Our final destination is the magnificent Sacsayhuaman, constructed from the most enormous blocks of granite that we have seen so far, some more than five metres high and weighing over 300 tons. It is here that we say a fond farewell to our trusty steeds, Capa Blanca and Bella, for we are on foot from now on. We dismount and hand the reins over to Antonio.

We approach the enormous wall of granite blocks in awe. There are three immense superimposed terraces in a zigzag pattern. We are standing amongst the jagged teeth of Cusco's puma, formed by the zigzag walls. The stonework is mind-boggling—how did they move those huge blocks and fit them so neatly together? They give the same impression as the stones at Machu Picchu, that they have been melted and squidged together.

It was built in the second half of the 15th century by the same Pachacutec Inca who conceived the whole design of central Cusco in the shape of a Puma. Some call it a fortress and some say it was a temple. It had not yet been completed when the Spanish arrived. Unfortunately, its proximity to Cusco and the size of its stones led to its use as a quarry for the construction of colonial Cusco. But it is good to know that the annual June Inti Raymi (Festival of the Sun) still takes place here.

We walk back to Cusco in the afternoon sunshine, looking forward to frequenting one of our favourite eateries. All this horse-riding and ancient monument viewing certainly builds up a good appetite.

* * *

We feel very comfortable in our delightful room at Hostal Marani. Life here has developed a certain rhythm for us, mostly based around going to lovely places to eat and we have carved a well-trodden route between our hotel via various eateries down to the town centre and back again. Just in our street, Carmen Alto, there are several good places to eat like piglets for very little money and we are making the most of them. Our favourites include the Internet café which serves a very splendid all-you-can-eat breakfast buffet for 1 sol (about 20p) each. Included in the price is one hour's free Internet access, so that takes care of a good portion of the morning. Then there is the posh restaurant where you can get a five course lunch for 1.50 sols—you get a drink, a starter, a main course of something like chicken or llama steak, a sweet and coffee to follow. We like to avail ourselves of this facility on a regular basis, as we like to dine in style, but cannot afford their evening a la carte menu.

Then we might venture off down into town on some errand or to do a bit of shopping. So we wander along to the Plaza San Blas, with its little church, where ladies in indigenous dress weave long colourful straps in hand-dyed wool on backstrap looms, which hook up to a tree and wrap around their bodies. Then we head down Cuesta San Blas, past the art and ceramic shops and the lady with the llama dressed in her Quechuan finery, hoping that you will pay her a dollar to take her picture. We go past the shops selling all sorts of handicrafts, artwork, brightly coloured clothing and every item you can imagine knitted in alpaca. A little further on we come to a couple of Quechuan guys from out of town, very friendly and smiley always chewing coca leaves and wearing the finest hand-knitted hats we have seen so far. They tell us proudly that they have knitted them themselves and have worn them in many special ceremonies.

Just round the corner is Jack's café on Choquechaca Street, which serves the best cup of coffee in town. We often pop in here if we are flagging after a hard morning's shopping, to sip lattes to the sounds of David Gray, which seems to be the only CD that the manager owns. But that is OK because it reminds Bill and I of the time when I lived in London and we were in the first flush of our romance. Whenever Bill came to stay, my neighbour Helen seemed to be playing David Gray and wistfully thinking about the time that she was propositioned by Hugh Grant in a pub, and wishing that she had not turned him down after all.

Now nearing the centre of town, we pass an ancient piece of wall built by the Incas in Calle Hatun Rumiyoq. There is always a young lad there ready to tell you all about it and make sure that you have seen the 12-sided building stone which is still slotted neatly into place despite all the odd angles, with not even a whisper of a gap between it and its neighbours. It is one of the huge stones from the walls of the cyclopean palace of Inca Roca. Now, it is part of the Archiepiscopal Palace, built up from the remains of the old palace.

Reaching Plaza de Armas, we scuttle beetle-like across the vast open space of the square, blinking in the bright sunlight, unused to its full glare having spent all morning in the shade of the narrow streets of San Blas. We feel safe in San Blas, but there is a much more edgy feel in the rest of town. So we try to make ourselves invisible to avoid arousing the attention of the many, many touts selling cigarettes, trinkets, postcards, or trying to get you into some restaurant or on a tour. We make a dive into Procuradores Street and head round the corner into Calle Tecsecocha, where there is another delight of Cusco, the Sunset Cinema Café, where one can purchase a beverage and a light snack, and sit watching a recently released film on a cinema-size screen with a digital sound system. We have seen the latest James Bond and, guess what, Lord of the Rings several times on rainy afternoons.

We puff our way back up Triunfo and Calle Hatun Rumiyoq, where despite the altitude and the steep gradient, Bill's pace always quickens and I know that we must be nearing the pastry shop, where he will probably purchase a couple of empanadas and something sweet and sticky.

Then nearing Plaza San Blas again, there may be a raucous fiesta, with people in bright clothing whirling about to music made on trumpets, guitars and drums. Or if it is quiet, we might stop and look in at the church which has an interesting story . . .

San Blas' little church was built in 1559 over the Incan sanctuary devoted to the cult of Ilapa, the thunder and lightning god. Inside the church is one of the greatest jewels of colonial art in the continent: the Pulpit of Saint Blas. It is an expertly crafted filigree of cedarwood. It is not known for certain who the artist was, but it is usually attributed to the most famous Quechuan woodcarver: Juan Tomas Tuyro Tupaq. According to a local legend, he was a leper from Huamanga (Ayacucho). The story goes that he had a dream in which the 'Holy Virgin of the Good Happening' told him that if he wanted to heal his leprosy he had to look for her in the small plaza of Arrayanpata in Cusco City. After a long journey and many mishaps, one day he found her painted on a wall of the Lirpuy-Phaqcha chapel, when suddenly the roof fell in. Falling on his knees and weeping in fright, he invoked the Virgin. Her rosary became rose petals which he gathered and rubbed over his body. This miraculously healed his leprosy. The piece of wall containing the painting was cut and moved to the Saint Blas Church, and the people then decided to build an altar and a pulpit for the Virgin. The grateful woodcarver promised to make the pulpit without charging any money for the work. It took him four years of hard work with wood from an enormous cedar tree that was cut in the Kusipata square (present-day Regocijo). But, on finishing his work the woodcarver broke his oath and asked the church's curate for 70 pesos in order to woo a local woman. Divine retribution for breaking his promise came while he was fastening the statue of Saint Paul over the pulpit's sounding board. He stumbled and fell off, dying soon after. His corpse was buried under the pulpit but some time later it was taken out and his skull placed before the feet of Saint Paul's sculpture, where it is seen today.

. . . And if we have not yet had our fill of food, there are another couple of gems on Carmen Alto to try. There is El Pie Shop which is, needless to say, Bill's favourite place. There is always a mouth-watering selection of freshly baked giant sweet and savoury pies. It is a very friendly place, where there is always someone willing to give you a game of chess or backgammon. We have whiled away many a rainy afternoon in there, but sometimes I have to winkle Bill out of there to save him from the potent home-made liqueur which gets handed round on cold days and the owner swears it has healing properties. I have not seen any evidence of that, but it certainly makes Bill loud and garrulous and then later, a bit grumpy as the hangover kicks in.

And for our evening meal, we usually visit a little family-run café on Carmen Alto, where there are two adorable chubby-cheeked children — a little boy that has only just learned to walk and a little girl who is always carrying around a puppy, almost as adorable as herself. Eating there is like living in the family's house. There is a curtained doorway into their living room. The curtain is always pulled back and you can see into the room where the kids are having their tea and the washing is hanging up and the telly is always on, playing something like Mission Impossible dubbed into Spanish. It is comforting to see life going on like this, but it also makes me homesick. Wonderful though Cusco is, I find myself longing more and more to get home and to get on with my 'real life' again. The prospect of having to find work when we get home with our coffers exhausted has been looming into my mind. And of course, there is so much left to organise for the wedding. Mum has been doing a sterling job, but there are so many things that a girl wants to do for her own wedding.

*   *   *

Feeling a little guilty at the debauched life of gluttony and laziness that we have fallen into, we set off today to explore more of the Sacred Valley on a tour through Pisaq, Urubamba, Ollantaytambo and Chinchero.

Just managing to squeeze in a hearty buffet breakfast, we hurry down to the Plaza de Armas, where we meet a portly gentleman with greying hair, dressed in a smart blazer. He is our guide, Armando. He motions for us to board the minibus which is already full with a selection of Gringos from other countries, and we chug our way up the steep road out of Cusco.

We settle back into relatively comfortable seats to be educated by the highly knowledgeable Armando about our destination for the day. He tells us that the Sacred Valley, known as Vilcamayo to the Incas, traces its winding route to the northwest of Cusco. The section known as the Sacred Valley, which we will be visiting today, lies between Pisaq and Ollantaytambo. The river, which starts life as the Vilcanota and then becomes the Urubamba, flows through the Sacred Valley and on past Machu Picchu into the jungle to merge with the other major headwaters of the Amazon.

The valley of the River Urubamba was a sacred place to the Incas. Its proliferation of springs, streams and wildlife of all kinds showed the Incas how special this place was to Pachamama, or Mother Earth, and the Urubamba itself was held to be an earthly representation of the Milky Way, symbolising the flow of life from the heavens to earth.

The Sacred Valley was the heart of the Inca Empire in economic terms as well. It was the Incas' breadbasket, providing maize and other crops such as quinoa, to feed Cusco and an ever-growing empire. In the Sacred Valley, the Incas worked in concert with the natural world to develop complex irrigation and agricultural systems.

I gaze dreamily from the window seeing rugged peaks, forming the sheer sides to the valley, with green terraces clinging impossibly to the slopes lower down, and the Urubamba sparkling merrily along at the bottom.

'If you look very carefully,' says Armando. 'You will see that the terraces are constructed to look like images of things that were sacred to the Incas. There is one that looks like a condor. And this one looks like a llama. There is also one that looks like a puma.'

I cannot quite make them out, but I think how the terraces and waterways add to the incredible beauty of the landscape, instead of taking away from it as most of the industry in the Western world does. The finest corn in Peru is still produced here, one that is highly nutritious and of excellent quality. We pass fields of potatoes and orchards growing apples, peaches and plums.

Armando tells us that there is still plenty of wildlife here and the animals include deer, viscacha, minks, skunks, foxes and pumas. But it is only the birds and the domestic animals that we see today. There are doves, thrushes, goldfinches and even hummingbirds. And there are cattle, sheep, pigs and horses in the fields nearer the road.

After an hour or so, the small town of Pisaq is our first stop. The buildings are typically colonial Spanish, laid out in a grid of streets surrounding the main square. The town is famous for its handicraft market and Thursday is market day. We get out of the minibus and wander about the stalls selling jewellery, ponchos, sweaters, bags and ceramic goods including the ceremonial goblets called 'Q'eros', and replicas of pre-Hispanic pottery. I buy two pairs of very fluffy slippers made from alpaca skin—one for me and one as a present for Mum. They will keep our feet toasty in the winter back home.

There is time for a coffee in a café overlooking the square before Armando gathers us to walk up to the Inca ruins on the slopes above the village. The ancient Inca citadel of Pisaq stands guard over the Southern end of the Sacred Valley. As we approach it along a stony trackway, I am struck by the colossal stone terraces that circle the mountain and balanced above this, at the edge of an outjutting limb of the mountain are the red stone ruins of ancient Pisaq. The ruins are another showpiece of the Incas' construction abilities. The ancient city is very extensive, being made up of different neighbourhoods and squares. Armando tells us that the town was divided into different status areas, with the priests living at the top. There are different building styles in each area, the highest quality being reserved for the highest status. The irrigation channels are still working amidst the impressive remains of the grand buildings. In the high status area there is the remains of a temple, where a vast stone lintel above the doorway frames a view of the sheer sided valley in front of us. The temple walls are built in a semi-circle and enclose a miniature version of the hitching post of the sun, carved from the natural rock and much like the one we saw at Machu Picchu.

Back in the minibus, another hour's drive brings us to the town of Urubamba, where we stop for an ample lunch. Sitting at the foot of the majestic snow-capped peak of Chicón in the heart of the Sacred Valley, Urubamba is known as the 'Pearl of the Vilcanota' because of the beauty of its surroundings and its pleasant climate. It was one of the main agricultural centres for the Incas.

After lunch we sleepily re-board the minibus and head for our final stop at Ollantaytambo. The river Urubamba flows between a series of Inca terraces that get steeper and narrower as the sides of the valley get rockier and more sheer. At the Northern end of the Sacred Valley, the ancient town of Ollantaytambo is overshadowed by the magnificent temple-fortress clinging to the sheer cliffs above it. The road we are travelling climbs a small hill to an ancient plaza.

Ollantaytambo was an important agricultural, administrative, social, religious and military centre in the era of the Tawantinsuyo. Legend has it that the name comes from an Inca chieftain named Ollantay who controlled the fortress here. He fell in love with the daughter of the Inca Pachacutec, Nusta Cusi Clooyu. This was a strict no-no in Inca society so they ran off together to the fortress at Ollantaytambo, which was then besieged by her vengeful father. Ollantay's forces were defeated by Pachacutec but the Inca let both of them live as he recognised the beauty of their love.

The town at the base of the mountain still maintains the integrity of its Inca design. Almost all the buildings are built on top of Inca foundations and so it is the only surviving example of Inca town planning. The town is laid out in the form of a cob of maize and is divided up into blocks. Each block has a single doorway into a central courtyard, with all the houses built around that courtyard. Armando shows us good examples of this just behind the main plaza. The women in the square are dressed in traditional clothing—their intricately woven shawls contrasting with the zigzag patterns of their black and red skirts and topped off with black and red hats. This is a living Inca city where the narrow streets have been inhabited constantly since the Incas' time.

We make our way downhill from the main plaza across the Río Patacancha to the Plaza Mañya Raquy, where we begin our climb to the fortress on the mountain. Within the skirt of the mountain that dominates the town, are the buildings of the Temple of the Sun, the Intihuatana and the 'Baño de la Ñusta,' (Bath of the Princess) where sparkling water runs through a channel cut into a natural boulder before falling several feet into a rectangular stone pool. It looks very inviting for a dip.

In the upper and western part of the city rises the mountain which houses the unfinished temples and terraces. Here we are to find out how the Incas built their amazing cities with the huge blocks of stone. This city was never finished as it was under construction at the time of the Inca Civil War, which was closely followed by the Spanish invasion. Ramps, levers, ropes, slicks made from clay and water and lots of manpower were used to get the vast blocks, quarried 9 miles away, up the mountain and into place—a great feat of architectural planning and engineering.

The main temple is partially destroyed, but the front facade is still standing, and is made of gigantic red monoliths. Bill and I have fun running in and out of the stone niches and posing for photos to be taken by one of our fellow tourists on the other side of the mountain.

And so, full up with ancient cities and culture, we make our way back to Cusco for a few more days of lounging about, drinking coffees and awaiting the day we have to take an 18-hour bus ride across the Andes back to Lima for our flight home.

We set off yesterday afternoon for that monumental bus ride that I had been dreading. It was advertised as taking 18 hours, but ended up taking 26 hours, because our numbskull of a driver got us stuck trying to ford a river as we crossed the Andes. It was 1am and despite much revving, followed by digging round the wheels, and pushing by gangs of local men and passengers we continued to be stuck. We watched with increasing frustration as all the other buses from Cusco to Lima got through successfully. Eventually, 8 hours later, a truck came to tow us out and it was late in the evening the following day by the time we had hair-pinned our way down through the Andes and finally trundled into our hotel in Lima. It is a very good job we left plenty of time before our flight leaves for home.

So here we are in Lima at the end of nearly 10 months travel. We are staying in the Mami Panchita guesthouse, run by friends of the people who own Hostal Marani in Cusco. It is a colonial style building set in its own grounds—clean and spacious with lots of polished wood and a bar with big comfy chairs and sofas to lounge about in. The hotel is in the quiet neighbourhood of old San Miguel—a district of Lima between the airport, Miraflores and the Old Town. It is a long way from the centre of town, but supposed to be safer. We have heard lots of stories about the level of crime and violence in Lima, particularly in the centre of town, but I am still shocked to see all the security measures that people have taken to protect their property. Every home has bars and shutters at the windows, high walls surrounding their gardens topped with vicious looking barbed wire or spikes of broken glass and great fortified looking gates that clang shut in the evenings to keep out marauding villains.

With this atmosphere of fear, we decide not to go into the centre of town. Besides which, at this late stage in our travels, we have seen plenty of museums, old churches and whatever else Lima has to offer the tourist. However, we did manage to venture out to the local shopping mall to get some last minute bargains and eat copious amounts of ice-cream—well we had to fill our time somehow.

There is a fresh-faced young couple staying at our hotel—Rick and Ange. We chat to them as we lounge on the comfy sofas.

'We've just got engaged and we're travelling round the world before we get married and settle down,' Ange tells us.

'Oh how lovely. How long are you travelling for?' I ask.

'Ten months. We're going down through South America, having a couple of weeks in Oz and then travelling through South East Asia and ending up in India,' says Rick.

'That's just like our route, but in reverse,' says Bill.

'Ooh, you must give us some tips of good places to go and places to avoid,' squeaks Ange excitedly.

'Oh well, where shall we start?' says Bill.

They are wearing brand new travelling shirts and shorts and their boots are clean and new. Their hair is cut neatly and their faces are still pale from an English winter. All their luggage is neat and brand-spanking new too. I look at us, we are a little worn and grubby round the edges. Our faces are weather beaten and neither of us has had a decent hair cut in months. Most of our clothes and luggage are fit for the bin now. I realise that Rick and Ange are just like us 10 months ago. I feel excited for them, but I would not want to swap places. Our adventure is complete and I am glad we are going home.

So many of my long held dreams have now been fulfilled by this journey. My dream to see India, where my father and my grandfather and my great grandfather once lived has come true. My dream to see the tea pickers in Sri Lanka, the land of my grandmother's people, has come true. My dream to see wild elephants and monkeys has come true. My dream to see the Himalayas has come true. My dream to travel along the Mekong River and to see river dolphins has come true. My dream to see the ancient civilisations of South America has come true. My dream to walk in the Andes has come true and my dream to go to the Amazon jungle has come true.

This journey has been one not only of place and time, but a journey of my relationship with Bill. The journey has certainly been a test of our relationship and I am very glad to say that it has passed the test and I am now more certain than ever that I have found my soul mate. We are like two misfits in the world, but by some happy accident we happen to fit with each other. We have made a good team. Generally how it has worked is that I would do all the research and planning and then Bill would put it into action. He was the one that always got us to the bus stop or the train station on time. He was the one that hoofed our luggage through difficult terrain. He was the one that always made sure we had enough to eat and drink on the journey. He was the one who always had that extra bit of energy to get us and our belongings safely to our destination. We had our sticky moments, but on balance they have been very few compared to all the times that we got along and supported each other. The sticky moments were mostly to do with Bill's occasional tendency to be impulsive with money and my tendency to judge that he had been frivolous. But that trait is also something that I love about him, because it stems from his exuberant nature and his generous heart, which is a perfect balance for my cautiousness.

So what now is left of my dreams? Now I am eager to fulfil the next part of the dream for my life—marrying Bill and settling down to have lots of babies. Of course, in this dream we will be living in a country cottage with roses round the door and vegetables in the garden. Our curly-haired children will be playing with our little dog, or chasing a fluffy kitten about. And as I bake cakes in the kitchen, I can look out of the window and see green hills rolling into the distance and hear birdsong in the meadow. And Bill will come home from a day's toil, whistling up the garden path, as the children shout, 'Daddy's home' and run out to jump into his arms.

* * *

We are on the plane leaving Lima, bound for Heathrow, where Mum and Dad will be waiting to pick us up. We will be staying with them in Herefordshire for a few days until the tenants move out of our house in Bristol. I am glad that it has worked out that way. It will be a bit of a soft landing for us to be looked after by Mum and Dad before hitting the harsh reality of finding work and starting our new life in Bristol. Dad has e-mailed to say that he has bought us a car out of the money we reserved from our travelling pot, so at least we will be mobile. My mind is whirling with everything that is left to organise before the wedding and I know Mum will be very glad to have me right there to get instant decisions.

'Let's play a game to while away a bit of time,' says Bill.

'Oh, yes, what's that?' I say.

'Top five of everything we did on our travels—you know like top five funniest moments, top five scariest moments, top five most embarrassing moments, best country, etc, etc.'

'OK, that sounds good, which one shall we start with?'

'How about funniest moments?'

We both think for a moment.

'Oh, yeah, remember dressing up as emperors and princesses in the Forbidden Purple Palace, in Vietnam? Ant in those satin platform boots was priceless, and the Vietnamese thought it was hilarious too,' says Bill. 'And there was Aunty falling in the sea with her camera in Sri Lanka. That was one of the best slapstick moments I've ever seen. And the funniest bit was the looks the rest of the family gave us—like, 'Oh Aunty! She's done it again. It's always Aunty that does things like that."

'One of the funniest things I've seen was you and Ant doing the sticky rice balls song and dance routine in the market in Vietnam, and the old lady squirting you with her water pistol. That was the thing about Vietnam, some of it was awful, like the wee-smelling train cabin, but we also had a lot of fun and the Vietnamese have got a really good sense of humour too. Well, all except that guide that took us on the tour to Bac Ha market. The other funniest moment for me was when we went to Amantani on Lake Titikaka and in the evening Lucilla got us all dressed up in traditional gear and took us dancing with the locals. You and Connor looked so funny with your pointy hats on. And the dancing was a hoot. We just laughed till it hurt.'

'Yes, I was hoarse from laughing so much. Ah ha, I've just remembered another funny moment. It was in Australia. We were staying at a hotel in the Snowy Mountains and I heard a commotion in the middle of the night. I heard you say, 'Oh, here I am then,' and I switched on the light to find you in the wardrobe instead of the bathroom. Good job you hadn't got your pants down before I put on the light,' says Bill.

'Well I think that has to go down as one of my top five most embarrassing moments, which takes us on to the next category. There were quite a few toilet related embarrassing incidents,' I say.

'Yes, there were. I remember when we were in Chile. We were in the market in La Serena and you had a bad tummy,' says Bill. 'That guy touted us to go in his restaurant and you said to me, 'Well at least I can use the loo there.' But the loo was only separated from the restaurant by a couple of saloon doors and I had to sit there pretending to look at the menu whilst there were these terrible noises and smells coming from under the half doors.'

'Oh believe me, that was just as embarrassing for me. I had to really pluck up my courage to come back out of that loo into the restaurant. I was desperately hoping there was a window and I could escape out the back, but no such luck.'

'Yeah, and there was the time that we were checking out that room when we arrived in Copacabana and you said you were going to check out the bathroom and then you did a big giant wee in there that sounded like a horse urinating. And I was trying to make small talk with the guy showing us the room to cover up the noise. And then you came out of the bathroom and said we weren't going to take the room. I thought it was the least we could have done for the poor guy after using his facilities,' says Bill.

'Well, I wanted a room with a view of the lake. It was a bit poor though, wasn't it? But I was desperate for a wee after our long coach ride. OK all the embarrassing moments so far have been about my toilet activities. What about you?'

'There was the horrible moment on the sleeper train from Pondicherry to Kanniyakumari, when I had my bad tummy, and I farted and pooed my pants,' says Bill.

'Oh, did you? You never told me about that at the time,' I say, giggling.

'No, I kept it pretty quiet because we hadn't been travelling together that long and I was really embarrassed about it.'

'OK, enough embarrassing poorly bum stories. Which category is next?'

'How about scariest moments? Being chased by the elephant in Mudumalai has to be THE most scary thing that I have ever experienced in my life. And I still feel ashamed that I didn't stop to rescue you first,' says Bill.

'Well, I'm not sure that there would have been a lot you could have done to stop a huge elephant. We might have both been killed. I just remember seeing you, running like the clappers in front of me. Your body was leaning at acute angles as you weaved from side to side going round bushes and your little feet were going round in circles so fast you looked as if you were pedalling a bike and you were kicking up a great cloud of dust. In a funny way, it helped me just to blindly follow you without having to think which direction to go in next. Otherwise I might have hesitated and fallen over and then I'd have been a gonner.'

'Any road journey in India has to be at the top of my list of scary moments,' says Bill.

'Yes, the jeep rides in Sikkim along the narrow twisty roads that were falling off the side of the mountain gave me the willies most of all, especially the one when our driver was the alcoholic goblin,' I say.

'Bandara telling us the story about the red-eyed devil in the jungle when we were staying at the old hotel in Nuwara Eliya, and halfway through the story the lights all went out and he just carried on, enjoying the extra spooky atmosphere. I tell you, I didn't want to get up from that table and walk down the dark corridor to our bedroom.'

'Rene's story in the Amazon about the jaguar smelling fear in your footsteps and the spirit of the jungle animals killing that man—that got me going.'

'Seeing you with Dengue Fever in Laos was very scary for me. I was really worried about you. I thought I might have to fly you home.'

'Um, sorry about that—I wasn't really aware of very much that was going on at the time. But I think your magic shiatsu treatment was what brought me through it so quickly. How about flying over the Amazon jungle? That was kind of exciting and scary at the same time.'

'Yeah, getting there on the rickety TAM flight was definitely scary. There was a moment when I thought the engines had cut out. I had visions of us crashing in the jungle and then we would have to eat each other to survive and I thought that airhostess had her eye on me and would eat me first,' says Bill.

'Being trapped under a canoe in Australia, when those two idiot women capsized us in their eagerness to go and flirt with the guides—that was one of my scariest moments.'

'Yes, that was pretty rubbish of them, wasn't it? Oh yeah, there was that bus journey from Potosi to Sucre in Bolivia, when the coca campesinos were blockading the roads and I was really scared you were going to poo your pants.'

'Oh, we're back on poorly bum stories again, are we? How about best country?'

'Well, India was both the best and the worst country for me. It's really got under my skin and I know I'll be going back there some time.'

'Um, I think I've had my fill of India for now, but I did love Sikkim and I loved the Himalayas—I loved staying between two hills where leopards live and bears roam in the woods and oh yes, I loved trekking and animal spotting near Mudumalai. Yes, I see what you mean—I love it and I hate it at the same time. But Bolivia has to be my favourite overall. The contrasts were amazing—we went to the Amazon jungle and we travelled high up into the Andes. There was Tiahuanaco and the fantastic Lake Titikaka and the mind blowing jeep trip across the altiplano and the salt flats.'

'Yes, you're right. I still dream about that trip. It was sublimely beautiful, but very weird at the same time. I remember the loco Argentineans stripping off in the hot springs that smelled like a bad fart and the pink flamingos and the weird shaped rocks and the fantastic colours and the vicunas. I think we're agreed, Bolivia is the favourite.'

'Yes, but Laos was pretty special too. It was so beautiful, but mysterious and magical at the same time with all the golden Buddhas and nagas. I'd love to go back when I'm not feeling ill and explore it a bit more,' I say.

'Yes, me too. The people were lovely there. Hey, we've had a brilliant time, haven't we?' Bill says.

'Yes, we have, and we've met some wonderful people too—Captain Bandara and the Veddas, Markus and Juli, Rajiv and the Todas, Kumar, Ant and Ems, Ed and Clare, René and Mabel . . .'

We both lapse into a quiet reverie for a while. The airhostess comes with our meals.

'Do you know what the best part of it was for me?' says Bill, pouring red wine into our plastic tumblers.

'No, go on then,' I say.

'Spending 10 months with you, my love, my angel, light of my life. Sharing all these amazing experiences with you by my side has just been wonderful.'

'Oh, go on you big soppy thing, you,' I say, nudging him in the ribs, but I see the little tear in his eye and know that he means it.

'Well there's going to be plenty more where that came from,' I say. 'We're getting married in three months time and we'll have the rest of our lives to have amazing experiences together. Do you know, Bill, I've had a bit of a realisation.'

'What's that, my dear?' says Bill.

'Well, even though I'm in my thirties, I guess I've never felt like a proper grown up before. I know I've found my soul mate,' I say, squeezing Bill's hand. 'And I'm really happy that I'm going to spend the rest of my life with you. But getting married feels like a really big step. I suppose it's because to be a wife and potentially in the future, a mother, I'll need to be really grown up. Before this trip, I don't think I was ready for that. We've both been tested many times on this trip, through stressful situations and mortal danger, or just being out of our comfort zones. And our relationship has really been tested too. I feel like somehow I've passed the test. It's been like a rite of passage, when I had to face all my fears and overcome them. So now I'm really ready for the next step in my life. I think what this trip has taught me is that each new day is a new beginning, and whatever it brings, good or bad, you've just got to get up in the morning and get on with it, with a relentless cheerfulness. I had a terrible tendency to procrastinate before, but I think I'm cured of that now. I think 'seize the day' is going to be my motto from now on.

'I'll drink to that,' says Bill, chinking his tumbler against mine and leaning over to give me a kiss. 'Yeah, and I hope we're still gallivanting off to Chile when we're in our nineties like your grandpa.'

'I can't wait to see him again and show him all the photos. I hope he's all right. I've just got a feeling that he's not going to be around for very much longer. It must be really hard for him, now that he's lost his independence'

'I think he's holding on to see us get married, Anna. And it will be a chance for him to see all the family together. Then he can go off to be with his lovely Iris again'.

We are both quiet for a few minutes while we finish our meals. I think about Grandpa and about my future life with Bill. Tummies full, we both settle down for a nap.

I wake up to see Bill gazing at me. 'You know, Anna?' he says, 'If you turn into a pillar of light before I do, I'm not going to wait twenty years without you. I'm coming straight after you.'

'Yes, me too, if you go first.'

Chapter 15
And They Lived Happily Ever After—Which is the Only Proper Way to Live

Harvey and Hazel
Invite you to help celebrate the marriage of their daughter,
Anna, to William Jope
At St Mary's Church, Clifford, Herefordshire
On Saturday 21st June, at 2.30pm
And afterwards at Rosamond Place

It is the night before the night before the Big Day. Anna is up late, putting the finishing touches to the most marvellous, magical, sparkling waistcoat that she is making for Bill to wear at the wedding. She has crafted it from the same beautiful fabric as her dress. Inside, she has sewn a secret pocket and in the secret pocket she has placed a piece of silk on which she has written all her love for Bill and her heartfelt desires for their life together. And as she wrote her wishes and desires, tears of joy sprang to her eyes. She dabbed her eyes with the silk, so that the magic of the joyful tears would become part of her prayer for their life together.

She hangs the waistcoat up, gives it a last kiss and puts it away in the wardrobe, before getting ready for bed. Her head is whirling as she lies down. There is still so much to do tomorrow—there is the seating plan to write out on a board and the little tiny jewels to stick on all the name cards and making the signs to the car park and the loos and balloons to blow up and the flowers to check . . . but she is so tired that soon she is fast asleep.

It is 1 am on the eve of the wedding and Karn and Anna are still up. They are putting rag curlers into Anna's hair, in preparation for the cascade of fabulous pre-raphaelite curls that Anna has planned for her wedding hair-do. The boys—Bill and his best man, Abava—went off earlier that evening to a bed and breakfast in Hay-on-Wye. It felt strange for Anna after spending all this time with Bill for him to leave her before the wedding. She felt sweetly tearful when he left, but it added to the ceremonial atmosphere as she and Karn got on with their last minute preparations.

Anna awakes at 5 am to find to her great joy that the Big Day is going to be a sunny one. She suddenly remembers that in all the commotion of the previous day, she did not have time to hem and press the gorgeous piece of sparkling fabric that she is going to wear as a wrap with the wedding dress that she has had made from the beautiful sari that she and Bill bought in India. Hazel finds her at 6 am drinking her second cup of tea and working away with the sewing machine and the iron.

'Let me finish that, I'm sure you've got plenty of other things to do,' says Hazel.

'Well, if you're sure you've got time, that would be great. You're so much quicker than me at this sort of thing anyway.'

In the end Hazel had been right about the wedding outfits and they had opted for a dark tails suit and waistcoat for Bill and an empire-line wedding dress made from the beautiful sparkling sari for Anna. She had been on a crash diet to lose all those excess pounds gained at the all-you-can-eat buffets and pie shops of Cusco, but was still a little sensitive about baring her midriff in a sari. She and Bill had realised that it would look much more in keeping in an English country church. The only concession to the exotic will be Karn in her lavender and gold sari, who has a very trim and toned midriff.

The day is already getting hot when Anna and Karn set off for the hairdressers in Hay-on-Wye. She feels very foolish arriving at *Jenesis Hair Studios* wearing shorts and a T-shirt, complete with her curlers still in and no make-up.

'God, I hope we don't bump into anyone we know,' she says to Karn as they get out of the car.

'Don't look now, but I think that's Bill's Mum and Dad coming down the street,' says Karn.

'Quick, hide me, I don't want to speak to them, looking like this.'

'Too late. Bill's Mum has spotted you and she's coming over.'

'Wooh, hooh,' waves Mrs Jope, beetling over. 'I've just bumped into the boys,' she says. 'I'll try and divert them away from the hairdressers. You wouldn't want Bill seeing you looking like that, would you?' Unfortunately everyone else in the street has already looked round to see what all the commotion is about. There is much pointing, staring and giggling.

'Thanks,' says Anna with a strained smile. 'Must dash—we're late for the hairdressers,' diving for cover through the doorway of *Jenesis*.

'Don't worry, Anna, I'm already on the case,' says Karn. 'I phoned Abava earlier to warn him to keep Bill well away while we're having our hair done. They're probably in the pub by now—he's taking his best man's duties very seriously.'

'Good morning, Anna. How are you feeling?' says Emma the hairdresser.

'Pretty nervous, actually.'

'I see you've already got the curlers in, so we'll have you looking lovely in no time at all.' She sits Anna in the chair and begins to undo the curlers. 'Um, I think some of them are still a bit damp. Better put you under the drier for a bit while I do the bridesmaid's hair.'

Anna sits under the drier for what seems like an eternity while Emma does and re-does Karn's hair for the umpteenth time. Anna's cheeks are getting redder and redder by the minute, partly from the indignity of having to sit under the hideous drying hood in her curlers and partly because the heat from the drier is roasting her head. She glances nervously at her watch every few minutes, watching the time ticking rapidly away.

By now, it is 11.30 am and she can stand it no longer. 'Emma,' she says. 'It must be dry by now. I'm getting roasted. Can I come out?'

'Oh, oh yes,' says Emma as if she has forgotten all about Anna, so absorbed she was in doing Karn's hair.

Finally, after about an hour, Emma has finished Karn's hair and she begins undoing the curlers from Anna's hair. One by one, the curlers come out, slowly revealing the full horror of what is going on on Anna's head. Not only are the curls so tight that her hair looks really short, but worse still, the heat of the drier has turned the ends into a hideous dry frizz.

'Oh my God. I look like bloody Shirley Temple having a bad hair day,' wails Anna.

'Don't worry,' says Emma, 'I can relax the curls a bit with some serum,' but the expression on her face is telling a different story.

Karn's wedding present to Anna and Bill is to pay for some candid 'behind the scenes' photos of things like them getting ready. Jane the photographer chooses this moment to arrive at the hairdressers. The candid photos seemed like a really good idea at the time—that is until Jane is pointing her camera into Anna's bright red, unmade up face, catching the trauma of the Shirley Temple moment on film. Jane clearly thinks it is highly amusing.

Anna looks at herself in the mirror. Her face is scarlet red, her hair is a dry birds nest on top of her head and the series of late nights trying to get everything finished in time for the wedding has given her the eye bags from hell.

'I'm hideous,' she wails. 'How am I ever going to look like a beautiful bride by 2.30pm?' The hair disaster, the tiredness, the nerves and the ever-ticking clock all combine to tip Anna's emotional state over the edge and she sits sobbing in the hairdresser's chair. Emma looks at Karn. Karn looks at Jane. Jane looks at Emma. Everyone shrugs. 'You'll be fine,' they all say in unison. 'Plenty of time yet. Come on, don't cry.' Jane suggests pile cream for the eye bags, but no-one has any pile cream.

'A bit of make-up, a bit of serum, a bit of hairspray and you won't recognise yourself,' says Emma as she sets to work. She sounds as if she is trying to convince herself as much as Anna. But before too long, with judicious misting of water and careful teasing and shaping, she manages to transform Anna from Shirley Temple into Kate Blanchett. The final touch is to add a tiara of tiny white lilies and diamante and suddenly she is looking like the fairy queen she had hoped for.

It is 12.30 as they walk back to the car—two hours and counting till the big 'I do'. Anna sits down on the pavement of the car park and has another big cry.

'Come on, Anna, it's just nerves,' says Karn. 'In two hours time you'll be marrying the man that you love. All you have to do is put on your dress and a bit of make-up.'

'Oh, it's the pressure of wanting everything to be perfect. It's been building for days,' sobs Anna.

'I know,' says Karn, giving her a big hug and some emergency chocolate rations. 'In fact it's probably been building for years. Isn't it every little girls dream to have the big fairytale wedding? And it's about to happen for you. So come on, on your feet now.'

Just as they are about to get in the car, someone says, 'Hello.' They look up to see a little old lady standing outside a cottage with roses round the door. Looking at the sparkling tiara, the old lady says, 'My dear, you look beautiful. Have you been chosen for something?'

Anna laughs and says, 'Yes, I've been chosen to be the lucky bride of William Jope. I'm getting married today.'

'Oh, how lovely. You look like a princess. Have a wonderful day,' she says as she waves them off in the car. With the kind words of the old lady, and the pep talk from Karn, Anna finally remembers what this day is all about. She <u>has</u> been chosen, at last she has been chosen, and this is her special day. She realises that Bill will still love her and marry her whether or not her hair looks like Shirley Temple and whether or not she has eyebags. After all, he has seen far worse on their travels together. All the stress and tension disappears. She starts to laugh and finally she is enjoying the day.

As she arrives back at home, everyone choruses together, 'Oh, your hair looks lovely.' Everything seems to be coming together. Her bouquet has arrived, the caterers are setting up in the marquee and the rest of her family seem to have the last minute preparations under control. Anna's brother-in-law, Andrew, is helping Hazel with the smoked salmon bruscettas for the enormous buffet Hazel has planned for the evening when 80 more people are due to arrive. Her sister, Jennie is preparing the strawberries they have just picked from a farm nearby and Anna's niece, Esther is busy decorating the seating plan with a gold pen and glitter. The ushers are all off changing into their morning suits. All she has to do now is to get ready.

She mentions the eyebags to Hazel, who says, 'Oh, don't worry darling, I've bought some marvellous eye cream from Christian Dior especially for the occasion. I have it on good authority that it works wonders on the top models after a heavy night out.'

'Oh thanks Mum, you're a wonder—you think of everything.'

She and Karn disappear into her room to complete the transformation from ordinary mortals into fairytale bride and bridesmaid. She looks at herself in the mirror before starting the makeover. The finished hair-do has begun the process, but she still has her work cut out to get that tired face looking bride-like. But as the nerves turn to excitement and whether it is the magic eye cream or the carefully applied make-up, or the glass of champagne that Karn has slipped into her hand, somehow her face seems to lose that tired drawn look and fills with a glowing vitality that hints at the joy that is beginning to well up within.

Beautiful Karn, Best Bridesmaid Ever

And then the finishing touches are added—toenails are varnished gold, perfume is applied, and jewellery fastened. She is just about to get Karn to help her into her dress when there is a knock at the door. Hazel steps in. Hair still wet from her hurried shower, she says, 'Come on Karn. We have to leave right now if we are going to get there on time.'

'But she's my bridesmaid and I need her to help me with my dress,' says Anna as Karn is being whisked from the room by a very rushed looking Hazel. 'It's OK for us to be a tiny bit late—people expect it.'

'It's OK for the bride to be a bit late, but not the rest of us,' says Hazel, as Karn is bundled downstairs.

'I'll help you,' says Jane, putting her camera down for a minute. But in the end it is Anna's Dad, Harvey, who helps her do up the zip and arrange the wrap around her shoulders.

'It's time that we were off now too, Anna. Are you ready?' says Harvey.

With a very firm 'Yes!' she lets him take her hand and lead her out to his shiny red Jag. They proceed along the gravel drive and through the stone gates, out onto the road in a very stately manner. Then they purr along on cream leather seats up the steep lane to St Mary's Church, flanked on either side by the white froth of Queen Anne's Lace and the vibrant pink of red campion.

Karn and Phil, the photographer, are waiting for them by the ivy-covered stone arch into the churchyard. 'You look fabulous,' says Phil, helping her out of the car.

'Good job you're a bit late,' whispers Karn. 'The last guests have only just made it.'

Anna takes a deep breath and holds her father's arm as they step through the archway onto hallowed ground. The churchyard is awash with sunshine, making the grass and the headstones glow. There is a hum of bees, and butterflies dance here and there amongst the wild flowers. Down a little path between the yew and the cedar stands the ancient church, nestling as it is amongst the glorious Herefordshire meadows, and in the distance stand the hazy shapes of the Black Mountains.

They set off down the path, gaining momentum as they go until nearing the church, they are proceeding at a lively running skip. Anna is greeted with a wonderful sight. The door to the church is open and amongst the flowers, there is a sea of happy, shining faces all eagerly waiting to catch a glimpse of her. And as she steps through a perfumed haze of lilies and honeysuckle at the church door, a strange thing happens. Until that moment everything has seemed a rush and time was flying by, but the moment her golden varnished and delicately sandaled foot steps over the threshold of the church, there is a strange whirring sound, like the cogs of the machine of time all slowing down and everything seems to go into slow motion so that she can savour every drop of these precious moments. The warmth of the love and good wishes from all the people in the church seem to lift her up and carry her along the aisle like a great wave of warm tranquil sea. There are gasps of wonder as she passes the congregation, as Dr Wilson plays *The Arrival of the Queen of Sheba.* The crystals on her dress and tiara are shimmering in the bright sunlight streaming in through the windows. She overhears a little girl say, 'Ooh, Mummy, is she a princess?'

And then she is standing next to her beloved Bill. She looks up at him to see tears of joy streaming down his face. She feels her heart swell in her chest and wonders how she can possibly contain the amount of love she feels for him without exploding into a thousand tiny pieces. She looks at the Reverend Marian Morgan, whose eyes are brimming too, and then she looks up and sees that most of the ladies in the choir are also crying.

Reverend Marian welcomes everyone and says an opening prayer. Somehow Anna manages to pull herself together enough to be able to sing the first hymn—*For the Beauty of the Earth.*

Marian speaks of the importance of marriage as the foundation of family life. She tells the congregation that Bill and Anna are about to make solemn vows to each other. Then Bill and Anna make promises to each other to Love, Comfort, Honour, Protect and stay faithful to one another as long as they both shall live.

'Who gives this woman to be married?' asks Marian.

'I do,' says Hawkeye, giving Anna's hand to Marian.

'Now, will you, the family and friends of Anna and William, promise to love and support them?' asks Marian.

'We will,' everyone choruses.

There are prayers and then Anna's sister, Jennie, reads from the Book of Corinthians about love. 'If I have faith that I may move mountains, but if I have not love, I am nothing . . . Faith, Hope and Love, but the greatest of these is Love.' They sing another hymn, *Lord of all hopefulness.*

Anna and Bill sit dreamily holding hands beneath an arch of flowers, as their friend Nick, with his radiant face and mane of golden hair, comes forward to give a poem, chosen by Bill for Anna—*Saints Bowing in the Mountains* by Hafiz.

Do you know how beautiful you are?

I think not, my dear.

For as you talk of God,
I see great parades with wildly colourful bands
Streaming from your mind and heart,
Carrying wonderful and secret messages
To every corner of this world.

I see saints bowing in the mountains
Hundreds of miles away
To the wonder of sounds
That break into light
From your most common words.

Speak to me of your mother,
Your cousins and your friends.

Tell me of squirrels and birds you know.
Awaken your legion of nightingales—
Let them soar wild and free in the sky

And begin to sing to God.
Let's all begin to sing to God!

Do you know how beautiful you are?

I think not, my dear,

Yet I could set you upon a stage
And worship you forever!

'Well how can I follow that beautiful reading?' asks Marian. 'Now put away your hankies because it's time for the sermon bit. This really is a wonderful day for a wedding and Anna and Bill and their families have worked really hard to make this day happen. But why are they here? Why have they gone to so much trouble and expense to come here, when they could have had a quiet little ceremony in a registry office somewhere? Knowing Anna and Bill, it is not just for show. This is not about the past. This is about what together they may become. By declaring their love and commitment to each other in the presence of God, they are made new, they leave behind their old lives and start afresh. This is the day on which new relationships begin, as their families and friends meet each other sometimes for the first time and new friendships are forged.'

Anna looks round to see Hazel smiling at her, with tears running down her face. Hawkeye is nodding in agreement and flashes a beaming smile at her.

'Today is about love,' says Marian. 'The love that Anna and Bill feel for each other is so clear. It is there in the way they look at each other, the way they touch each other. Their concern and the respect they show for each other is a joy to see. They have spent a year away travelling together and that must have exposed them and their relationship to great stress and danger. There was the danger that their relationship could have fallen apart under the challenges thrown at them. But it didn't. It grew and became even stronger. And now, here they are, two very special and spiritual people, demonstrating their love and trust in each other.'

Then Marian invites Anna and Bill to make their vows to each other. They make promises to each other that they will be together from this day forward, to have and to hold, for better for worse, for richer for poorer, in sickness and in health, to love and to cherish each other according to God's Holy Law.

Abava mischievously pretends to drop the rings down a grill in the church floor, but then smiles a winning smile and hands them to a momentarily shocked Marian. She gives him a motherly tut before asking for God's blessing on the rings.

'I give you this ring as a sign of our marriage. With my body I honour you. All that I am, I give to you. All that I have, I share with you, within the love of God, the Father, Son and Holy Spirit,' Bill and Anna both say as they place the golden bands on each other's fingers.

And as they say their vows, Anna feels as if everything else is fading into the background and that she is alone with Bill in some far off heavenly place.

'I therefore proclaim that they are man and wife,' says Marian, wrapping a silk cloth around their joined hands. 'Those whom God has joined in holy matrimony, let no man put asunder. You may kiss the bride.'

A great cheer rises from the congregation and everyone claps the new couple.

Brother-in-law, Andrew sings Anna's favourite hymn, *Amazing Grace*. And as his rich deep voice, the colour of mahogany resonates around the church and through her body, she can finally hold back the tears no longer. Great fat drops of pure joy spill over and run down her cheeks and onto the floor. And her tears are joined by Bill's tears and by all the other tears cried in that church on that day until a river of joy is running down the aisle and out of the door.

Marian leads them to the altar and asks God to pour out his blessing on them. As Anna kneels with Marian's hand on her head, she feels as if great shafts of light are beaming in through her head and spiralling down through her body, making her sway in a trance-like circle. The choir sings, '*The Lord bless you and keep you.*'

Marian says more prayers for Anna and Bill's marriage, that they may cherish and nurture their children, that they may always show hospitality to others and that they may have the kindness to help any neighbour in need. Andrew sings, '*Oh Perfect Love,*' as they go to sign the register.

As Anna and Bill walk back up the aisle as man and wife, she sees Grandpa's beaming face amongst the throng of smiling faces and she is glad that he is here, despite his failing health, to witness her special day. Outside the church she goes to greet him.

'Grandpa, I'm so glad you could come,' she says.

He gives her a big kiss and says, 'Anna, I've been on plenty of difficult journeys in my time and nothing could have stopped me from getting to your wedding. We've all been waiting a very long time for this day. And now that it has happened we are very glad. What a wonderful day. I know you two will be very happy together. Oh and by the way, I really did enjoy the letters that you sent on the World Wide Newspaper!'

Then Anna goes to find Hazel. She kisses her and says, 'Mum, thanks for everything. You've worked tirelessly and endlessly to make everything perfect for us. You've thought of things that never would have occurred to me. And it's all worked out just right. This is the happiest day of my life.'

'Oh, well, it's just what any mother would do for her daughter. It was a beautiful service, wasn't it? And Marian did really well. I'm so glad for you, Anna,' says Hazel, with a little tear and gives her a big hug.

The churchyard is full of sunshine and happy children playing amongst the butterflies, as friends and relatives (and a few old flames) are greeted and photos are taken.

'Isn't it wonderful to have all the people we love gathered in one place,' says Bill gazing around at the happy throng. Amongst the guests are Markus and Juli, the two lovely Germans from their Sri Lankan adventures with the Captain, and Clare and Ed, who helped them get through the Bolivian Pampas ordeal. The only ones missing are Ant and Ems, who sent their apologies from Australia.

As Bill and Anna leave the church through a cloud of confetti, Harvey hands the keys of his precious Jag to his new son-in-law.

'My goodness, that's a pretty good wedding present,' says Andrew.

'Oh, it's just on loan,' says Bill.

When their posteriors are nestled comfortably against the leather, Andrew leans his head in the window. Bill points to the hyperdrive button and says, 'I just start her up and then press that button, right?'

The colour drains from Andrew's face. 'No mate! Oh, you're just joking—thank goodness for that. Just take it easy, the gaffer would have a fit if anything happened to his pride and joy.'

'I will,' says Bill. 'I seem to have been saying that a lot lately!' He smiles and takes off before anyone else can ram more confetti down the back of his shirt. They process regally down the steep little lane through the lush greenness of a Herefordshire June towards the marquee in the meadow next to Hazel and Harvey's house, where a feast is laid on.

'Hello Wifey,' says Bill to Anna, reaching over to squeeze her hand.

'Hello Hubbey,' she smiles back at him.

'We did it then.'

'Yes we did.'

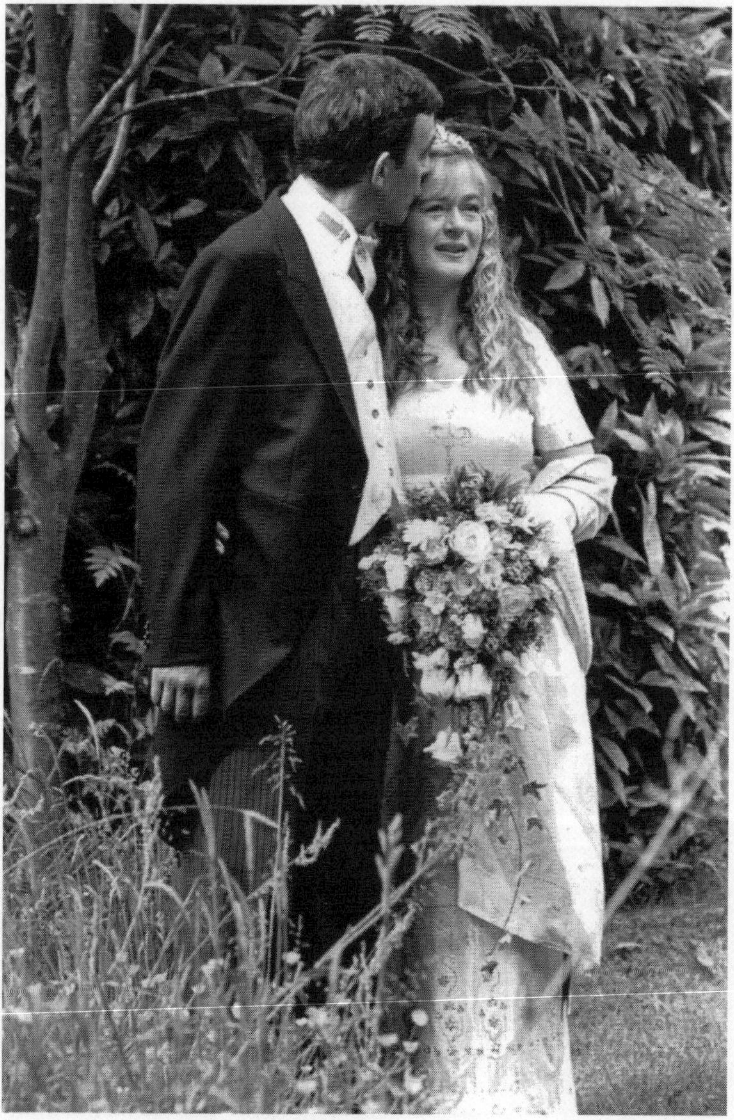

Dear Wedding Guests,

> Yesterday it was sweet madness,
> Reciting poems for hours
> And talking about love to anything that moved.
>
> Yet I believe another wonderful day,
> And perhaps even a sweeter height of rare, inspired insanity
> Has just begun.

Hafiz

We had a wonderful honeymoon in the West Penwith peninsula of Cornwall. We stayed in Porthcurno and on the second day, walked to the Minack Theatre, set spectacularly on the cliffs overlooking the sea. As we approached the lady who was directing people to their seats, she asked us to stop for a minute while she radioed her colleague.

'Yes, I've got two here for The Dream. Shall I send them over?' Then she turned to us and said, "Go over there and ask for The Dream."

We walked to the other side of the amphitheatre and were directed to a little lovers' seat perched high above the stage and dedicated to A Midsummer Night's Dream. We both feel incredibly lucky and grateful that we have been granted **Our Dream**. Thank you for sharing it with us.

With much love

Anna and Bill xx

Acknowledgements

To my beloved parents, Hazel and Hawkeye, such tolerant, generous and long suffering souls, I cannot begin to thank you enough. My sincerest apologies for using any of your foibles as a source of humour in this book.

To Karn, dearest sister and Maid of Dishonour, you never fail to reflect the truth of life back to me and continue to show me the beauty, the good and the light in all things, even when life has dealt me the hardest of blows. For your part in this story and for your unquenchable support, I am forever grateful.

To Bushman Bandara, Markus Fischer and Juli Brode, I cherish the sweet memories of the time we spent together in Sri Lanka—such adventure, such laughter, such a rich experience. Let's meet up and do it all over again! And to Markus, thank you for letting me use your beautiful photos.

To Clare and Ed, without your humour and stalwart good selves, the Pampas experience may well have sent me over the edge.

To Ant and Ems, I am still looking forward to seeing the ad for 'Authentic Aussie Tour Guides – Holidays with a difference in Vietnam.'

To Duncan Fatz, my undying thanks go to you for ploughing through the rough field that was my first draft. Your wise words and brutal honesty helped me cut much of the nonsense that would have had readers quickly closing the cover.

To Tamsyn Grant, thank you for connecting with the humanity of this book and restoring my faith that I had actually produced something worthy of publication. And thank you for laughing at all the silly things that make me laugh too.

To Karen Floyd, thank you for believing in me and demanding that I get off my arse and get this out there. No more lights hidden under bushels. And thank goodness your Spanish is better than mine!

To Monty Halls, dearest old mucker, thank you for always having faith in my writing ability and for providing an exciting start to the story.

To Sara Coleridge, a thousand thank yous for your creative inspiration with the cover, not to mention all your help and support with the emotional journey of parenthood.

To Dave Prescott, huge thanks for showing this terrible technophobe how it's done.

To all at Author House, especially Kathy Lorenzo, my deepest thanks for helping me to finally get my words in print. I look forward to many more collaborations.

Last, but most certainly not least, to Bill, dearest companion of my heart, sharing the joy of all these moments with you has been the most enriching experience of my life. Without your unstoppable enthusiasm, I would probably still be sitting behind a desk in grey old London, editing boring medical reports. These memories and experiences have been etched onto my soul forever and have certainly shaped me into a better, wiser and stronger person.

Picture credits

All photographs copyright Anna Bromley except those taken by Markus Fischer on pages 56, 61 and 65.

Further information

To see lots more beautiful colour photos of our trip, and to read my blog, go to www.anna-bromley.com.

You can also take a look at my Facebook page, 'Wild Animals and Wedding Outfits,' and follow me on Twitter.

Printed in Great Britain
by Amazon.co.uk, Ltd.,
Marston Gate.